Typography
& Typesetting

Typography & Typesetting

TYPE DESIGN AND MANIPULATION USING TODAY'S TECHNOLOGY

Ronald Labuz

VNR **VAN NOSTRAND REINHOLD**
——————— New York

Printed in the United States of America

Designed by Joel Weltman, DuffeyWeltman
Communication Design, New York
Associate Designer, Adelina Bissolo

Van Nostrand Reinhold
115 Fifth Avenue
New York, New York 10003

Van Nostrand Reinhold International Company Limited
11 New Fetter Lane
London EC4P 4EE, England

Van Nostrand Reinhold
480 La Trobe Street
Melbourne, Victoria 3000, Australia

Macmillan of Canada
Division of Canada Publishing Corporation
164 Commander Boulevard
Agincourt, Ontario M1S 3C7, Canada

16   15   14   13   12   11   10 9 8 7 6 5 4 3 2

Library of Congress Cataloging-in-Publication Data
Labuz, Ronald, 1953–
    Typography and typesetting.
    Bibliography: p.
    Includes index.
    1. Type and type-founding.   2. Printing,
Practical—Style manuals.   3. Type-setting.
I. Title.
Z250.L13   1987   686.2'25   87-10499
ISBN 0-442-25966-2

To my colleague
James O'Looney

Teaching from the heart
he teaches more than he knows

CONTENTS

TYPOGRAPHY TODAY

Written communication depends not only on words but on the clear and effective presentation of words. For over five hundred years, the most legible way to communicate a written message has been with *typography,* the selection and arrangement of typeset letters on a printed page. Typography is an art and a science, a skill and an expression. Through several technological revolutions its essential purposes have remained the same: to express a thought and to evoke a feeling.

There are many other ways, of course, to convey ideas or emotions visually. Cave paintings such as those at Altamira in Spain are the earliest preserved examples, but obviously they are not typography. So, what distinguishes typography from other forms of communication?

Type and Typewriting

Type is proportionally spaced lettering used to create words, sentences, and blocks of text. Type is *not* typewriting. Examine figure 1-1. In the typewriting sample, each letter takes up the same amount of horizontal space; in the typesetting sample, the letter widths vary, contributing both to the greater dignity and beauty of type.

Type and typewriting differ in other ways. The names of both are derived from the Greek word *typos,* which means *letter.* Yet type is far more versatile. Some type styles, for instance, establish a certain mood in a way that typewriting styles cannot (fig. 1-2).

A typographer designs with type. In general, the typographer attempts to accomplish several goals in deciding what a written communication should look like. First, the style should be appropriate to the audience. When designing books for children, knowledgeable typographers will use type styles with large, open letters that are easily identifiable.

Second, the type should be suitable to the subject matter. Everyone has received or seen a wedding invitation produced in a delicate script type style. That script is a perfect complement to the grace of the wedding ceremony; it would be out of place in an advertisement for used cars.

Third, type should be legible. For any written message to convey meaning or evoke a response, it must first be understood. If the typographer fails to follow basic rules, he or she may easily create pages that communicate poorly. Fortunately, those rules, which will be discussed in detail in later chapters, are neither complicated nor numerous.

Finally, type should be aesthetically pleasing. The individual creativity of the typographer means that there is usually no single correct way to design a page. Although there are rules of suitability and legibility, the creative sense that produces the artistic page cannot be so easily coached. It must be cultivated through trial and error. The rules, once learned, are the starting point. After acquiring a solid background, the beginner moves beyond the basics to develop an individual artistic style.

```
situations typically
obtaining informatic
gical or legal probl
```

situations typically encounte
obtaining information from cl
gical or legal problems. Canc

1-1.
Typewriting versus typesetting.

Roman

Egyptian

Sans serif

Script

Miscellaneous

1-2.

**The various moods
of the typeset
letter.**

Typesetting

Typesetting is the production of type. There are several ways to produce, or set, type. Irrespective of the method chosen, typeset letters are proportionally spaced and are always selected by typographers to meet the specific needs of the job at hand. A typesetter typically follows the directions of the typographer as to which type style to use, what size type to produce, how much spacing to allow, and how the typeset letters should be arranged on the page.

Typesetting, then, is a mechanical craft. Typography is a creative act. Yet it is not unusual to find that the typesetter and the typographer of a job are indeed the same person.

In general, there are two varieties of typesetting, or composition: hot type and cold type. As its name suggests, hot type is formed by heat (specifically, through the use of molten metal). Cold type refers to alternative forms of typesetting, all of which have been developed since the middle of this century. Although it may seem convenient to refer to type as being either hot or cold, many industry experts argue that the term *cold type* is a misnomer from the past—*cold type* now refers to so many different forms of typesetting technology that the phrase is nearly meaningless.

HOT TYPE—FOUNDRY

Type was originally set by hand. Handsetting is the arrangement of individual letters in position in a tray. When a single line is completed, a second line is set, and so on until the entire job is composed. Because these letters can be arranged and rearranged, they are known as *movable type*.

In the Western world, handsetting with movable type was perfected by Johann Gutenberg of Mainz, Germany, in the 1440s. The basic mechanical features of this technique have changed very little for more than five centuries. Indeed, handsetting was the only method of composition until the 1880s.

Handset letters are usually *foundry type*. A type foundry is an establishment that casts letters from metal molds. In the first four hundred years of typesetting history, the foundries rigidly controlled typographic style by manufacturing and selling a very limited number of typefaces. Printers and typesetting companies purchased *fonts,* or complete collections of letters, numbers, and punctuation marks of a single size and style, and distributed the fonts into cases (fig. 1-3).

When setting type by hand, the typesetter, or *compositor,* removes individual metal letters from a case and places them in trays called *composing sticks* (fig. 1-4). Pieces of metal called *quads* allow for horizontal spacing within the lines of type, and *leads* and *slugs* are used to adjust for vertical spacing between the lines.

As letters are selected to form words and lines, they are transferred to a flat tray called the *galley.* A *galley proof,* or test image, is made to check whether any errors have been made in composition. The compositor makes the necessary corrections.

When the corrections are completed, the type is locked up in a metal frame called the *chase.* All type plus any accompanying illustrations, such as woodcuts or engravings, are assembled in the chase. The compositor must be certain that all parts of the job are the same height, forming a plane that is "type high," or .918 inches. If the job is not uniformly type high, those pieces that are lower will not be imprinted with the same amount of ink and will thus appear lighter than the rest of the form. Finally, the chase is used directly as a printing image or a duplicate plate

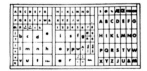

1-3.

Type cases.

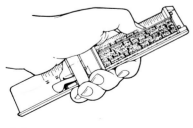

1-4.

Composing stick.

is made from it (fig. 1-5). Because the type in the chase can be made into several kinds of plates, the raised letters of handsetting do not necessitate a raised printing method (typically, letterpress). *Gravure* and *offset* printing processes can also accommodate foundry type.

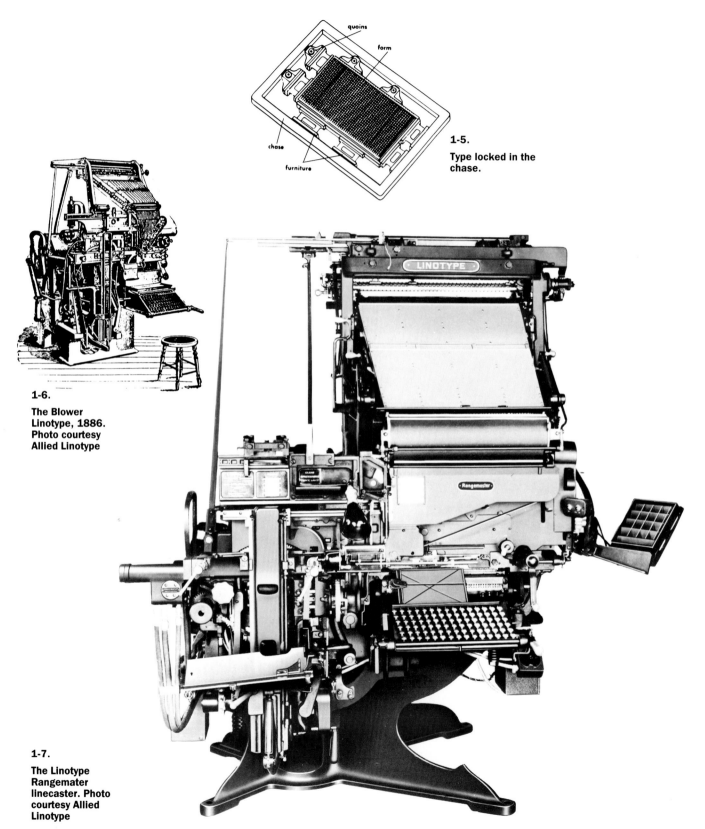

1-5.
Type locked in the chase.

1-6.
The Blower Linotype, 1886. Photo courtesy Allied Linotype

1-7.
The Linotype Rangemater linecaster. Photo courtesy Allied Linotype

HOT TYPE—MACHINE COMPOSITION

In 1884, a German immigrant to America, Ottmar Mergenthaler, perfected the Linotype, the first mechanical system that effectively produced type. Within twenty years, this *linecasting* typesetter transformed the composition rooms of America's newspapers and printing plants (figs. 1-6 and 1-7). A Linotype operator sits at the keyboard, much like a secretary uses a typewriter (the two keyboards are, however, very dissimilar). As characters are entered on the Linotype keyboard, a casting machine molds individual lines of type.

The principle of linecasting was relatively simple: a page was created more easily by assembling full lines of type rather than individual letters, and composition was quicker. But it took over fifty years of experimentation to perfect the technology. Early models of mechanical typesetters either did not work at all or were simply too slow. Mark Twain lost a fortune investing in the Paige typesetter, a Mergenthaler competitor that never went into production.

What did Mergenthaler accomplish that others did not? He perfected a system that allowed for a *circulating matrix.* A matrix is an individual lettermold which, combined with other matrices, forms the line to be cast in one piece. When a Linotype operator strikes a key on the keyboard, a matrix drops down from the overhead *magazine.* The matrices are collected in a tray until the limits of a line are reached. When a line is filled, the operator pushes a lever; the lever is a mechanical signal to the machine to begin the linecasting.

After a line is cast, the matrices for that particular line are no longer needed. However, because an endless supply of matrices is a physical impossibility, each matrix must be recirculated to its original magazine if it is to be used again. Mergenthaler's solution was simple and reliable. Each matrix was cut with a different set of notches (similar in appearance to a key). As the matrices moved along a rail, called the distribution bar, they found their unique grooves and fell back into their proper places in the magazine. The setting and linecasting processes were then repeated.

The Linotype replaced individual letters with full, independent lines of type as the building blocks of pages. Machine composition revolutionized both the setting of type and the preparation, or *makeup,* of type into complete pages.

Advancements were fast in the rapidly mechanized nineteenth and early twentieth centuries. In 1887, Tolbert Lanston invented the Monotype, a linecasting machine that produced both body (text) and display (headline) typesetting. By 1911, Washington Ludlow was marketing his Ludlow Typograph, a second display linecasting system. In 1914, the patents for the original Mergenthaler Linotype expired, and a competing company, Intertype, began to produce a linecaster almost identical to the original.

Although many small print shops still use linecasting and even handsetting methods, the vast majority of type is no longer set in metal today. The greatest revolution in typesetting technology occurred after World War II, in the late 1940s and early 1950s.

COLD TYPE—PHOTOTYPESETTING

The third way to set type, following handsetting and linecasting, is phototype. As the name implies, phototype uses photography as its basic principle. There are several ways in which this is accomplished, but the first successful phototypesetting machine, the 1947 *Fotosetter,* simply replaced

1-8.
The Fotosetter.

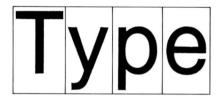

1-9.

Phototypesetting
***(top)* versus photo**
display typography.

1-10.

Direct impression:
carbon and cloth.

the metal lettermolds of the Linotype with photographic negatives. Instead of casting lines of metal type, the lines were photographed (fig. 1-8).

The basic principles of phototypesetting were not new. As early as 1871, Ringwalt's *Encyclopedia of Printing* included a report on "phototypography." Experiments continued throughout the late nineteenth century, but the success of the Linotype made the perfection of phototypesetting a low priority in the early twentieth century.

By the 1950s, offset lithography began to replace letterpress in American print shops as the printing method of choice. In order to print handsetting or linecasting by offset lithography, high-quality *reproduction proofs* were made. These proofs served as the master from which, first, the negatives and, then, the plates necessary to the offset lithography process were made. The photographic production of type eliminated the need for reproduction proofs, allowing for direct-to-plate offset production. The popularity of hot-type composition methods slowly diminished. But photo-type only gradually became standard procedure until the late 1960s, when the computer dramatically accelerated the pace with which phototypesetting became the preeminent technique.

As with many other industries, the computer radically changed typesetting. Linotype operators, at their best, produced about four lines per minute. Today's computerized typesetters have maximum speeds of up to 6,000 lines per minute. The technology has quickly evolved through several generations, from the film strips of the 1960s through the digital scanning of the 1980s. Those generations, and the 35-year history of phototype, will be discussed later, but one important factor facilitated the need for the laser speeds of the 1980s: memory.

No one can type 6,000 lines per minute. In today's phototype-setting shops, operators using several computer terminals keyboard typographic codes and documents. When a job is completed, memory is stored magnetically on floppy diskettes, tape, or rigid disks, which allow memory to be moved to the phototypesetter for composition. It is not unusual to construct a system with dozens of input terminals and one incredibly fast photo unit.

Today, typesetting input takes several forms: the traditional work pattern in the typesetting company; the new "cottage industry" of typesetters who work at home on their own terminals and periodically deliver their memory to the typesetting company; the customers who type their own jobs and send electronic memory rather than paper copies to the type-setter; the up-to-date type house, which uses word processors for typesetting input; the data-base typography of large corporations set in-house instead of by commercial type houses; and the electronic publishing industry, which transmits memory directly to intelligent copiers for multiple images. The traditional typesetter, one man at the machine, is gone. He has been replaced by computerized speed and technological improvement.

COLD TYPE—PHOTOLETTERING

Photolettering devices set headline type (correctly referred to as *display* type). Phototypesetters are very efficient in producing *body,* or *text,* type, but they simply do not create the excellent display lettering that is necessary for high-quality typography (fig. 1-9).

The advantage of photolettering devices is that they produce many sizes and styles of type at low cost. Some manufacturers offer up to five thousand different typefaces. Moreover, many machines are capable of skewing letters to produce special-effect characters that are condensed, staggered, slanted, expanded, or even curved.

COLD TYPE—DIRECT IMPRESSION

Typesetting with a typewriter is variously known as strike-on composition, direct-impression typesetting, and, simply, typewriter composition. Direct-impression typesetting requires that a carbon ribbon be used to produce a sharp, clean impression on reproduction-quality paper. Cloth ribbons are not acceptable (fig. 1-10).

Several companies have produced direct-impression typesetting devices, but only one, IBM, still has machines on the market. Singer, Friden, and Varityper have all ceased production, in part because the decreasing cost of phototypesetting machines has virtually eliminated direct impression's only advantage over phototypesetting, the initial cost of equipment.

In general, direct-impression typesetting does not provide perfect quality or a wide range of type styles and sizes. The difference in quality, however, is often not noticeable to persons untrained in typography (fig. 1-11).

COLD TYPE—OTHER METHODS

There are three other sources of type: dry transfer lettering sheets, cut-out lettering sheets, and hand lettering.

Dry transfer lettering is often used in graphic design to produce professional *layouts.* It is also popularly used by small, low-budget print shops for display lettering (fig. 1-12). Sheets of letters are printed with a pressure-sensitive material on the back, which, when rubbed with a ballpoint pen or burnisher, transfers the letter from the sheet to a working surface. Errors can be corrected by removing letters with a soft eraser or rubber cement pickup.

Cut-out lettering is printed on low-tack adhesive paper, so that individual letters can be separated from the sheet, peeled from the protective backing, and placed in position. Lettering is placed with great accuracy before burnishing.

Hand lettering must be drawn in ink by professional letterers or calligraphers. This technique is usually limited to logos, trademarks, or custom designs, but occasionally it is used in place of typesetting to satisfy a specific demand (fig. 1-13). When hand lettering is required, the image is inked on heavy board and then photographically reduced to sharpen the image, eliminate minor imperfections, and protect the original rendering from possible damage.

The IBM typewriter composition sys varying in memory capacity. The fir entry typesetter—as the keyboarder The second typesetter in the IBM lir (ESC). It has machine memory—the two pages of information, which car

I think that new printing types ba of historic letterforms and design special printing conditions of too expression of the time in which avoid the word "modern." I simp must reflect the spirit of tod

1-11.

Direct impression *(above)* versus phototypesetting.

Letraset *instant letter...*

AAAAAAAAAAA.
BBBBBBBBBBCCCC
DDDDDDDDDDEE
EEEEEEEEEEEEEE
GGGGGGGGHHHHH
IIIIIIIIIIIIIIIIIIIIIIII

1-12.

Letraset lettering sheet.

1-13.

Calligraphy for Committee In Support of Solidarity.

College Education (1)		
X_{i1}	$(X_{i1} - \overline{X}_1)^2$	X_{i2}
90	$(90 - 90)^2 = 0$	80
95	$(95 - 90)^2 = 25$	75
90	$(90 - 90)^2 = 0$	85
85	$(85 - 90)^2 = 25$	80
	$\Sigma = 50$	80
$\overline{X}_1 = 90$		

1-14.

Example of technical typography.

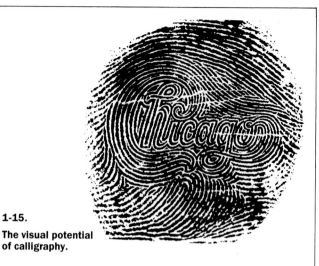

1-15.

The visual potential of calligraphy.

Bedford Computer Corporation	Consolidated Balance Sheets		
December 31.		1981	1980
Assets			
Current Assets			dollars in thousands
Cash and temporary cash investments		$1290	$ 135
Accounts receivable			
Trade (less allowance for doubtful accounts of $50 in 1981 and $48 in 1980)		1567	793
Company affiliated through common ownership		28	18
Inventories		2688	1147
Prepaid expenses		17	15
Deferred income taxes		80	12
Total Current Assets		5670	2120
Property and Equipment — At Cost			
Leasehold improvements		58	4
Furniture and fixtures		48	36
Production equipment		176	9
Vehicles		71	40
Equipment leased to others		112	83
Total		465	177
Less Accumulated depreciation and amortization		106	43
Property and Equipment, Net		359	129
Other Assets		55	94
Total Assets		$6084	$2343

1-16.

Tabular composition from Bedford Corporation Annual Report, 1981.

Frank Sinatra

" There are very few singers whom musicians respect. And Sinatra is tops with musicians, he's the one they really admire, because he sings the way a great saxophone player plays. Sinatra was a rock star before there was Presley, before there was rock 'n' roll. He was *the* pop star. He also had the image of being a swinger. And that was cool. It had a certain diddly-bop to it. I remember those album covers with his jacket falling off his shoulder, and the hat cocked at an angle. I still see that image when I hear Sinatra sing. But that's not what impressed me about the man—I didn't read *Photoplay*. The voice is what got to me. "

—Billy Joel

1-17.

Typographic variations: roman, italic, bold, and bold italics. From *Esquire*, June 1986.

3.23 DELUXE INTERIORS

PROOF THAT MAZDA'S QUEST FOR EVER-HIGHER LEVELS OF PERFORMANCE DOES NOT END WHERE THE INTERIOR BEGINS.

Below, you see the remarkable inner world of the 323 Deluxe Sedan. Here you'll find rich cut-pile carpeting, sumptuous velour upholstery, and room to relax and stretch out in uncommon comfort. Yet the true task of this well-appointed interior is to help you take full advantage of the 323's superb performance capabilities. And every facet of the interior's design has been crafted with consummate care to achieve this goal.

Bountiful driving conveniences.

Settle into the deeply contoured driver's seat and you'll instantly notice the way it holds you firmly yet comfortably in place. Or the way the thickly wrapped steering wheel presents itself at just the right angle for optimum comfort and control.

What you may not notice at first glance are the myriad of driving conveniences that are at your command. On the floor beside the driver's seat are remote releases for the locking fuel-filler door and trunk lid. The side mirror is adjustable by remote control. The rearview mirror is the day/night type to cut reflected headlight glare. There's a covered coin box to the left of the steering wheel. And the windshield wipers include the intermittent-action feature so handy in a light mist or drizzle. And all of the above are, of course, standard equipment.

1-18.

Rules in excellent typography.

1-19.

Typographic style in advertising.

The Value of Typography

Each year, business produces over 72 billion pieces of written communication. In the 1980s, that communication has increasingly been typeset instead of typewritten. Because of that change, and because of the simplification of the technological process of typesetting, more people than ever before are involved in the production of typesetting and the art of typography (fig. 1-14). There are several reasons for the growth of typography as a solution to communications problems.

Legibility. Type styles are specifically designed to be legible: shape of letters, density, spacing, and clarity of characters all contribute to the overall ease of comprehension. Type designers, the creators of type styles, are rigorously trained in the psychology and science of our perception. By using the results of studies that have determined how we read, how we react to certain shapes and colors, and how patterns affect written communications, type designers blend science with art to produce typefaces that combine aesthetic appeal and effective communication.

Visual Appeal. Type is more attractive than typewriting. In business, hundreds of pieces of paper may cross a desk in any given day. The attractively produced and designed message has a greater chance of being noticed than typewriter text. The message that looks professional and authoritative is more likely to be read by the corporate manager faced with a dozen competing brochures.

Interest. A significant purpose of a book, magazine, advertisement, or newspaper headline is to "tease" the reader. Typesetting permits the use of eye-catching type styles, superior charts and graphics, and optical diversity first to capture and then to retain the reader's interest (fig. 1-15). A typeset chart, for instance, is far more interesting than a typewritten row of figures (fig. 1-16). Words that are emphasized with italic or bold variations of a typeface are more appealing than underlined or capitalized typewriting or word processing (fig. 1-17). Today's typesetting machines also allow for vertical and horizontal *rules* that organize the page visually and attract the eye (fig. 1-18).

Emotive Impact. Typewritten text styles all look similar. The variety of typefaces permits the typographer unlimited creative freedom. Any image can be imparted by typeface selection: solidity or refinement, glamor or strength, festivity or seriousness. It is not an accident that the typographic design of a stock offering is very different from that of an ad selling women's clothing (fig. 1-19).

Compaction. Type is not only more graphically effective than typewriting; it can be more cost-effective as well. Because typeset characters are proportionally spaced, they take up less room than typewritten characters. The exact figure will vary depending on what type size is used, but typeset copy occupies approximately 40 percent of the space required for the same amount of typewritten copy (fig. 1-20).

For example, if a corporation is preparing a 100-page typewritten report and 250 copies will be printed, the job, if typewritten, will require 25,000 sheets of paper. However, if the report is professionally typeset, compaction will result in a report that is only 60 pages long. This means that in the same press run of 250 copies, only 15,000 sheets of paper will be required. Not only will typesetting save a significant amount of paper, but printing, postage, and handling expenses will also be reduced.

Productivity. Finally, the automation of the office has resulted in a new understanding of productivity. Office managers are concerned not only with how quickly material is produced, but with how well it works. Because typesetting is more legible, more attractive, and more professional

n 1955 a novel was published with the title *The Man in the Gray Flannel Suit.* Almost immediately, those words became an American catchphrase. The man in the gray flannel suit came to represent all that was perceived to be wrong with American business—the conformity, the stodginess, the lack of true creativity, the unquestioning obedience to executive authority.

The book became a best seller, and was republished in some twenty-six languages. The book's author, Sloan Wilson, commenting upon the phenomenon of the book years after its publication, said, "Suddenly the book, or at least the title, became something of a joke in the United States. I remember a television skit in which Art Carney climbed out of a sewer in dirty overalls and said to Jackie Gleason, 'What did you expect, the man in the gray flannel suit?'... *Mad* magazine had a takeout on gray flannel. The title [was] good for a big yuck when

```
     In 1955 a novel was published
with the title The Man in the the
Gray Flannel Suit. Almost immedi-
ately, those words became an
American catchphrase. The man  in
the gray flannel suit came to
represent all that was perceived
to be wrong with American business--
the conformity, the stodginess, the
lack of true creativity.
     The became a best seller, and
was republished in some twenty-six
languages. The book's author,
Sloan Wilson, commenting upon the
phenomenon of the book years after
its publication, said, "Suddenly
the book, or at least the title,
became something of a joke in the
United States. I remember a tele-
vision skit in which Art Carney
climbed out of a sewer in dirty
overalls and said to Jackie
Gleason, 'What did you expect, the
man in the gray flannel suit?'....
Mad magazine had a takeout on gray
flannel. The title [was] good for
a big yuck when any comedian
mouthed it."
```

1-20.

Compaction.

1-21.
The tradition of
book typography: 1895

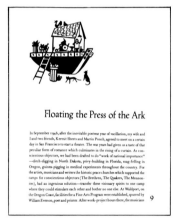

1-22.
Traditional book typography.
Typographer: Adrian Wilson,
***Printing for Theater*, 1957.**

1-23.
Experimental typography.
Typographer: Robert Massin,
La Cantatrice Chauve
by Eugene Ionesco, 1964.

than typewriting, it is widely recognized as the superior medium for conveying a message.

Moreover, typesetting is more memorable than typewriting. Researchers at ITT had discovered that typeset paragraphs are remembered longer and understood better than typewritten ones. Although the initial expense of typesetting equipment is greater, a proven return on investment is evident both in typographic appeal and cost-efficiency. As a result, the explosion of corporate and in-house typography is expected to continue.

The Industry: Who Uses Type?

There are several thousand companies in the United States and Canada that specialize in setting type. But inexpensive, easy-to-use typesetting machines are expanding the number of type rooms in today's printing industry. Forty years ago, a conventional type house possessed Linotypes and Ludlows and foundry type cases. A large initial investment was required, and the typesetting industry was populated with a relatively small number of establishments.

Today, typesetting options are growing as typesetting equipment is becoming less expensive. Decreasing prices are a common result of rapidly changing technology. After the initial research and development costs of new machines have been recouped by the manufacturer, prices go down and the manufacturers continue to sell equipment profitably. There are more than eighty thousand in-house graphics facilities in the United States, many of which set type for the corporation, advertising agency, professional association, or magazine that has established the facility. Many of the more than forty thousand printers sell type as a profitable sideline and as a service to their customers. Quick printers, newspapers, and magazine publishers also offer typesetting services. Because the initial investment for typesetting equipment can be under $20,000, hundreds of entrepreneurs throughout the United States and Canada have established one-person typesetting businesses in small offices or even in their own homes—an impossibility in the days of hot-metal composition.

Output options have expanded with the number of organizations using type. As technology becomes even more affordable, typesetting will continue to proliferate. The changing structure of the industry may result in fewer specialty type houses and many more in-house type shops, but the basic work patterns of typesetting will not be altered. Books, newspapers, magazines, and advertising must still be designed and set.

BOOK TYPOGRAPHY

Book design, the oldest typographic tradition, continues to be a vital part of the typesetting and printing industry (fig. 1-21). In fact, 10 billion dollars are spent annually on book publishing alone.

Typography is important to the book in three distinct areas: the cover and jacket design, the text, and the illustrative material (charts and graphs).

Hardcover dust jackets and paperback covers, like the credits that appear at the beginning of a motion picture, establish an appropriate mood. The movie titles for a Western may be set in a typeface that evokes the Old West. Similarly, the jacket design of a book can be whimsical or serious, antique or modern, depending on the book's content.

Text, or body, type is chosen far less for its emotional impact than for simple legibility. There is a debate about the relative merits of evocative typography. But within the constraints of the book's size and design,

1-24.

Newspaper mastheads: typography as a reflection of historical periods and diverse reading audiences.

1-25.

Digitek 3000 with attached Preview Terminal. Photo courtesy Itek Composition Systems

the typographer selects a typeface that best reflects what the book is about.

Charts, tables, and graphs are exempt from any debate regarding emotive appeal. Typeset illustrative material is designed to present information that can be interpreted immediately. A well-designed graph can convey statistical information that would otherwise be difficult to understand.

Book typography, then, must be emotive, legible, and informative as the situation demands. Those three functions offer a construct into which all typography must fit. But, although it tends to be less adventurous than the magazine or advertising fields, the book publishing industry has the opportunity to produce revolutionary as well as traditional typography (figs. 1-22 and 1-23). Most publishers are aware of typographic standards and attempt to offer books that are designed and produced well. Design strategies are discussed and executed either by in-house graphics personnel or by free-lance book designers. Very few publishers actually typeset their own books, and almost no major houses physically print what they publish. Contracts are usually signed with type houses and book manufacturers (printers who specialize in book printing and binding) on a competitive bid basis, so that the type house or printer that offers the lowest cost estimate does the job.

NEWSPAPER TYPOGRAPHY

Two kinds of typographers are necessary for the production of any newspaper: newspaper designers and graphic designers.

A newspaper designer establishes a visual philosophy for a paper, which can be traditional or contemporary, staid or friendly, depending on what the publisher and editors of the paper require (fig. 1-24). Newspaper designers are trained to use seemingly insignificant details, such as changes in typeface and type weight and the use of horizontal rules. Although these differences are usually imperceptible to the reading audience, they cause a demonstrable change in the reader's attitude. A minor alteration in headline typography can increase—or, possibly, decrease—a newspaper's circulation.

The graphic designer works within the format created by the newspaper designer. At all large and medium-sized dailies, and at most smaller newspapers, the designer typically works at a layout terminal, where each page is designed on a day-to-day basis within the parameters set for the front page, editorial page, metropolitan page, and so on (fig. 1-25). Thus, graphic designers working for newspapers are very restricted. Type sizes, typeface selections, length of typeset lines, length of type columns, and even the size and position of photographs are often predetermined. Those restrictions, however, are a challenge that many designers enjoy. Each day the newspaper must fit the given format yet still be typographically interesting.

Graphic designers are further restricted by the technology used to produce newspapers. Newspaper presses are designed for speed, not high quality. Photographic reproduction is comparatively poor, and the printing quality of color illustrations is often sketchy. When designing any piece for a newspaper, typographers must keep in mind that small details and type sizes will not reproduce as well as large, strong designs. Although some papers (such as the Gannett Corporation's *USA Today*) have made remarkable strides toward excellent color reproduction, newspaper typography is predominantly a black-and-white affair. Fashion ads appearing in newspapers are usually illustrated with line or wash drawings because they reproduce better than photography.

1-26.

U&lc, a source of
continuously
excellent
typography.

MAGAZINE TYPOGRAPHY

As one might expect, the typography of magazines is quite similar to that of newspapers. Magazine designers create formats and graphic designers work within established guidelines. In general, there are three kinds of magazines: general circulation publications, trade journals, and house magazines. General circulation magazines, such as *Time, TV Guide, Field and Stream,* and *Ladies' Home Journal,* are intended for a wide reading public. Trade journals, on the other hand, are planned to meet the needs of a specific audience. For example, graphic designers might subscribe to *The Typographer, Graphic Arts Monthly,* or the International Typeface Corporation's *U&lc.* Even more specialized, house magazines have a limited readership with a controlled circulation. *The American Ceramic Society Journal* and *DuPont* are sample publications in this area. Even though they may have relatively limited audiences and, in some cases, small budgets, trade and house magazines can be as typographically excellent as general circulation magazines. See, for example, sample covers of *U&lc* (fig. 1-26).

     Whatever the magazine, the designer has an intriguing new problem to solve: how to make the *banner,* which is nearly always on the cover, immediately recognizable. A successful banner is a merger of color and letters, which produces a lasting impression that does not derive from linguistic communication.

     Like a logotype or trademark, the banner shouts out the name of the product to the potential consumer. *Time* magazine's four red letters make the magazine identifiable even before the individual letters have been discerned. When the banner works as well as that, the reader will pay much less attention to any other type on the cover; a photograph or drawing becomes more important than words in conveying the content of the publication.

     A serious problem for magazine designers is where to place dozens of advertisements with varying typography to form a coherent whole. Highly successful magazines have very strict advertising typography standards, whereas less prosperous journals may be forced to accept substandard advertising design in the interest of profit. Fortunately, most advertising typographers realize that magazines offer a premier opportunity both to sell their clients' services and to display their own talents. Indeed, magazine typography provides a great deal of opportunity for excellence and innovation (figs. 1-27 through 1-30).

1-27.

Page spread from
Avant Garde,
designed by Herb
Lubalin.

1-28.

Cover of *Bauhaus* **magazine, designed by Joost Schmidt.**

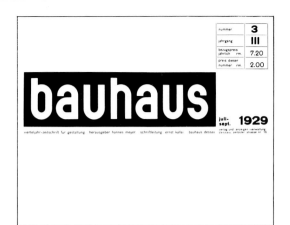

1-29.

Contemporary magazine design: March 1986, *Magazine Design and Production.*

The Corporate Side of Electronic Publishing

Electronic technical publishing systems offer corporations many benefits

BY JAMES KLAUBER

Many companies and organizations are in the publishing business, although not all of them know it. According to one corporate publishing expert, the yearly publication output of the top 10,000 American companies exceeds that of the commercial book publishing industry.

Many of these corporate publications are technical documents and books, such as user documentation, training and repair manuals, and catalogs. These special documents typically have been produced using expensive, labor-intensive, time-consuming methods. But today, revolutionary electronic publishing systems are coming on the market that promise to change the way technical documents are produced forever.

Technical documents have several characteristics that distinguish them from other kinds of corporate publications. Unlike annual reports or product brochures, technical publications tend to have consistently formatted pages rather than individually designed pages. Unlike typical office documents such as memos and reports, technical documents usually are fairly lengthy, averaging about 100 pages. Unlike promotional literature directed to customers, technical documents are more educational or technical and can be published for employers as well as customers. And, unlike most other corporate publications,

which are published only once, technical publications often must be stored, updated, and republished frequently.

The average technical document has a high percentage of graphics, averaging between 20 and 25 percent. Line art, charts, graphs, and tables are more common than photographs. Frequently produced under very tight deadlines, many technical documents also undergo frequent revisions throughout the production cycle because of product changes, engineering developments, and so on.

Technical documents include a wide variety of publications, including maintenance manuals, product specifications, engineering documentation, installation and assembly manuals, user documentation and reference manuals, price and parts lists, catalogs, proposals, and contracts.

Technical documents usually are produced within corporations either by in-house graphic arts departments or by publishing groups dedicated to technical documents. Outside resources also can be called upon, but most technical publishing functions are handled in-house.

Until recently, publishing these corporate technical documents has been an expensive, laborious, and time-consuming process that required highly skilled, highly paid

Continued on page 54

MARCH 1986 53

1-30.

Whitespace in advertising.

MANNY PEREZ
DIRECTOR

SCOTT KULOK
DIRECTOR

Perez and Kulok. If you're in advertising perhaps you've heard about them. Each in his own way has always been known for television advertising that gets noticed.

Manny Perez. 14 years at Young & Rubicam. He's directed. He's produced. He's art directed. He's even been a creative director, and, for the past six years he headed up the largest commercial production department in the business. He's won every award the advertising industry has to offer. What Perez can now offer the industry is an intense dedication to high standards and a unique understanding of all the creative elements which add up to provocative, powerful, and, best of all, tasteful advertising.

Scott Kulok. The attention and acclaim that Scott Kulok has won from his peers at Young & Rubicam (and Wells, Rich, Greene, and Scali, McCabe, Sloves) didn't just happen by chance. It comes from a professional and personal commitment to outstanding television advertising. The awards he has received as art director, producer, and director serve as evidence of a very rare talent.

Perez, Kulok and all the people at Filmfair are singularly dedicated to making television commercials that move, persuade, touch, excite, and involve the viewer. In short, advertising that works. Judy Wolff will be pleased to show you the reels and discuss how the talents of Manny Perez or Scott Kulok may benefit your next production.

FILMFAIR NEW YORK
35 East 20th Street, New York, N.Y. 10003 212-505-0500

JUDY WOLFF
SALES REPRESENTATIVE

TARA McCARTHY
EXECUTIVE PRODUCER

1-31.

Illegibility as a typographic device.

ADVERTISING TYPOGRAPHY

Advertising typography is typography designed to sell. The first step in selling the product or service of the client is to catch the attention of the reader. Advertising typography therefore emphasizes the role of display type over text type and illustrative elements. Even when a brilliant drawing or photograph is used to draw attention, the ad cannot work until the product or service being advertised is identified with letters and words. Advertising is thus primarily typographic. Even television advertising always contains several typographic statements of the product's name.

There are no rules in advertising typography, except that the client must be satisfied. More than in other fields of typography, advertising layouts are approved by a single client who pays the bill. Thus, advertising must be created to suit the subjective tastes of the client and his customers.

Type in print advertising need not be legible (fig. 1-31), or horizontal (fig. 1-32), or even in an understandable language (fig. 1-33). The type must only be appealing. There are exceptions, of course, but advertising typography is the least reliant upon convention. Novelty and creativity are the bywords of the advertising typographer.

1-32.

New Wave slants.

1-33.

Foreign-language advertising typography.

JOBWORK

Jobwork is a catch-all phrase used to refer to design projects that do not fit into some large category, such as bookwork, publication design, or advertising. And that encompasses a great deal: brochures, annual reports, catalogs, directories, letterheads and envelopes, business cards, forms and labels, coupons, menus, package designs, record jackets, calendars, and posters. In a sense, the beginning typographer who focuses on jobwork has to be the most creative and knowledgeable member of the profession. Working with a variety of clients on many different kinds of jobs, he or she must have (or develop) at least a rudimentary understanding of a dozen different printing specialties. What is the standard size of a business card? How fast can a forms manufacturer produce 10,000 copies of an invoice? How big is a number 10 envelope? Who does comb binding? How should the typography for a brochure die cut be executed? Is thermography acceptable for a wedding invitation or must the more expensive engraving process be used? These are the sorts of day-to-day questions a typographer working in a job shop must answer. Jobwork is demanding and ever-changing—a perfect position for the beginning typographer who wishes to learn the entire field before specializing.

THE ANATOMY OF TYPE

Throughout the history of typography, typefaces have been developed for specific purposes. Every typeface is part of a common heritage, which has produced a terminology describing the various parts of the letter and the page. As early as the fifteenth century, typographers and calligraphers were communicating with special technical terms. Today, this technical language must be mastered by anyone interested in type.

The history of typography can be a burden. Much of the terminology we use has survived from the days of handsetting and linecasting. For example, typographers usually refer to capital letters as *uppercase* and small letters as *lowercase* because, when letters were handset, capitals were distributed farther away from the typesetter, in the upper part of the case. Small letters, which were needed more often, were located in the lower case, within easy reach. These and many other words are legacies of a typesetting method that has long been supplanted. A primary reason for the study of typographic history is that an awareness of the past helps us to understand the words we have inherited.

The Parts of a Letter

Any discussion of type anatomy is complicated by the lack of a recognized nomenclature. Adding to this confusion, the terminology used to describe letter shapes (and many other characters, such as punctuation marks and numbers) varies from country to country. Despite the arcane and often difficult language of printing processes, the language of typography is simplified by general terms for the four major elements of the letter: the serif, counter, ascender, and descender. These *typeface characteristics* offer type designers a variety of possibilities for manipulating each character.

SERIFS

A stroke is a straight line that makes up part of a letter. Various letters have horizontal, vertical, or diagonal strokes. The letter *M,* for instance, always has at least four strokes: two vertical and two diagonal. The *M,* however, may also have *serifs.* The serif is a short cross-stroke that projects from a main stroke (fig. 2-1).

Serifs are a curious historical bequest from the Romans, the first civilization to fully develop characters that look much like ours. When Roman stonecutters carved words into the Coliseum, the Column of Trajan, and other monuments, they finished off the rough edges that their tools left at the tops and bottoms of letters with a special instrument that created a crisp horizontal line. Fifteen hundred years later, Renaissance humanists were interested in preserving the Greco-Roman heritage. They copied the style of Roman lettering in their own typeface designs, thus perpetuating the tradition of serifs, if only for their aesthetic value. Twen-

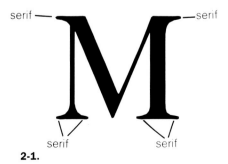

2-1.

Example of serifs in the letter *M.*

15

2-2.
Sans serifs (left)
versus serifs.

Wood type is wonderful. While nine-teenth century faces have long been relegated to special collections of printing memorabilia, these large letters are still fondly remembered. The size of wood type is not expressed in points but in picas, or "line."

Wood type is wonderful. While nineteenth century faces have long been relegated to special collections of printing memorabilia, these large letters are still fondly remembered. The size of wood type is not expressed in points but in picas, or "line."

2-3.
Four kinds of serifs:
a. bracketed, b.
barbed, c. wedged,
and d. square.

PQRS PQRS PQRS **PQRS**
a   b   c   d

2-4.
Open and closed
counters.

2-5.
Open and closed
bowl.

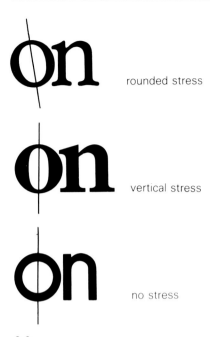

2-6.

**Three kinds of
stress.**

rounded stress

vertical stress

no stress

tieth-century researchers, however, have discovered that the serif does perform a useful task: the short horizontal strokes act as arrows, pointing the reader's eye toward the right.

Before 1800, all typefaces had serifs. Typefaces without serifs are known as *sans serifs* (from the French *sans,* meaning without). One of the first decisions a typographer must make is whether to use a serif or sans serif design (fig. 2-2). If the serif is chosen, the typographer must select one of several different varieties available (fig. 2-3). A strong, wedged serif will contribute a very different impact from a delicate hairline.

Serif selection indicates how critical is an intelligent understanding of type characteristics. A novice typographer may look randomly at a few typeface specimen sheets and simply pick out a typeface that "looks good," unaware that the selected face may not *act* on the page the way it appears on the specimen sheet. A professional typographer, on the other hand, chooses typefaces on the basis of his or her knowledge of what each characteristic contributes.

Serifs with brackets or fillets are traditional, safe, and rather staid. A hairline serif is graceful and nearly feminine. Wedge serifs are much more powerful, but evoke a style reminiscent of the nineteenth century. Cupped serifs are contemporary, relaxed, and almost comic. Square serifs have an exaggerated bulk that is energetic and forceful. Rounded serifs, the most popular choice of typographers, carefully ameliorate the chunkiness of the square serifs, because they combine strength and familiarity. Calligraphic serifs are freely styled and informal.

COUNTERS

A counter is a hollow space that forms an integral part of a letter. Letters such as *a, b, d,* and *o* have closed counters, whereas the letters *c, n,* and *v* have counters that are open (fig. 2-4). The curved stroke that physically creates a counter is a *bowl* or void. The designer may create a slightly open bowl, as in the *g* of figure 2-5, to give the letter an antique look.

The most important decision concerning counters is the choice of *stress* (fig. 2-6). Stress is the degree of slant with which the counter of a letter is designed. There are three types of stress: rounded, vertical, and geometric (figs. 2-7 through 2-9). Geometric stress is actually no stress at all. In general, rounded stress is the most legible option. Because vertically and geometrically stressed letters consist of less white space and more mass, letters designed with these stresses are more dazzling and thus more attractive to the eye. There are, of course, degrees of variation among the three options, but all typefaces, whether they are serifs or sans, have some form of stress.

2-7.

Rounded stress.

2-8.

Vertical stress.

2-9.

Geometric stress.

GHJKLMNO

GHIJKLMNO

GHIJKLMNO

2-10.

The x-height.

ASCENDERS AND DESCENDERS

Perhaps the simplest term to understand in typography is the *x-height,* the height of a lowercase *x* (fig. 2-10). A common error among students first learning typography is to equate the size of letters with the x-height. However, there is actually little connection between x-height and type size.

The basic references for type size are the ascenders and descenders. Ascenders are the parts of letters such as *b, d, k,* and *t* that rise above the x-height. Descenders fall below the x-height, as in the letters *p* and *q* (fig. 2-11).

Type is measured in a system of *picas* and *points.* There are 12 points to the pica and approximately 6 picas to the inch. Type size is expressed in sizes ranging from the tiny 6-point type to the 10-point type commonly used in specifying books to 72-point display and so on (fig. 2-12). When determining the point size of a letter, one must be certain to measure from *the top of an ascender to the bottom of a descender* (fig. 2-13).

Because of the manner in which type size is measured, the relative lengths of ascenders and descenders become quite important. Some faces have a very large x-height (and therefore short ascenders and descenders).

2-11.

Ascenders and descenders.

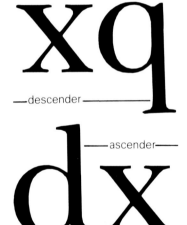

2-12.

Type sizes, to 72-point.

72 ABCDEFGHIJKLI

60 ABCDEFGHIJKLMNC

48 ABCDEFGHIJKLMNOPQR

36 ABCDEFGHIJKLMNOabcdefghijkl

24 ABCDEFGHJKLMNOPQRSTUVabcdefghjklmnopqr

18 ABCDEFGHIJKLMNOPQRSTUVWXYZabcdefghijklmnopqrstuvw

12 ABCDEFGHIJKLMNOPQRSTUVWXYZabcdefghijklmnopqrstuvwxyz

10 ABCDEFGHIJKLMNOPQRSTUVWXYZ abcdefghijklmnopqrstuvwxyz

8 ABCDEFGHIJKLMNOPQRSTUVWXYZ abcdefghijklmnopqrstuvwxyz

6 ABCDEFGHIJKLMNOPQRSTUVWXYZabcdefghijklmnopqrstuvwxyz

2-13.

Measuring type size from ascender to descender.

2-14.

Comparison of four different x-heights.

pxf pxf

Baskerville Helvetica

pxf pxf

Optima Caledonia

---

12 POINT, TWO POINTS OF LEAD

Garamond suggests quali
distinction. It is one of the fi

12 POINT, TWO POINTS OF LEAD

A dominant recent them
tionship of one shape

2-15.

Twelve-point Garamond versus twelve-point Helvetica.

Others have very small x-heights with accompanying long ascenders and descenders (fig. 2-14).

The x-height chosen by the type designer in large part determines the general feel of the type. Faces with large x-heights tend to be very open, airy, and legible. Those with small x-heights appear to be more compact and restricted, but take up less space—an important consideration when one designs books, newspapers, and magazines. Compare the two typefaces in figure 2-15. Contrary to appearance, they are actually the *same size*. Faces with a *small* x-height will look *much smaller* than identically sized faces with large x-heights. Indeed, it is quite possible for 10-point type of one design to be visually equivalent to 14-point of another (fig. 2-16).

OTHER TYPE CHARACTERISTICS

The type designer must consider several less important characteristics of letters. For example, the *apex* occurs in any letter, such as *A, V, M,* and *W,* in which two vertical or diagonal strokes meet each other (fig. 2-17). An apex can have any of several shapes: flat and pointed are two of the most common. A hollow or rounded apex can give a completely new character to a typeface that might otherwise be relatively bland.

The *arm* is a horizontal or diagonal stroke that moves away from the main body of the letter. The letters *E, F, L,* and *T,* have horizontal arms; *K, X,* and *Y* have diagonal arms (fig. 2-18). The lower diagonal strokes of the *K* and *X* are the *legs.*

The *bar* is any horizontal stroke necessary for the formation of a letter. A serif is not considered a bar, because it is not an integral part of the letter. Even in sans serif type, certain letters, such as *e, f, t, A, H,* and *T,* require a bar. The bar may be designed as a hairline, medium, or heavy stroke (fig. 2-19).

2-16.

The "visual size" of type largely depends on the x-height. All examples are set in 13-point type.

Alternate Gothic No.1 TYPEMASTER V3073 ABC123abc%#½×˚?!&   Lost Horizons

Bodoni Bold Italic   TYPEMASTER V3082   ABC123abc&!?$

Casual Serif   TYPEMASTER   V30-136   ABC123abc & ?   Contrasting Ideals

Futura Book Italic TYPEMASTER V3049 ABC123abc$?&!Martyr

2-17.

Apexes.

2-18.

Horizontal and vertical arms.

2-19.

Bars.

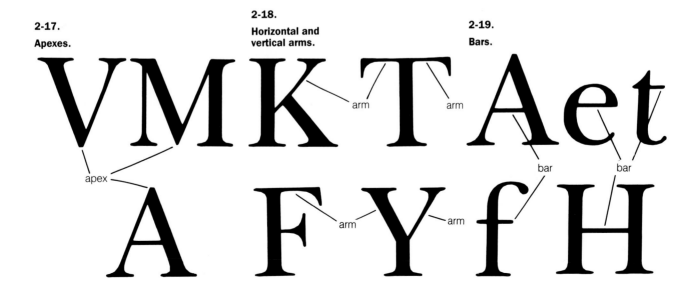

The *beard, nick,* and *spur,* similarly, are all short strokes that project from a major stroke (figs. 2-20 through 2-22). Like the serif, however, they are ornamental rather than essential parts of the letter. The sans serif *G* can be designed with or without a beard. The serif *G* may or may not have a spur.

　　The lowercase *g* has more idiosyncracies than any other letter. The *ear* is a small stroke extending from the upper right side and ending in an optional *ball*. The *link* connects the upper bowl to the lower *loop*, a characteristic found only in a few letters (fig. 2-23). Beginning typographers who are attempting to identify typefaces can put the singularity of the *g* to good use. Notice the subtle differences in the various letterforms in figure 2-24. Type designers have worked and reworked the *g* and all the other characters to distill one particular style. That style is created when the shape chosen for the bowl of the *g*, for instance, is repeated in the bowls of the *a, b, c, d,* and so on through the entire alphabet. Learn the *g* of a particular typeface and any other character in the font will be more recognizable.

2-20.
Beard.

2-21.
Nicks.

2-22.
Spurs.

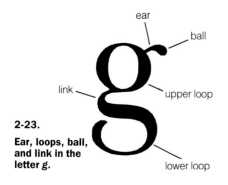

2-23.
Ear, loops, ball, and link in the letter *g*.

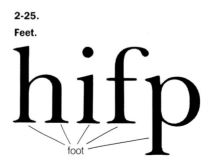

2-24.
Variations on the letter *g*.

2-25.
Feet.

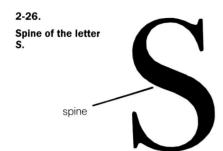

2-26.
Spine of the letter S.

spine

The *foot* and *head* are the lower and upper parts of letters. The style chosen for the foot may be repeated in other letters but some, like the *t*, may require individualized feet. The shape chosen for the foot of a *t* is usually repeated, although reversed, in the head of the *f* (fig. 2-25).

The *shoulder* is a curving stroke, or arc, arising from a stem. Letters such as *m* and *n* have these short letterforms, which follow the hairline, medium, or heavy stroke pattern set by the stem. The curving stroke in the middle of the uppercase and lowercase *s* is the *spine* (fig. 2-26).

Tails are diagonal short strokes, either above or below the baseline, that finish such letters as the *j, y, R,* and *Q* (fig. 2-27). The tail of the *Q* may be horizontal or curved.

Terminals are the several different kinds of finishing touches at the end of a stroke. There are many shapes, including the ball, barbed, pointed, sheared, and teardrop terminals (fig. 2-28).

Arms, legs, spines, shoulders, ears, feet, beards, and hairlines. Many professionals believe that if beginners in typography learn the parts of type, they will more quickly master the art of selecting the most appropriate

2-27.
Tails.

tail

tail

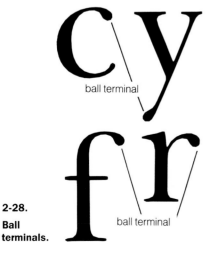

ball terminal

ball terminal

2-28.
Ball terminals.

typeface for a given job. If alphabets are chosen with a particular sort of stem, bowl, and terminal in mind, the typographer who knows how those letterforms function will have solved the design problem. A client may require the impression of stability. If so, a typeface with moderately rounded stress, serifs, heavy bars, closed counters, and a pointed apex is a wise choice. A second client may be attempting to draw customers to his store with type that projects a more festive image. In that case, vertical stress, open counters, large x-height, rounded apex, and teardrop terminals are appropriate.

Effective typeface selection is accomplished in two stages. After the typographer becomes aware of how typefaces are constructed, based on a good knowledge of the parts of each letter, he or she must learn how those parts create messages and elicit emotions. That knowledge will be gained with some practice, talent, and common sense.

LOMBARDIC
Textura
Fraktur
Schwabacher
Rotund
Freeformed

2-29.
**Black letter
typeface designs.**

Venetian
Old Style
Transitional
Personal Style
French Modern
English Modern
New Style

Readability Faces
Legibility Faces

2-30.
**Roman serif
typeface designs.**

Clarendons
New Clarendons
Egyptians
Slab Serifs

2-31.
**Square serif
typeface designs.**

Grotesques
New-Grotesques
Geometric Sans Serifs
Styled Sans Serifs
Stressed Sans Serifs
Softened Sans Serifs

2-32.
**Sans serif typeface
designs.**

Formal Pen
Informal Pen
Small-Serif
Sans-Serif
Formal Brush Letter
Informal Brush Letter
Freehand Brush Letter
ROUNDBALL LETTER
Commercial Script
Ronde
Informal Brush Script
Freestyle Brush Script
Roundball Script

2-33.
**Script and cursive
typeface designs.**

Shadowed
Drop-Shadow
OUTERLINED
RAISED
Ribboned
INCISED
WHITETOP
Squared
CHAMFERED
THICKENED
Rounded
Rugged
Textured
BEVELED
TUSCAN
STENCIL
REVERSED
Woodcut
Typewriter
Outline
PATTERNED

2-34.
Novelty typeface designs.

Typeface Designs

Throughout the history of type, typefaces have been developed in specific patterns called typeface designs. There are many different theories as to how type designs should be classified. Although a universally accepted classification system is much needed, there is no current winner among the various options.

A brief account of recent classification methods suggests the general desire to achieve some sort of standard and the difficulties inherent in that task. In 1954, Maximilian Vox, a French typographer, divided all type into six designs that were further elaborated into ten basic designs by the Association Typographique Internationale in 1961. The British Standards Institution created a third plan in 1965 using nine divisions. A few years later, a West German group, the Deutsche Industrie Norman, constructed a classification system of, again, nine major categories with 35 subgroupings. Meanwhile, in the United States, J. Ben Lieberman completed his Typorama in 1967, containing nine basic designs subdivided into 30 categories.

By the late 1960s, typographers had understood that a systematic classification would be difficult at best, especially for beginners in typography (who perhaps *need* it the most). In his book *Printing Types* (1971), Alexander Lawson of the Rochester Institute of Technology suggested "a rational system," which, with one very small change, will be used throughout this book. Lawson divides the roman serifs into old style, transitional, and modern. For the sake of brevity, these three groups will be discussed here as a single category: roman serifs. The differences between old style romans and transitionals will be clarified in the next chapter.

In this slightly revised version of Lawson's system, there are six major typeface designs: black letter, roman serif (Lawson's old style, transitional, and modern romans), square serif, sans serif, script/cursive, and novelty (figs. 2-29 through 2-34).

The beginning typographer should immediately make a choice among major designs before moving on to specific typeface selection. Novelty typefaces would certainly not be used in any case where a roman serif might be suitable and vice versa. After the design is chosen, typeface selection will already be somewhat limited. With thousands of typefaces from which to choose, eliminating inappropriate design categories is one of the best initial steps in making a correct typeface selection.

Variations, Fonts, and Families

Assume you have chosen Helvetica for a particular job. Created by Max Miedinger in 1954, Helvetica is perhaps the most popular contemporary style. However, it is just that—a type style and not a typeface. Helvetica, like most major faces, exists in different versions, called variations (fig. 2-35). A variation is a typeface based on an original pattern, which is different from the original style in at least one of four ways: weight, proportion, angle, or texture. These changes result in versions that are slanted, lightened, darkened, stretched, widened, or reversed.

Weight is perhaps the most noticeable of the four major variations and is itself subdivided into numerous categories. For example, the British Standard typeface weights are extra light, light, semilight, medium, semibold, bold, extra bold, and ultrabold. Among many other weight classifications are such strange ones as elephant, massive, and slim. The two most common are book (between light and medium) and black (heavier than ultrabold). European designers, especially the Swiss, have recently begun to

Helvetica   **Helvetica**
Helvetica   Helvetica
Helvetica   *Helvetica*
Helvetica   Helvetica
Helvetica   *Helvetica*
Helvetica   **Helvetica**
Helvetica   **Helvetica**
Helvetica   **Helvetica**
Helvetica   **Helvetica**
Helvetica   **Helvetica**
Helvetica **Helvetica**
Helvetica   **Helvetica**
Helvetica Helvetica
Helvetica   Helvetica

Helvetica
Helvetica Inserat
Helvetica Inserat
Helvetica
Helvetica
Helvetica
Helvetica
Helvetica Rounded
Helvetica Rounded
**Helvetica
Rounded**
Helvetica Rounded
Helvetica Rounded

2-35.

**The variations of
Helvetica.**

eliminate the confusion of myriad typeface names by assigning weight and italic variations a number. Univers, designed by Adrian Frutiger in 1957, was the first typeface to be created with this system.

The bolder and extremely light versions of a typeface are best used for display purposes, because they are not particularly legible in large amounts of copy. Regular and medium versions are better alternatives as body copy typefaces.

Typeface proportion refers to the general dimension of the face. A design that has been stretched horizontally or vertically will look completely different from the original face. Variations according to proportion are ultracondensed, extra condensed, condensed, normal, expanded, extra expanded, and ultra expanded. Other common variations include extended, compressed, and wide.

There are only two possible variations corresponding to angle: regular and italic. Sans serif italics are often referred to as *obliques* to distinguish them from true italics. The oblique, designed for most sans serifs, is simply a slightly slanted variation of the parent typeface. The true italic of serif typefaces is slanted, but often contains letterforms that are somewhat different from the parent typeface. The *a, g,* and *v* are often redesigned in the italic variation.

As figure 2-35 suggests, a typographer has the choice of *each* of these three design variables. He or she can select faces such as Helvetica Light Italic and Helvetica Bold Condensed Italic. Moreover, type can be altered in accordance with the fourth major variation, texture: outline and reverse faces are two of the most common reverse variations. Outline faces consist of a line sketching the perimeter of the letter, while the interior is left open. Reverse letters are, most commonly, white characters on a black background.

Once the typeface has been selected and the typographer has chosen the correct variation, further problems await. The type size, along with all the other necessary typesetting parameters (including linespace, wordspace, letterspace, and measure), must now be decided. What does this mean in real numbers? There are 16 major point sizes: 6, 7, 8, 9, 10, 11, 12, 14, 18, 24, 30, 36, 42, 48, 60, and 72. Many of today's typesetting machines offer even greater variety. Yet if there are 36 variations of a selected typeface, and if each variation is available in at least 16 sizes, then there is a minimum of 546 combinations *in the Helvetica family alone.*

FONTS

Those 546 combinations of Helvetica are called *fonts,* the term for the complete collection of all the characters of a typeface in one size. A font may include uppercase letters, lowercase letters, small caps (capital letters the size of lowercase), lining figures (numbers that are all the same height), old style figures (numbers with ascenders and descenders), superscripts and subscripts (sometimes called superiors and inferiors), fractions, mathematical and scientific symbols, punctuation marks, ligatures (two letters joined as one character, as in *fi* or *fl*), diphthongs (two vowels pronounced as one sound, as in æ or œ), accents and diacritical marks, foreign-language characters, reference marks, and monetary symbols. When a type designer creates a typeface, he or she may include all these characters or, depending upon the demands of the particular design, may exclude some characters from the face. Figure 2-36 displays a complete collection of characters of 11-point Baskerville.

ABCDEFGHIJKLMNOPQRST
UVWXYZ abcdefghijklmnop
qrstuvwxyz
$123456 .,;:!?&-/()'' 1234567890
fi/⅛¼⅜½⅝¾⅞

2-36.

**A complete font of
11-point
Baskerville.**

2-37.
The Cheltenham family.

Cheltenham Oldstyle
Cheltenham Wide
Cheltenham Medium
Cheltenham Bold
Cheltenham Bold Condensed
Cheltenham Bold Extra Condensed
Cheltenham Bold Outline
Cheltenham Oldstyle Condensed
Cheltenham Italic
Cheltenham Medium Italic
Cheltenham Bold Italic
Cheltenham Bold Condensed Italic
CHELTENHAM BOLD EXTRA CONDENSED TITLE
Cheltenham Bold Extended
Cheltenham Extrabold
Cheltenham Inline
Cheltenham Inline
Extended
Cheltenham Inline
Extra Condensed

THE FAMILY

The idea of a type family was perfected by Morris Fuller Benton of the American Type Founders (ATF). Organized in 1892, ATF was a merger of more than twenty different type founders that had previously manufactured designs independently which closely resembled one another. Benton was given the task of creating order from the vast array of competing designs. His solution was to bring together all of the typefaces based on one design and to standardize them under a generic name. Old Style Antique and Catalogue Antique, which were cast by two different companies, became parts of the Bookman family. The most popular new family was Cheltenham, which grew from two members in 1904 to more than twenty variations eight years later (fig. 2-37).

A typeface family is thus a collection of variations based on a single design. Before 1892, typefaces were scattered and their names were inconsistent. Today, the family is designed as a consistent whole. Italics, lights, and bolds are rightly considered to be essential parts of a complete typographic product, and variations of a new typeface are incorporated into one intact family (fig. 2-38).

Benguiat Medium
Benguiat Medium Italic
Benguiat Bold
Benguiat Book Condensed
Benguiat Book Condensed Italic
Benguiat Book Italic
Benguiat Book
Benguiat Medium Condensed
Benguiat Medium Condensed Ital.
Benguiat Bold Condensed Ital.
Benguiat Bold Condensed
Benguiat Gothic Book
Benguiat Gothic Med. Italic
Benguiat Gothic Book It.
Benguiat Gothic Medium
Benguiat Bold Italic
Benguiat Gothic Bold

2-38.
Members of the Benguiat family.

3-1.

Cave drawings of
Altamira, Spain,
discovered in 1879.

3-2.

A famous example
of native American
picture-writing. The
story reads: I left

home *(1–2)* in a
canoe *(3)* to be
gone for ten days
(4). I arrived on an
island where two
families lived *(5)*. I

met a friend *(6)*,
and we went
together in a canoe
(7) to another
island *(8)*. We
hunted with bows

and arrows *(9)* and
killed a sea lion
(10). We returned
(11) by canoe *(12)*.
After ten days *(13)*,
I arrived home *(14)*.

3

A SHORT HISTORY OF TYPE

The 26 letters that are the building blocks of written English have evolved over the course of several millenia. Although printing is a far more recent phenomenon, the development of type styles—the refinement of the symbols we use to express ourselves in writing—is a process that began when man first started to communicate.

Pictographs

The first graphic messages were drawn twenty-five thousand years ago as a series of pictures that told a story. Those that have been preserved may have represented the hopes of the artist for a successful hunt, because they usually show animals running, fighting, and dying (fig. 3-1). Known as pictographs, ancient examples are found throughout the world: Norse rock-tracings in Sweden, prehistoric cave paintings in France and Spain, Chinese characters copied from life (for instance, the Chinese pictograph for *house*, looks like a house), and American Indian picture-stories (fig. 3-2).

Obviously, pictographs are not letters. They communicate only through a literal representation of the objects described. A vocabulary of concrete images is therefore more easily represented than abstract ideas. In other words, it may be relatively simple to draw a picture of a house or a goat, but it is more difficult to draw pictures for concepts like hope and despair. Moreover, pictographic narrations of any length require a great deal of physical space.

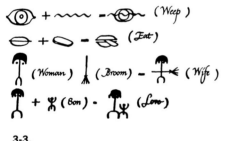

3-3.
Ancient ideographs.

Ideographs

As civilizations grew more sophisticated, they developed ideographs to represent basic ideas. For example, the picture of a moon set above three slashes signified three months and a picture of a man set above eight slashes signified eight men.

By 5000 B.C. in Sumeria, 2000 B.C. in China, and 3500 B.C. in Egypt, two systems had evolved to express abstract ideas. First, complex ideas were symbolized by the combination of two simpler concepts: the picture of water drawn over the picture of an eye represented grief (fig. 3-3). Second, abstractions were illustrated by pictures of concrete objects with which they were associated. A symbol of a star represented the heavens or a peace pipe represented peace.

The Sumerians, Chinese, Aztecs, Mayans, native Americans, and Egyptians all used ideographs. The Japanese and Chinese alphabets are still based on them. In other countries, ideographs continue to be used in logo design and signage (fig. 3-4).

3-4.
Today's ideographs.

3-5.

The hieroglyph for Cleopatra, inscribed in 196 B.C.

3-6.

A hieratic manuscript from the Egyptian *Book of the Dead*, written before 200 A.D.

3-7.

The Phoenician alphabet.

3-8.

The transition from *apis* to A.

Phonograms

Many people followed the same pattern to form alphabets. But our own alphabet owes most to the ancient Egyptians, who combined pictographs, ideographs, and phonograms in a system known as *hieroglyphics*. The Egyptians never did abandon the use of pictures to represent objects or ideas, but they were the first to use pictures that represented *sounds*.

Phonograms developed from pictographs and ideographs. Thus, the wavy line representing water (used in the ideograph for grief) came to be associated with the *n* sound, because the Egyptian word for water was *nu*. Similarly, the sign for mouth (or *ros* in the ancient Egyptian language) eventually evolved into a representation of the *r* sound.

By creating symbols that represented sounds, the Egyptians developed a prototype for the letters that we use today. Although the Egyptians never gave up their pictographs and ideographs, the use of phonograms was refined. Initially, there were several hundred sound-pictures (30 for the letter *A* alone), but that number was reduced to 45, and, finally, to 25 (fig. 3-5). New forms of the hieroglyphs, the hieratic and the demotic, were developed. But the Rosetta Stone, which enabled linguists to decipher Egyptian writing, demonstrated that pictographs combined with the phonogram were still in use as late as 200 B.C. (fig. 3-6).

The Phoenicians

Around 1200 B.C., the Phoenicians gained their independence from Egypt. Phoenicia was a trading nation, doing a brisk shipping business throughout the Mediterranean. They needed a businesslike alphabet to keep their accounts. By borrowing from the Cretans, the Egyptians, the Hittites, and the Babylonians, the Phoenicians created the first writing system composed exclusively of letters.

The Phoenicians borrowed the concept of the letter from the Egyptians. The Egyptian phonogram for *A* was based on the word for ox, *apis;* the Phoenician word for ox was *aleph,* based on the Egyptian. Likewise, the Egyptian word *beth* (meaning ibis) was commandeered by the Phoenicians to become the *b* sound.

Instead of drawing every object in the world, the Phoenicians used 21 characters to represent words. This system suited their business purposes admirably (fig. 3-7). Letters made their accounting easier to understand, quicker to perform, and simpler to learn.

The Greeks

In contrast to the business-oriented Phoenicians, who left no body of literature, the Greeks employed the alphabet in large part to preserve a literary and philosophical tradition. By 1000 B.C., they had adopted a writing system that was adopted from the Phoenicians, and they had begun to transform it to create the true beginning of our alphabet.

The Phoenician system did not satisfy the demands of Greek culture. For instance, it had no vowels. If one is trading fruit, *bshl dts* is a quick and understandable way to record the transaction of a bushel of dates —an item of information devoid of complexity or ambiguity. The Greeks, on the other hand, expressed a cultural requirement by adding five vowels to the Phoenician alphabet. The consonants were renamed in Greek. Indeed, centuries later the first two characters, alpha and beta, inspired the name we now use to refer to the entire system of symbols: the alphabet.

Figure 3-8 shows the transition from the Egyptian pictograph for

READ TO THE RIGHT
AND THEN TO THE LEFT
AND THEN RIGHT AGAIN
AND THEN TO THE LEFT

3-9.
Boustrophedonic writing.

ΑΒΓΔΕΖΗΘΙΚΛΜ
ΝΞΟΠΡΣΤΥΦΧΨΩ

3-10.
The alphabet officially adopted by the city-state of Athens in 403 B.C.

the word *ox* to the Greek letter alpha. The Phoenician aleph seems to be the reverse of the Greek alpha because the Greeks wrote *boustrophedonically,* a wonderful word that means "as the ox plows." Just as an ox reverses its direction after plowing each row of sod, the Greeks wrote the first line of a text from left to right, the second line from right to left, the third line from left to right, and so on (fig. 3-9). Over the centuries, several Phoenician letterforms (like the aleph shown in figure 3-8) were transposed by the Greeks. Our modern letterforms are the result.

By 403 B.C., the Greek alphabet was standardized. An official version of the writing system had been decreed that year by Athens and it was slowly adopted throughout the other city-states of Greece. As you can see from figure 3-10, the alphabet of two thousand years ago strongly resembles the one Greeks use today. However, the ancient Greeks did not have punctuation, lowercase letters, or spaces between words. Those refinements would come later, as would the remaining letters that round out our own system of 26.

The Romans

The Roman alphabet contained 23 letters. Copying from the Etruscans, who had themselves adopted the Greek alphabet, the Romans took the letters *A, B, E, Z, H, I, K, M, N, O, T, X,* and *Y* intact. They remodeled the *C, D, G, L, P, R, S,* and *V,* and revived two Phoenician letters abandoned by the Greeks, the *F* and *Q.* The orderly Romans placed the *F* and the *Q* in the alphabet next to the two letters that most resembled them, the *E* and the *O.* The *Z* comes at the end of our alphabet because, for a time, the Romans discarded it. When they found that the letter was indispensable, it was returned to the alphabet, only this time it went to the back of the line.

The most important contribution of the Romans to our own alphabet was the visual refinement of capital letters. Those incised in the Column of Trajan have been called the perfect expression of a letter. Indeed, they are the basis of all of our typefaces. Yet the Trajan capitals are not geometrically designed: their beauty comes from the subtleties of their curves and strokes, not from their adherence to the classic standard of letter proportion (fig. 3-11). Several artists and calligraphers, including Luca Pacioli, Albrecht Dürer, and Geoffroy of Tory, have attempted to construct geometric formulas for type designs. But none has matched the perfection of the Trajan capitals, which represent the transformation of the comparatively brutish symbols of the Greeks into artistic designs (fig. 3-12).

The Romans were also the first to name letters *A* and *B* instead of alpha and beta or aleph and beth. As discussed, they also contributed the short finishing cross-strokes called serifs. The serifs were used in handwriting as well as stonecarving.

Every lettering style owes its intrinsic form to the tools used to make characters. Babylonian wedge-shaped cuneiform letters were made by pressing wedges into wet clay; the Egyptians chiseled their uncomplicated hieroglyphic characters into stone; the more graceful hieratic script of later Egyptian civilization was drawn on papyrus with reed pens; and the rough Greek letters were drawn in wax with a stylus. Roman letters feature the first examples of thick and thin strokes and graceful curves. Thicker strokes are usually referred to as major strokes; the thinner stroke of the same letter is the minor stroke. Researchers have theorized that the tool required to produce these embellishments was a double-pointed pen. By shifting the angle of the pen, the Roman could produce lines of any width. When a stone was to be carved, a sketch of the letter was first made with this tool

3-11.

The Roman capitals
of the Column of
Trajan.

3-12.

Greek letters versus
Trajan capitals.

VELAMENACAN
VOTAFVTVRAE

3-13.

Quadrata square
capitals.

ΛΟΝΙΑSΙΝ·ΜΟΝΤΙ
VΙΟ:VΙΚΟΡΗΟΕΒΙC

3-14.

Rustica capitals.

3-15.

Everyday Roman
hand.

3-16.

Uncial alphabet.

and then chiseled. Throughout the fourteen hundred years between the design of the Trajan capitals in 114 A.D. and the work of Gutenberg, calligraphers using similar wedge-shaped tools continued to produce these thicks, thins, and curves that were the models for our first typefaces.

Roman Manuscript Hands

From the second through the fifth centuries, Roman letters developed in several ways. The Trajan capitals were created as stone carvings, but at the same time, various forms of calligraphy were evolving. Printing, of course, had not yet been discovered in the West, so any reading material was painstakingly copied by hand by writing specialists known as *scribes*. The Roman scribes produced public documents, literature, and other commissions by wealthy manuscript collectors.

The first style developed by the scribes, the Quadrata square capitals, was a formal alphabet that owed much to the Trajan design (fig. 3-13). The serifs and stresses of Quadrata letters, however, required careful, meticulous calligraphy practical only for the most important inscriptions and documents. Moreover, the Quadrata letters were wide, taking up a great deal of space on the expensive vellum parchment used by the Romans as a writing medium.

3-17.

Semi-uncial script from the *Book of Kells* (circa 8th century).

Not surprisingly, beauty was quickly sacrificed in the scripts that were used to letter less important works. By the fourth century A.D., scribes invented the Rustica capitals for quicker, easier, and less expensive writing. In contrast with Quadrata, Rustica letters are narrow and less ornate (indeed, *Rustica* is the Latin word for *simple*) (fig. 3-14). Note the dots in the middle of the lines, which represent one of the first uses of punctuation. Of course, not all letters were intended for ornate pages. Everyday hands also developed that were as different from the Quadrata and Rustica as today's handwriting is from printing typefaces like Helvetica or Souvenir (fig. 3-15). Most important for the history of type, the less formal hands featured the first use of a form of small letters.

Lowercase letters continued to be developed in the *uncial* hands—a compromise between the elegance of Quadrata and the spare economics of Rustica. The uncial was often used by monk-scribes for copying theological texts, especially the Bible. After the fall of Rome in 456, monks were the great preservers of religious and secular knowledge alike. Many monasteries contained special rooms called scriptoria for the exclusive purpose of copying and illustrating books. Producing bibles, Books of Hours, and public documents, the monks protected and disseminated the legacies of Europe's intellectual and cultural tradition for a thousand years.

3-18.

Semi-uncial script.

Over time, scribes created forms that were simple to write yet retained the intrinsic beauty of more elaborate hands. The rounded letterforms of the uncial and its descendant, the *semi-uncial*, or *half-uncial*, suited both needs (figs. 3-16 through 3-18). The semi-uncial is often classified as a lowercase alphabet—the first complete one in history. Scribes used the lowercase simply for its ease in writing and greater legibility.

During the thousand-year history of the scribes, the basic alphabet of lowercase and uppercase letters was formed. The *U* and *W* were developed from the *V* by the year 1000, and the *J,* based on the *I,* was added by 1500. Spacing between words was not generally adopted until the eleventh century; punctuation marks became prevalent with the invention of printing four centuries later.

The Early National Hands

Although the sack of Rome in 456 A.D. is given as the official end of the Empire, centralized power had begun to falter long before that time. During the period of this long decline and the centuries following it, communication broke down between different parts of Europe. Monks isolated from one another by geographic obstacles and sheer distance slowly began to use different letterforms. The regions in which individual styles were developed were not nations, yet the various styles that appeared at the time are nonetheless referred to as *national hands.*

The three most significant early national hands were developed in Ireland (the Celtic), France (the Merovingian), and western Germany (the East-Frankish) (fig. 3-19). Less important hands that had some impact upon later styles included the Lombardic of Italy and the Visigothic of Spain.

The *Book of Kells* shown in figure 3-17 was written in the Celtic hand. It reflects the beautiful work of the monks of Ireland, among the finest of the period spanning the sixth through ninth centuries. While in other parts of Europe the classic styles deteriorated, great care was taken to preserve the original forms in Ireland. The *Book of Kells* was completed in the early ninth century—two to three hundred years after the semi-uncial was first developed.

Other national styles, however, reveal a steady degeneration of the letterforms. The Merovingian and East-Frankish styles eventually became illegible to anyone not trained to read them. The very purpose of copying —preserving a culture—was endangered by the increasing stress upon intricacy of the letterforms rather than legibility.

3-19.

National hands: *a.* **Celtic,** *b.* **Gothic, and** *c.* **Roman.**

Alcuin and the Caroline Minuscule

By 775, writing throughout Europe had become so haphazard that important secular documents and religious works were in danger of being distorted by illegibility and poor copyists. The cultural achievements of the Roman Empire had given way to a dangerous provincialism.

Charlemagne, who ruled the Franks and, later, the Holy Roman Empire from 768 to 814, was as enthusiastic a scholar as he was a soldier and king. Determined to revive the cultural glories of the Classical era, he decreed in 789 that a monumentally ambitious project be undertaken: every existing manuscript, religious and secular, contemporary and ancient, was to be copied.

Charlemagne's project first required the development of a standard writing style not only to reproduce existing texts but to create new ones. For that purpose, he appointed Alcuin, a monk who had been born in York, England, around 732. Charlemagne's choice was a wise one: trained in the British Isles, Alcuin used the beautiful Celtic and Anglo-Saxon semi-uncials as the basis for his new style, which has come to be known as the Caroline Minuscule (after the Latin name for *Charles,* Carol). Figure 3-20 illustrates the style.

A *minuscule* is a set of lowercase letters that are more than merely small versions of *majuscules,* or uppercase letters. The Caroline hand marked the beginning of individualized lowercase and uppercase alphabets. In addition, uppercase letters, for one of the first times in history, signaled the beginnings of sentences. Ornate frills and flourishes, which decreased legibility, were avoided. We who are used to spare printing types are quite comfortable reading this script of 1,200 years ago. We can recognize in the Minuscule, as in the Trajan capitals, direct ancestors of the alphabet we use today.

3-20.
Caroline minuscule.

The Post-Caroline Hands

Charlemagne's influence did not last indefinitely. By the eleventh century, scribes were again producing letters in different styles throughout Europe. Over time, however, the different hands coalesced into two major categories.

GOTHIC

The Gothic style evolved in northern Europe in the twelfth century. By 1400, it was used throughout areas that now correspond to present-day Germany, France, and England. Popularly called Old English, the style is more accurately known as *black letter,* the term used in England in the fourteenth and fifteenth centuries (fig. 3-21). However, the gothic hand went by many names, depending on the region: in Germany, it was known as *textur;* in France, as *lettre de forme.*

Gothic letters consist of heavy vertical lines that were easy to draw. Stylistically related to the mystical Norse runes of pre-Christian northern Europe (fig. 3-22), the letterforms are difficult to read if one is unfamiliar with the style. Indeed, the dot on the *i* was added when it became impossible to distinguish the *i* from a stroke of the *m, n,* or *u.*

3-21.
Gothic script

3-22.

Norse runes,
fourteenth century.

3-23.
Examples of Rotunda, the "half-Gothic."

3-24.
Humanistica minuscule.

3-25.
Humanistica cursive.

3-26.
Later Humanistica script.

In the south, scribes who used the Gothic style did not take it to its logical conclusion. Rather than develop a consistently heavy, vertical hand (as had been used in the north), the scribes of northern Italy, France, and Spain created the "half-Gothic," or *Rotunda* (fig. 3-23). This style is more reminiscent of the rounded Caroline minuscule and the heritage of the Roman capitals than of the severe northern Gothics.

ROMAN

Rotunda represented the first radical break from the black letter Gothic. Rebellious Italy refused to copy the northern styles. Under the sponsorship of the Church and the governors of Italian city-states, scribes and calligraphers of the fourteenth century created an alternate hand known as *Roman*.

The Roman style was one of many developments that grew out of the Italian Renaissance, a period characterized by a revived interest in the Greco-Roman heritage and an emphasis on humanism as its major intellectual force.

Renaissance humanists sought to influence all cultural media, including art, architecture, literature, and even lettering. More than simply rejecting the paradigm of the Gothic and half-Gothic style, calligraphers wanted to replace it with the most usable ancient style they could unearth. For minuscules, they turned to the Caroline, the oldest example known. Their choice of majuscules was obvious—the letters were engraved on their own architectural monuments. Seizing upon these two models, the Humanists created a new style that was actually a combination of two venerable oldsters. The hand is called *Humanistica* (figs. 3-24 and 3-25). A comparison with the Caroline minuscule of figure 3-20 shows the obvious links.

The stylistic links *should* be obvious. In 1425, an important Renaissance Humanist, Niccolo Niccoli, founded a school in Florence that taught the Caroline Minuscule of 789 (renamed the *lettera antiqua*). For a short time, the Caroline hand was copied exactly. The scribes quickly realized, however, that the lowercase Caroline did not mesh perfectly with the Roman capitals. They added serifs, lengthened ascenders and descenders, and made the letters crisper and cleaner. Later models of the Humanistica demonstrate that within 75 years after Niccoli's school was founded, the style had radically changed (fig. 3-26).

During the same period, a second important writing style, the *cancellescara,* or chancery script, appeared. A less formal outgrowth of the Caroline style, the script was used by papal secretaries, including the painter Raphael, for writing the Pope's briefs and correspondence. With its narrow, rounded letters and angular feel, cancellescara is the most beautiful Renaissance script.

Gutenberg

Even people who are not interested in the history of printing have heard of Gutenberg. Ironically, his name is usually known for the wrong thing. Gutenberg did not invent printing. Nor did he invent movable type, the printing technique by which his magnificent Bible was produced. But Gutenberg can be credited with contributions to printing that revolutionized the production and distribution of written materials.

To print is to produce multiple copies from a single master image, which can take many forms. For example, before Gutenberg set up shop in Mainz, Germany, in the fifteenth century, playing cards were being printed throughout Germany from carved blocks of wood. Indeed, scrolls were produced in China and Japan by this method as early as the seventh century. Obviously, the limitation of printing books with wood blocks was that each page had to be carved as a piece—an extremely difficult and time-consuming process.

Movable type, on the other hand, is a method based on individual characters—for example, the letters used in handsetting—which can be arranged and rearranged in any configuration. There is evidence that the principle behind this technique may be four thousand years old—the age of a clay disk with pictographic forms that was discovered on Crete in 1908. A more recent forerunner of Gutenberg was Pi Sheng, who in 1041 created movable Chinese characters from hardened clay. In Korea, movable type was cast from metal by the thirteenth century. The earliest printed book extant is a Korean work dated 1337.

Some printing historians claim that movable type was introduced to Europe by a Dutch printer, Laurens Janszoon Koster. An Italian historian of the seventeenth century contended that Pamfilo Castaldi of Milan deserved the credit. But printing history indisputably shows that Gutenberg's press was the source of all subsequent technology in the practice of handsetting. From his shop in Mainz came a method that was quickly reproduced throughout fifteenth-century Europe.

What did Gutenberg do? Independent of all other methods, he developed a system that greatly improved the efficiency and appearance of movable type. The salient features of Gutenberg's method were:

- a practical way to cast individual letters in quantity and in a controlled size
- an ink that was viscous enough to stick to the metal letters (Chinese ink was not)
- a frame in which the letters were held (the first chase)
- a printing press adapted from a wine press
- a method to deliver paper to the press
- a registration system that allowed individual sheets of paper to be fed uniformly to the press

Gutenberg's discovery and perfection of a working printing system may have required 20 years of research. There is evidence that he began experimenting in 1435. His first book that bore a date, a psalter, was finished in 1457.

Conclusive evidence for the dates of Gutenberg's experiments in printing appear in the record of a 1439 trial of a lawsuit in which he was involved. Among the facts that turned up over the course of this trial were that Gutenberg had commissioned an artisan named Konrad Saspoch to construct a press, that the goldsmith had purchased large quantities of lead, presumably to experiment with the casting of letters, and that as early as 1436, he had purchased from a fellow goldsmith, Hans Dunne, material "solely for that which belonged to printing."

Some time between 1444 and 1448, Gutenberg moved from Strasbourg, where he had been living since 1428, to his birthplace, Mainz. A Latin grammar may have been completed over the course of those four years, when his exact whereabouts are unknown. But we do know that the financial difficulties he encountered in pursuing his projects began in that period. In 1448, he borrowed 150 gulden from a relative. Again in need of money in 1450, he borrowed 800 gulden from a wealthy Mainz merchant, Johann Fust, to "complete the work on books." That loan, guaranteed by a mortgage against Gutenberg's type and press, was followed by a second one of 1,200 gulden to enable him to complete his master work, the *Bible.* In 1454, printed papal indulgences appeared in Mainz—the first commissioned work ever completed. The next year, Gutenberg was in trouble.

Fust sued to recover his loans and Gutenberg lost his equipment in the foreclosure. Peter Schoeffer, Gutenberg's assistant and Fust's son-in-law, took over the press and the next year completed the 42-line *Bible* (so named because it contains 42 lines in each column) (fig. 3-27). In 1457, the names of Fust and Schoeffer appeared on the *Mainz Psalter,* a beautiful work with calligraphy by Schoeffer that was printed by the new partnership (fig. 3-28). Gutenberg himself continued to print: the *Catholicon,* a Latin dictionary completed in the 1460s, is credited to him.

Gutenberg died in 1468, two years after Fust, but Schoeffer continued to print for many years. His two most famous works, *Hortus Sanitatis,* a German herbal, and *Chronik der Sachsen,* a history, appeared in 1485 and 1492 respectively. After Schoeffer's death in 1502, his son and grandson carried on the family printing tradition, which lasted until at least 1555.

Gutenberg's type shows the importance of the long history of letterforms. The first printing face is an exact duplicate of the Textur Gothic, whose historical antecendents lay in the East-Frankish national hand, the

3-27.

a. Page and b. detail from the Gutenberg *Bible.*

3-28.

The *Mainz Psalter.*

3-29.

A manuscript page written in Textur. Compare with the Gutenberg *Bible.*

3-30.

Subiaco, the first roman typeface.

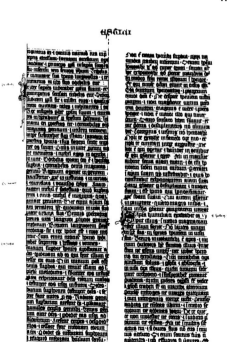

Belliger ad celoſ ampla trop
Quoſ habuit penale chaoſ: ia
Et quoſ morſ peteret: boſ no
R ex ſacer ecce tui radiat pa

3-31.

**The second face of
Sweynheim and
Pannartz.**

qui omnibus ut aquarum ſubmerſis cum filiis ſuis ſimul ac nurıbus
mirabili quodã modo quaſi ſemen huãni generis conſeruatus eſt: quế
utinã quaſi uiuam quandam imaginem imitari nobis contingat: & hi
quidem ante diluuium fuerunt: poſt diluuium autem alii quorũ unus
altiſſimi dei ſacerdos iuſtitiæ ac pietatis miraculo rex iuſtus lingua heᵇ
bræorũ appellatus eſt: apud quos nec circunciſionis nec moſaicæ legis
ulla mentio erat. Quare nec iudæos (poſteris enï hoc nomen fuit)neqʒ
gentiles: quoniam non ut gentes pluralitatem deorum inducebant ſed
hebræos proprie noïamus aut ab Hebere ut dictũ eſt: aut qa id nomen
tranſitiuos ſignificat. Soli qppe a creaturis naturali rõne & lege inata
nõ ſcripta ad cognitioné ueri dei trãſiere: & uoluptate corporis cõtepta
ad rectam uitam pueniſſe ſcribunt: cum quibus omibus præclarus ille
totius generis origo Habraam numerãdus eſt: cui ſcriptura mirabilem
iuſtitiã qui non a moſaica lege (ſeptima eïm poſt Habraã generatione
Moyſes naſcitur) ſed naturali fuit ratione conſecutus ſũma cum laude
atteſtatur. Credidit enïm Habraam deo & reputatũ eſt ei in iuſtitiam.
Quare multarum quoqʒ gentium patrem diuina oracula futurũ: ac in
ipſo benedicẽdas oẽs gentes hoc uidelic& ipſum quod iam nos uideũs
aperte prædictum eſt: cuius ille iuſtitiæ perfectioẽm non moſaica lege
ſed fide cõſecutus eſt: qui poſt multas dei uiſiones legitimum genuit
filium: quem primum omnium diuino pſuaſus oraculo circũcidit: &
cæteris qui ab eo naſcerétur tradidit: uel ad manifeſtum multitudinis
eorum futuræ ſignum: uel ut hoc quaſi paternæ uirtutis iſigne filii reᶠ
tinẽtes maiores ſuos imitari conaret: aut qbuſcũqʒ aliis de cauſis. Non
enim id ſcrutãdum nobis modo eſt. Poſt Habraam filius eius Iſaac in
pietate ſucceſſit: fœlice hac hæreditate a parẽtibus accæpta: q uni uxori
coniunctus quum geminos genuiſſet caſtitatis amore ab uxore poſtea
dicitur abſtinuiſſe. Ab iſto natus é Iacob qui ᵖpter cumulatũ uirtutis
prouẽtum Iſrael etiam appellatus eſt duobus noïbus ᵖpter duplicem
uirtutis uſũ. Iacob eïm athleta & exercétem ſe latine dicere poſſumus:
quam appellatione primũ habuit: quï practicis operatoibus multos
pro pietate labores ferebat. Quum auté iam uictor luctando euaſit: &
ſpeculationis fruebat bonis: tũc Iſraelem ipſe deus appellauit æterna
premia beatitudinéqʒ ultimam quæ in uiſione dei conſiſtit ei largiens:
hominem enim qui deum uideat Iſrael nomen ſignificat. Ab hoc. xii.
iudæorum tribus ᵖfectæ ſũt. Innumerabilis de uita iſtorum uirorum
fortitudine prudentia pietateqʒ dici poſſunt: quorum alia ſecundum
ſcripturæ uerba hiſtorice conſiderantur: alia tropologice ac allegorice
interpretãt: de qbus multi cõſcïpſerũt: & nos in libro qué inſcripſiûs

3-32.

**Eusebius, designed
by Nicolas Jenson.**

enim id ſcrutãdum nobis mõdo eſt. P
pietate ſucceſſir: fœlice hac hæreditate
coniunctus quum geminos genuiſſet
dicitur abſtinuiſſe. Ab iſto natus é Ia
prouétum Iſrael etiam appellatus eſt
uirtutis uſũ. Iacob eïm athletã & exer
quam appellatione primũ habuit: quï
pro pietate labores ferebat. Quum au
ſpeculationis fruebat bonis: tũc Iſrae

a

Et picis in morem ad digitos lenteſcit habendo. Eiuſmodi
figuratio parum admiſit ex ſe perfectum: nec conuenit ad
mittere ut aut poſſit: aut debeat cum cæteris temporibus p
totam declinationem uim incipiendi ſignificare. Abſurdũ
é ergo ea quæ ſunt inchoatiua perfecto tempore definire: &
mox futurum declinando inchoatiua eſſe demõſtrare. Nec
enim poteſt cum tota uerbi ſpecies inchoatiua dicatur alia

b

3-33.

**(a., b.) The later
faces of Nicolas
Jenson.**

Caroline minuscule, and the Gothic writing style (fig. 3-29). Yet Gutenberg's choice of a typeface was inevitable. Gothics were the only calligraphic style used in Germany at the time. Moreover, Gutenberg was a businessman catering to public taste. Buyers obviously wanted to read works produced in a familiar hand. The concept of mass production itself was alien enough: when Gutenberg's Bible was sold in Paris, claims were made that the printed copies must have been the work of the devil. Certainly no scribe could produce two perfectly identical books.

Gutenberg realized, of course, that his natural competitors were the calligraphers. He therefore produced books that were similar both in quality and appearance to their best work. Scribes were obviously threatened by this revolutionary development, but they continued to produce manuscripts well into the sixteenth century.

Incunabula

The word *incunabula* is derived from the Latin word for cradle and refers to any printing produced before 1500. The technological secret of printing was closely guarded, reserved to printers working in and around Mainz, from between 1440 and 1460. In 1462, the city was sacked and the printers scattered throughout Germany and Italy, bringing their knowledge of printing techniques with them. By 1500, more than eleven hundred printing presses had been established throughout Europe. They had produced more than thirty-five thousand different titles and a total of twelve million books. That far exceeded the total output of all the scribes in two thousand years.

SWEYNHEIM AND PANNARTZ

Within four years after the attack on Mainz, two German printers, Konrad Sweynheim and Arnold Pannartz, established a press in a Benedictine monastery at Subiaco, near Rome. Like Gutenberg before them, Sweynheim and Pannartz created a printing type that resembled a national style, in their case the prevalent writing style of Rome—the Humanistica.

The first roman, or typeface based on the Humanistica, has been labeled *Subiaco* by later historians (fig. 3-30). This initial attempt of 1465 shows a clearcut influence of the black letter gothic. By 1468, however, Sweynheim and Pannartz had cast a new typeface more firmly based on humanist and Roman letters (fig. 3-31).

JENSON AND THE VENETIANS

The names of Sweynheim and Pannartz are well known because of the innovativeness rather than the quality of their work. Their face was not an aesthetic success and had little influence upon later type design. The first roman to be crafted by a master designer, Nicolas Jenson, would not appear until 1470.

Jenson worked in Venice. His typefaces were the pattern for all romans for over half a century and were so widely copied that *any* roman typeface dating from before 1500 is now called a *Venetian*. Jenson's first face, completed in 1470, is *Eusebius,* named after the author of the text for which it was originally used (fig. 3-32). Between 1470 and 1480, Jenson printed more than one hundred fifty books in several different type styles. The later styles are remarkably similar to romans designed today, five hundred years later (fig. 3-33).

Diquead qͤſto ſincero & ſanct
gno parlare, humilmente fecime
exiguo auſo di ſubito parendo. S
tro, poſime adſedere, Cum la mia

3-34.

**Designed by Griffo,
the roman face
used by Aldus.**

P hillyrides Chiron, A mythaoniusqͤ; Mel
S æuit et in lucem ſtygiis emiſſa tenebris
P allida Tiſiphone, morbos agit ante, metu
I nqͤ; dies auidum ſurgens caput altius effi

3-35.

**The Aldine italic
(1500).**

ALDUS AND THE SCHOLAR-PRINTERS

By 1480, printing had spread to England, Switzerland, France, Holland, Belgium, Austria, Hungary, Spain, Denmark, Poland, Sweden, and Portugal. Many printers were humanists themselves: from Subiaco came the orations of Cicero and an issue of St. Augustine. Caxton, the first printer in England, produced the works of Chaucer. Jenson created editions of the Greek and Roman classics. The first book printed in Venice was a work by Cicero, and the second was a work by Pliny. Book buyers and book makers alike were interested in ancient texts.

The most famous of the humanist printers was Aldus Manutius, a scholar, translator, editor, and author. Although Aldus, along with his type designer Francesco Griffo, continued the tradition of the roman typeface (fig. 3-34), his major contribution to printing was the pocket book.

Before 1500, all books were large volumes too heavy to be carried about. Instead, they were intended to be read aloud. Aldus was to change the appearance of books, however, by creating small texts that were similar in size to modern-day paperbacks. The simplicity of this innovation is deceptive: Aldus had to confront the critical problem of fitting a large quantity of information into a smaller format. His solution was based on two ideas. First, he commissioned Griffo to create a type that was smaller than the existing single-sized faces, thereby pioneering the concept of type sizes. Second, after experimenting with several designs, Aldus discovered that by slanting type (as in cursive writing), more letters could be fit into a given space. Basing his experiments on cancellescara, the Chancery script, Aldus created the typeface shown in figure 3-35. In Italy, the face was almost immediately named the Aldine. Elsewhere, because of its Venetian birthplace, the style was called the *italic,* the name by which we know oblique letters today. Although Aldus did not use a slanted face for emphasis, as we do, the Aldine Italic is nevertheless one of the first type variations.

These innovations enabled Aldus to produce cheap, portable books that made the classics available to anyone who could read. The pocket book idea spread throughout Europe, where it was supported by—and encouraged—an increasingly literate population.

Printing was only fifty years old when Aldus began to produce his pocket books. Typefaces of the time continued to *look like* the work of scribes. As noted, many readers demanded a printing type that resembled the familiar and elegant handwriting of calligraphers. Only in 1531 would the first face not explicitly based on handwriting be created.

The Roman Classifications: 1500–1800

Between 1500 and 1800, the major typographic phenomenon was the development of the romans. Many typographic classification schemes include four distinct varieties of roman: the Venetians (created before 1500), Old Style romans (created between 1500 and 1750), transitional romans (created between 1750 and 1780), and modern romans (created after 1780). In this book, however, all four styles will be referred to as the roman serif. By 1500, two of the six major design categories, the black letter and the roman serif, had evolved. The next major design would not be created until after 1800.

OLD STYLE ROMANS

When Aldus and Griffo designed the first important typefaces of the sixteenth century, they reaffirmed the supremacy of Italy as the source of typographic innovation. Their influence spread throughout Europe, as the printing trade itself continued to proliferate. Eventually, the center of typographic creativity shifted to the west, toward France.

Geoffroy Tory and Claude Garamond rest at the fulcrum of that transition. A bookseller, philosopher, translator, poet, and editor, as well as typographer, Tory studied the work of Aldus in Venice and brought his new-found knowledge back to his native France. He was author of *Champ Fleury* (1529), one of the first works devoted to the study of type design. Tory's own typefaces are historically important because they are among the first to be designed on rigidly geometric principles. But his major contribution was the link he forged in a long typographic tradition. By modeling his own faces on the type style he had borrowed from Venice, he established the roman serif as a prototype that lasted throughout more than two hundred years of French type design.

Claude Garamond, another Frenchman, is given credit for creating the first true printing typeface not designed to imitate handwriting. Garamond also began a tradition (still in practice among type designers today) of giving his own name to his designs. The Garamond face shows obvious connections, via Tory's typefaces, to Aldus' roman (fig. 3-36). It is classified as the first Old Style roman, a style easily identified by its small and elegantly shaped letters and the absence of contrast between major and minor strokes.

In the sixteenth through nineteenth centuries, printers did not have an extensive type library from which to choose. Garamond, designed in 1541, was the dominant printing typeface for two hundred years, although many later designers reworked the face. Indeed, the type we know as Garamond today (which is the type that appears in this book) is usually based on a 1614 redesign by Jean Jannon.

At about the time when Garamond was designing masterworks in France, Dutch and English printers had established what we now call the Dutch/English school of Old Style romans. The most significant figures of that school were Christopher Plantin of Antwerp (fig. 3-37) and William Caslon of England. In 1557, Plantin commissioned Robert Granjon to produce the first *accompanying italic* for use with the roman (fig. 3-38). In the same year, Granjon also designed the first cursive, a typeface that simulates handwriting. Cursives joined the black letter and the roman as the third major design category. Meanwhile, in 1539, Juan Pablos of Mexico City established the first press in the Western Hemisphere.

The Dutch/English school has a long history. William Caslon issued his typeface in 1734, foreshadowing the transitional roman (fig. 3-39). Transitional romans differ from their old style forerunners in the relative straightness of their serifs and strokes and greater contrast between major and minor strokes. The success of the face was instantaneous, and Caslon quickly supplanted Garamond in printers' type rooms. Used in the first printings of both the Declaration of Independence and the United States Constitution, the Caslon face suffered a decline in popularity in the 1800s but was revived in full force in this century. Many printers still stand by an old motto, "When in doubt, use Caslon."

reſtituit.Fuit hic(vt Annales ſe cius qui ab inſigni pietate mag nente illo pernobili claſſico exc in Syriam contendit,communi atque opibus cú Guliermo Mor à proceritate corporis, Longa ſ

3-36.
Garamond's original version of the first Old Style roman.

NTONIVS Perrenotus, S.R.C.tit. Sancti Petri ter, Cardinalis de Granuela,prefatæ Regiæ & C à conſiliis ſtatus, & in hoc Regno locum tenens neralis,&c. Mag.co viro Chriſtophoro Plantino ſi, & præfatæ Catholicæ Maieſtatis Prototyp gio,dilecto.gratiam Regiam & bonam voluntat

3-37.
Plantin, designed by Granjon.

Simon Voſtre & tant d'autres, dont M. Arthu Chriſtian nous résume ici les travaux, firer merveille dans cette œuvre nouvelle.

Encouragée par plusieurs monarques, l'in primerie n'avait, jusqu'au commencement a XVIᵉ siècle, inſpiré en France aucune méfian

3-38.

Granjon's accompanying italic.

3-39.

Caslon's specimen page.

3-40.

Baskerville's specimen page.

ABCDEFGHIJKLMNOPQRSTU
abcdefghijklmnopqrstuvwxyz
ABCDEFGHIJKLM.NOPQRSTUV
abcdefghijklmnopqrstuvwxyz

3-41.

Bulmer.

TRANSITIONAL ROMANS

The Old Style persevered for nearly two hundred fifty years. But, in 1757, John Baskerville of Birmingham, England, shocked the typographic world by producing a design that was different from any other face that had preceded it. Baskerville, the first *transitional roman,* is a dazzling typeface with increased contrast between thick and thin strokes, a nearly vertical stress in the counters, and very sharp serifs (fig. 3-40).

When Baskerville was introduced, the face was denounced by many contemporary printers and typographers, especially in Great Britain, as too "sparkling" (in part because of the increased contrast of the face and in part because of the brilliant paper Baskerville created for the type). Within forty years, Baskerville's popularity exceeded Caslon's and eventually forced the Caslon type foundry to go out of business. In time, the Baskerville face also lost favor among typographers. Like Caslon, it would be revived in this century after a long decline. Baskerville is now used in more books that win design awards than any other typeface.

Baskerville influenced several other designs in the transitional style. The letters designed by Simon Fournier (who invented the point system), the type used by William Bulmer's Shakespeare Press, and the Scottish Romans are the most notable (fig. 3-41).

MODERN ROMANS

Baskerville's ascendency did not last long. In the 1780s, two type designers, Firmin Didot of France and Giambattista Bodoni of Italy, developed the *modern romans.* Because Bodoni was the much more important printer, he is often given most of the credit for the innovation of this design.

The moderns are a study in contrasts (figs. 3-42 and 3-43). In letters like the *A,* Baskerville's influence is carried to an extreme. Thin strokes are hairlines, whereas thick strokes are strong and heavy. The circular feeling of the old romans had given way to a full vertical stress, especially in letters such as the *a* and *o,* whose counters are vertical instead of rounded. Printers now had a choice between three very different roman typefaces. Some diehards continued to use the Old Style; most, however, were proponents of the transitional or the modern styles. But more startling changes were to happen to typefaces soon.

Influences of the Industrial Revolution

At the end of the eighteenth century, machines and steam power began to make drastic differences in everyday life. New machine-made products increasingly replaced the handiwork of artisans, supplanting a tradition that had been carried on since the Middle Ages. For the first time, objects could be mass-produced and distributed efficiently.

Every manufacturer strives to command the greatest portion of the marketplace. The Industrial Revolution created a large group of entrepreneurs who competed with one another to sell their products to a growing number of consumers. Moreover, improvements in transportation enabled individual manufacturers to convey their goods greater distances and thereby to service more people.

Among the many results of the competition fostered by the industrial revolution was the rise of advertising. With mass-production came the demand for printed publicity, which in turn changed the world of the typographer.

3-42.

Bodoni, modern roman.

3-43.

Didot, modern roman.

3-44.

Victorian typefaces.

ABCDjkl

Quousque tandem abutere, Catilina, patientia nostra? quamdiu nos etiam furor is te tuus eludet? quem after CONSTANTINOPLE £1234567890

3-45.

Robert Thorne's Fat Face—the first bold variation.

Before 1800, books constituted the majority of printing work, with an occasional news sheet or pamphlet as the odd job. After the introduction of the machine, printers produced newspaper ads, circulars, posters, catalogs, time tables, trade cards, labels, and stationery. Then, as now, manufacturers demanded typefaces that shouted out the names of their products. Instead of legibility, the qualities of attractiveness, novelty, and noticeability became critical. From 1800 to 1890, most type designers cared very little about the aesthetics of type. The emphasis was on loudness, not artistry.

Many type historians firmly believe that the typefaces of the nineteenth century are, as a whole, the worst designs in history, unsurpassed in their ungainliness and ugliness (fig. 3-44). Because Queen Victoria of England reigned throughout much of the nineteenth century, these typefaces are called *Victorians*. The reason behind their appearance is quite simple: if one advertiser's printer used a bizarre typeface that was quite noticeable, that advertiser's competitor demanded a typeface even *more* noticeable. This typographic escalation logically lead to wildly embellished designs.

The movement toward more and more flamboyant designs resulted in several new type forms. In 1805, Robert Thorne produced his *Fat Face* (fig. 3-45). A cursory comparison with Bodoni reveals that Fat Face is a bolder variation, indeed, the first bold typeface ever produced. At the time it was created, however, Fat Face was regarded as a new design. The idea of grouping typefaces into families would wait for Morris Fuller Benton in the 1890s.

In 1815, an English type founder, Vincent Figgins, designed a face with square serifs (fig. 3-46). Because the heavy blocks reminded the English public of the Egyptian pyramids (Napolean had recently completed a military campaign there), the faces were popularly known as Egyptians. Today the style is called the *square serif*.

A year later, in 1816, William Caslon IV (the original Caslon's great-grandson) produced the first type without serifs (fig. 3-47). Caslon did not popularize the new design—in fact, the typeface was ridiculed by typographers and customers alike for its radical novelty and somewhat amateurish brutishness. However, by 1832, William Thorowgood and Robert Thorne had each revived the idea of the sans serif. Thorowgood called the style Grotesque, the common term still used in Great Britain. Gothic also became—and continues to be—a popular name for the style. To avoid confusion with the gothics of Gutenberg's Germany, *sans serif*, a phrase invented by Figgins, is the preferred term.

In America, the ornate and sometimes giddy faces of the Victorian era formed the last of the six basic designs, the *novelty* faces. Type was stretched, twisted, covered with ornamentation, cut into pieces, and given three dimensions. The possibilities seemed endless (figs. 3-48 and 3-49).

Typography was suffering. Unschooled, boisterous designs were the norm as type stopped being attractive and simply became loud. This downward trend continued until the 1890s, when it finally precipitated a reaction that was the most important typographic event since Gutenberg.

ABCDEFGHIJ KLMNOPQR STUVWXYZ&,.:;.- £1234567890

Two Lines Pica, Antique.

3-46.

Vincent Figgins's square serif.

W CASLON JUNR

3-47.

The first sans serif, designed by William Caslon IV in 1816.

3-48.

The excesses of Victorian typography.

No. 1.

No. 2.

Ornamented, Johnson & Smith, 1834.

Ornamented No. 1, Johnson & Smith, 1834.

Double Shade, Johnson & Smith, 1834.

Ornamented, Johnson & Smith, 1834.

Italic Antique Shaded, Johnson & Smith,

3-49.

Victorian novelty flourishes.

William Morris

The typographic giants of the first half of the twentieth century included Frederick Goudy, Stanley Morison, Bruce Rogers, Daniel Berkeley Updike, Eric Gill, W. A. Dwiggins, and Will Ransom. These men had more in common than a shared love of letterforms. They all owed something to the legacy of William Morris.

THE ARGUMENT.

UCIUS Tarquinius (for his sive pride surnamed Superb ter hee had caused his owne in law Servius Tullius to be murd'red, and contrarie to tl maine lawes and customes, quiring or staying for the people's suffrag possessed himselfe of the kingdome: went

a.

Born in 1834, Morris was a poet, painter, designer, and social reformer whose careers spanned the many years of the Victorian Age. Morris and his Pre-Raphaelite Brotherhood of Edward Burne-Jones and Dante Rossetti have been called revolutionaries. He founded The Socialist League and edited *The Commonweal,* its journal. In his art and his writings, he argued against the commercialization and vulgarization of design by the machine.

But Morris's ideals were not so much revolutionary as they were reactionary. His subject matter was consistently the past: his poetic works include "The Defense of Guenevere" (1858), translations of the *Aeneid* (1875) and the *Odyssey* (1881), and both translations and adaptations of the traditional Icelandic *Volsunga* saga. Fighting against the rising tide of the machine, Morris consistently looked to the past for his paradigms.

His thoughts on type and printing were influenced by his neighbor on the Thames at Hammersmith, Emery Walker. On November 15, 1888, at the Arts and Crafts Exhibition in London, Walker gave a lecture on the history of printing, and particulary, book printing. He praised Caslon and the fine printing of the fifteenth through seventeenth centuries. He defended Old Style romans and Venetians from the contemporary onslaught of the transitional and modern romans, Baskerville, Bodoni, and Didot. With the aid of lantern slides of incunabula, Walker converted Morris. From 1888, until his death in 1896, Morris sought to restore the long-lost standards of craftsmanship to typography and bookmaking.

HERE ends the tale of the Wood beyond the World, made by William Morris, and printed by him at the Kelmscott Press, Upper Mall, Hammersmith. finished the 30th day of May, 1894.

3-50.   b.

a. Golden and b.
Troy typefaces,
designed by
William Morris.

Morris's interest in typography surfaced with his founding of the Kelmscott Press in 1890. As noted, book production in the nineteenth century was subordinated to the printing of advertising posters, handbills, and catalogs. With the death of the master printer William Bulmer in 1830, book design and typography began a long period of decline that was to last almost until the twentieth century.

Morris idealized the fifteenth-century craftsman, the guild, and, most important, the practice of creating even ordinary, everyday objects by hand. He disparaged the decline of quality he ascribed to machine-made production. In his novel *News from Nowhere* (1891), Morris describes a utopian future: haymaking is a major occupation, handicrafts have been revived, and government has disappeared. Simple and unchanging, his utopia was essentially a glorified representation of medieval society. The Morris revolution is often called the Arts and Crafts Movement because it produced a new emphasis on handmade crafts that we are still enjoying today.

THE KELMSCOTT PRESS AND CHAUCER

Morris put his theories into action by founding a press from which he verbally and visually proclaimed his views. Fifty-three titles were produced by the Kelmscott Press in its seven years of existence. Many display the medieval influence of calligraphy and manuscript illumination. The ultimate reactionary crafts master, Morris made certain that his ideas of form and style were perfectly harmonized in every phase of a book's production. Not content with simply designing pages, he commissioned typefaces specifically for the Kelmscott books, modeled after Jenson's Venetian and Peter Schoeffer's early black letter (fig. 3-50). Photographs of early medieval manuscripts and incunabula type styles were carefully studied before any new typefounding was begun. Paper for the press was made under Morris's own supervision from linen rag, with wire molds woven by hand in order to reproduce the irregularities of paper made in Bologna in the fifteenth century. Ink was imported from Germany. Only the densest blacks and clearest reds could summon the spirit of the fourteenth century. Of course, all presswork was done manually by master technicians using Albion hand presses (fig. 3-51).

The magnum opus of Kelmscott is Morris's edition of Geoffrey Chaucer's *Canterbury Tales*. For this, Morris used a slightly larger version of the typeface Troy, a bold, clear face based on Schoeffer's Gothic. Cut by Edward Prince, the face is the paradigm of Morris's theory of fine typography, *evocative printing*.

Simply put, evocative printing holds that type, as well as all other elements of a book, should elicit from the reader the appropriate emotional or intellectual state indispensable to the fullest appreciation of the literary work at hand. For example, Troy was designed and arranged to evoke the time of Chaucer. Although Morris stated that his books should be easy to read, the pages of the Kelmscott Chaucer are not, at first glance, particularly legible. Yet the fault rests with our habit of reading quickly, not with Morris's typography. Kelmscott Press editions were designed to allow a relationship to develop gradually between reader and book. By using borders, decorative initial capitals, handmade inks and papers, the finest of

3-51.

Text page from Kelmscott.

pains they adorned it, this unromantic, uneventful looking land of England, surely by this too our hearts may be touched and our hope quickened.

OR as was the land, such was the art of it while folk yet troubled themselves about such things; it strove little to impress people either by pomp or ingenuity: not unseldom it fell into commonplace, rarely it rose into majesty; yet was it never oppressive, never a slave's nightmare or an insolent boast: & at its best it had an inventiveness, an individuality, that grander styles have never overpassed: its best too, and that was in its very heart, was given as freely to the yeoman's house, and the humble village church, as to the lord's palace or the mighty cathedral: never coarse, though often rude enough, sweet, natural & unaffected, an art of peasants rather than of merchant princes or courtiers, it must be a hard heart, I think, that does not love it: whether a man has been born among it like ourselves, or has come wonder

3-52.

Page from Morris's
Innocentium; set in
Golden.

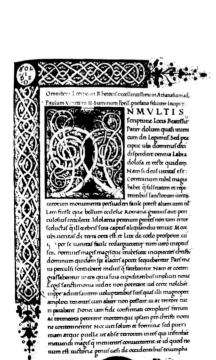

3-53.

The first page of the
Kelmscott *Chaucer*,
with woodcut by
Burne-Jones.

3-54.

Medieval
manuscript page in
humanistic
minuscule.

3-55.

Text page in
Golden.

THE ARTS AND CRAFTS OF TODAY.
BEING AN ADDRESS DELIVERED IN
EDINBURGH IN OCTOBER, 1889. BY
WILLIAM MORRIS.
'Applied Art' is the title which the Society has
chosen for that portion of the arts which I have to
speak to you about. What are we to understand by
that title? I should answer that what the Society
means by applied art is the ornamental quality
which men choose to add to articles of utility. Theoretically this ornament can be done without, and
art would then cease to be 'applied'... would exist
as a kind of abstraction, I suppose. But though this
ornament to articles of utility may be done without,
man up to the present time has never done without
it, and perhaps never will; at any rate he does not
propose to do so at present, although, as we shall

ODI profanum vulgus & arceo;
Favere linguis: carmina non prius
Audita Musarum sacerdos
Virginibus puerisq; canto.
Regum timendorum in proprios greges,
Reges in ipsos imperium est Iovis,
Clari Giganteo triumpho,
Cuncta supercilio moventis.
Est ut viro vir latius ordinet
Arbusta sulcis, hic generosior
Descendat in Campum petitor,
Moribus hic melioreque fama
Contendat, illi turba clientium
Sit maior: aequa lege Necessitas
Sortitur insignis & imos;
Omne capax movet urna nomen.
Destrictus ensis cui super impia
Cervice pendet, non Siculae dapes
Dulcem elaborabunt saporem,
Non avium citharaeq; cantus

3-56.

**The face of the
Ashendene Press.**

GOLDEN COCKEREL
THIRTY-SIX & TWENTY-FOUR
point titling above, and these lines are set in 18 point roman.
The type was first used for 'The Four Gospels' in 1931 and
is now on loan from Thomas Yoseloff Limited to Will and
Sebastian Carter at the Rampant Lions Press, Cambridge,
where these lines have been set. ★ There is a very battered
14 point also, not really worth using, but there is no italic.

3-57.

**Specimen of the
Golden Cockerel
typeface.**

DOMINE omnipotens, Deus patrum nostrorum Abraham, et
Isaac et Jacob, et seminis eorum justi, qui fecisti coelum et ter-
ram cum omni ornatu eorum; qui ligasti mare verbo praecepti
tui; qui conclusisti abyssum, et signasti eam terribili et laudabili nomine
tuo; quem omnia pavent et tremunt a vultu virtutis tuae, quia importa-
bilis est magnificentia gloriae tuae, et insustentabilis ira comminationis
tuae super peccatores; immensa vero et investigabilis misericordia pro-
missionis tuae: quoniam tu es Dominus, altissimus, benignus, longanimis,
et multum misericors, et poenitens super malitias hominum. Tu, Domine,
secundum multitudinem bonitatis tuae promisisti poenitentiam et remis-
sionem iis, qui peccaverunt tibi, et multitudine miserationum tuarum
decrevisti poenitentiam peccatoribus in salutem. Tu igitur, Domine
Deus justorum, non posuisti poenitentiam justis, Abraham, et Isaac et
Jacob, iis, qui tibi non peccaverunt, sed posuisti poenitentiam propter me

3-58.

**Bertam Goodhue's
Merrymount type.**

vellums for binding, and the appropriate typeface, Morris emphasized that a book like the *Canterbury Tales* is a literary treasure that deserves our time.

Evocative printing is a milestone in the history of typography, not because it is the one correct theory, but because it was the *first* theory. The novelty lay in Morris's belief that typography was important enough to be the subject of analysis, that it was an art as well as a craft (fig. 3-52).

Morris's work cannot be fully appreciated merely as an illustration in a book about printing. To truly understand the magnificence of the Kelmscott *Chaucer,* one must see and feel it. There is no better example of Morris's belief in the unity of a harmonized printed work: binding, head-bands, type selection, paper, ink, and press impression each contribute to the whole. The handmade rag paper helps carry one back to 1473 Bologna. Inking is a dense black, as though calligraphic pens and brushes might have been used. Burne-Jones's 87 woodcut pages (fig. 3-53) and the dozens of borders and initials are also reminiscent of medieval manuscripts (fig. 3-54). The pigskin boards and silver clasps look like a fifteenth-century binding.

More than three years were needed to complete the printing of the Kelmscott *Chaucer,* which was finished just three months before Morris's death in 1896. The outcome is a spectacular incorporation of several crafts to produce an artistic masterpiece.

A classic use of Troy, the *Chaucer* is considered the best work of the Kelmscott Press. Not all of the Kelmscott books were intended to evoke medieval England, however, so, appropriately, not all of Morris's titles were set in Troy. Golden, a clean and legible type based on Jenson's Venetians, was first used in the romance, *The Story of the Glittering Plain* (fig. 3-55) and for Kelmscott's more contemporary works: volumes by Rossetti, Ruskin, Herrick, Shelley, and Morris himself. Subject matter, not simple aesthetic crankiness, dictated legibility and type selection.

The Impact of Kelmscott

Morris revived the study of typography. Before the work of the Kelmscott Press, no school taught typography or graphic design, and even typographers failed to devote much attention to proper typographic patterns and techniques. After Morris, however, classes were offered in graphic design. Type manufacturers supplied printers with the classic typefaces that had long been forgotten. Most important, typographers began to realize that design involved more than simply arranging letters on a page. In England and America, many printers quickly followed Morris's lead and set up shops dedicated more to art than to profit. These efforts, which continue today, are known as the *private press movement.*

THE PRIVATE PRESSES

Among the first of a long succession of private presses that soon sprang up in England were the Ashendene Press of St. John Hornby, established in 1894; the Vale Press of Charles Ricketts (1896); and the Golden Cockerel (1896), which is most notable for the work of Eric Gill (figs. 3-56 and 3-57).

In America, the first distinguished press was Merrymount, founded by Daniel Berkeley Updike in 1893 (fig. 3-58). Updike later wrote the two-volume *Printing Types,* still considered the authoritative history of the subject.

The private press movement soon influenced popular, everyday

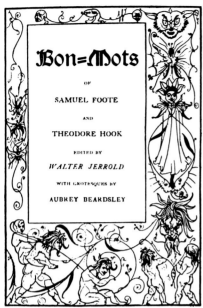

3-59.

The Everyman's Series; design by Aubrey Beardsley.

typography. In 1894, J. M. Dent & Sons of London began *The Everyman's Series* (fig. 3-59), which made the beautiful typographic and illustrative styles of the private press movement affordable to the general public. In 1895, Elbert Hubbard founded the Roycrofters in East Aurora, New York, producing furniture, books, and other articles by hand in an atmosphere reminiscent of medieval crafts shops (fig. 3-60). Sometimes disparaged by contemporaries and historians alike for using inferior methods and materials, the Roycrofters and the Everyman's Series were both immensely popular in their time. Because he attempted to popularize the private press ideals, Hubbard was forced to compromise some of those same principles. But one book written by Hubbard and published by the press, *A Message to Garcia,* sold over 50 million copies and is rated as the fifth best-selling book in history. That circulation brought the private press aesthetic home to many Americans.

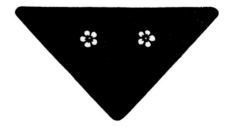

3-60.

Page from Elbert Hubbard's Roycrofters.

PRIVATE PRESS THEORIES IN ENGLAND

Although Morris's theory of evocative printing was not universally accepted, it dominated the private press movement from 1890 to 1920. If some of the private presses rebelled against Morris, all owed a great deal to Kelmscott. The work of the Vale Press is a case in point. Rather than explicitly follow Morris's typeface classifications, the Vale Press used half-uncials that were a marked change in style. Nonetheless, the overall appearance of Vale pages retained a close allegiance to Kelmscott.

The Ashendene Press of St. John Hornby, like the Doves Press to follow, was also influenced by the typography of William Morris. Hornby, in fact, used a typeface based on the Subiaco of Sweynheim and Pannartz that was originally designed for Kelmscott by Emery Walker.

Walker's own Doves Press, however, was one of the first artistically successful presses to break away from the influence of evocative printing. In 1890, Walker had been invited by Morris to be a partner in Kelmscott. He declined, but very little happened at Kelmscott without Walker's advice. Walker established Doves in 1900 and produced the press's best work, the Doves *Bible,* in 1905. Based on Jenson, the *Bible's* type is much crisper than any of the faces designed by Morris, and it is often pointed to as a precursor of the clean styles of the 1920s and 1930s.

Owing much to the Kelmscott philosophy that typography could be art, Doves and Ashendene still rejected the specifics of the theory of evocative printing. Both Hornby and Walker disagreed with the use of extensive borders, floriated designs, and decorative initial capitals. Instead, they stressed form, a plainness of design, and crisp, undecorated pages (fig. 3-61). By 1918, the move toward simplicity had made its way into commercial printing. Emery Walker had made the ideal of simplicity a reality in the works of the Doves Press, and the preeminent typographic theorists of the 1920s were about to follow his lead. The paradigm of Kelmscott was rejected, but Kelmscott was still the source, the catalyst, of that theoretical reversal. Evocative printing was the fountainhead of a new category of typographic talk: theory about what typography should do.

PRIVATE PRESS THEORIES IN AMERICA

American private presses took up the ideas of Kelmscott, and, unlike the English presses, never rejected them. The ideal was vibrantly advanced and always respected. Morris was the starting point from which Americans made typographic gains.

The first member of the movement in America, the Merrymount Press of Daniel Berkeley Updike, was quickly followed by dozens of private presses. Frederic Goudy, who first saw the work of the new English private presses at McClurg's Bookstore in Chicago, started the Camelot Press in 1895 and designed his first typeface for it. Goudy later founded the more successful Village Press and went on to become the most important American type designer in the first half of this century.

In the 1900s, Goudy was the intermediary between Morris and the average commercial printer. He was not a popularizer (as was Elbert Hubbard) but an apostle. During this period, Goudy, like Morris before him, always insisted upon careful workmanship and a reverence for the past. When asked, for example, by Kuppenheimer and Company to design a typeface, Goudy ordered the American Type Founder's version of Morris's Golden to use as his pattern.

Unlike the work of the Roycrofters, Goudy's craftsmanship was always respected by fellow printers. Goudy therefore could, and did, be-

¶ These Books printed, as a fi
field of literature remains open to
there is an immense reproducti
cheap form, of all Books which i
stood the test of time. But such
a substitute for the more monun
the same works, & whether by
some other press or presses, suc
duction, expressive of man's ad

3-61.
**The face of Emery
Walker's Doves
Press.**

3-64.

Typeface designed by Daniel Berkeley Updike for the Merrymount Press.

3-62.

Frederic Goudy, from the Village Press.

RELIGION IN LITERATURE AND RELIGION IN LIFE. BEING TWO PAPERS WRITTEN BY STOPFORD A. BROOKE, M.A., LL.D.

THOMAS Y. CROWELL & COMPANY
NEW YORK. ANNO DOMINI MDCCCCI

The Alphabet

AND ELEMENTS OF LETTERING

CHAPTER I : The Beginnings of the Alphabet*

OF ALL THE achievements of the human mind, the birth of the alphabet is the most momentous. "Letters, like men, have now an ancestry, and the ancestry of words, as of men, is often a very noble possession, making them capable of great things": indeed, it has been said that the invention of writing is more important than all the victories ever won or constitutions devised by man. The history of writing is, in a way, the history of the human race, since in it are bound up, severally and together, the development of thought, of expression, of art, of intercommunication, and of mechanical invention.

* The author of *The Alphabet* advances no claim that in "The Beginnings of the Alphabet" he has presented any new facts. As his own particular line of study starts at the point where our roman letter forms came into existence, it seems desirable to touch briefly on the earlier history of those forms, accepting and using the conclusions of scholars, since he himself has neither the facilities nor the scholarship necessary to a successful study of Assyrian, Babylonian, or Egyptian picture writings and their development. The chapter is intended only to cover briefly the means of recording thought prior to the beginnings of Greek and Latin writing. The

[5]

3-63.

Bruce Rogers's Centaur type.

❡ THE CENTAUR. WRITTEN BY MAURICE DE GUÉRIN AND NOW TRANSLATED FROM THE FRENCH BY GEORGE B. IVES.

I Was born in a cavern of these mountains. Like the river in yonder valley, whose first drops flow from some cliff that weeps in a deep grotto, the first moments of my life sped amidst the shadows of a secluded retreat, nor vexed its silence. As our mothers draw near their term, they retire to the caverns, and in the innermost recesses of the wildest of them all, where the darkness is most dense, they bring forth, uncomplaining, offspring as silent as themselves. Their strength-giving milk enables us to endure without weakness or dubious struggles the first difficulties of life; yet

WHILE FIRE LOOKS ON AND SMILES

MEN who smoke, or carry lighted cigars, cigarettes, pipes or matches while handling gasoline are inviting Fire, and thousands of blackened ruins bear testimony to their unpardonable carelessness.

Fire is a public enemy against which we are fighting a defensive battle. We *must* be more careful. We must do everything in our power to protect our homes, schools, public buildings and places of business, and to safeguard the investment that they represent. The Hartford Fire Insurance Company will help you in your efforts to prevent fire and will make good your loss if fire does come.

There is a local agent of the Hartford near you. He will see to it that you are protected by the service and policies of a Company that has been serving property owners faithfully for 114 years.

HARTFORD FIRE INSURANCE COMPANY, Hartford, Conn.

3-65.

Advertising typography of the 1930s was dominated by the faces of Frederic Goudy.

3-66.
Frederic Goudy,
Village Press work.

ABCDEFGHIJKLMNOPQRSTUVWXYZ
abcdefghijklmnopqrstuvwxyz
1234567890,;-.;'!?$ &

ABCDEFGHIJKLMNOPQRSTUVWXYZ
1234567890.,::-'!?$&

3-67.

Goudy Old Style
(top) and
Copperplate Gothic.

come a voice that echoed Kelmscott's demand for the return of fine print-ing. Moreover, Goudy's pages are stylistically closer to Morris than are Hubbard's. Decorated initials and borders are commonplace in the works of the Village Press. That work includes a publication of William Morris's *Hollow Land.* Indeed, Goudy himself said that Morris was "one of the out-standing figures of the Nineteenth Century, and in printing, it may be, the greatest figure since Gutenberg" (Goudy, 1934: 191). Goudy's early work demonstrates the breadth of Morris's influence (fig. 3-62). That influence was passed on to two of Goudy's apprentices, Will Ransom and W. A. Dwiggins.

Bruce Rogers, one of the great American book designers of the period, was also profoundly influenced by Morris. Rogers noted that upon seeing the Kelmscott books for the first time, his interest in book produc-tion became intensified, and he abandoned the idea that a book could be made beautiful through illustration alone. When Rogers began working on the Riverside Press limited editions, one of the first books he produced was an edition of Chaucer. His most famous type design, Centaur, like Morris's Golden, was modeled on Jenson (fig. 3-63).

Like Goudy, Rogers brought the influence of Kelmscott to com-mercial printing, but Goudy and Rogers were not the only missionaries for Morris in America. Daniel Berkeley Updike, Carl Rollins, and T. M. Clel-land all spread Morris's ideas. Updike's *A Day at Laguerre's* (1892) may be the first Arts and Crafts book published in America. His Merrymount Press was the earliest American press to pattern itself explicitly on Morris's Neo-Gothic mannerisms: red and black inks, black floral borders, woodcuts, decorated initials, and faces based on Jenson and other Venetians all recall Kelmscott (fig. 3-64). In 1928, Updike published *A Chronological List of the Books Printed at the Kelmscott Press.*

The Personal Style

After 1920, typographic trends swung like a pendulum between the ex-tremes of decoration and simplicity.

Although Frederic Goudy was profoundly influenced by Morris, by the 1920s he had developed his own theory of typography—the *Personal Style.* Goudy no longer believed that a graphic designer or typographer should look back to the past for a paradigm. Rather, the best designs reflected the designer's personal and contemporary concerns. The master typographer used the page to reflect the spirit of his or her time. The artist's unique contribution was the most important factor in the typo-graphic equation.

Goudy's own work represents the most effective example of the Personal Style. Nearly 60 percent of all advertising in the 1920s and 1930s was set in a Goudy face (figs. 3-65 and 3-66). So successful was Goudy that he became the first full-time type designer in history. Unfortunately, he reflected his own time *too well.* His faces evoke the 1920s and 1930s to the extent that they now seem outdated today and are rarely used (fig. 3-67). One exception, his display face Broadway, is still occasionally seen (fig. 3-68).

3-68.

Frederic Goudy's
Broadway type.

ABCDEFGHIJKLMNOPQRSTUVWXYZ 1234567890.,.!?'::-

ABCDEFGHIJKLMNO
PQRSTUVWX
abcdefghijklmnopqrstu
vwxyz $123456
..,;:!?&-/()''   1234567890
fi/⅛¼⅜½⅝¾⅞

3-69.

**Stanley Morison,
Times New Roman.**

ABCDEFGHIJKLMNOPQRST
UVWXYZ abcdefghijklmnopqrstuvwxyz
$123456   ..,;:!?&-/()'' 1234567890
fi/⅛¼⅜½⅝¾⅞

3-70.

Eric Gill, Perpetua.

3-71.

**Bauhaus
typography
popularized the
sans.**

The New Style

Reaction to the Personal Style came quickly from both England and Germany. The New Style designers of England vigorously rejected the idea that a typographer's pages should be tied to a single chronological point. They argued that, like good art, good typography and graphic design are timeless. What is effective today should be effective years from now.

This response gave rise to a new typographic movement that took its name from a typeface that had been designed by Stanley Morison specifically for the pages of the London *Times*—Times New Roman (fig. 3-69). But the first typeface to result from the New Style was Perpetua, very aptly named by the designer Eric Gill, who intended it to be used perpetually (fig. 3-70). Gill followed Perpetua with Gill Sans, a sans serif that is perhaps the most imitated face in history. Later, the typeface Univers continued the tradition.

If Morison and Gill were the important type designers of the New Style, Beatrice Warde was its major propagandist. Warde gave the American counterpart of the British New Style, the Crystal Goblet School, its name. She believed that type should not decorate pages. Rather, it should be like a crystal goblet, a clear receptacle that delivers but does not obscure its contents. In a famous formulation, she insisted that type should be invisible. Its purpose was not to suggest an illustrative design, but to convey words clearly.

The Bauhaus

After World War I, artists throughout Europe grouped themselves into several competing movements: Russian Constructivism, Italian Futurism, English Vorticism, French Dadaism, and Dutch de Stijl—to name only the best known. But the most important by far in the history of typography was the German Bauhaus. The Bauhaus issued a forceful rejection both of evocative printing and the Personal Style.

The Bauhaus was not simply an artistic theory. Bauhaus designers created within a wide range of media, including architecture, poetry, painting, sculpture, and furniture, as well as typography. The ideals of this cultural movement, artistic commune, printing shop, design school, and aesthetic academy were concisely set forth in several manifestos, and the theory was deceptively simple: whatever is artistic must be functional. An artistically correct page must not contain flourishes and florets, for type need only do the job of signifying meaning to the reader. That is its function.

The Bauhaus emphasis on sparseness, order, symmetry, and function produced surprising results (figs. 3-71 through 3-73). Although one might expect the movement's stringent guidelines to give rise to sterile, uninteresting designs, Bauhaus typography is among the most striking ever created. The influences of geometrical symmetry and abstract art produced a look that is at first shocking, but after one examines the theoretical background that underlies it, is recognizably orthodox. Russian constructivist typography, which began with a similar philosophy, produced similar results (fig. 3-74).

Two important results of Bauhaus theory were the revival of the sans serif and the emphasis on form. This severe formalism produced one strange conclusion: the "universal type" of Herbert Bayer (fig. 3-75). Taking Bauhaus theory to an extreme, Bayer argued that since we do not speak in capital letters, we need not write with them, and proceeded to eliminate all uppercase characters from his design. Several Bauhaus books were

3-72.

H. N. Werkman,
announcement.
1926.

3-73.

Laszlo Moholy-
Nagy, prospectus
for Bauhaus
school, 1923.

Das Buch, welches anläßlich der ersten Aus-
stellung vom 15. August bis 30. September 1923
des Staatlichen Bauhauses zu Weimar nach
dessen 3½jährigem Bestehen erscheint, ist in
erster Linie Dokument dieser Anstalt; es reicht
aber, dem Charakter der Anstalt entsprechend,
weit über eine örtliche oder spezifische Ange-
legenheit hinaus ins allgemeine, gegenwärtige
und zukünftige Gebiet künstlerischen Schaffens
und künstlerischer Erziehung.
So wie das Staatliche Bauhaus das erste wirk-
liche Zusammenfassen der im letzten Jahrzehnt
gewonnenen Einsichten in künstlerischen Ent-
wicklungsfragen bedeutet, so nimmt das Buch
spiegelnd Teil an diesen Fragen und bedeutet
jedem, der sich über den Stand dieser Dinge
unterrichten will, hierzu ein willkommenes Mittel.
Darüber hinaus bleibt ein geschichtliches
Dokument. Denn das Bauhaus ist, obwohl zu-
nächst einzigartig, keine insulare Erscheinung,
sondern ein kräftiger Trieb, der sich voll ent-
faltet und auch völlig sich ausbreiten wird. Das

a

3-74.

(*a.*, *b.*) El Lissitzky,
examples of
constructivist

typography for the
Berlin magazine
*Veshch/
Gegenstand/Objet,*
1922.

b

3-75.

Herbert Bayer,
universal type.

ABCDEFGHIJKLMNOPQRSTUVWXYZ
abcdefghijklmnopqrstuvwxyz
1234567890

3-76.

**Paul Renner,
Futura.**

ABCDEFGHIJKLMO
abcdefghijkmnopqrs

3-77.

**Max Miedinger,
Helvetica, 1954.**

abcdeghijklmnopqrstuvwxyz
ABCDEFGHJKLMNOPQRSY

3-78.

**Adrian Frutiger,
Univers, 1957.**

printed with the universal type. However, readers quickly discovered that capital letters *are* functional. Without them, one sentence runs into the next, and punctuation alone cannot prevent ideas from seeming confused. The universal type was quietly discarded.

A more important innovation by Bayer was the *geometric sans serif,* originated in 1927 with Futura (fig. 3-76). Although the original geometric sans serifs have diminished in popularity, they did much to raise the status of the sans from a specialty face that was only occasionally used in display to, by 1970, a common text type.

In 1933, Adolph Hitler ordered the Bauhaus out of Germany. Many of the designers, including the movement's founder, Walter Gropius, carried on their theory and practice in the United States. The University of Chicago became the new center of Bauhaus philosophy. Throughout the 1940s and 1950s, many American typographers produced functional and highly formalized designs in the Bauhaus style.

Swiss Typography

In the 1950s, typographers from Switzerland echoed the New Style of the 1920s. Demanding clean designs without embellishment, they formulated a typographic statement so influential that it was echoed by typographers for six decades.

Max Miedinger created the most popular typeface of our time, Helvetica, in 1954 (fig. 3-77). A modern sans, Helvetica is used throughout the world in books, advertising, signage, letterheads, and television graphics. Adrian Frutiger designed a similar style, Univers, in 1957 (fig. 3-78).

Swiss typography resembles Helvetica. Champions of the use of whitespace as a design element, the Swiss created airy, clean pages that complemented their airy, clean typefaces. In the late 1950s, when most American typographers were still using Bodoni set with four points of lead in body copy, the Swiss offered a compelling alternative (figs. 3-79 and 3-80).

By 1980, Swiss typography was the mainstream. Characterized most notably by the use of sans serif in body copy, the Swiss expressed the differences between evocative and New Style as the difference between the syntactic and the semantic element of the page: the syntactic element places importance on the way type is arranged; the semantic element, which the Swiss believed to be more critical, emphasizes the legibility of the words themselves. The arrangement of words, they insisted, should maximize legibility. In this endeavor, Swiss typography has fostered the typographic science known as *legibility research.* The results of that research are given in the next chapter.

The Waves of the Sixties

Throughout the 1960s, the proponents of syntax ruled American typography. With the advancement of communications technology came rapid changes in art and design. The artistic movements of the decade were readily evoked by designers and typographers and mirrored in posters, which had become a popular artistic form.

For example, optical art, in which lines or geometric patterns create the illusion of motion, was a painting style that also influenced typographers and illustrators (fig. 3-81). But op art typography was quickly replaced by the psychedelic designs of the late 1960s (fig. 3-82). By the 1970s, Swiss typography had made its way across the Atlantic and was

3-79.

Paul Rand, design for Kaiser-Frazer.

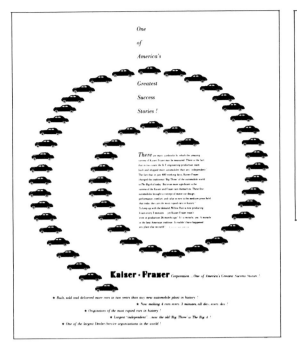

3-80.

Carlo Vivarelli, magazine cover, 1958. The grid of the Swiss style.

3-81.

Op art.

3-82.

The influence of psychedelic typography.

3-83.

New Wave: the
Bedford Corporation
annual report,
1981.

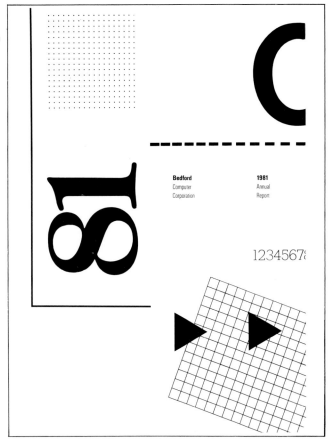

3-84.

New Wave in the
New York Times.

3-85.

The letterspacing of
New Wave
typography.

3-86.

Bob Clarke, Utica
Transit Authority
advertisement,
1985.

beginning to bring some serenity to American advertising. That serenity, however, did not last long.

The New Wave

The tenets of New Wave typography are directly opposed to those of the New Style. Rather than stressing legibility or considering the page as a mere vehicle for the message, New Wave typographers, who came into prominence in the late 1970s, emphasized playfulness and visual interest at the expense of verbal communication. Semantics had given way to syntax. Although they appear to be wildly free, New Wave designs are actually created within a strict set of visual symbols and patterns (figs. 3-83 through 3-85).

Slanted type patterns, the use of condensed, bold, and italic sans serifs, a grid background, the strange use of bold sans serifs as initial caps, and the absence of illustrations or photography are hallmarks of the style. New Wave typography lives and dies by its type. Functioning at the conceptual level, the message is conveyed not by type as word but by type as illustration. Lines of type are often reproduced at incongruous diagonals, repeated in different sizes and colors, or floated off the edge of the page into oblivion (fig. 3-86). Individual letters and characters are scattered, apparently randomly, about the page (fig. 3-87). In short, the type is relentlessly visible, a total violation of Beatrice Warde's Crystal Goblet Style.

The New Wave also rejects Swiss typography, most violently in its letterspacing. Display letters on New Wave pages are often separated from one another by as much as an inch. This total repudiation of *kerning* is purposeful: the message is that these pages are as much a rejection as they are a statement. New Wave has most often been used in advertising. Obviously, it would not work in editions of Shakespeare and Milton. One of the early classics in the style, however, was the Bedford Corporation's 1981 annual report—which enlivened a typographic area that is usually a bastion of graphic conservatism (see fig. 3-83).

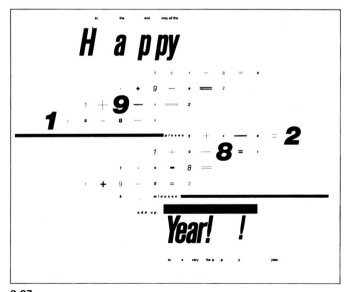

3-87.

Walter Kopec, New Year's greeting. 1982.

ABCDEFGHIJKLMNOPQ
RSTUVWXYZ
abcdefghijklmnopqrstu
vwxyz $12345
.,;:!?&-/()'' 1234567890
fi/⅛ ¼ ⅜ ½ ⅝ ¾ ⅞

3-88.

**Hermann Zapf,
Optima.**

The Persisting Personal Style

Amid the changes of typographic fashion, the Personal Style retains a significant influence. The most important typographer and type designer of the last three decades, Hermann Zapf, has worked to reflect the 1960s and beyond. His 1958 Optima typeface is a modern classic (fig. 3-88). Other important Zapf type designs include Kompakt, a popular display face, the script Virtuosa, and the romans Aldus Book, Melior, and Palatino.

Two Zapf works, *Manuale Typographicum* and *Typographic Variations,* display several hundred examples of his designs. Not only are the pages of these books consistently honest and clear, but they are consistently relevant (figs. 3-89 through 3-91).

Like Goudy earlier in the century, Zapf successfully represents his own time. In a technical age, the constants in Zapf's work are clarity and the appropriate use of technology. Optima and Palatino are among his most popular typefaces. His own graphic work, and the work of those who have been influenced by his style, have been tremendously popular in the last two decades. Zapf's successes point out most emphatically that typography is not static. The ebb and flow of flamboyant versus clean typography will continue. But Zapf's own designs show that crispness and legibility are not necessarily antithetical to attractiveness. The critical importance of Zapf's typography is its synthesis of relevance and clarity.

ABOUT ALPHABETS

SOME MARGINAL NOTES ON

TYPE DESIGN

by HERMANN ZAPF

THE M.I.T. PRESS, CAMBRIDGE/MASS.

AND LONDON, ENGLAND

3-89.

**Hermann Zapf, title
page of *About
Alphabets.***

ABCDEFGHIKLM
abcdefghiklm

N
n
o
O

John Baskerville | *Amongst the several mechanic arts that
have engaged my attention, there is no one which I have pursued
with so much steadiness and pleasure, as that of letter-founding.
Having been an early admirer of the beauty of letters, I became
insensibly desirous of contributing to the perfection of them* |

pqrstuvwxyz
PQRSTUVWXYZ

ABCDEFGHIJK
abcdefghijk

L M
l m

n o
N O

pqrstuvwxyz
PQRSTUVWXYZ

3—90.

**Hermann Zapf, from
*Manuale
Typographicum.***

abcdefghijklmnopqrstuvwxyz
ABCDEFGHIJKLMNOPQ
RSTUVWXYZ & Æ Œ Å ff ft
1234567890 (ä) ›å‹ [ö] 1234567890

*Genom boktryckeriet hade man ett nytt, förut okändt, medel att sätta i omlopp och utsprida
satser och undersökningar. Det var omöjligt att längre spärra tanken inom ett särskilt skrå,
eller qvarhålla den lössläppta forskningen. Hon gick genom lyckta dörrar. Det hade växt vingar
på den unga örnen, och han pröfvade dem alltjemt och steg emot solen.   Esaias Tegnér*

3-91.

**Hermann Zapf, from
*Manuale
Typographicum.***

THE ART AND SCIENCE OF LEGIBLE PAGES

Ideally the typeset message will possess two qualities: *readability* and *legibility*. Readability, which refers to an easily understood writing style, depends solely upon the talents of the author and editor. The typographer alone provides legibility, the capacity of a well-set letter, line, or page to be easily read. The design of our letterforms, the use of appropriate body and display faces, and the typographic pattern selected by the typographer all contribute to legibility. The legibility of a typeface thus depends both on the intrinsic qualities of the face's letterforms and on the way in which the type is manipulated on the page.

ITC and Typeface Design

The novice typographer and typesetter will quickly become familiar with the International Typeface Corporation (ITC), the most important contemporary typeface supplier.

ITC, founded in 1970 by Aaron Burns, Edward Rondthaler, and Herb Lubalin, is responsible for the majority of our popular new faces. Its contemporary classics include Avant Garde (1970), a redesign of Souvenir (1970), Benguiat (1973), Friz Quadrata (1973), American Typewriter (1974), Korinna (1974), Bauhaus (1975), Zapf Book (1976), Eras (1976), and Clearface (1979). As the names of several of these faces reveal, ITC designers have included all the luminaries of recent type design, including Hermann Zapf, Herb Lubalin, Tom Carnase, Edward Benguiat, Jovica Veljovic, Aldo Novarese, Tony DiSpigna, and Tony Stan. ITC is also responsible for one of the best magazines discussing typography and design trends, *U&lc* (distributed free to any member of the design and typography community).

But ITC is not the only company carrying the banner of contemporary type design. Berthold AG has revived classic faces, including Bodoni, Caslon, and Baskerville, and has contributed new faces, such as Walbaum (1979) and Akzidenz Grotesque (1983). The Haas Foundry released Haas Unica in 1980. Linotype has continued to commission designs, including Frutiger in 1976, Serifa in 1977, and Versailles in 1982—all the work of Adrian Frutiger, the designer of Univers. Max Miedinger, the designer of Helvetica, created Linotype's Neue Helvetica in 1983.

Has the proliferation of typefaces stopped? Certainly not. In 1980, the World Typeface Center (WTC) was founded by Tom Carnase. Among the best of WTC's work has been Carnase Text, WTC Goudy, and Thaddeus.

Contemporary faces have been tremendously successful. But that success has inspired the creation of "lookalike" faces, pirated versions of original designs. There are three international conventions and agreements dealing with typeface design protection: the Paris Convention (1883), the Hague Convention (1934), and the Vienna Agreement (1973). Unfortunately, these agreements have proven to be unenforceable. The Hague Convention has been ratified only by France, East and West Germany, Switzerland, Italy, Spain, Belgium, the Netherlands, and a handful of other countries. The Vienna Agreement has been signed only by West Germany and France. The United States, unfortunately, offers no significant protection for new type designs.

The letter of the law specifies that a typesetting equipment company need redraw (and rename) the letters only slightly. When specifying type, it is important—both for the integrity of typeface selection and the integrity of typography as a whole—to make certain that the typeface being set is the original. Beyond the matter of typographic sensibilities, however, is that of simple honesty. The type house and the typographer have an ethical responsibility both to their customers and to type designers to use original versions of contemporary faces.

Specifying Type for Legibility

After the typographer makes an appropriate typeface selection, the manuscript must be converted into type. The typesetter follows the commands set forth in a series of typographic specifications. These "specs" are expressed in one of several measurement systems used by the typesetting and publishing industries. These systems must be mastered by the beginning typographer—they are the basic language of typographic expression.

Three methods are used to measure type: the point and pica system is employed throughout the graphic arts and graphic design fields; the unit system is used by typesetters; and the agate is a measurement of newspaper classified advertising space.

THE POINT SYSTEM

In 1785, Firmin Didot of France, the creator of a famous modern roman typeface that bears his name, perfected the point/pica system first invented in 1737 by Simon Fournier.

The system is based on the *pica,* a unit of measurement equal to almost one-sixth of an inch (six picas are actually .9962 inches), and divided into 12 points. Figure 4-1 illustrates the relative values of picas, points, and inches.

Although the point/pica system may appear to be confusing, consider yourself lucky that you are not measuring type before Fournier and Didot, when each type had a different *name.* For example, what we now call 10-point type was then called Long Primer, 8-point type was Brevier, 14-point was English, 36-point was Double Great Primer, and 42-point had the impressive name of Seven-Line Nonpareil. Today, many type professionals in Europe measure type in millimeters. Other Europeans use the *cicero,* a unit one-sixteenth larger than the American and British pica.

Points and picas, the only units used in this country, were not adopted in the United States until the late nineteenth century. Before that time, different type manufacturers used different terms to refer to the same size and, worse, they used the same term to refer to different sizes. Confusion resulted when a typesetter attempted to combine foundry type from two different manufacturers. These problems led the American Type Founders to systematize the method we use today.

Type that is 14-point or smaller is usually specified for setting paragraphs of text and is thus known as *text type* or *body type*. Anything larger than 14-point is display type. Typefaces are often designed exclusively for either purpose, although many faces can be used for both text and display.

Very large type is measured in picas instead of points. However, its size is expressed, not in picas, but in *lines.* Thus, type that measures 288 points (24 picas) from top of ascender to bottom of descender is *24-line* type.

4-1.

Type measurements: inches, picas, and points.

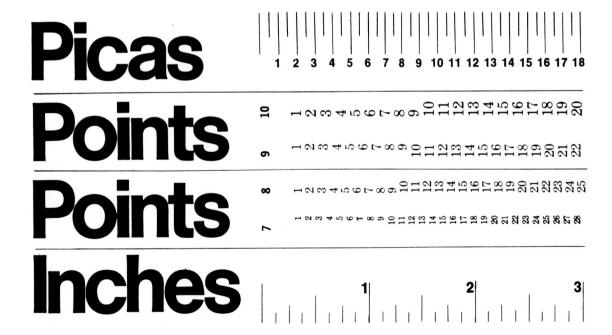

4-2.

Body and display type.

Choosing Type Sizes

Body type should be between 9- and 12-point. Smaller sizes will make large amounts of text illegible. If a smaller size is required, be certain to select a face with a large x-height. This will make the type itself appear larger and easier to read.

You should, of course, be aware of the audience. Who will be reading the text you are designing? Books and magazines intended for young children or for the elderly should be set in 12- and 14-point body type.

After selecting the body type size, display type must be specified. A general rule of thumb is to choose a size that is from 1½ to 3 times larger than that specified for the body (fig. 4-2). Setting 48-point display with 8- point body type is poor typography, because the display will overpower the page . A line of 24-point display and 10-point body type is much better. One of the more common typographic errors is the use of type sizes that are too large. An excellent way to learn the intricacies of the typographic art is to experiment with a single typeface and merely one or two sizes as a starting point. Move away from that limited selection only after you have determined how the legibility and overall appearance of the typeface is affected by a change in size.

Choosing Linespace

The second typesetting parameter to be selected is the linespace, or the distance *from one baseline to the next* (fig. 4-3). It is *not,* as beginning typesetters often believe, the distance between lines of type (from bottom of descender to top of ascender) or from baseline to top of ascender.

Linespace is a relatively new term for what hot-metal typographers call *leading* (pronounced "ledding"). In the days of hot-metal typesetting, compositors created extra space between lines by inserting strips of lead between the horizontal rows of type.

Today, many typesetters still refer to extra space between lines as leading, often mystifying those who are unaware of typesetting's hot-metal past. In phototypesetting this extra space is simply the difference between the type size and the linespace. If 12-point type is set with a 14-point linespace, there are two points of leading. If the linespace is 16 points, there are four points of leading.

When specifying linespace for body copy, the standard rule is to use from one to four points of leading. Type that has no leading (meaning that the type size and linespace are the same) is *set solid*. This specification is usually not recommended, however, because the lines of type will appear too close to one another to be legible (fig. 4-4). You may, however, set type solid if the face has extremely long ascenders and descenders or if the face is being set in a light weight (fig. 4-5).

In general, the leading should be about 20 percent of the type size. Thus, for 9- and 10-point type a leading of one or two points is usually ideal; for 11- and 12-point type, two to three points is required. This rule, however, has many exceptions. Heavier typefaces and faces with large x-heights require more leading than do light faces with small x-heights (figs. 4-6 and 4-7). One must remember that typography is an art: the goal of

4-3.

Measuring linespace.

linespace

of a merger or acquisition — baseline
and can represent the buyer — baseline
or the seller or both. A — baseline
Precision Banker can also — baseline
handle a leveraged buyout
from initial negotiation to

The earliest types were conscious copies of hand-written characters. The printers were so anxious to emulate the scribes, they even adopted the numerous tied letters, or ligatures, the scribes resorted to when approaching the end of a line. The original Gutenberg fonts, for example, contained forty or more of these tied letters. However, the steel tools of the punchcutters were far removed from the

4-4.

Type set solid. Sans faces must be leaded to be legible.

Aldine Roman has a delicate beauty of letter which makes it an outstanding face. It has an even balance throughout between thick and thin lines. Because of its strong visual appeal, Aldine Roman can be employed as a text type face for an extensive variety of applications.

Aldine Roman has a delicate beauty of letter which makes it an outstanding face. It has an even balance throughout between thick and thin lines. Because of its strong visual appeal, Aldine Roman can be employed as a text type face for an extensive variety of applications.

4-5.

Light typeface set solid *(top)* and with one point of lead.

Century is an unusually legible face characterized by its harmonious balance, which helps produce a clear, clean type impression. Because of its graphic appeal and legibility, this type face has been widely used for textbooks and manuals as well as advertising matter. Newspapers and periodicals which report the news in great detail very often specify Century for body type.

Century is an unusually legible face characterized by its harmonious balance, which helps produce a clear, clean type impression. Because of its graphic appeal and legibility, this type face has been widely used for textbooks and manuals as well as advertising matter. Newspapers and periodicals which report the news in great detail very often specify Century for body type.

4-6.

Typeface with large x-height set solid *(top)* and with one point of lead.

Press Roman is a practical type face featuring excellent form and clarity. Characteristically, Press Roman has no pronounced thick or thin lines as found frequently in other type faces It is a sturdily constructed face, rich in feeling, that can be employed for numerous purposes.

Press Roman is a practical type face featuring excellent form and clarity. Characteristically, Press Roman has no pronounced thick or thin lines as found frequently in other type faces. It is a sturdily constructed face, rich in feeling, that can be employed for numerous purposes.

4-7.

Typeface with small x-height set solid *(top)* and with one point of lead.

maximum legibility means that the typographer must be flexible in adhering to formal rules. Fashion can also dictate the amount of leading specified. The wide linespacing popular in the advertising of the 1940s and 1950s, for example, is now out of style (figs. 4-8 and 4-9).

Spacing between display and body should be at least six points larger than the display type size, so as not to cramp the text (fig. 4-10). For example, if you are using 18-point display, at least 24 points of linespace are required between the lowest display baseline and the first baseline of text. Chapter 8 provides a more thorough discussion of linespacing specifications.

4-8.

Advertising typography in the 1940s was often widely linespaced.

4-9.

Advertisement from 1960. Another example of wide linespacing.

Think small.

18 New York University students have gotten into a sun-roof VW; a tight fit. The Volkswagen is sensibly sized for a family. Mother, father, and three growing kids suit it nicely.

In economy runs, the VW averages close to 50 miles per gallon. You won't do near that; after all, professional drivers have canny trade secrets. (Want to know some? Write VW, Box #65, Englewood, N. J.) Use regular gas and forget about oil between changes.

The VW is 4 feet shorter than a conventional car (yet has as much leg room up front). While other cars are doomed to roam the crowded streets, you park in tiny places.

VW spare parts are inexpensive. A new front fender (at an *authorized* VW dealer) is $21.75.* A cylinder head, $19.95.* The nice thing is, they're seldom needed.

A new Volkswagen sedan is $1,565.* Other than a radio and side view mirror, that includes everything you'll really need.

 In 1959 about 120,000 Americans thought small and bought VWs. Think about it.

4-10.

Inadequate linespacing between display and text.

4-11.

Line length: *a.* **too short,** *b.* **too long, and** *c.* **appropriate.**

The Fotosetter phototypeset-ting machine was con-s t r u c t e d similarly to the standard hot-m e t a l linecaster. Its operation was almost iden-t i c a l , substituting a camera lens for the metal pot.
a.

Up to 1950, machine-set type and handset type were complete-ly compatible in an industry which enjoyed steady growth. There was naturally some overlapping of type designs from foundry to machine, but the guidelines were reasonable and in most cases respected. After 1950, however, the industry became involved in technological ferment which has by no means ended.

c.

b.

In 1911, the Ludlow typograph was first marketed. A slug-casting machine utilizing hand-composed m used primarily for display typesetting. When the basic Linotype patents expired, a competing machine—alm the original and called an Intertype machine—became available (1914). The composing room then settled do five year period of consolidation. Original models underwent numerous refinements, but no major new con troduced to speed up typesetting. Type manufacturing for typefoundries and composing machines under changes.

4-12.

Caslon *(top)* **versus Eras Book: x-height affects type appearance as well as appropriate line length.**

The main purpose of letters is the practical one of making thoughts visible. Ruskin says that all letters are frightful things and to be endured only on occas ion, that is to say, in places where the sense of the in scription is of more importance than external orna ment. This is a sweeping statement, from which w e need not suffer unduly; yet it is doubtful whether

The main purpose of letters is the practical one of ma king thoughts visible. Ruskin says that all letters are frig htful things and to be endured only on occasion, that is to say, in places where the sense of the inscription is of more importance than external ornament. This is a sweeping statement, from which we need not suffer unduly; yet it is doubtful whether there is art in indivi

Choosing Line Length

The width of a typeset line is the *line length* or *measure.* The only type specification given in picas, line length is the distance from the right margin to the left. It is perhaps the least subjective specification. Through research we have definitive rules as to how long a line should be for maximum legibility.

Book, newspaper, and magazine typographers are concerned as well with the total vertical depth of typesetting. Measured in picas, the vertical depth is estimated by the typographer before a job is set. An accurate estimate is essential. If, for instance, the total depth of a magazine or newspaper article is 20 percent more than estimated, it will be impossible to fit the text into the space provided in the design. The type must then be reset in a smaller size to fit, which is both expensive and time-consuming.

When determining a proper line length, one should remember that reading is easiest when a complete thought is contained in each line. If the measure is too narrow, the ideas, like the type conveying them, will appear choppy and difficult to follow. Similarly, the typographer must avoid lines that are too long. When one reads, the peripheral vision of the left eye is anchored to the left margin of the page. If the measure is too wide, the reader loses that peripheral anchor. The eye moves back along the baseline, instead of down, and the same line is read over again (fig. 4-11).

As with leading, the correct line length depends on the type size and x-height. The measure should be set from between approximately 1½ to 2½ alphabets long. To convert this into usable figures, *the line length should generally be 1½ to 3 times the type size.* For 10-point type, then, a 15- to 30-pica line length is appropriate; 12-point type will require line lengths that are between 18 and 36 picas. If your page size is larger than 36 picas, a double-column format is usually advisable.

Typefaces with extremely large x-heights should "violate" these numerical guidelines on the high side. Souvenir and Century Book, for instance, can be set with wider margins than can faces, such as Bembo or Garamond, that have smaller x-heights (fig. 4-12). The 2½ rule is not absolute. Some of our best typography violates all the rules, but before rules can be broken intelligently, typographers must understand them.

If your typography calls for a line length greater than 45 picas, you should re-examine your specifications. Most phototypesetting machines are engineered to set widths of 45 picas or less. The vast majority of typesetting is set from 15 to 30 picas.

THE UNIT SYSTEM

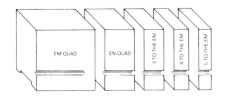

4-13.

Em and en quads in handsetting.

Used to determine the space between typeset words and letters, the unit system is based on a square called the *em.* The em is yet another inheritance from handsetting. An "em quad" was a piece of metal used for spacing between words or for pushing lines flush to the left or right margin.

The em quad is a space equal to the type size squared. A 12-point em, for instance, is 12 points high by 12 points wide. The en quad is a smaller unit of space equal to one-half of an em, or in the case of 12-point type, six points wide. Ems, ens, and the "thin space" (whose size varies according to the typesetting manufacturer) are the only fixed spaces used in most computerized phototypesetting equipment. In handsetting, 3-to-the-em, 4-to-the-em, and 5-to-the-em spaces (commonly abbreviated as 3-em, 4-em, and 5-em spaces) denote measurements that are one-third, one-fourth, and one-fifth of an em, respectively (fig. 4-13). There is a difference, however, between spaces and quads; in handsetting, a 3-em space is a

3-to-the-em piece of metal, whereas a 3-em *quad* is a piece of metal that is three ems wide.

Phototypesetting eliminates the use of metal but retains the concept. A 12-point em is a square of white space 12 points wide and 12 points high. Through photographic enlargement and reduction, ems are created for every size of type (fig. 4-14). The em can be subdivided just as easily into ens and smaller component parts called *units.* The faces designed for phototypesetting are created within a system composed of a specific number of equal units ranging in number from 4 to 64 (fig. 4-15).

Metal type was originally cast according to an 18-unit system (the em was divided into 18 equal parts). This continues to be a popular system among phototypesetting manufacturers. After a system is chosen, each character in the font is itself assigned a fixed number of units by the type manufacturer. This value, called the *set width* or simply the *set,* is programmed into the computerized phototypesetter (some machines use a device known as the "width card"). When a letter is set, the machine's camera photographically exposes the character and then automatically moves the number of units assigned by the set width (similar to a typewriter moving the carriage over to allow the typing of the next letter). The next character is then exposed. Figure 4-16 gives an example of the different set widths assigned to each character in an 18-unit system.

The spacing between letters and words is among the most important qualities that distinguish professional from shoddy typography. Rather than repeat a routine formula, the effective typographer specifies letterspacing and wordspacing values for each job by using a system of measurement proportional to the type size. As you develop typographic skills, you will also develop an understanding of your own preferences in letterspacing. Recent typographic trends have swayed between very loose display letterspacing and severely kerned (or tightly set) display (fig. 4-17). Figure 4-18

4-14.

Ems from 6-point through 48-point.

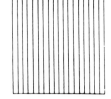

36-POINT EM DIVIDED INTO 18 UNITS

72-POINT EM DIVIDED INTO 18 UNITS

4-15.

Ems of 36 and 72 points divided into 18 units.

4-16.

The 18-unit system.

i, j, l	4
f, t, I, . , ,	5
r	6
c, k, s, v, x, y, z, J	9
a, b, d, e, g, h, n, o, p, q, u, L 1, 2, 3, 4, 5, 6, 7, 8, 9, 0	10
F, T, Z	11
A, B, E, K, P, V, X, Y	12
w, C, D, H, N, U, R	13
G, O, Q	14
m, M	15
W	17

shows examples of 8-point, 10-point, and 12-point type with a letterspacing value of minus one unit, which means that the letters have been slightly kerned.

As you design typography or set type, you may come to the realization that a slight kerning is the style you prefer. If so, assuming that you are using a unit system, you can simply ask for minus one unit of letterspace as a matter of routine. If the unit system did not exist, however, specifying letterspacing would be terribly complicated, for a minus one unit means something different with each type size. In an 18-unit system, one unit in 8-point type is $\frac{1}{18}$ of eight points, or about $\frac{4}{9}$ of a point. By the same calculation, one unit in 10-point type is about $\frac{5}{9}$ of a point, and one unit in 12-point type is $\frac{2}{3}$ of a point.

If the unit system were not in place, you would have to memorize each of those values—and many more. Simple experimentation with various letterspaces might take months because every type size would require a different quantity. The unit system resolves that problem with proportion. The phototypesetting machine will adjust to the set width of the type size you have specified, simplifying day-to-day typography.

Choosing Letterspace

As with linespace and line length, the proper amount of letterspace depends a great deal upon the typeface chosen. Condensed type can be set much tighter than regular and extended variations. As noted, recent typography has clearly moved away from the loose letterspacing of the past, so your choice will depend upon both typographic fashion and personal taste.

Text letters should *never* overlap. Kerned letters may be quite close to one another in very tight spacing, but they must not touch (fig. 4-19).

N o w   i s   t h e

Now is the time for al good men

4-17.

**Effects
of varied
letterspacing.**

Today, our children are computing basic math. Tomorrow, they'll be programming the future. But before they can fill the computer screen with new information, we'll have to help fill their minds. With ideas. Information. Dreams.
With the stimulation only a first-rate college education can provide. But they'll need your help. Because only with your help will colleges be able to cope with the high cost of learning.

Today, our children are computing basic math. Tomorrow, they'll be programming the future. But before they can fill the computer screen with new information, we'll have to help fill their minds. With ideas. Information. Dreams.
With the stimulation only a first-rate college education can provide. But they'll need your help. Because only with your help will colleges be able to cope with the high cost of learning.

Today, our children are computing basic math. Tomorrow, they'll be programming the future. But before they can fill the computer screen with new information, we'll have to help fill their minds. With ideas. Information. Dreams.
With the stimulation only a first-rate college education can provide. But they'll need your help. Because only with your help will colleges be able to cope with the high cost of learning.

4-18.

**8-, 10-, and 12-
point type set with
minus one point
letterspacing.**

4-19.

Letterspacing.

TOUCHING

TIGHT

NORMAL

LOOSE

4-20.

Contemporary
letterspacing:
kerning.
Typographer:
Robert Wakeman.

4-21.

Contemporary
letterspacing: New
Wave. Anne Cole
Fashions.

A N N E   C O L E

C   O   L   L   E   C   T   I   O   N

NEW YORK, 1411 Broadway, 32nd Floor, (212) 398-9696, LOS ANGELES, California Mart, Suite C-1355, (213) 623-4307

4-22.

**Ragged right
margin versus
justification.**

*ten führen wir in unserem Programm
bereits die Original-Walbaum-Antiqua
im Titelsatz von 48p Schriftguß abge-
leitet, die Walbaum-Buch, deren Aus-
gangspunkt der 16p-Grad im Schriftguß ist, dem nun abschließend die Text-
fassung in Form der Walbaum Standard folgt. Dieser letztgenannte Schnitt
basiert auf dem Vorbild des 8 und 10p-
Grades des alten Handschnittes, dessen
einzelne Größen alle von starker Indivi-
dualität geprägt sind. Mit der Walbaum
Standard geben wir den Buchherstel-
lern und Katalogdruckern ein sorgfältig
ausgewogenes Schriftbild an die Hand,
das auch reprotechnisch keine Probleme
durch „Ausbrechen" der feinen Serifen
und Haarstriche aufwirft. Diese neue
Fassung, in der Bearbeitung von G. G.
Lange, dient sowohl der Gesamtaus-
gabe der Werke von Adalbert Stifter, als
auch im werblichen Bereich zahlreichen
Komzeptionen. Die Walbaum hat seit
Jahrzehnten unter Kennern einen festen
Platz. Das Gußoriginal entstand um
1804 in Weimar. Das Haus Berthold
erwarb im Jahre 1919 die Originalma-
trizen von der Firma Brockhaus in
Leipzig, die sie nach Auflösung der
Walbaum'schen Gießerei erworben*

Berthold-Schriften überzeugen durch Schärfe u
nd Qualität. Schriftqualität ist eine Frage der Erf
ahrung. Berthold hat diese Erfahrung seit über
hundert Jahren. Zuerst im Schriftguß, dann im
Fotosatz. Berthold-Schriften sind weltweit gesc
hätzt. Im Schriftenatelier München wird jeder
Buchstabe in der Größe von zwölf Zentimetern
neu gezeichnet. Mit messerscharfen Konturen
um für die Schriftscheiben das Optimale an Kon

1.86 mm (7 p)   20   30   40

Berthold-Schriften überzeugen durch Schärf
e und Qualität. Schriftqualität ist eine Frage
der Erfahrung. Berthold hat diese Erfahrung
seit über hundert Jahren. Zuerst im Schriftg
uß, dann im Fotosatz. Berthold-Schriften sind
weltweit geschätzt. Im Schriftenatelier Mün
chen wird jeder Buchstabe in der Größe von z
wölf Zentimetern neu gezeichnet. Mit messe
rscharfen Konturen, um für die Schriftscheib

2.00 mm (7.5 p)   20   30   40

Berthold-Schriften überzeugen durch Schä
rfe und Qualität. Schriftqualität ist eine Fra
ge der Erfahrung. Berthold hat diese Erfah
rung seit über hundert Jahren. Zuerst im
Schriftguß, dann im Fotosatz. Berthold-Sc
hriften sind weltweit geschätzt. Im Schrifte
natelier München wird jeder Buchstabe in
der Größe von zwölf Zentimetern neu geze
ichnet. Mit messerscharfen Konturen, um

2.15 mm (8 p)   20   30   40

4-23.

**Variations in
wordspacing from
line to line.**

work in stress evaluation and repair. Qualified
personnel conduct sessions in medical, physical and
physiological therapy. Under their guidance, hard-
charging executives have the opportunity to

Book Collectors Scout Rarities

Book Collectors Scout Rarities

Book Collectors Scout Rarities

Book Collectors Scout Rarities

4-24.

Wordspacing: *(from bottom to top)* loose, normal, tight, and very tight.

The oldest specimens of Greek printing consist of detached passages and citations, found in a few of the first printed copies of Latin authors, including Lactantius in 1465; the Aulus Gellius and Apuleius of Sweynheim and Pannartz of 1469, and some works of Bessarion at Rome without date.

4-25.

Poor wordspacing as a result of insufficient measure.

In display type, letters sometimes run together as a special effect (fig. 4-20). Because they take up more space, letters that are rounded will touch adjacent letters before straight ones will.

Letterspace considerations are more important for display type, whose letters, being larger, are much more noticeable. The typical letterspace decisions for display range from touching to very tight, tight, normal, loose, and very loose. The last is a New Wave phenomenon characteristic of the typographic style prevalent in the early 1980s (fig. 4-21). Alternatively, unit specifications can be used; in fact, they are preferable, because *minus four units of letterspace,* for instance, is a much more precise instruction than *very tight letterspace.*

Choosing Wordspace

Wordspace, too, is measured in units and specified by the typographer. It is probably more important than letterspacing because errors in judgment have a greater effect. The wordspace is always larger than the letterspace. If mistakes are made, they will be quite noticeable.

Wordspacing is also important in allowing for *justification,* or the alignment of the right as well as left margin (fig. 4-22). Traditionally, all book, magazine, and newspaper typography has been set justified, but in the last 25 years, more and more typographers have specified *flush left/ragged right* typography, or the alignment of the left margin alone. The debate between justified and unjustified typography continues to be among the loudest in type circles. Partisans on either side claim their favorite is more legible and more pleasing to the eye.

The facts? Researchers have discovered that readers are not aware of whether the type they are reading is justified. Indeed, a Dutch newspaper changed overnight from justified to flush left/ragged right, and its audience did not even notice. Justified type is only slightly more legible than well-set unjustified type, yet the latter is 14 percent less expensive, primarily because it requires fewer corrections. In justified copy, more words are hyphenated at the ends of lines, necessitating closer inspection for the inevitable errors in word division. Perhaps more important, unjustified typesetting contributes a contemporary look to the page.

Justification requires that wordspacing and letterspacing values be varied as needed to bring the final word of the line to an even right margin. As figure 4-23 shows, the amount of wordspace changes from line to line of copy. It is therefore specified as a minimum and maximum unit value. Unless the typographer is very familiar with the typesetting system being employed, he or she should describe the desired effect with words such as loose, normal, tight, and very tight (fig. 4-24). Loose and very tight wordspacing is best used only for small amounts of copy, if at all. Remember that where a large quantity of copy is to be set, aesthetics must be subordinated to legibility. Although, as a designer, you may prefer the appearance of very tight wordspacing, it makes long paragraphs of copy difficult to read. Be wary also of very short line lengths, which create wordspacing problems (fig. 4-25).

THE AGATE SYSTEM

The *agate* system is the simplest of the three methods for sizing type and is used exclusively for measuring the column length of classified advertising space. There are about 5½ points to the agate and 14 agates to the column inch.

The system is employed essentially for billing purposes. Classified ads are often purchased by the agate line. Larger display ads are usually purchased by the column inch.

Type size, linespace, and the other necessary specifications *create* the appearance of the page. The fine points are not niceties that can be avoided. Rather, they contribute to the professionalism and perfection of typography. The basics of typeface, type size, linespace, and line length are the core of the typographic craft. When a typographer has mastered that foundation, an essential step has been taken toward achieving a genuine artistic style.

Legibility Research

The legibility of a letter depends on the ease with which a reader can decipher it as a symbol—readers must identify letters to read them. Any part of a letterform, then, that increases identifiability will also increase legibility.

The novice typographer in search of a typographic style is not, however, aided by a simple definition. Rather, he or she needs a logical strategem for making design decisions. One answer is suggested by the way we read. Research has determined that the eye moves across a page in *saccadic jumps*. It focuses on a small group of words for about one-quarter of a second and then leaps to the next group in the line (fig. 4-26).

Research has also shown that the reader actually looks most closely at the top halves of letters . This information should lead typographers to choose typefaces whose top halves are as identifiable as possible. *Identifiability* is a subjective term; but typographers must know what faces are identifiable if correct decisions are to be made.

Information useful in making these decisions comes from legibility research, a field associated with the psychology of perception. For several decades, social scientists have discovered two sets of data that are useful to typographers: first, the alphabets that are most legible; second, the typographic patterns that produce the most legible typesetting.

Many typographers disagree about the value of legibility research. Typographic scientists like Rolf Rehe of Design Research International and Miles Tinker, one of the first psychologists to publish widely in the field, obviously believe that legibility research is a valuable contribution to the typographic industry. More traditional typographers, on the other hand, believe that research has not discovered anything that Baskerville, Caslon, and Goudy did not know. But even these typographers agree with the validity of the principles derived from research.

Legibility research can certainly claim two triumphs. First, if typographers have learned through experience what typographic research is now "proving," then research is at least demonstrating the validity of typographic theories of the past. William Morris was correct when he suggested that typography that rigorously adhered to design principles could dramatically affect a reader's perception. Second, much legibility research has been done in fields that are new or untested. Children's books, television typography, the design of works to be read by persons with sight handicaps, and outdoor advertising typography are all good examples. If letters are to appear on a billboard 12 stories above ground level, how large must the letters be? What typefaces work best? What kind of face is most effective on a poster placed on a moving bus? These are the sorts of questions that legibility research can answer. Experience cannot provide answers to questions about new problems.

Legibility research, then, has a legitimate role to play in typo-

This is an example of how eye (saccadic) movements may progress during reading. Circles indicate the focusing points for each stop (fixation), while the squares show the approximate area covered by the eye during a fixation. Broken lines indicate saccadic jumps, and solid lines are (re-reading) regressions.

4-26.
Saccadic jumps.

graphic decision making, especially for the beginning typographer. Perhaps it is true that the rules we learn from research may be mastered by simple experience, but experience takes time. That we learn is more important than the method through which we acquire knowledge. Mastery of the craft is the ultimate objective, however that mastery is obtained.

The results of legibility research can be found in the two most important journals in the field: the British publication of the International Council of Graphic Design, *Icographic,* and *Visible Language* (formerly *The Journal of Typographic Research*), published by the Cleveland Museum of Art. Miles Tinker's *Legibility of Print,* published in 1963, is still an important work, as are *The Visible Word* by Herbert Spencer (1969), and his later *Study of Legibility.* A more recent work of equal value is Rolf Rehe's *Typography: How to Make It Legible* (1974). Hundreds of research reports are available. Many are noted in Rehe's book, which contains a bibliography of nearly two hundred items, and in Spencer's *Visible Word,* which lists 464 citations.

What does the research tell us? The next several pages provide an overview of several of the most important research studies, presented according to subject in alphabetical order. Some of the information may be obvious to professional typographers, yet obviousness does not dilute its importance.

ADVERTISING TYPOGRAPHY

Advertising set completely in display type sizes is no more attractive and will retain the reader's attention no longer than advertising set both in display and body type sizes. Whitespace is far more attractive than increased type size.

It may be economically worthwhile to purchase a larger ad, with more whitespace, to increase reader attention.

The average person will spend 10 seconds looking at an ad and will read less than 10 percent of it. That percentage will decrease with the number of words on the page, which is to say that the more words there are in an ad, the fewer the average person will read. More copy will be read on verso pages than on recto pages.

THE ALPHABET

A radical redesign of the alphabet based upon the principles of legibility would result in typefaces that are easier to read. Any such proposal, however, is impractical. The alphabet is a cultural given which cannot be changed at will.

CHILDREN'S BOOKS

Fifth graders read 10- to 12-point type as well as or better than type set in larger sizes. Thus, the large type sizes found in some children's books are necessary only in books intended for those under 10 years old.

COLOR

Black type is most legible printed on off-white paper with a yellowish tone; bright white papers manufactured for halftone reproduction are not conducive to easy reading.

The following combinations are particularly difficult to read: red on black; black on red; white on yellow; yellow on white or cyan .

In rank order according to ink color, the following ink and background combinations are most legible: yellow on blue, red, or magenta; cyan on blue, white, or red; green on any color; magenta on blue, white, cyan, or green; red on cyan, green, blue, or white; and blue on red, magenta, or blue.

DISPLAY TYPE

There is no significant difference in legibility between 14- and 30-point type. If the typographer decides upon 18-point instead of 30-point, the additional white space created will increase legibility.

EXCELLENCE IN TYPOGRAPHY

The great majority of readers confronted with poor typography and good typography identified the latter immediately.

There is a close correlation between typographic legibility and reader preference. Readers favored legible typography.

FIGURES

Old style figures are more legible than modern lining figures and should be specified whenever possible. Numbers are less legible than letters. Arabic numerals are always more legible than Roman numerals or numbers written in word form.

Readers prefer tables over diagrams, but diagrams provide for easier learning. They should be set in at least 8-point. If tables are set, at least one pica of white space should separate each tabular column.

INDENTS

Paragraphs set with a 2- to 3-em indent are easier to read than paragraphs without indentation. Additional linespace between paragraphs may be an acceptable substitute for indentation.

JUSTIFIED VERSUS UNJUSTIFIED

There is no significant difference in legibility between justified typography and typography set ragged right/flush left. Reading speed is unaffected by unjustified columns, and readers do not express a preference for either typographic pattern. Indeed, poor readers may read unjustified typography more easily. Moreover, as noted, production costs for ragged right are considerably less than for justified composition. Uniform letterspacing in ragged right composition may increase legibility. Overall, unjustified typography can be recommended whenever the typographer decides it is appropriate.

LETTERSPACING AND WORDSPACING

Some letterspacing is necessary. Space between letters helps the reader to differentiate between characters and increases letter recognition. Where a consistent quantity of space is specified, a letterspace the width of the lowercase *i* is the best choice.

When kerning, spacing that is visually proportional to the letter's width affords the highest degree of legibility.

LIGATURES

Ligatures are not merely historical anachronisms. Typography with ligatures is easier to read than typography without them.

Because the saccadic jump encompasses approximately one inch of horizontal space, the use of ligatures allows additional characters to be fit into that space and thus increases reading speed.

LINESPACE

Type with linespace is read more easily than type set solid. The optimum quantity of linespace varies both according to type size and to the individual typeface specified. Anywhere from one to four points, however, should be allotted for type sizes that range from 9 to 12 points.

The optimum linespace for 10-point faces of medium x-height and width is two or three points, depending on the typeface. Boldface type must be linespaced greater than lighter variations.

As a general rule, more space should be specified between lines of type than between words.

LOWERCASE VERSUS UPPERCASE

Lowercase letters are much more legible than uppercase, but there is no difference in legibility between headlines set in all lowercase and those set in upper- and lowercase.

The initial capital letter in upper- and lowercase typography is significant in signaling the beginning of each sentence.

Display lines set in all capital letters are difficult to read. Body copy set in all caps is completely illegible. Words set in all caps are read letter by letter rather than by saccadic jumps. Reading is approximately 15 percent slower.

MEASURE

The most legible measure depends upon the type size and typeface chosen. Lines that are too short or too long are both difficult to read.

For typefaces ranging from 9- to 12-point, lines that contain from 10 to 12 words are most legible. In practice, this requires an 18- to 24-pica measure. If smaller type sizes are used, a proportionally smaller measure should be specified.

Two-column typography is easier to read than one-column type set on a comparatively wide measure.

REVERSE TYPE

Type set white on black is approximately 15 percent more difficult to read than type set black on white. Over three-quarters of all readers prefer black on white. If reverse type is specified, it should not be set smaller than 12-point.

SERIFS VERSUS SANS

Regardless of the opinions of Swiss style and New Wave designers, serif typefaces are slightly more legible than sans serifs.

Two-thirds of the readers expressing a preference favored serif typefaces. Serifs seem to increase both legibility and recognition value.

SHAPES OF LETTERS

Condensed or expanded letters are not as legible as those of "normal" width. The condensed versions are particularly difficult to differentiate.

Geometrically designed sans serifs are especially difficult to identify because each letter is shaped similarly.

TELEVISION TYPOGRAPHY

Because the televised image is digitized in a relatively coarse fashion, serifed typefaces with thin strokes should not be specified. Because fine letterforms fill in easily, medium weight sans serifs or square serifs should be specified.

Typefaces specifically designed for television typography are no more legible than already existing typefaces.

TEXTBOOKS

Legibility is especially important for readers who are learning new material. Important means of enhancing the legibility of textbooks include: emphasizing portions of text, setting synopses of information in the same typography as the body, and presenting information in an outline format.

Students who use primary and secondary school textbooks tend to prefer two-column formats. In addition, typography that stresses typographic visuals (outlines, charts, and graphs) is much more legible than straight text.

Good typography and good design increased reading awareness significantly.

TYPE SIZE AND X-HEIGHT

The most legible type sizes are 9-, 10-, 11-, and 12-point. However, if the typeface has a small x-height, 11- and 12-point should be specified. Conversely, 9- and 10-point sizes should be chosen for typefaces with large x-heights.

Smaller type sizes will not permit easy recognition of letters. For reference material, however, a smaller type size may be necessary to fit a large quantity of information into a book or pamphlet.

VARIATIONS

Medium-colored, "gray" typefaces are more legible than boldface or light variations. Regular versions are easier to read than italic, bold, condensed, or expanded variations.

Though italics are aesthetically preferred by typographers, the boldface variation is a better choice if emphasis is the only concern. However, an abundance of bold lettering is wearisome to the eye.

WHITESPACE

In advertising typography, whitespace is a valuable attractive force. The greater the amount of whitespace, the larger the number of readers who will pay attention to the ad.

In text, improvements in the distribution of whitespace increase ease of reading more than improvements in writing style.

5

TYPOGRAPHIC APPLICATIONS: BOOK DESIGN

Fundamentally, there are four different kinds of typography: book design, publication design (newspapers and magazines), advertising typography, and jobwork. Many experienced typographers and most type houses specialize in one area. However, everyone working in the field should have a basic knowledge of each major typographic category. The beginning typographer can expect to be confronted with a variety of different typographic problems. An understanding of basic vocabularies, design strategies, and typographic rules will equip the novice with the tools for creating solutions.

The field of book design itself can be categorized into various specializations. Designers of scientific textbooks, for instance, are far more concerned with the legible design of charts and graphs than are designers of novels. Private-press book typographers work in a very different way from typographers designing books for trade publishing houses. There are, nevertheless, shared fundamentals that all book typographers understand and use.

No matter what kind of book is being created, the parts are the same. Most important in the context of this book, the fact that the book designer is a typographer is understood by all segments of the book industry. Unlike magazines and advertising, which rely heavily on visual as well as verbal information, most books are composed primarily of words.

Terminology

Book typography has a vocabulary all its own. The novice book designer will do well to memorize the most important terms used in the industry:

- A *verso* is a left-hand page; a *recto* is a right-hand page.
- The page number is referred to as the *folio,* and may appear at the top of the page (center, left, or right); at the bottom (center, left, or right); or in the margin.
- The top of the book is called the *head;* the bottom, the *foot.* In most books, the book or chapter title is repeated on every page, either at the top (where it is called a *running head*) or at the bottom (where it is called a *footer*).
- The first page of a chapter (called the chapter opening) contains a *chapter head,* which identifies the chapter number and title and which in almost all cases has a consistent design throughout the book. In fine book typography, chapter openings always appear on a recto page.
- Two numbered pages make up the front and back of a *leaf.* A *sheet* usually consists of several leaves, and the number of leaves is determined by how many times the sheet is folded:

An unfolded printed sheet is called a *broadside;*
A sheet folded once creates a *folio* of four pages;
A sheet folded twice creates a *quarto* of eight pages;
A sheet folded three times creates an *octavo* of 16 pages;
A sheet folded four times creates a *16-mo* of 32 pages (and 16 leaves);
A sheet folded five times creates a *32-mo* of 64 pages (and 32 leaves);
A sheet folded six times creates a rare *64-mo* of 128 pages.

- Confusingly, experienced typographers often refer to books that are 6 by 9 inches and 8½ by 11 inches (two popular sizes) as octavos and quartos (*8vo* and *4mo*) respectively. However, octavo, quarto, folio, 16-mo, and 32-mo should refer only to the number of times the paper is folded. Popular book sizes have become identified with the terms *quarto* and *octavo* because book paper, or *stock,* is manufactured in standard sizes. Although there are many standard sizes, if a leaf requires three folds, the book is an actual octavo.
- Publishers often refer to books as *folio* and *quarto editions.* In general, the terms *folio* and *quarto* are used quite loosely by book publishers. A folio edition commonly means an oversized book that is larger than a quarto, which is in turn larger than an 8vo.
- Books are produced in *signatures,* collections of pages sewn or glued together in the binding. The arrangement of the signature pages is known as the *imposition.* For example, the imposition of a 32-page signature is such that page 32 faces page 1, page 31 faces page 2, page 30 faces page 3, and so on. The imposition is also important when designing newsletters and brochures. An easy way to remember imposition is to remember that the sum of the facing pages will be one greater than the total number of pages in the signature. The best way to be certain about an imposition, however, is to create a *dummy,* a set of pages folded and numbered in exactly the same way as the signature. After the dummy is created, one can refer to it to make certain of the imposition.
- Book sizes are expressed in inches in the United States, and millimeters in Britain and elsewhere throughout the world. Whichever method is used, the dimensions of the finished book (for example, 6 by 9 inches) are called the *trim size.* Note that, in the United States, trim sizes are expressed as width by length (6 by 9). In Britain, they are expressed as length by width. Sheets are trimmed, or cut, in several stages of book production: they are cut down to practical sizes for printing; further reduced when their edges are bound; and undergo a final trim when the outer edges of the book are evened.

The Parts of a Book: Front Matter

A book consists of three basic parts: front matter, body, and back matter. The front matter (sometimes called the preliminary matter or prelims) consists of all or a combination of the following:

Half title (bastard title)	Preface
Announcement (fact title)	Foreword
or frontispiece	List of illustrations
Title page	Acknowledgments
Copyright page	
Dedication	
Table of contents	

THE WORLD OF
ALDUS
MANUTIUS

5-1

Half-title page.

5-2.

**Title page with
announcement.**

HALF-TITLE PAGE

The half, or bastard, title, is the first page to contain type. Always a recto, it features only the title of the book (the subtitle, if any, is omitted). This should appear on the upper fourth of the page (fig. 5-1). Half-title type should be no larger than 18-point; often it is the same size as the type used for chapter openings.

ANNOUNCEMENT OR FRONTISPIECE

Opposite the title page, the announcement, fact title, or card is a list of books previously written by the author. The announcement is a rather new member of the front matter, largely replacing the frontispiece, a photograph or engraving that is related to the topic of the book (for example, a biography's frontispiece is usually a photograph of the subject). Announcement type should be set the same size as the text type used in the body (fig. 5-2).

BOOKS BY

ALEXANDER AND NICHOLAS HUMEZ

Alpha to Omega
The Life & Times of the Greek Alphabet

Latin for People / Latina pro Populo

The Boston Basin Bicycle Book
(WITH EDWARD AND JANICE GOLDFRANK)

A · B · C

ET

CETERA

The Life & Times

of the Roman

Alphabet

by Alexander &

Nicholas Humez

David R. Godine · Publisher
BOSTON

TITLE PAGE

The title page includes the full title of the book; the author's name; and the publisher's name, place of business, and logo or emblem. Again, this page is always a recto.

Typographically, the title page sets the tone and artistic style for the entire book. So important is it that entire books have been devoted to the design of this page alone. Samples from master typographers will themselves serve as valuable lessons (figs. 5-3 through 5-8).

The type sizes to be used must be selected with the importance of the various elements in mind. The title should be set in the largest size on the page. The names of the author and publisher, which are less significant, should be less prominent. They are often set in the same size. The

5-3.

Title page: *The World of Aldus Manutius.*

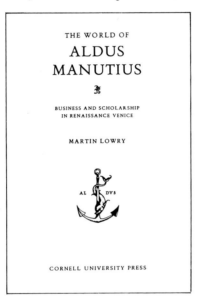

5-4.

Title page: *The Letter Forms and Type Designs of Eric Gill.*

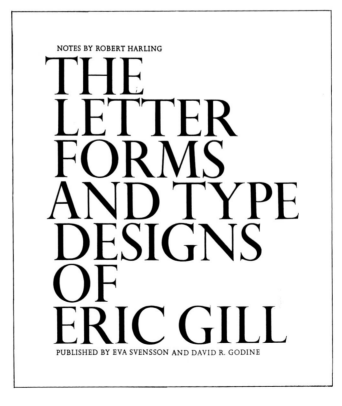

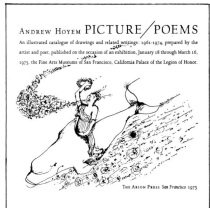

5-5.

Title page: *Picture/Poems,* **1975.**

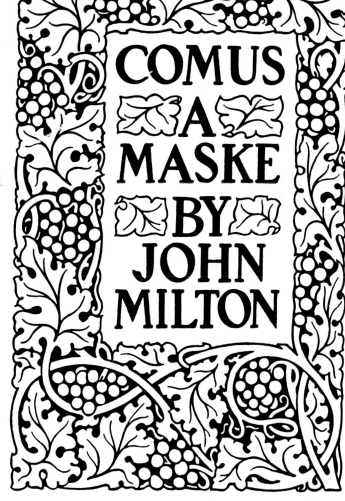

5-6.

Title page: *Comus.* **Typographer: Clarke Conwell.**

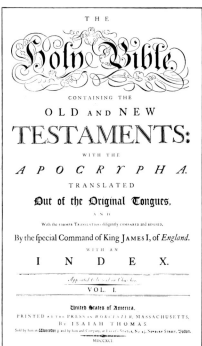

5-7.

Title page. Typographer: Isaiah Thomas, 1791.

5-8.

Title page: the "Bishop's Bible," 1591. Typographer: John Legate.

publisher's place of business and the date of publication, if included, merit the smallest type sizes: 10- or 12-point is usually adequate. The typographer must not commit one common mistake—setting the word *By* (as in *By Herman Melville*) in the same size as the author's name and thereby calling undue attention to an insignificant preposition. There are four possible solutions: cite the author's name without the use of the word; set the word *By* on a separate line in a smaller size; de-emphasize the word in the same line by setting a lowercase *b*; or, best of all, combine the last two suggestions and set *by* in smaller type on its own line. This may seem to be a small nuance, but all details are important in the design of the most significant page of the work.

The design of the title page should not exceed the dimensions of the text type specified for the body and should reflect the typography of the book as a whole. If, for example, illustrations are an important part of the book, an illustration might be used on the title page.

As with type size selection, the design should reflect the relative importance of the title page elements. The title should appear in the *optical center* and upper third of the page, with the author's name featured just below but still in the top half. A healthy amount of whitespace should separate the author's name from the publisher's name and emblem, which appear at the foot of the page. The last line on the title page should define the bottom margin of the book and should align with the last line of type on text pages. When possible, the title should align with the top line of a text page.

Although borders and rules were once very popular on title pages, contemporary taste in typography leans toward the crisp, undecorated page. Today's title pages may contain a single hairline rule to demarcate the publisher's imprint. Any additional decoration, unless specifically evocative of the book's subject matter, is probably a poor choice.

COPYRIGHT PAGE

The copyright page is located on the reverse of the title page and is therefore always a verso. It should contain the following information: a copyright notice; the date of publication; the name and address of the publisher; the edition number; a copyright warning; cataloging-in-publication (CIP) data, available from the Library of Congress; and the book's ISBN. The CIP data helps librarians correctly catalog the book for library shelves. The ISBN (International Standard Book Number) is assigned by the publisher and is used by bookstores and other agencies ordering the title. If the book was manufactured in the United States, the copyright page should also contain the words *Printed in the United States of America* to avoid manufacturing import duties. Finally, the page includes credits to the book designer and jacket designer, and photographic credits for the jacket design. If the publishing house believes it is appropriate, the type house, printer, and binder will also be noticed.

Because of the great number of items, and because many (such as the CIP) are not available until very near the actual production deadline, the copyright page is often given little attention by the typographer. That is a mistake. The copyright page is the first page examined by librarians and bookstore buyers. As much care should be taken with it as with any other part of the front matter (figs. 5-9 and 5-10).

5-9.

Copyright page.

5-10.

Copyright page.

DEDICATION

The dedicatory phrase may appear either on the copyright page or directly opposite, on its own page. If a full page is given to the dedication, the page should be a recto.

The type should be approximately the same size used for the announcement and text. If the dedication occupies its own page, it should be placed at the head of the page or in the optical center. If it will be set on several lines, the first line should align with the top of a text page.

TABLE OF CONTENTS

The contents page is a numbered recto. The designer must use creativity and care to design a table of contents that is both easy to use and attractive. The table must show the relationships between the various parts of the text easily and quickly. If the book has three major sections divided into 24 chapters, the table of contents should make this readily apparent. The contents should be displayed in a text size (usually 10- or 12-point). The header (whether it is *Table of Contents, List of Contents* or, simply, *Contents*) should be in the same size as the chapter opening heads.

Chapter numbers should be displayed at the left, followed by the chapter title. If there are more than nine chapters, an en space should be set before the number in chapters 1 through 9, so that single-digit numerals will align with the second digit in numerals 10 and above. For example, the numeral in chapter 9 should be directly above the 0 in chapter 10. This will also permit all the periods following the chapter numbers to align.

Chapter titles must be absolutely accurate. The page numbers are set after the mechanicals for the book are completed. Only then will the exact sequence of pages be known. Last-minute changes in chapter titles must be incorporated. The page number of each chapter should be checked and rechecked.

The chapter numbers, chapter titles, and page numbers can be visually connected in many ways (figs. 5-11 through 5-13). Popular meth-

Contents

5-11.

Table of contents.

ods include the use of *leaders* (although some typographers consider them to be visually obtrusive on contents pages), extra leading between chapter titles, and boldface type. If the table of contents is to include headings and subheadings, the typographer has a greater opportunity to distinguish between chapters.

The typography of the table of contents should not overpower the text. Rather, this section should be designed within the typographic boundaries of the body.

LIST OF CONTENTS

5-12.
Table of contents.

Contents	Inhalt	Sommaire
7 On visual transformation	7 Zum Thema «visual transformation»	7 Considérations sur le thème «visual transformation»
9 Structures of formation	**9 Strukturen der Gestaltung**	**9 Structures de la conception formelle**
11 Work and play with elements	11 Arbeit und Spiel mit Elementen	11 Travail et jeu avec des éléments
12 Topology	12 Topologie	12 Topologie
20 Constructions in area and space	20 Konstruktionen in Fläche und Raum	20 Constructions planes et dans l'espace
28 Educational manipulations	28 Didaktische Manipulationen	28 Manipulations didactiques
32 Variations on a theme	32 Variationen auf thematischer Basis	32 Variations sur base thématique
35 Isometric landscapes	35 Isometrische Landschaften	35 Paysages isométriques
40 Abstract forms in art and cultural publicity	40 Abstrakte Formen in Kunst und kultureller Werbung	40 Formes abstraites dans l'art et la publicité culturelle
47 Present-day tendencies of style in design	**47 Aktuelle Stiltendenzen im Design**	**47 L'esthétique industrielle moderne**
48 Company print, advertising, title pages, brochures	48 Firmendrucksachen, Inserate, Prospekte, Titelblätter	48 Imprimés d'entreprise, annonces, prospectus, pages de titre
60 Trade fair and exhibition style	60 Messe- und Ausstellungsstil	60 Style des foires et expositions
62 Alusuisse	62 Alusuisse	62 Alusuisse
63 Dow Chemical Europe	63 Dow Chemical Europe	63 Dow Chemical Europe
70 IBM Information and information material	70 IBM Information und Informationsmaterial	70 IBM Information et matériel d'information
76 Communications equipment	76 Kommunikationsgeräte	76 Instruments de communication
78 Visual organisation of working and leisure areas	78 Visuelle Gestaltung von Arbeits- und Freizeiträumen	78 Conception visuelle des locaux de travail et de loisirs
79 Abstract art in a pharmaceutical company	79 Abstrakte Kunst in einem pharmazeutischen Betrieb	79 Art abstrait dans une entreprise pharmaceutique
82 Fountains in a courtyard	82 Wasserspiel in einem Atrium	82 Jeux d'eaux dans un atrium
84 Design of a Keep-Fit Club	84 Gestaltung eines Fitness-Clubs	84 Conception d'un fitness-club
86 Plastic sculptures for an indoor swimming pool	86 Kunststoffskulpturen für ein Hallenbad	86 Sculptures en polyester dans une piscine couverte
90 Electro-image	90 Elektro-Image	90 Electro-image
97 Change of style in symbolism	97 Stilwandel in der Symbolik	97 Evolution stylistique de la symbolique
107 Sight, overview, insight	**107 Sicht, Übersicht, Einsicht**	**107 Perception, aperçu, aperception**
108 New methods of information	108 Neue Informationsmethoden	108 Nouvelles methodes d'information
110 Exhibition pavilion of the telecommunications ground station at Leuk	110 Ausstellungspavillon der Telekommunikations-Bodenstation Leuk	110 Pavillon d'exposition de la station de télécommunication au sol de Loèche
114 Evaluation of satellite pictures	114 Auswertung von Satellitenaufnahmen	114 Interprêtation de prises de vues transmises par satellite
114 Land use mapping	114 Landnutzungskartierung	114 Analyses cartographiques
116 False colour manipulation	116 Falschfarben-Manipulationen	116 Manipulation avec des couleurs fausses
118 Statistics: Population structure visualized on town maps An urban concentration as an example	118 Statistik: Auf Stadtplänen visualisierte Bevölkerungsstrukturen am Beispiel einer urbanen Konzentration	

5-13.
Table of contents.

FOREWORD

The foreword is almost never written by the author, but by an authority on the subject matter who explains why the book is an important contribution and appraises the author's standing in his or her field.

Like the preface to follow, the foreword should be designed to be consistent with chapter opening pages. The first foreword page is usually a recto, but this decision may depend on the length of the foreword and the standing of its writer.

PREFACE

There is much confusion, even among members of the publishing industry, as to the distinction between the preface, the foreword, and the introduction. In general, the preface is a short preamble that may serve to acknowledge the help of other individuals or organizations or may summarize the methods used to collect information. Most important, however, the preface should give the reader an idea of the book's *purpose.*

The design of the preface should echo the foreword and the chapter openings (fig. 5-14). This section should open on a recto.

LIST OF ILLUSTRATIONS

A list of illustrations tends to be added at the editor's discretion, depending on whether he or she believes that it will assist the reader. It should briefly identify the book's illustrations and, of course, include the page number on which each illustration appears. If an illustration appears on an unnumbered page, it should be identified by the number of the page that it faces or follows, as, for example, *Facing page 124* or *Following page 124.* If plate numbers or figure numbers are used in the text, they should be included in the list of illustrations.

This section directly follows the table of contents either on a verso or recto. The typographic style should closely follow that of the contents page.

ACKNOWLEDGMENTS

Acknowledgments are made to persons and organizations helpful to the author in preparing the manuscript. In a work discussing art or photography, acknowledgments will also be made to museums and individuals who permitted the author to reproduce artwork.

Acknowledgments often appear in the preface. If they are extensive enough, they may occupy their own section, which may open on either a recto or verso.

ADDITIONAL FRONT MATTER

Other possible front matter includes lists of abbreviations (which may also be included as back matter), lists of contributors (often with short biographies), lists of symbols, and *errata.* The errata is a list of all mistakes made in the book. If the book has already been printed and the errata are important enough, an errata sheet is sometimes tipped in (pasted in) just after the copyright page.

5-14.
Preface.

The acknowledgments and lists should be as typographically understated as possible, so that the information they contain will be legible and accessible. Some information may be included because it is legally necessary (as with acknowledgments); other facts will aid the reader. Thus, while front matter should be subordinated to the main body of the book, it should not be neglected by the typographer. Design should match the general pattern established in the tables of contents and illustrations, but a slightly smaller type size is sometimes used if the lists are quite long.

When designing the front matter, the typographer should not include more than one section on a single page. Acknowledgments should be either included in the preface or set as an acknowledgments page—not placed randomly wherever there is room, such as on the last page of the table of contents or on the dedication page. The dedication and credits, which may appear on the copyright page, are the only exceptions to this rule. Depending on the number of pages in the book as a whole, this combination may be financially necessary. If, for example, the book is printed in 32-page signatures and it is exactly 160 pages without a dedication page, the aesthetic value of setting the dedication on its own page may not justify the cost of adding an extra 4-page signature to the text.

PAGINATION

Only one rule must be religiously followed for the numbering of book pages: every recto page must bear an odd number and every verso page an even number.

The first page of the book rarely has an arabic numeral. Virtually all publishers paginate the front matter with lowercase roman numerals (i, ii, iii, and so on), and label the first page of the body as page 1. Moreover, many pages are not numbered, including the title and half-title pages, copyright page, dedication page, part-title pages within the body, blank pages, and pages that consist totally of illustrations. Although such pages are not imprinted with a page number, they do figure into the pagination sequence. For instance, the first numbered page in a book could bear the roman numeral v, indicating that four pages preceded it. If the front matter does not have page numbers, the first numbered page may be printed with the arabic numeral 11. Examine several books closely and notice the different pagination systems.

The Body

For 350 years, all typography was book typography and most book typography concerned body text. One can study many fine examples from a rich tradition (figs. 5-15 through 5-18). The typographer is concerned with several different problems in designing the book proper: the introduction, part-title pages, chapter openings, headers and footers, folios, heads and subheads, captions, and footnotes. If the book is to be aesthetically successful, all of these elements must be treated uniformly and coherently.

INTRODUCTION AND PART-TITLE PAGES

The introduction is treated exactly like a chapter, and the introduction opening should be designed in the same way as a chapter opening.

Part-title pages separate sections consisting of several chapters within a book. Depending on the organization of the contents, they usually feature the same display type used on the title page and in chapter openings, and may contain a decorative emblem or illustration that ties in with the overall design or theme of the work.

5-15.

Chapter head. Typographer: William Kittredge, The Lakeside Press.

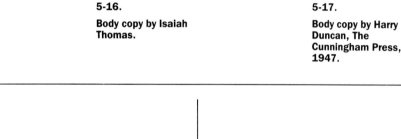

5-16.

**Body copy by Isaiah
Thomas.**

5-17.

**Body copy by Harry
Duncan, The
Cunningham Press,
1947.**

5-18.

**Title and body copy
by El Lissitzky,
1923.**

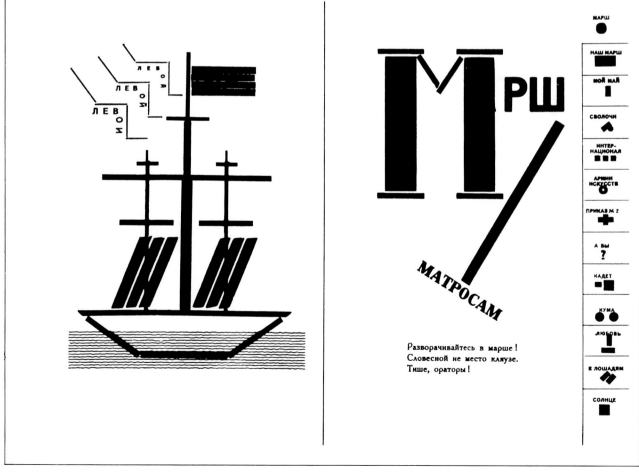

5-19.

The use of rules in newspaper design, from the Boston *Globe*.

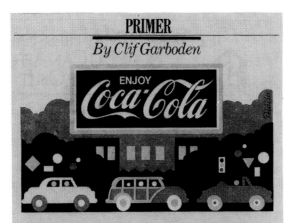

PRIMER

By Clif Garboden

The Coke sign

Think back to 1953. If you can't remember much, you're not alone. Ike was president, the French army was spending Yankee dollars in Indochina, the other Yankees took a subway Series in six, and the networks introduced *Topper, Make Room for Daddy,* and *Name That Tune.* And one more thing: The Coke sign went up at the intersection of Cambridge Street and Soldiers Field Road. There it stayed until 1984, when it and the bottling plant it graced came down to make room for the Embassy Suites Hotel. Have you missed it? There's no question that this huge red-and-white mass of neon and incandescent lights was part of the landscape. It did more than hype cola; it gave us the time and temperature — usually incorrectly. And it . . . well, it *meant* something. For one thing, even by the early '60s it reminded us that 1953 was a long time ago. And it touted Brighton's brush with big-name industry. To the natives it meant hometown. And to millions of students who dribbled off the Mass. Pike headed for Cambridgeport and Allston and the Back Bay, it represented the end of a journey, the end of Christmas vacation, the return to finals, and everything that was their hometown away from home. When they saw the Coke sign, it all came back — traffic, no place to park, crooked streets, crooked landlords, September-to-May romances, cockroaches. In short, that monument to sweet carbonation offered a fitting welcome back to the life this Athens on the Charles afforded its student population. Like everything else the academic hordes were allowed to use, the Coke sign bespoke a long-faded and well-dated charm. As 10-foot ceilings are to living rooms the Coke sign was to outdoor advertising. It must have been nice, or at least okay, in its day.

expression of mid-'80s modernism, to a hotel designed expressly so that women execs can conduct business in their rooms without spreading papers out on the bed.

Brighton state Representative William Galvin likes the sign. He calls it artistic, and he thinks it should be a bona fide landmark. In May he introduced legislation that would allow the sign to rise again — not atop the Embassy Suites, of course, but in the neighboring Conrail yard. Like the CITGO sign before it, this alleged eyesore on the river (Galvin suggests that the Embassy Suites is a far greater affront to the skyline) would be protected, like any endangered species that would otherwise be wiped out for being ugly.

Typesetting Parameters. When deciding on mnemonic codes, typesetters often make the mistake of creating codes that reflect, naturally enough, the terminology of the typesetter. But the typesetter will not be using the codes. The word processing operator should not be forced to learn the arcane terminology of typesetting. Simple words can and should be substituted for technical terms to make things easier for the word processor.

For instance, $LL should be translated to mean "line length," rather than the typographic term "measure." $LS can mean "line space," rather than "leading" or "lead." $SZ can refer to "type size," a more graphic description than the preferred typographic term "point size."

How will these codes work together? A string such as $LL20$SZ10$LS12 means the type will be set 20 picas wide, in 10 point type with a 12 point line space. If you supply word processing personnel with a clear code chart *and* correctly translate the codes, they will be able to handle the typeset coding.

Typographic Patterns. There are two types of patterns on typeset pages: *standing patterns,* which affect large sections of copy, and *single line codes,* affecting only one line of copy.

For standing patterns, continue the strategy of eliminating technical typesetting terms by ignoring technical terms, such as quad left. Use $RR to mean ragged right copy, $RL for ragged left, and $CC for centered composition. When several lines are set ragged or centered and you wish to return to justified composition, use $RX (ragged off).

The single line code most often used is $FL, meaning flush left. The appropriate code for flush right is $FR.

Spacing. The ems and ens proposed for standard word processing paragraph indents are $EM and $EN. Any code beginning with $I will be reserved for other indents. To indent from the right margin, use $IR. $IL is indent left, and $IC indents equally from both the right and left margins. To set the number of picas to be indented, follow the $I codes with a two-digit number. Thus, $IL04 means a left indent of four picas.

To turn an existing indent on and off, use $IO for indent on and $IX for indent off.

As discussed earlier, letter spacing and word spacing are best left to typesetting professionals. But it is possible for word processing personnel to adjust line-spacing values: use $PP and $MP for plus or minus one point of line spacing ($+P or $−P are also possibilities).

Tabs. Tabs are among the more difficult problems for word processors to solve. Reserving $T for tabbing will help clear up coding problems.

$TX clears all existing tabs. $TS_____(for tab set) establishes a tab number and tab length. For example, $TS0113 means that tab 1 (01) is 13 picas (13) long. $TB will move the copy forward one tab, replicating the way tabs work in word processing. Finally, $TR is used as a tab return (returning while staying within the tab length specified).

Typesetter Commands. Typesetting commands are usually machine-specific, but $EX and $CO are obvious codes for "Execute" and "Command," if

145

5-20.

Rules in book typography.

5-21.

The use of rules. From *Innovators of American Illustration*, edited by Steven Heller. New York: Van Nostrand Reinhold, 1986.

BRAD HOLLAND

Brad Holland (born on October 16, 1943, in Fremont, Ohio) began his career as an illustrator in such odd environs as a Chicago tattoo parlor and the Kansas City headquarters of Hallmark Cards. He arrived in New York in 1968 and was immediately given an assignment by Herb Lubalin for Avant-Garde. With success within his grasp, he periodically left the overground for the underground, always with the intention of expanding his boundaries. Not content to be tied to one governing style or point of view, his graphic incarnations have been numerous; but with each change of line or of concept, he has caused a rippling effect throughout the illustration field. Holland has influenced many artists and art directors. His belief in the power of illustration as a vehicle for personal expression has contributed to its now diverse applications.

It's hard to say how I started in this business. It seems like I just barged in, and nobody ever chased me off, so I stuck around. You know, there're always more artists than there's room for. You never see articles in the *New York Times* about how the Russians or the Japanese are getting ahead of us in art. So you just have to wedge yourself in where you can. When I set out, hardly anybody made it in this racket before the age of forty. It was like the Masonic Order or the Brotherhood of Raccoons. You worked your way up by degrees to the higher orders, had a comfy middle age, and ended up painting portraits somewhere. So it was hard for somebody as young as I was to break in. I got so used to being called "The Kid" in those days that I still answer to the name.

When you started drawing, did you have any knowledge of illustration? No. I'm not sure I do even now. See, where I grew up everything was pop culture. Howard Pyle, Michelangelo, the Katzenjammer Kids—it was all art to me. But I didn't know how a person earned a living doing that stuff. I knew most of those guys had been dead for years. But Walt Disney had these programs on TV, showing how they made their movies and that seemed a little more accessible. So in the seventh grade I started getting work ready to send to Disney. I knew I'd have to do something to earn a living in a few years, and I knew I didn't want to go to college.

5-22.

Hung initial cap.

Oil and gas revenues for 1982 were $14.3 million, up from $10.6 million for 1981. However, an operating loss of $9.9 million was recorded for 1982 as compared to an operating profit of $3.3 million for 1981.

This decrease is primarily due to a write-down of the Company's investment in oil and gas properties of approximately $8 million, a write-down of the Company's tubular goods inventory of approximately $2 million, and to significantly higher depreciation, depletion and amortization expenses incurred throughout the year. Nicklos uses the "full cost" method of accounting for exploration costs, and under this method a write-down of the investment in oil and gas properties is required whenever cumulative capitalized exploration costs exceed the estimated future net revenue from production of proved reserves plus the estimated value of unproved proper-

Students of Eugene Lang College: There is no single way to describe them. They are 150 individuals with 150 different reasons for choosing this distinctive institution. Gus Baker, a graduate of a distinguished, private school in New England, was looking for an outstanding liberal arts college with a special character. Gus was not only interested in *what* he would learn, but *how* he would learn.

Steve Riff once thought he could educate himself. He was right—at the time. After a brief stint in a college out west, he worked his way cross-country in a second-hand van, using his stacks of books as an improvised boxspring for his mattress. After two years on the road, Steve was yearning again for interesting classmates and teachers.

Myung Kang was a straight-A student, and a leader in extracurricular activities: student government, French club, Community School Board. She was ready for greater challenges. The Admissions Committee agreed that Myung possessed the maturity and talent to begin college after her sophomore year in high school.

What brought Gus, Steve, and Myung together—what brings *all* the students of the College together—is one shared belief: that a college education must be as provocative, demanding, and inspiring as life itself. They have found such an education at Eugene Lang College. Here, with a student/faculty ratio of 8:1, students and teachers work together as partners in intellectual discovery. You meet, not across the vast expanse of a lecture hall, but in small, intensive seminars based on an open exchange of ideas.

You are given the freedom to design a program of study comprised entirely of these highly-focused undergraduate seminars in the humanities, the arts, the social sciences, and the natural sciences and mathematics. You also have the opportunity to combine

5-23.

Hung initial cap.

CHAPTER OPENINGS

Chapter openings should form a consistent pattern to secure the parts of the book together into a visual whole. At one time, recto chapter openings were obligatory—recto pages are noticed first by those leafing through a book, and a verso chapter opening (including a blank verso) was avoided at all costs. Today, the decision is left to the publisher, but, when possible, the typographer should try to manipulate his or her design so that chapters regularly open on right-hand pages. A previous chapter can often be laid out to consume one more or less page, thereby allowing the next chapter to begin on a recto.

After the title page, the chapter head is the one constant display element in all books—and for many, the only part of the body that is set in display type. It should typographically define the beginning of the chapter.

The word *chapter* is often omitted from the text of the chapter head, and a simple arabic or roman numeral is used to indicate the chapter number. The typeface selected for the chapter number and title usually belongs to the same family as that chosen for the text. The type should be set in a size at least twice as large as the text type—boldface is rarely necessary.

The title and chapter number are often placed in the optical center of the chapter opening page, with ample whitespace segregating the head from the beginning of the text. A rule extending across the entire width of the text will further separate the display from the body (figs. 5-19 through 5-21).

The typographer must now decide how to design the text opening. The first letter or words of each chapter may receive special treatment so that they will be visually emphasized. For example, a *raised initial* simply involves setting the first letter in a type size larger than that used for the rest of the text. The more complicated *hung initial* involves indenting up to four lines of text (figs. 5-22 and 5-23). Finally, the first two words of the chapter may be set in small caps for an understated effect (fig. 5-24).

VIII

A Brief History of Typography

THE SCOPE of this book does not permit the inclusion of a comprehensive review of every aspect of typographical history, but in this short chapter we shall give an outline of the main periods of evolution and a few notes on the more important figures involved. The subject can be divided into four basic periods for ease of study. These cover the following stages of development, but the dates which are given do not indicate an exact point in time at which a change occurred, serving only as a convenient division of history into periods containing major advances in style or technique.

(*a*) The first period extends from about 1450 to 1530 and covers the discovery of the technique of printing from movable type, and the growth of typographic style away from an early dependence on the manuscript book.

(*b*) The second period runs from 1530 to 1800 during which the art of printing came to maturity and the printed book was the dominant form of expression. This period also included the evolution of all the autographic methods of illustration from woodcut to lithography, and the important phases in the development of roman type design. The subdivision of printing into several basic and distinct crafts also occurred in this stage of printing history.

(*c*) The third period covers the years between 1800 and 1914 that saw the application of new mechanical techniques and the growth of printing from a craft to an industry as a result of the Industrial Revolution. This was also the time in which entirely new demands were made upon the aesthetic disciplines of the craft, and the printed book lost its position of dominance to journals, magazines, advertising literature and other forms of ephemeral printing.

(*d*) The fourth stage from the early 1920s until the present day includes the growth of the modern movement in design and its effect upon typographic and applied graphic art, as well as the important influence of various kinds of revivalism.

THE BEGINNINGS

THE KNOWLEDGE that images can be transferred from a relief surface is probably as old as civilisation. Exactly where or when the first

143

5-24.

Initial caps in a chapter head.

Whatever decision is made by the typographer, all chapter openings in a book should be designed consistently.

HEADS AND SUBHEADS

Captions that introduce sections of material within a chapter are called headings, or heads. Subheads correspond to divisions within each main section and are designed to reflect the hierarchical organization of material clearly.

All heads and subheads should be separated from the text by the use of whitespace and by a distinct treatment of type. There should be more whitespace above heads and subheads than below. If equal space is used, it will be more difficult to discern the organization of the chapter.

Heads can be set as much as two to three points larger than the text type size. They may also be set in boldface, italics, or all caps. The main heads and various levels of subheads must all be distinct from one another. If a main head is set in boldface type two points larger than the text size, the first subhead may be set in upper- and lowercase boldface that is the same size as the text, and a second subhead, if necessary, may be set with identical specifications in roman. This is merely one among dozens of combinations of type variations and sizes, but the important point is to establish a descending hierarchy of emphasis for the reader (fig. 5-25). Given the variety of solutions available, the typographer should specify heads to be set in the same family as the face used for the body.

RUNNING HEADS

A running head is set along the top of each text page to identify basic information about the book. The three most common varieties of running heads include the book title on every page; the book title on the verso and the chapter title on the recto; and the chapter title on the verso and an indication of the page's contents on the recto. This last option is by far the most useful for the reader who is leafing through the book to find a particular bit of information. It is also the most time-consuming and difficult to create, because the editor must summarize the information of each recto page. The choice of method is usually based upon the subject matter of the book. In a volume of poetry, the repetition of the book's title throughout is perfectly appropriate, whereas in a technical or reference work, the reader expects some help in locating specific passages.

Running heads not only aid the reader in finding particular parts of a book, but they also form a visual bond between two facing pages. A book without running heads will appear typographically disjointed.

The running head is sometimes placed along the outside margin or at the foot of the page. Wherever its location, it must be separated from the text either by some decorative device (a rule is the most common) or by whitespace. Page numbers can be incorporated into the running head in a variety of ways (figs. 5-26 through 5-29). When placed at the bottom of the page, as in figure 5-29, the running head becomes a *footer* and the page number becomes a *drop folio*.

If whitespace is used to separate the heads from the text, a minimum of six points should be specified. This quantity will ensure the intended visual effect and can be conveniently programmed into *autopagination* systems, which will incorporate the running heads onto the page gal-

5-25.

Hierarchy of heads and subheads.

5-26.

Running head.

ment—the whole Saarinen family took part in the project. Part of the Cranbrook complex included the Kingswood School for Girls, and each member of the Saarinen family had a part in its successful completion: Loja supervised a dozen weavers to create the fabrics for draperies and upholstery; Pipsan decorated the auditorium and dining hall interiors; and Eero, then aged twenty, was responsible for the bold sculptural forms of the furniture.

Finally giving up his intention to become a sculptor after having studied in Paris for two years, Eero enrolled at the Yale University School of Architecture, graduated in 1934 with honors, and spent the next two years on a fellowship traveling throughout Europe. This was a wonderful opportunity for him to study European architecture in detail with the freshly trained eye of an architect. Upon returning to Cranbrook, Eero assumed major responsibilities both at Cranbrook and at Eliel's architectural firm.

Eero found Cranbrook infused with a new energy as a result of a group of exceptionally talented young designers that had clustered around Eliel: Charles Eames, an exponent of technological humanism, Harry Bertoia, directing metal crafts; Florence Schust (later to become famous as Florence Knoll); and Harry Weese and Ralph Rapson, who came to study architecture and city planning. Of these, Charles Eames was to have the most dramatic effect on Eero. They became close friends and collaborators who, together and separately, made invaluable contributions to the furniture industry and the American vision of interior design.

Saarinen's work built on that of Mies van der Rohe, Le Corbusier, Loos, Gropius, and the Bauhaus. While their steel-tube and laminated wood furniture provided the models for some of his own creations, Saarinen was plagued by the dissonance caused by the dissociation of the legs from the body of the chair. It was an issue that was to cause him years of experimentation, finally culminating in the Pedestal group of 1957, with which he achieved the visual unity of construction and materials he had been seeking, if not the technical unity.

In the spirit of organic design, it was Saarinen's goal to conceive a truly organic chair in which all parts—construction and materials—blended in a unity of design. He attempted this initially with Charles Eames, and the result was the winning of first prize in the 1940–41 Museum of Modern Art Organic Design in Home Furnishings competition. Saarinen and Eames jointly won first prize in category A, Seating for a Living Room, and in category B, Other Furniture for a Living Room. (For further information about the entries, see the section on Charles Eames.)

The combined approach of Eames and Saarinen revolutionized the traditional concepts of the chair, their three-dimensional molded plywood making possible the formation of seat, back, and arms in one consolidated shell. But the legs were still a problem for Saarinen. He made another attempt at unity in 1946 with his Womb chair (Plate 49), but this, again, was a compromise.

Saarinen carried the tenets of organic design even further than Charles Eames, by insisting that a chair should not only be unified as an object but should also attain unity with its user and its architectural setting. Saarinen believed that a chair was incomplete without a person sitting in it. In like manner, he considered the design of the chair in relation to the proportion and scale of walls, floors, ceilings, and the room's overall spatial proportions.

Saarinen's Womb chair is considered by many to be one of the most comfortable contemporary chairs ever made. When conceptualizing the Womb chair, Saarinen was guided by two considerations: comfort and the unity of space and architecture. Like Eames, Saarinen was intensely concerned with human anatomy and its relationship to furniture. Realizing that we no longer sit rigidly as our Victorian forebears had done, he set out to design a chair that would accommodate the way in which we really sit, not the way in which we ought to sit. Eames and Saarinen had in common the idea of designing a chair for slouchers.

It has been noted that the Womb chair was an outgrowth of the collaborative effort between Saarinen and Eames that had won the 1940 Organic Design competition. The first step was taking a molded plastic shell armchair, then upholstering it in foam rubber with loose seat and back cushions. This version was designed for Knoll Associates in 1948. Saarinen noted:

A comfortable position, even if it were the most comfortable in the world, would not be so for very long, . . . the necessity of changing one's position is an important factor often forgotten in chair design. So, too, is the fact that an equal distribution of weight over a large surface of the body is important.

Saarinen has described the Womb chair as:

. . . [an] attempt to achieve psychological comfort by providing a great big cup-like shell into which you can curl up and pull up your legs (something that women seem especially to like to do). A chair is a background for a person sitting in it. Thus, the chair should not only look well [sic] as a piece of sculpture in the room when no one is in it, it should also be a flattering background when someone is in it—especially the female occupant.

---

something lovely, in contrast, is something he would have heard from hundreds of British English speakers throughout his life; he could well have learned this usage as a very young child. His 'mistake' is not linguistic, but SOCIAL in character: he has used an expression that marks him, to Stephen Daedalus, as belonging to the wrong sort of social group — in this case, to a lower social class than his station in life would predict.

I have pointed out two differences between these 'mistakes': one case contains INADVERTENT errors that violate rules of LINGUISTIC structure, the other involves language that is INTENDED to be just as it is, but may incur (from at least some hearers) a negative judgment as to the SOCIAL position of the speaker. For inadvertent violations of linguistic principles, I should like to reserve the term (speech) errors. For the remainder there is no standard term, and I have no good candidate.

1.1   Below are two literary representations of dialogue — the first (involving three speakers) from William Faulkner's The Sound and The Fury, the second from Charles Dickens' Pickwick Papers. List the features of these speeches that might be labeled 'mistakes' and critically examine the accuracy of this label.

(a) . . . . "What you gwine do ef hit rain?"
"Git wet, I reckon", Frony said. "I ain't never stopped no rain yit."
"Mammy always talkin bout hit gwine rain." Luster said.
"Ef I dont worry bout y'all, I dont know who is", Dilsey said. "Come on, we already late."

(b) "Fine, fresh hearty fellows they seem", said Mr. Pickwick, glancing from the window.
"Wery fresh," replied Sam; "me, and the two waiters at the Peacock, has been a pumpin' over the independent woters as supped there last night."
"Pumping over independent voters!" exclaimed Mr Pickwick.
"Yes", said his attendant, "every man slept vere he fell down; we dragged 'em out, one by one, this mornin', and put 'em under the pump, and they're in reg'lar fine order, now. Shillin' a

5-29.

**Running footer.
From *Mistakes*,
Arnold Zwicky.
Columbus:
Meridian
Publishing, 1979.**

5-27.

**Running heads:
book title verso and
chapter title recto.**

year of grace, 1884, probably did not think it of any importance that in the preceding year a finely educated young lawyer, occupying a second-story room in a near-by building, had grown weary of sitting in his office, reading law books and magazines and growing poorer each day and had departed for other fields. He had made application for admission to practice in the federal court, but had never put up the fee, perhaps due to his impecunious circumstances. Atlantans called Woodrow Wilson a dreamer and the world confirmed the judgment. But what magnificent dreams!

It was a six-column paper, issued six days a week, skipping the Monday edition. During the week it would be an eight-page paper, going to fourteen or more pages on Sunday, considered a pretty good paper in those days.

There was a friendly feeling between the printers of the Constitution and the members of the news staff, a feeling engendered by the fact that some of the staff had been typesetters before becoming journalists. In this class was Bill Arp (Major Charles H. Smith), who had been a

---

5-28.

**Running heads:
chapter title verso
and heading recto.**

The Press, The Footstep, Girts, &c.

just in the place where the further hinder Rail of the Carriage stands projecting over the Rib-Rail, when the Iron of the Tympan may just rise free from the Fore-side of the Plattin; for then that projecting will stop against the Iron Pin.

The Stay of the Frisket is made by fastning a Batten upon the middle of the Top-side of the Cap, and by fastning a Batten to the former Batten perpendicularly downwards, just at such a distance, that the upper-side of the Frisket may stop against it when it is turned up just a little beyond a Perpendicular. When a Press stands at a convenient distance from a Wall, that Wall performs the office of the aforesaid Stay.

Ball-Stocks are Turn'd of Alder or Maple. Their shape is delineated in Plate 9. at g: They are about seven Inches in Diameter, and have their under side Turned hollow, to contain the greater quantity of Wool or Hair, to keep the Ball-Leathers plump the longer.

On. p. 75

The Lye-Trough (delineated in Plate 9. at k) is a Square

Of Racks for Paper

about nine Inches long, and four and an half Inches broad; and the length of the Bristles about three Inches.

To perform the Office of a Lye-Kettle (which commonly holds about three Gallons) the old-fashion'd Chafers are most commodious, as well because they are more handy and manageable than Kettles with Bails, as also because they keep Lye longer hot.

The Tray to Wet Paper in is only a common Butchers Tray, large enough to Wet the largest Paper in.

The Weight to Press Paper with, is either Mettal, or Stone, flat on the Bottom, to ly steddy on the Paper-Board: It must be about 50 or 60 pound weight.

For Pelts or Leather, Ball-Nails or Pumping-Nails, Wool or Hair, Vellom or Parchment or Forrel, the Press-man generally eases the Master-Printer of the trouble of choosing, though not the charge of paying for them: And for Paste, Sallad-Oyl, and such accidental Requisites as the Press-man in his work may want,

Equipment and Materials

Drawing and Drafting Tools

51

Drawing and Drafting Tools

It would be both impossible and pointless to attempt an exhaustive listing of these essentials. Our short list aims to cover the most useful knives, scissors, compasses, ruling pens, rules, drafting machines, triangles, templates, and magnifiers.

Knives

It's not the body, but the blades that cost you money over the years, and if you've used the standard No. 11, you know they don't last long at all. Our advice is to invest in surgical steel blades and a fine oilstone, and you can stop running out to the store for those endless packs of 100 ordinary blades.

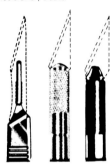

Surgeon's Scalpel

Obviously, this tool has been designed to be highly manipulatable and comfortable in the hand for prolonged and delicate work. Surgical handle No. 3 holds all the surgical blades normally used in graphic work — Nos. 10, 11, and 15. The Schein blades are extra sharp, flexible, and relatively durable — and you don't need the sterile versions.

Cost: $2.45 (No. 3 handle); $13.75 (100 pack No. 11 blades)

Henry Schein, Inc

X-acto No. 1 Knife

The standard graphic arts tool that will accomplish most lightweight cutting work in the studio. A light aluminum handle takes the normal No. 11 blade, as well as the Nos. 10 and 16. There is a super No. 1 version that comes with blade shield and blade lock for easier blade changing, and a version with safety shield and

5-30.

Oversized folio.

client, photographer, production manager, and printer all have copies.

Our second presentation is a very tight dummy. For this, I write and set sample headlines and body copy, as well as style settings for the charts, financials, and notes. We get good color or black-and-white stats of exactly the kind of photos we are planning to set up. The illustrations and charts are drawn in tight comp form. We use color type transfers, color zip, and PMS paper and assemble the whole thing in book form so that it can be presented at a board meeting and will give even the most visually inexperienced client an exact concept of how their report will look.

Next, after the photography is completed and the copy is written, we'll show them page layouts of the entire book with everything—stats of the actual photos, galley proofs of the type, tight pencil drawings of the charts—taped in position. When we go to mechanicals, everything has been approved and there are minimal changes at the last minute.

37

5-31.

Folio set flush with top text line.

were thrown back by the Greeks). A great naval battle, in which the Etruscans and the Carthaginians fought on the same side, for once, against a Greek force, took place off Sardinia around 540 B.C. and left Corsica for the nonce in Etruscan hands while Carthage felt free to subjugate Sardinia; but in 524 B.C., a land force of Etruscans and their allies failed to take Cumae, which was successfully defended by the Greek general Aristodemus. Moreover, even alliance with Carthage could not arrest the rapid growth of Greek influence in Sicily, and the defeat of Carthage by the Syracusans at Himera in 480 B.C. was followed six years later by the destruction off Cumae of an Etruscan naval force, in token of which Hieron of Syracuse sent several bronze Etruscan helmets to the temple of Zeus at Olympia.

With Rome no longer a part of the Etruscan power bloc after the expulsion of Tarquin the Proud, Etruria began retrenching – Greek imported goods become scarcer and scarcer from this point on – and soon the Etruscans had to cope with onslaughts from the north as well, as the first of the Celtic invasions began which would culminate in the overrunning of Tuscany and the sack of Rome itself in the early fourth century B.C. The Etruscans seem never to have had an internal organization going much beyond a loose confederation of sovereign city-states, much like that of Greece, and this was to prove their undoing as city after city slipped away from the alliance to be absorbed by the growing power of Rome. Despite an alliance with Gaul, Etruria lost out to Rome during the course of the third Samnite War, the Samnites having been an Oscan people engaged in their own futile stand against early Roman expansionism. A decisive defeat was inflicted on the Etruscans and their allies in 295 B.C. near the town of Sentinum – tradition has it that one of the Roman consuls, Publius Decius Mus, offered himself up as a ritual human sacrifice to the gods of the underworld and of the earth for their efforts.

Volsinii, the last great Etruscan town to hold out, was taken over by Rome when a slave revolt broke out and the Romans, called in by the Volsinian patricians, won the

Et
ria
51

5-32.

Folio set in outer margin.

leys automatically. Even if autopagination is not used, standard linespacing will simplify the production of mechanicals.

Running heads should be set in small caps or italics to distinguish them from the text (obviously, if a substantial quantity of text is itself set in small caps or italics, a different choice should be made). Again, the typeface should be from the same family as the text type. Overall, the running head should be a visual that is not particularly visible—strong enough to be easily seen if the reader wants to find a particular passage in the book, yet not so strong as to overpower the other, more important, elements of the page.

FOLIOS

Folios, or page numbers, are often designed in conjunction with the running head. If so, the folio is usually placed on the outer edge (sometimes called the foredge) of verso and recto pages alike. Folios should never be placed in the gutter adjacent to the spine, because the reader will have difficulty finding them there.

Folios are usually set in regular or italic type; boldface variations are rarely used. Unlike all other textual elements, there are occasions when folios are set in a different type family from the text (fig. 5-30). Like the running head, the folio should be apparent when needed but otherwise visually unobtrusive.

If the folio is not part of the running head, it may be placed (1) in the outer margin at the approximate optical center, (2) at the foot of the book in the outer margin, or (3) at the foot of the book, centered. Typographers should examine the approaches of other designers before making their own decisions (figs. 5-31 through 5-33). Wherever the folio is placed, it should be clearly discernible from the main body (especially if the text is heavily illustrated).

5-33.

Folio centered in head margin.

The folio on the chapter opening page receives special attention. If an elaborate chapter head is used, competition with the folio can be eliminated by placing the page number at the bottom center of the text, separated by a whitespace of one to two text lines.

Folios demand well-considered treatment because they are very important to the text. Not only do they enable readers to reference or relocate specific information, but books designed without folios are difficult to produce. The order of pages can be easily confused, and the consequences are devastating if the book's contents are gathered out of sequence. However, folios are routinely omitted from nontext pages, such as blank pages or pages made up entirely of illustrative matter. When appropriate, the mechanical artist should insert a blank sheet with the words *Blank Page* written in non-repro blue. In government publications, the words *Blank Page* are actually set and printed.

After determining the position of the folio, the designer must consider whether to use old style or lining figures. This choice presumes that the text type is a serif (old style numbers are not manufactured for sans serif faces). Some serifs are manufactured with only one style of numeral. Both styles are sometimes unavailable in a single font. If required, either lining or old style figures may be "borrowed" from a different typeface. The figures of Baskerville, for instance, are not visibly different from those of Caslon or Times.

If the folio is part of a running head set in small caps, an old style figure should be used (the lining figure will rise above the small caps and overpower them). In general, old style figures have a more serious tone and are less conspicuous than lining figures.

CAPTIONS

Captions describe or identify illustrations. They can also serve as a credit line that acknowledges the supplier of illustrative material.

Because illustrations for a book usually have widely different sizes, the novice typographer may specify each caption to be set to the width of its accompanying figure. However, as with the typography in the book as a whole, caption typography should be internally consistent. Captions set in different measures will result in pages that appear to be haphazardly designed and disjointed. The typographer should decide upon one measure for all captions. If that measure is less than a dozen picas, the captions should be set ragged right (even if the text is justified). Because the captions are set in relatively small type, the ragged right lines will be much less noticeable than the choppy lines created by a too-short justified measure. A caption should never be set longer than the width of the illustration.

Captions should be set at least two point sizes smaller than the text, but the type should be no larger than 8-point. They should be immediately distinguishable from the text. If the illustration is a full bleed, the caption can be placed on the opposite page; if the illustration takes up two facing pages, the caption can be placed on the next page. A mortise, or white box cut out of the illustration with type dropped in, is unsightly and should not be used.

The placement of captions should be fairly consistent. If one caption is centered to the right of its accompanying illustration and another is located at the bottom left, the page will look unpleasant and readers will have trouble matching captions with the appropriate illustrations. The standard location is below the illustration, flush left.

Somewhat similar to captions, *marginal notes* are a running description of the contents of the text, which are set in the outer margin. Although once very popular, marginal notes are now only occasionally used. If they are required, they should be set smaller than the text type (italics are sometimes used). Private press books often have marginal notes printed in a second color, usually red.

QUOTATIONS

Quotations are either set as an integral part of the text or separated from the text by whitespace and an indent. The decision of when to segregate quotations is a matter of publishing house style. A general rule is that if the quotation is longer than five text lines, it should be indented (or, in the words of the trade, set as an *extract*).

Short quotations should be enclosed within open and closed quotation marks as part of the running text. Extracts may be set in a smaller size or italic (fig. 5-34). Extracts should be linespaced at least one full text line before and after the quotation and indented two to four picas from both margins.

FOOTNOTES AND ENDNOTES

Notes should be set at least two points smaller than the text type but no larger than 8-point. They should be included only in scholarly works and, if possible, they should be grouped either at the ends of chapters or as back matter (in which case, they are properly referred to as *endnotes*). If footnotes are absolutely necessary, the layout of the book cannot be completed until corrected galleys are set and the exact amount of space the footnotes will require on each page is determined.

Long footnotes create another sort of problem. They may dominate the page, even though their purpose is to supplement the text. Yet the only solution, carrying forward the footnote to the next page, is distracting to the reader. Typographically, it would be better to eliminate footnotes altogether, but that would require readers to flip back and forth as they were reading (which, again, is distracting). There is no simple solution here. However, assuming no editorial decision to the contrary, endnotes are the better typographic choice.

If notes appear in the back matter, they should be listed according to chapters as well as pages for easy cross-reference. Several different systems are used to identify footnotes, including a series of asterisks and daggers on each page, sequential numbering in each chapter, and sequential numbering throughout the text. If either of the last two options are used, superior figures are specified to mark the notes. Extreme care must be taken to specify and set numbered notes correctly. If sequential numbering is used, one small error may mean that the entire book will have to be reset.

Back Matter

The back matter of the book consists of reference material helpful to the reader, including appendices, endnotes, glossary, bibliography, contributors' list, index, and colophon.

APPENDIX

An appendix contains information that, although not essential to the book proper, may be of help to some readers. Explanations of research methods, texts of documents, tables of technical data, and expositions of particular points raised in the text are some examples. Typographically, the appendix

5-34.
Extract set in italic.

is treated exactly as a chapter. For example, if chapter opening pages are rectos, appendices should open on the recto. Type sizes should be the same as in the body copy proper.

GLOSSARY

The glossary defines technical terms used in the text with which the reader may be unfamiliar.

Glossaries are often set in type that is one or two points smaller than the type used in the main body of the book. It is permissible to set the glossary (and the back matter to follow) in two columns, even if the body is set in a single-column format. The glossary should be arranged in alphabetical order. If it is quite long, the typographer should consider marking the beginning of each letter in the alphabet. This will not only break the monotony of uninteresting pages, but it will make it easier for the reader to locate a word in the list.

BIBLIOGRAPHY

The bibliography opening page should be consistent with the opening page of the glossary and index. If there is room, the opening page should be a recto, preceded by a blank verso if necessary.

The *MLA Handbook* and the *Chicago Manual of Style* are two authoritative guides to bibliographic style that have set the standard for many publishing houses. The type size may be one to two points smaller than the body copy size. The use of boldface and italics in bibliographic citations depends on the guidelines provided in the publisher's house style manual.

INDEX

The index is the last portion of the book to be designed and prepared. Because it must contain references to typeset pages, the index can be prepared only after the book is completely set and pasted up into pages.

The typography of the index will depend entirely upon how many pages the typographer has to devote to this portion of the book. Indexes may be set in four columns of 6-point type if space is limited, or in two columns of 10-point type if many back matter pages remain. It is the responsibility of the typographer to design the index before it is actually done. This will permit the indexer to help in meeting the space demands by preparing a more or less lengthy index, as the situation requires, and it will allow immediate typesetting once the prepared index has been checked by the author or editor.

The alphabetical divisions of the index should be made explicit with an initial letter or with whitespace that is no more than twice the linespace being used. A regular typeface, set in a smaller size than the text type, should be used in index citations. Textual references should be clearly distinguished from references to illustrations. A good strategy is to set textual references in regular type and illustration references either in italic or bold.

The footnotes, glossary, bibliography, and index are designed as a whole and often only after the remainder of the book has been set. At that point, the publishing house and the typographer know how many printed pages must be allotted for the front matter, body, and appendices. Often, the remaining back matter is then "assigned" a specific number of pages.

Why? Assume a book is being printed in 32-page signatures. If the publisher knows the front matter, body, and appendices will take up 245 pages, 11 pages remain to bring the book up to 256 pages, or eight complete signatures of 32. If the remaining back matter takes up more, or less, than 11 pages, the book will contain useless—and expensive—blank pages.

COLOPHON

Appearing on either the copyright page or, more correctly, the last page of the book, the colophon includes the names of the designer, illustrator, printer, and binder, along with such information as the typeface, type size, and paper used and other production details (figs. 5-35 and 5-36).

The colophon is a typographic fine point that is becoming a rarity in all but private press work. First used by Fust and Schoeffer, it has a long connection with the history of typography (fig. 5-37). The colophons of Bodoni, Morris, Updike, and Goudy are signatures of the typographers; they also give essential information for those interested in historical production specifications.

A Note on the Type

This book was set on the Linotype in Janson, a recutting made direct from type cast from matrices long thought to have been made by the Dutchman Anton Janson, who was a practicing type founder in Leipzig during the years 1668–87. However, it has been conclusively demonstrated that these types are actually the work of Nicholas Kis (1650–1702), a Hungarian, who most probably learned his trade from the master Dutch type founder Dirk Voskens. The type is an excellent example of the influential and sturdy Dutch types that prevailed in England up to the time William Caslon developed his own incomparable designs from them.

Typography and binding design by

WARREN CHAPPELL

5-35.

Colophon by Warren Chappell.

This book was planned by Bruce Rogers and composed in English Monotype Van Dijck by Mackenzie & Harris, Inc., San Francisco, California. Presumably, the original of this type was cut about 1671 and is attributed to Christoffel Van Dijck, the famous Seventeenth Century Dutch punchcutter and an associate of the Elzevir type foundry. Jan Van Krimpen of The Enschedé Foundry in Holland assisted the Monotype Corporation of England in redrawing Van Dijck for present day use. Presswork is by The Haddon Craftsmen, Scranton, Pennsylvania, on a Curtis Colophon Special Finish Ivory paper stock from Perkins & Squier, New York City. Binding is by The Haddon Craftsmen.

5-36.

Colophon by Bruce Rogers.

5-37.

Fust and Schoeffer's printing device.

Exterior

After the front matter, body, and back matter have been completed, the exterior of the book—the jacket, cover, and spine—remain to be designed.

JACKET

Jacket design is a particularly important category of the graphic design field. It is not unusual for the typographer of the book proper and the jacket designer to be different people. This is especially true if the design of the jacket is illustrative rather than typographic (as it usually is). The decision is made by the publishing house.

The dust jacket is not strictly book typography. If typography must bow to one of two gods—legibility or impact—the jacket comes down on the side of impact. It should be a miniature billboard—really, an example of advertising typography. The jacket is a sales tool and its primary aim is to draw attention. Legibility, of course, may be one tool used to attract the eye and, if it does so, the typography has done an admirable job. But the jacket designer's first goal must be to make the potential buyer select one particular book from among hundreds of competing ones. Color, mass, and size may be more important in this arsenal than the quick identification of title, author, and content (fig. 5-38).

To avoid an overly busy design, and to attract attention quickly, the jacket should be relatively simple, usually containing no more than three design elements. The spine text should be readable from a minimum of 15 feet away. The jacket design may or may not be consistent with the book typography.

COVER AND END PAPERS

A paperback cover is effectively the same as a hardcover dust jacket—it too is an advertisement for the book, which an illustrator or graphic designer may be commissioned to execute. If the book is hardcover (casebound), however, the problem of the cover (case) is nearly always the typographer's. Most casebound editions are bound in cloth, which is available in a range of colors and finishes. (Recently, paper cases have been gaining in popularity.)

The entire cover is printed in one impression, folded, bound onto boards, and, finally, glued to end papers, which are attached to the sewed-in signatures and thus secure the pages within the covers. End paper stock is heavier than the paper used for book pages, but it often has the same texture and color. Historically, end papers were elaborately decorated with a marbled pattern. Today, most designers use white end papers. Depending upon both the production budget and the nature of the book, a good choice might be an end paper that matches the color of the cover.

The front cover may be embellished with a decorative emblem, the author's signature, or the book title. There are two basic ways of putting the typographic message on the cover: it can be printed in various colors of ink or stamped with a brass die. The die may be inked, or the cover may be *blind stamped* with an uninked die, so that the message is simply pressed into the cover material.

SPINE

After the colors of the cloth and ink have been selected for the case, the typographer must decide what lettering will appear on the spine. The title

5-38.
Jacket typography.

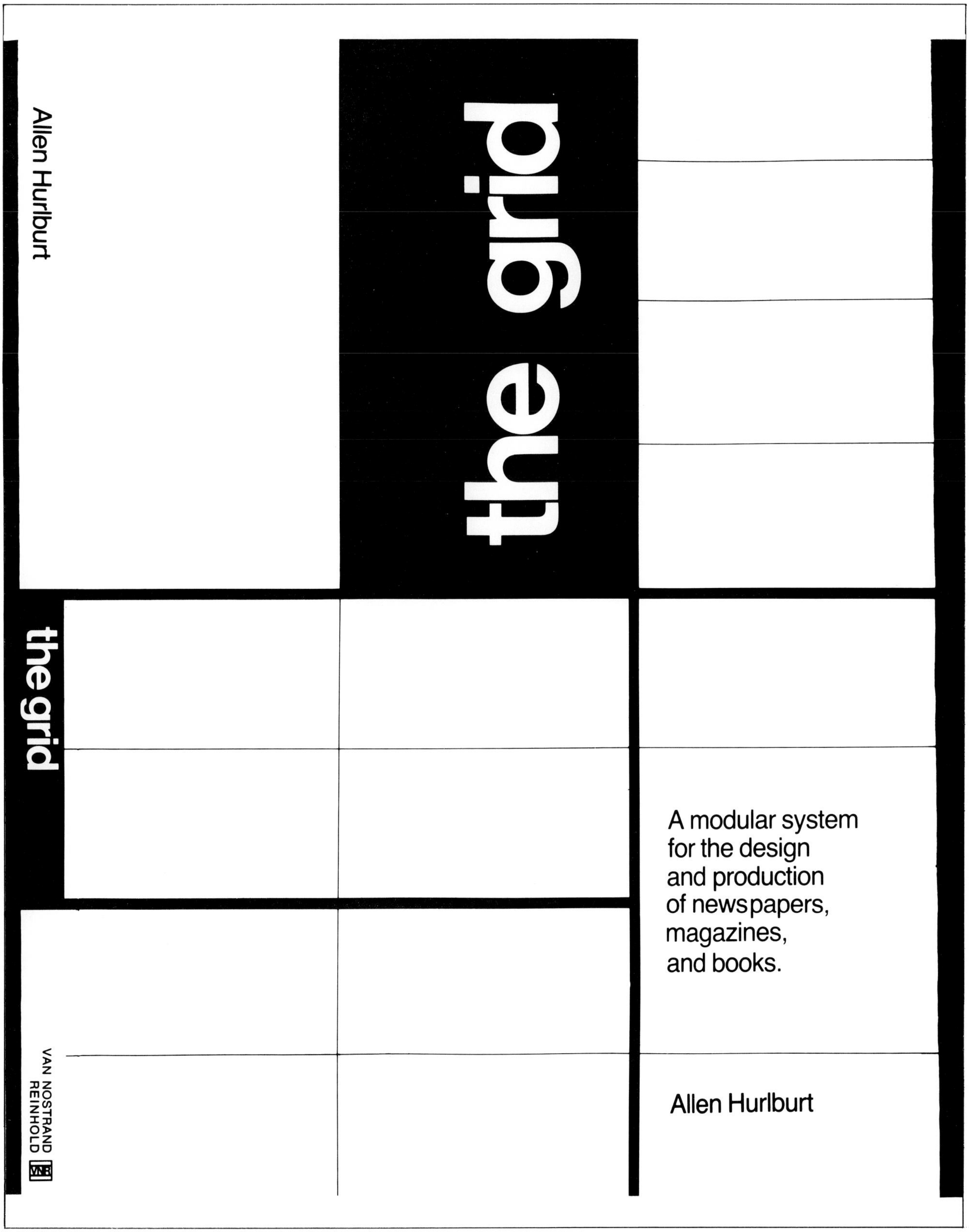

the grid

Allen Hurlburt

the grid

A modular system
for the design
and production
of newspapers,
magazines,
and books.

Allen Hurlburt

VAN NOSTRAND
REINHOLD

of the book, the author's last name, and the publisher's name and logo are standard choices. Unless the book is written by a very famous person, the title should receive prominence, with the author's and publisher's names given less emphasis. The author's name is never set smaller than the publisher's, though the reverse is often the case. If the publisher's name is long, it may be set on several lines. Occasionally, it is omitted from the spine and only the company logo is reproduced.

The typographer must decide whether the typographic elements will be vertical, horizontal, or a combination of both. The title is often set vertically with the author's name set horizontally at the top and the publisher's name set horizontally at the bottom. The type size chosen for the title varies widely, but it should be large enough to be immediately legible. There are many variations on this theme, and the novice should take a look at a number of examples before deciding upon a solution (fig. 5-39). If the title is set vertically, the type should read from the top to the bottom. Some designers violate this rule for no apparent reason and to the detriment of legibility. When we place a book on a flat surface, it is nearly always with the front cover facing up, meaning that type set on the spine from top to bottom is recognizable rather than upside down. Moreover, when we look for a book on a shelf, we naturally read down rather than up. Even if a book's jacket is removed, the front cover is rarely viewed (and the back cover even less often). So, generally, we look to the spine for identification. It should be a major concern of the typographer. If the book is thick enough, or the title is short enough, the title should be designed horizontally. Horizontal letters are always easier to read than vertical letters.

5-39.

Paperback cover and spine typography.

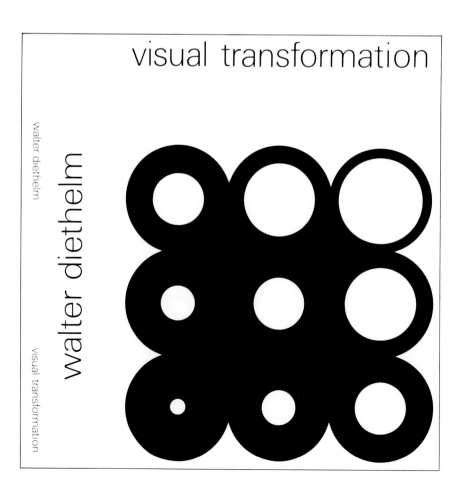

Rules and Theories of Book Composition

The typographer must decide whether a book should be set justified or ragged right, choose the appropriate typeface, select the type size and linespace, and determine the width of the measure. These decisions form the crux of book design and they should be guided by typographic rules determined by the research discussed in chapter 4. The standard rules of composition are not stringently followed by all typographers for all jobs. Nor will they lead to awards for innovative typography. They will, however, result in competent and legible typesetting. A review of the basic rules of book composition follow.

Line length. Research regarding how we read has pointed to very specific recommendations concerning optimum line lengths. The 2½ rule suggests, for example, that 10-point type is most legible on a measure 25 picas long. If the book is large, a two-column format should be considered.

Type size. A commonsense rule is to use sizes that are large enough to be read. The most popular type sizes are 10-point and 12-point. Chapter heads should not overpower the body type. If 10-point or 12-point type is specified for the main body, 8-point (and not illegible 6-point) should be used for footnotes.

Linespace. When specifying linespace, use one or two points of lead. Lines that are "aired out" more than two points may appear disjointed, whereas less than one point of lead may result in an extremely black—and illegible—page.

For the linespace between display type in heads and text type in body, specify a quantity that is twice the size of the type to which you are moving. Thus, if your display line is set in 30-point and the text is in 12-point, a 24-point linespace after the display line is appropriate.

Typeface. The selection of typeface is the most important and most difficult typographic decision. There are very few guidelines to direct the novice typographer, and the best rules—common sense and good taste— are usually learned through practice. In general, however, remember that italics and bolds should be used only for emphasis; regular type versions are more legible than variations; serifs tend to be more legible than sans serifs; and condensed and expanded variations should not be specified for bookwork.

THE GOLDEN SECTION AND PROGRESSIVE MARGINS

The book typographer's first job is to prepare a layout for two facing pages. At this point in the design process, the typographer works with two bits of knowledge: the size of the book and what the book is about. From this information, he or she must create an overall concept that presents and complements the author's ideas.

Perhaps surprisingly, one of the first significant design decisions is the width of the margins. Margins serve at least four functions: they frame the text; provide a space for illustrations and folios; enable the reader to hold the book without hiding the text; and allow for trimming. The typographer should specify margins that are at the very least three-eighths of an inch wide.

Different books require different margins. Mass market paperbacks have narrow margins to reduce the number of pages and keep costs low. Quality books tend to have wider margins, which result in a more elegant appearance and higher production costs. The typographer should discuss general economic considerations with the publisher before beginning to design the work.

There are several classic theories as to how margins should be designed. The oldest is known as the *golden section*. Jan Tschichold, one of the most innovative Bauhaus designers, discovered that many medieval manuscripts and incunabula shared a uniform proportion (fig. 5-40). The inner, outer, head, and foot margins were determined according to the formula 2:3:4:6. (If the inner margin was 2 inches, the head was 3 inches, the outer margin 4 inches, and the foot 6 inches.) Tschichold found that these proportions were followed no matter how large the inner margin happened to be.

According to the golden section, the width of the page should be proportional to its depth by a ratio of 2:3, meaning that a 6- by 9-inch book conforms perfectly with this proportion. The ratio of text to page area is also 2:3, so the text area of a 6- by 9-inch book that is 4 inches (24 picas) wide should be 6 inches deep. The final rule of the golden section is that the text should be as deep as the sheet is wide, as again is the case in our example.

These golden section proportions determine that the text dimensions of a 6- by 9-inch book will be 24 picas wide and 36 picas deep. There will be a 2-inch margin at the foot, 1⅜ inches at the outer margin, 1 inch at the head, and ⅝ of an inch at the inner margin (fig. 5-41). Examine several books and you will discover that the ancient golden section is still applicable to today's typography.

A newer, closely related theory is the idea of *progressive margins*. As with the golden section, progressive margins become larger beginning with the inner margin and working counterclockwise on verso pages and clockwise on recto pages. They also increase in size as the trim size increases.

5-40.

Jan Tschichold's golden section.

5-41.

Example of golden section design.

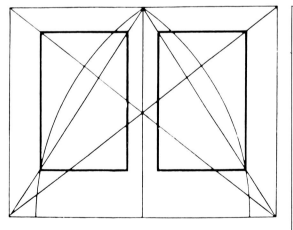

184   *The Roman Face Preferred*

Script types are imitations of different styles of handwriting, but every one of them, even the most flourished, was modeled on some fashion of roman letter preferred or used by early copyists.

Italic is but a simplified style of disconnected script. Its capitals differ from roman mostly in their inclination.

Black-letter is a degenerate form of roman, in which angles are substituted for curves. Its capitals are probably imitations of the hasty flourishes of an inexpert penman.

Gothic, without serifs, the simplest and rudest of all styles, seems an imitation of roman capitals cut in stone.

Italian is a roman in which the positions of hair-line and thick stroke have been transposed.

Title, or fat-face, is a broad style of roman with over-thick body-marks.

Antique is a roman in which the lines of all the characters are nearly uniform as to thickness, with square corners and of greatly increased boldness.

Ornamentals of every style, and even the newest varieties of eccentric types, show some conformity to the roman model.

The roman face is always in most request, for roman is the character preferred as a text-letter by all English-speaking peoples and all the Latin races. Its only serious rival in general literature is the fractur, or the popular face of German type; but even in Ger-

The proportions can vary. For example, if the inner margin is 1 inch, the head margin could be 2 inches, the outer margin 3 inches, and the bottom margin 4 inches. The basic difference between the golden section and progressive margins is the absence of a uniform proportion.

For many books, the golden section simply will not work. Many typographers purposefully specify a very large outer margin to allow for illustrations, running heads, or folios (fig. 5-42). In a textbook, a wide outer margin can also serve as a place for the reader to write notes or reminders.

The typographer must decide whether each page will be symmetrically designed. One possible problem of an asymmetrical design is the show-through from one side of the sheet to the next. If, on the other hand, every page is designed with exactly the same proportions on every margin (in violation of the golden section), rectos and versos will be virtually identical. In the event of a pagination problem, the order of pages can be easily changed.

THE GRID THEORY

The pages of a book should be a coherent whole. As the typographer works on the layout, he or she should apply a consistent formula so that the design of each page appears to have been inevitable rather than contrived. By far the most valuable framework used in the layout of a book is the grid theory.

The grid is nearly universal today. When developing a solution to a particular layout problem, the typographer first examines the text and illustration requirements, taking note of the sizes and shapes of any photographs, logos, and repeated typographic patterns. The dimensions of the *grid cell* are then decided. The cell is a carefully formalized vertical and horizontal unit usually the size of the smallest significant element on the page. More complicated grid cells may also be diagonal.

5-42.

Disproportionally wide margins in book typography.

THE ECONOMICS OF TYPOGRAPHY AND NEW PROCESSES

composition, and generated from the computer in un-justified composition) is also the signal for the film to be drawn forward a specified distance so that the next line is composed in the film area immediately following that used for the previously-exposed line. The correct term for describing this distance is 'film feed', which can be abbreviated to FF or ff followed by the distance, thus ff12 would represent a distance *from baseline to baseline* of 12 points. All depth measurements in film-setting are made from baseline to baseline as the exposed character has no body to form automatic datum points, and its relation to the character below and above is decided solely by the movement of the film. Film is generally loaded in rolls of 50 or 100 ft, although the

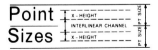

The measurement of a typeface, the x-height base line is the 'base line' referred to in the text.

Massachusetts Institute of Technology   City and Regional Planning
June 19 - 30
Summer Session 1987

5-43.

**Book typography
construction using
the grid system.**

After the size of the cell is determined, the typographer renders the grid in ink on either illustration board or card stock. Copies of the now tangible grid are made and used in laying out the pages. *Every* textual element, including folios, running heads, captions, body copy, and chapter heads, must be specified to fit into the cellular pattern (fig. 5-43). As the typographer lays out the book, the parts of the page will inevitably align into a unified design.

The grid governs both the position and, in some sense, the size of all design elements. If, for instance, the typographer has determined that the grid cell of an 8½- by 11-inch book will be 1 inch (6 picas) wide and ½ inch high, the measure used to set every part of the copy must be a variable of 6 picas. Text type can be set 12 picas (two cells), 18 picas (three cells), or 24 picas (four cells) wide, but it must *not* be set 16 picas wide. Moreover, illustrations are sized according to the grid. All photographs, in this example, will be reproduced in variations of 1 by ½ inch. A photograph, therefore, may be scaled to 6 by 4½ inches, but a 6- by 4⅛-inch photograph would violate the integrity of the grid.

The grid, then, is a structure providing a proportional relationship. For modern typographers, this structured approach is more favored than the intuitive method often used in the past. It is quite apparent, however, that the golden section is a clear precursor to the grid. The difference, of course, is that the grid theory does not constrain the typographer to a given pattern. Rather, the typographer designs the pattern to fit the demands of the project. This, in fact, is the greatest advantage of grid theory. While incorporating a structure, the system is at the same time quite adaptable, unifying a variety of disparate elements.

After the initial typographic decisions are made, the typography of the book is actually quite commonplace. The typeset pages are checked for errors while the typographer prepares the layout. A complete layout of each page, called the *dummy,* is the next step (see chapter 7). Whether or not the grid theory is used, the publisher should be asked to supply layout sheets. If the book consists primarily of text, ask for twice the number of sheets as the number of anticipated pages. If there are more than a few illustrations, request an additional 50 percent. Each page is dummied on an individual sheet, which is usually printed in nonreproducible blue ink. The layout sheets should be imprinted with two pages to allow for the design of facing pages (called a *spread*).

If the grid theory is used, the layout sheets will ideally have grid cells imprinted on them. Otherwise, the margins of the text, along with lines for footers, running heads, and folios, should be printed in nonrepro blue, saving the typographer the time of measuring the distances between each of these elements on every page.

The layouts should be prepared by pasting in copies of galley proofs. All *widows* and *orphans* must be corrected, and no more than two lines in a row should end in a hyphen. Three or more hyphens look unpleasant and distracting. More important, each line (especially the last) of every facing page must align with its opposite. This step not only ensures that the page will be aesthetically pleasing, but it also eliminates possible show-through from one side of the page to the other.

After the layout is complete and the corrections from galley proofs have been incorporated into typesetting memory, corrected galleys are set. The mechanical artist will receive the layout sheets along with the new galleys. Mechanicals will be prepared to the exact specifications found on the layout sheets.

6

TYPOGRAPHIC APPLICATIONS: FROM NEWSPAPERS TO JOBWORK

Publication Design

Publication design is a rather new phrase for magazine and newspaper typography. The lifeblood of magazines and newspapers, as of the book, is the written word. Publication designers, however, have other concerns beyond legibility. Visuals, such as photographs, illustrations, and charts and graphs, are far more important elements in the magazine than in most books. In general, a book is considered a purer typographic form.

Even with these basic differences between book typography and publication design, the essential difference has not been noted: publication designers must work with two distinct typographic elements at once: editorial copy and advertising copy. The greatest challenge of any publication designer is meshing advertising, created by dozens of different designers, with editorial copy to form a coherent, sustained image for the publication.

NEWSPAPER DESIGN

The U.S. Department of Commerce estimates that the total value of shipments in the newspaper publishing industry for 1987 was $30.7 billion, as compared with $16.6 billion for magazines and $12.2 billion for book publishing. More people buy and read newspapers than any other source of printed information.

Newspaper typographers must produce entirely functional results. It is impossible to cover all the details of newspaper design here, but the typographer interested in the subject should consult one of the several excellent textbooks listed in the bibliography. Those by Edmund Arnold are especially useful.

The basic typographic decision to be made in any newspaper format design is whether the paper should be a broadsheet or a tabloid. The broadsheet usually has a six-column format, although the five-column format is becoming more popular. The tabloid, which is half the size of a broadsheet, is at most five columns wide; the four-column format is often specified.

Tabloid is a pejorative term in some circles. The earliest tabloid papers concentrated on the scream headline and the weird story (as some still do). Editors and designers of "respectable" tabloids, such as Long Island *Newsday,* have done much to redefine the word. These papers are very much influenced by magazine design (fig. 6-1). Closer in size to a magazine than to a broadsheet newspaper, the new tabloids combine impressive visuals and strong typographic devices to create a *visible* rather than merely functional statement. Bold use of photography, screen tints, drawings, rules, dropouts, and color have characterized the tabloid, which has now begun to influence the design of such broadsheets as *USA Today.*

6-1.
Tabloid format.

The most important part of the newspaper is the first page above the fold. This is the most noticeable section on the newsstand and the first to be examined by the reader. The designer must be concerned with four elements: the flag (name of the paper, appearing at the top or optical center) (figs. 6-2 through 6-4), the headlines, the photography, and the text.

Illustrative elements in the paper should meet the "dollar bill" test. If a dollar bill can be laid flat without touching any illustration, the typographic design is inadequate. Too much type has been placed in the area without enough of the visual relief afforded by visuals. The typographer has a wide range from which to choose: photographs, rules, boxes, and headlines are the most common (figs. 6-5 and 6-6).

A unified style is even more important in newspaper typography than in book design. Captions and bylines must be absolutely consistent within each newspaper; all headlines should be set in the same typeface family; and the mastheads of the various sections should be stylistically parallel (fig. 6-7).

The newspaper designer should establish a *headline schedule,* a list of all available display sizes and variations used by the newspaper. The editor,

6-2.

Traditional newspaper flags.

6-3.

Contemporary newspaper flags.

6-4.

Ornamented newspaper flags.

6-5.

Typographic rules in the Arlington Heights *Herald*.

working with the schedule at hand, will assign headline weights according to the importance of the individual story (as decided in editorial meetings). The designer then incorporates these specifications into the layout of the page. The most important story in the paper might be set three columns wide in 36-point bold. Less important stories will then be set in smaller type sizes with fewer columns. A basic rule is to make certain that two headlines do not run into each other. If two headlines must be set on the same horizontal, some sort of illustrative device, whether a photo or a box rule, must be used to divide them.

The typographer designing an advertisement that will appear in a newspaper must be cognizant of the poor quality of paper and ink used in the newspaper printing process. Halftones should be 85-dot screens. Illustrations should have relatively bold lines. The typefaces chosen for newspaper advertising should not contain thin letterforms, which will tend to thicken in the printing process and distort the typeface.

Newspaper advertising should, over time, create an identity for the client. Examine a newspaper from a large city. You will notice several companies with established images. Because many companies advertise regularly in a newspaper, they need not pay more for a memorable identity, which depends as much on typographic ingenuity as on continual exposure.

6-6.

Evidence of the grid theory in newspaper design.

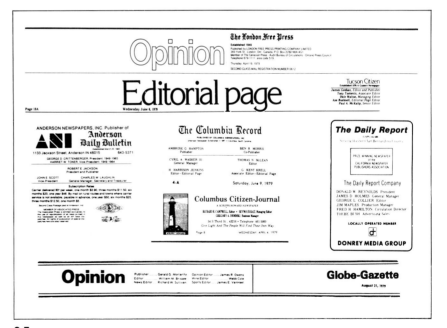

6-7.

Masthead styles.

MAGAZINE DESIGN

The wide range of magazine typography, from the slick professionalism of *Time* and *Mother Earth News* to the functionalism of *Ceramic Abstracts,* fundamentally distinguishes magazine design from newspaper typography.

A graphic identity for a magazine is established externally by the *banner.* The banner can be so effective that it ceases to be solely verbal. Foreign language editions of magazines like *Reader's Digest* and *Time* are still immediately identifiable by speakers of English.

The magazine should have an internal identity as well (figs. 6-8 and 6-9). Heads, illustrations, photographs, and other forms of graphics are the primary elements used to develop this image (figs. 6-10 and 6-11). Unlike the book typographer or newspaper designer, the magazine designer is often responsible for suggesting or creating ideas for graphics.

Of course, the typography must also be supportive of the identity, while competing with the magazine's advertising. Exciting typography is the rule rather than the exception (figs. 6-12 and 6-13). Article heads can be ingeniously designed to fit the particular story (fig. 6-14). Initial caps are also well used, along with quotations, rules, boxes, and subheads.

Student typographers are frequently offered the opportunity to develop publications for local nonprofit organizations. Though such work earns the designer little or no money, the opportunity is invaluable. Any typographer interested in magazine design should also study books published on the subject; the works of Allen Hurlburt and Jan White are among the very best (see bibliography). Also, anyone interested in magazine typography should create his or her collection of excellent examples. Tearsheets of particularly exciting magazine spreads and, indeed, a magazine library, are indispensable references in achieving ever more creative solutions.

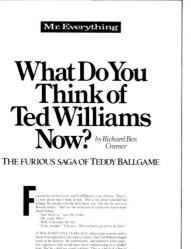

6-8.

Typography from
***Esquire*, June**
1986.

6-9.

Typography from
***Connoisseur*, June**
1986.

6-10.

Typography from *Magazine Design and Production,* 1986.

Artists' workstations:
THE STATE OF THE MARKET

Computer graphics workstations for two-dimensional design and art have been focusing mainly on two areas of performance: small stations intended to produce data and presentation graphics in the form of slides and other hard copy; and large stations intended for production of newspapers and magazines, once the design layout has been done by other means.

BY ALYCE KAPROW

6-12.

Typography from *U&lc.*

THE DOLLAR MARK

TYPO-GRAPH-IC·TID-BITS!

In 1850, Joel Munsell, a New York State newspaper publisher collected a great deal of typographic trivia and published it in a volume called, appropriately, "The Typographical Miscellany." In addition to such items as the longevity of printers and a French printing plant run by blind craftsmen, we present the following for your education & enjoyment.

6-11.

Magazine graphics.

Life seen as a brief moment. Above: Woman in Three Stages (1899). Right: Self-Portrait with a Skeleton Arm (1895).

WHAT ONE COLLECTOR HAS FOUND IN THE GREAT NORWEGIAN EXPRESSIONIST

BY MARIANNE TUTEUR

MUNCH'S SPELL

6-13.

Typography from *Graphis,* March/ April 1986.

IBM

Design
Business and
Education

Design
Wirtschaft und
Bildung

Design
Commerce et
Formation

6-14.

Magazine article typographically introduced.

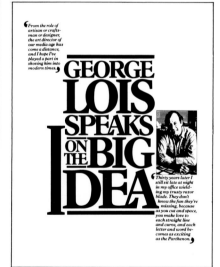

"From the role of artisan or craftsman or designer, the art director of our media age has come a distance, and I hope I've played a part in shoving him into modern times.

GEORGE LOIS SPEAKS ON THE BIG IDEA

Thirty years later I still sit late at night in my office wielding my trusty razor blade. They don't know the fun they're missing, because as you cut and space, you make love to each straight line and curve, and each letter and word becomes as exciting as the Parthenon.

6-15.

The potential strength of a single letter in a newspaper ad.

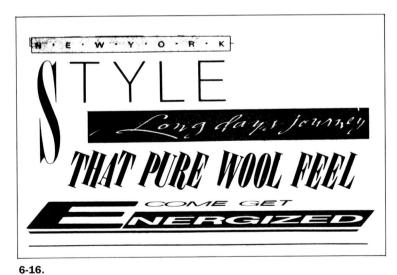

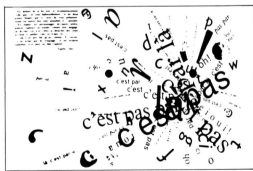

6-16.

The use (and abuse) of type in newspaper advertising.

ADVERTISING TYPOGRAPHY

Typographers working in advertising agencies and art studios are generalists, creating many different kinds of advertising. There are at least seven basic varieties: newspaper and magazine advertising; television advertising; transportation and outdoor ads; catalogs and directories; point-of-purchase advertising; direct advertising pieces; and sales aids.

Newspaper and Magazine Advertising

A major difference between the retail advertising that appears in newspapers and the ads that appear in magazines is that newspaper advertising is almost exclusively black-and-white. Typographers designing advertising must carefully determine the mechanical requirements of the particular publication. Specifications for size and columnar dimensions vary greatly within, as well as between, the two media.

The three major design elements are type, illustration (either drawings or photographs), and whitespace. In newspaper and magazine advertising alike, generous use of whitespace is one of the best ways to attract attention .

If type is intended to catch the reader's eye, the typographer must remember that readers will often simply skim a magazine's or newspaper's pages. Directing the reader to the advertisement is frequently accomplished through the bold use of display type, generous spacing between typeset lines, or large type sizes (fig. 6-15). Ads should not contain too much display. Several lines set in large type will compete with one another and all emphasis will be lost (fig. 6-16).

Television Advertising

Typography is obviously a secondary consideration for the movement-oriented television commercial. In nearly every commercial, however, typography will play *some* role: most advertisers flash the name of the product or service at least once (and often, several times) during the span of the television advertisement. Because of the quick visuals, television typography is not understated. It must be big, bold, and impressive.

Transportation and Outdoor Advertising

Transportation advertising, or "car cards," are placed directly on buses, taxis, subways, and commuter trains, either inside, in frames above the windows, or on the vehicle's exterior frame.

Outdoor advertising is a large subindustry that produces billboard posters and rents advertising space from product manufacturers. Advertising agency artists or typographers design the billboard in miniature. The designs are then copied by personnel of the outdoor advertising agency and reproduced on oversized lithographic presses or, in some cases, directly painted onto billboards.

Transportation and outdoor advertising operate at a disadvantage. Most consumers disregard such ads as sources of information. Indeed, many consumers consider them an environmental intrusion. The designer of the outdoor or transportation ad must therefore be concerned foremost with gaining the reader's attention. Accordingly, car cards often feature stunning color graphics or engaging typography (fig. 6-17). Outdoor ads take a blunter approach: type is reproduced in huge dimensions to stun the passing consumer with sheer mass.

6-17.
Transportation advertising.

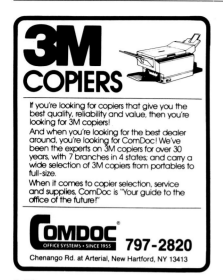

6-18.

Example of effective advertising in a telephone directory.

Typographers who work on either advertising form must again be certain to determine the required dimensions carefully. Excess verbiage must be restrained. Messages must be short and to the point.

Catalogs and Directories

Catalogs and directories involve two varieties of typography. If the catalog is a company publication selling or displaying merchandise, the typographer creates a format much like a magazine designer. However, the catalog or directory advertisement may simply be an insertion in, for instance, a telephone directory. Size is then controlled by the design requirements of the directory and by the amount of space purchased.

Telephone directories, by the way, offer excellent studies of typography. Because of the very cheap paper used to produce telephone books, illustration and photography play a limited role and type becomes the most important vehicle for carrying a message. Beginners in typography can learn lessons from the uneven quality of most directories, where errors include several different type styles in the same ad, too much display type, and poor type style selection. Fortunately, the poorly designed work is offset by professionally competent typography (figs. 6-18 and 6-19).

Point-of-Purchase Advertising

Point-of-purchase advertising is an attempt to persuade the consumer to purchase specific merchandise on the spot. Supermarkets are prime users of this advertising medium, but department stores, book stores, and every kind of specialty shop also feature two-dimensional and three-dimensional displays (figs. 6-20 through 6-22). Point-of-purchase displays are designed by the advertising agency for a manufacturer, who distributes them to appropriate locations.

Two-dimensional, point-of-purchase display possibilities include posters, window streamers, banners, counter cards, pole signs, wire hangers (which are suspended from the ceiling along aisles or walkways), and specialty items such as wall plaques, decals, and glass or electronic signage.

Three-dimensional displays are usually self-contained constructions, such as counter display units, floor displays, bins containing merchandise, and cardboard units that assemble into cartons to hold merchandise. Display cartons often require ingenuity on the part of the typographic designer, who must account for all the folds and dimensions of the unit when he or she creates a design.

The typographic requirements of point-of-purchase advertising are similar to those of outdoor and transportation ads. Type must immediately

6-19.

A poorly designed telephone directory ad.

6-20.

Point-of-purchase ad.

6-21.

Three-dimensional point-of-purchase display (assembles to become carton).

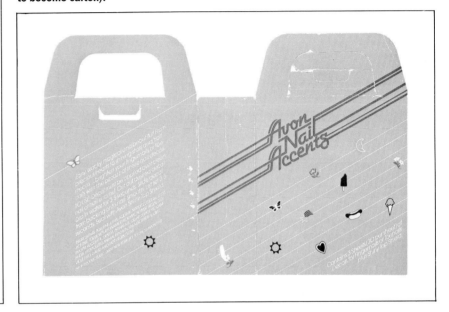

6-22.

Three-dimensional point-of-purchase restaurant display.

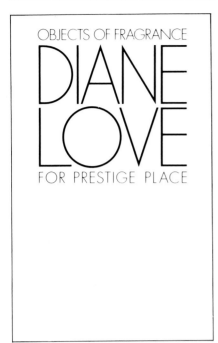

6-23.

Example of direct mail advertising for a perfume manufacturer.

6-24.

Magna Computer Systems.

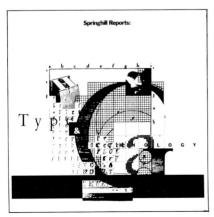

6-25.

Springhill Reports.

sell a product to the consumer. Large type sizes, color, and special typographic effects are often used to attract the eye of the potential buyer.

Direct Advertising

Direct advertising is distributed to the consumer of a product or service, either in person or through the mail. Both methods involve the same sorts of printed pieces to convey a message. For typographers and typesetters in the advertising field, direct advertising is the most common type of assignment (figs. 6-23 through 6-25). The simplest mode of direct advertising, the business letter, is the only one that should not be typeset. All other forms must be professionally designed and typeset in order to relate the necessary message of quality and competence to the consumer. The typography depends on the nature of the business being advertised: banks and insurance companies wish to create a different visual impact than fashion boutiques and department stores.

Leaflets are single printed sheets, usually folded and sometimes printed on both sides. The broadside, as noted, is a larger printed sheet. For convenience it is often folded several times. Booklets or pamphlets are about eight pages or less, bound with a paper cover and saddle-stitched (stapled on the fold). Brochures are similar to booklets, but contain more pages and are often bound with a board cover. Envelope stuffers are single sheets featuring a product or service. They are frequently included in monthly billings. Self-mailers are printed on both sides and folded. One side is used for addressing and stamping (no envelope is required); the other contains the advertising message. Finally, the least ambitious of all direct advertising is the handbill. Cheaply printed on one side and distributed either door-to-door or in front of a store, handbills often contain coupons or announcements of a special event.

Direct advertising is popular because it is inexpensive and effective. It is an interesting area for typographers both because of the diversity of materials one can use and the challenge of the open marketplace.

Sales Aids

Much less interesting typographically are the materials designed by an organization to assist the sales staff. Sales manuals and catalogs contain price lists, technical information, and service specifications to be retained by the sales staff or distributed by sales representatives to customers.

Typographers may also help create sales presentations, which can be slick multimedia events or more simple and less expensive easeled charts and graphs. The "flip-flop" is a series of cardboard pages designed as a coherent presentation. More expensive routes include photographic slides and motion pictures. In every case, the typographer or letterer will be consulted to make typeface and type size decisions.

Jobwork

Most jobwork, of course, is not as glamorous as book jacket design or advertising. But, like advertising, jobwork is oriented toward selling a business's identity or product. As such, it is essentially the work of two people: the typographer and the typographer's client. Unlike the fine artist or the type designer or even (at times) the book designer, the job typographer must learn to work with the client. This is not always an easy task and it is certainly not always appreciated. But, as commercial artists, we must deal with commerce. The client must be satisfied. As one typogra-

6-26.

Bob Clarke, SUNY brochure, 1986.

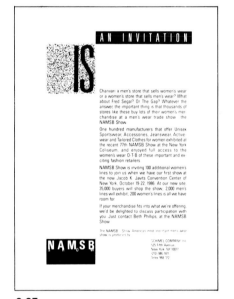

6-27.

Postmodern jobwork typography.

pher has put it, "The only thing worse than dealing with the client is not dealing with the client. I like to eat."

When beginning to design any type of jobwork, the typographer must determine the answers to several questions. What does the client need? How much is the client willing to spend for printing? How many copies are required? What is the intended audience for the job? Will payment be made on a per-hour or a per-job basis? Will the job require a color reproduction process? What kinds of illustrations or photographs will be supplied by the client? How large a project does the client envision? Most important, who will make the final decision to accept a design? There are clients who simply will not be satisfied by *anything* the typographer produces and who are best left to other designers. Worse, perhaps, is the committee that attempts to make a design decision. In all cases, the typographer must attempt to work with a single person who has the authority to say yes. Attempting to satisfy the tastes of all the members of a seven-person committee is a lost cause.

After these questions are answered in an initial meeting with the client, the typographer can begin to work on creating a solution that is mutually acceptable. But how do the client's answers affect the typographic design?

Need. The typographer must assess the needs of the client and adjust the work accordingly. The design of a throwaway flyer for a supermarket should be different from that of a prospectus offering the sale of municipal bonds. The typographer must become familiar with the aim of the job and, more specifically, determine whether the client is trying to inform, to sell, or to promote. Occasionally, clients wish to have far too few, or far too many, copies of a job printed. If 100 copies are specified, it is the responsibility of the typographic designer to inform the client that the per-copy cost of printing 100 copies will be much higher than that of printing 500 or 1,000 copies. The typographer is not simply a layout artist; there is a professional obligation to *inform* the client about both the design and the printing process.

Cost. Early on in the design process, the typographer and the client must have a shared understanding as to costs. It makes little sense to design a flashy four-color annual report and then find, after days of work, that the client cannot afford an elaborate design because of a limited budget. The typographer should impress on the client that solid one-color work is often far more effective than poorly designed color work (figs. 6-26 and 6-27).

Audience. A brochure for a children's museum should be designed very differently from a brochure for a fabricator of engine parts. Who is the client attempting to reach? Typography should be selected with a specific audience in mind. However, before discussion, it is not always perfectly clear, either to the client or the typographer, who the audience is. To cite one example, the brochure for a children's services agency may be intended for any or a combination of several different audiences: foundations from which the agency is seeking funds; families of children who need the agency's services; community citizens who need to be informed about the agency; board members who are actively seeking community support for the agency; or the children themselves. The typography that will best reach children (for example, large, open square serifs and sans serifs) will be far different from that created to impress a foundation president (for example, a transitional roman with conservative styling).

Payment. Everyone has an opinion about design, but many people outside the graphics professions do not understand how long a design may take to create or how much real work is devoted to an excellent solution.

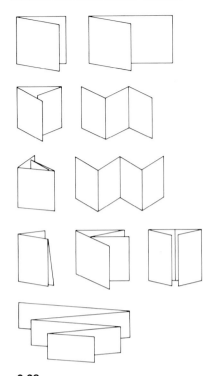

6-28.
Folds.

6-29.

**The Quaker Oats
Company.
Typographer: John
A. Flesch. 1984.**

To avoid conflicts, the typographic designer and the client should discuss the method of payment and anticipated fee. If the typographer will be working continuously for the client, creating a monthly newsletter, for example, a monthly retainer fee may be the appropriate solution.

The typographic approach will depend upon information available only from the client, to which end a good working relationship between typographer and client is essential.

BROCHURES

The typography of brochures is as limitless as the typography of books or magazines. There are hundreds of different kinds of brochures. Defined broadly, the brochure can be anything from a typewritten price list to the slickest annual report for a multinational corporation.

In actual production, the brochure presents only one special problem: unlike many other types of jobwork, it is always folded, and the typographer should become familiar with the many different kinds of folds (fig. 6-28).

PACKAGE DESIGN

Although closely related to advertising typography, package design is part of a very different field known as industrial design. Like advertising typography, package design is an attempt to use type and color to draw attention to a product. The package designer creates an interesting solution not only within the constraints of a package's shape and size but also within those of the manufacturer's corporate identity (see next section). The solutions are often among the best and most lively typography to be found anywhere (fig. 6-29).

Package design is a very profitable occupation because payment for the work is based upon the long-range effect of the solution. Unfortunately, the typography at times is noticed but not appreciated. As with many other forms of typography, the intent of package design is to attract. But after the consumer is attracted to the design, the product is bought and consumed, and the package is thrown away.

CORPORATE IDENTITY AND CORPORATE GRAPHICS

Corporate identity is a unified image for a corporation or organization. Every large company has a recognizable logo or trademark, but corporate identity goes beyond a mere symbol. The typographer who creates an identity interweaves that symbol throughout the corporation's graphics: letterheads, envelopes, individual containers, shipping cartons, vehicle signage, advertising and sales materials, and office and store signage (figs. 6-30 through 6-32). The "package," then, is not simply a box or a bottle. It is the entire company.

Typographers and graphic designers who work on establishing a unified corporate image are among the best-paid members of the industry. It is not unusual for a major corporate identity program to cost hundreds of thousands of dollars. Of course, corporations do not change their identities often. The corporate mark is intended to be a permanent, easily identifiable symbol. It is both expensive and risky to change an image.

There are several sorts of corporate identity marks. A logotype based upon an alphabet can become a symbol in itself. Indeed, such symbols work even when the consumer does not understand the letters that are being used (fig. 6-33). Other corporate identity programs have been cre-

6-30.

Corporate identity:
Prime Computer
AG, Switzerland.
Typographer:
Odermatt & Tissi.

Drick

REG. VARUMÄRKE   SWEDEN

ISRAEL – HEBREW

6-31.

Corporate identity:
New York
Committee of
Young Audiences.
Typographer: Herb
Lubalin.

THE NEW YORK COMMITTEE OF YOUNG AUDIENCES 400 WEST END AVENUE, NEW YORK, N.Y. 10024 212 874-5503

Bevete

MARCHIO REG.   ITALIAN

Пейте

ТОВАРНЫЙ ЗНАК   RUSSIAN

6-33.

The identity of the
Coca-Cola
Corporation is
immediately
recognized
worldwide.

6-32.

Corporate identity:
IBM. Typographer:
Paul Rand.

6-34.

Herb Lubalin, logotype for proposed magazine, *Mother and Child*.

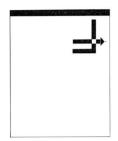

6-35.

Experimental letterhead, El Lissitzky. Original in red and black.

6-36.

Traditional letterhead.

ated by typographers who have used the corporation's product as the basis for a permanent symbol (fig. 6-34).

Typesetters and typographers quickly realize that novelty is a lasting characteristic of the profession. Letterheads, business cards, and other stationery are among the most challenging of typographic problems. Some typographers tend to specialize in letterhead design or corporate identity, in part because these lucrative areas make specialization economically feasible. The typography of the letterhead is usually clearcut and sharp, but recent designs have been increasingly daring (figs. 6-35 and 6-36).

A second area of corporate graphics is the annual report, one of the most important publications for any large business. Reports are submitted to potential and existing stockholders and employees, as required by law. They are profitable endeavors for typographers and printers alike. Because no expense is spared by corporations wishing to convey an impressive image, these yearly financial reviews are often the source of stunning typographic innovation (fig. 6-37). They can also be the most conservative of pages, depending, of course, on the image the corporation wishes to portray (fig. 6-38).

Ronald M. Labuz   *Typography*

Department of Advertising Design
Mohawk Valley Community College
1101 Sherman Drive, Utica, New York 13501
(315) 792-5492   (315) 733-8709

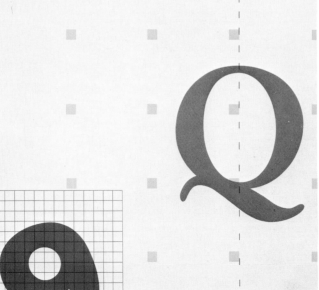

6-37.

Bedford Corporation annual report, 1981. An early classic of the New Wave typographic style.

6-38.

Compugraphic Corporation annual report, 1982.

6-39.
Modern logotypes.

Although most beginning typographers will not be designing annual reports early in their careers, they would do well to begin a collection of them. Corporate annual reports are available to the public for the asking. They often contain the best typography ever produced for the corporation.

Letterheads

A letterhead is typography in microcosm: the work can be humorous or serious, prudent or ornate. Few typographic forms allow the master designer to express his talent so comprehensively on a single page. Working with only three lines of type (the client's name, address, and telephone number) and, possibly, a trademark, the typographer must be able to show the client to the world in whatever fashion the client wishes.

Trademark is the legal term for the singular device that is indentified with a corporation, institution, or product. There are several kinds: a *symbol* is a mark without type, such as the American eagle; a *pictograph* is a public symbol typically used in signage (fig. 6-39); a *lettermark* forms the shorthand name of the company in type (NBC, IBM, and GE); and a *logo* is the full name of a corporation or institution spelled out in type (Kodak's is a good example). Many designers and typographers, however, use the word *logo* to refer to any trademark.

The client's visual identity is of the utmost importance for the letterhead design. When the typographer has discovered how a company wants to represent itself, half the problem is solved; he or she then searches for the correct combination of trademark and typeface to fit the client's demands. Obviously, many corporate clients already have well-developed logos and symbols. In these cases, the typographic problem is simply one of rearranging or modernizing the elements on the page.

Many clients will require that letterheads be printed in the very specific color used in their signage and corporate graphics. The typographer must make certain that the printer follows directions for color reproduction faithfully. Care should also be taken to allow the letterhead to be used easily: most correspondence is typed with a left margin that extends at least an inch from the edge of the sheet. A wide design on the left margin might consume too much space.

The designer of a letterhead and envelope will be choosing paper for the job as well. There are a wide range of specialty papers manufactured for stationery. Large corporations often have their letterhead design printed on several different grades of stock for several different purposes. Similarly, several different sizes of envelopes may be needed, depending on the kind of correspondence.

Business Cards

Often designed along with a letterhead, the business card serves the same purpose: identity. The most common error made in designing business cards is setting the type too small. Whitespace should be included, but many cards make excessive use of this element at the expense of typography. Remember that the business card is a reference. The person distributing the card and the person receiving it have a common goal: they want the information on the card to be easily readable. The most important information on the business card may be the telephone number, which is often set too small to be legible.

Complicating this illegibility are the economics of modern printing. The engraved business card is seldom affordable, and the engraving process has largely been replaced by thermography. This involves placing a

6-40.

F. Starowieyski, calligraphic poster.

6-41.

Arther Baker and Mike Stommen, poster for Western Michigan University Center.

plastic powder upon wet ink to produce a raised image that is sometimes called "false engraving." Before using thermography, the typographer should show samples to the client, who might be displeased with the slightly pebbled finish that results. Also, because heat is used in thermography, letterforms set in 6- and 8-point type tend to fill in. Offset lithography, although it does not produce a raised impression, may be the right answer.

POSTERS AND SIGNAGE

Posters have been very important to the history of typography for the past century and they continue to be popular collector's items. The typographic poster, which is quite different from the movie or political poster, is a visual statement of an individual typographer's particular style (figs. 6-40 and 6-41). Often, posters do not advertise anything other than the skill of the typographer or the type house.

Major signage projects include store and vehicle signs, but there are less obvious opportunities as well: maps and signs are needed for museum displays, commercial areas, college campuses, public transportation, and tourist bureaus. Quick impact and legibility are the most important features, but store signage also usually reflects the nature of a particular business. Thus, a jewelry shop will display a sign set in very austere, dependable type, whereas a sporting goods store or candy shop will attempt to convey a less weighty impression. As with all typography, signage requires sensitivity to the manufacturer's message. An understanding of the needs of the client and a willingness to satisfy those requirements with appropriate typeface selections are the two cornerstones of any successful typographic solution.

MENUS

This chapter on typographic applications will conclude with menus, if only because Daniel Berkeley Updike, the author of the best history of printing types, considered menu design in a way every typographer should consider all typography. The typographer must be a researcher, an ergonomics engineer, a psychologist, and an interior designer. The advice Updike gives in his book *In the Day's Work* (1924) applies not only to jobwork typography but to the typographic design process as a whole:

One can only plan successfully these smaller pieces of work by considering minutely what they are meant to accomplish. Let us take a menu. What questions would be uppermost in one's mind in planning that? The first that would occur to me would be the hour of the meal and where it was to be served. Was it to be by day or by night? If by day, by artificial light or not? The color of the card and the size of the type would be somewhat dependent upon this. Was there any particular scheme of color in the decorations of the table? Because my menu must either match or at least not be discordant with it. Was it to be a big table with ample room for each guest, or a small one? Was the menu to be laid on a napkin or to stand upright? That would dictate my choice of size; for a menu is an incident, not a feature, at a dinner, and should not be so large as to be in the way if laid down, nor so big as to knock over glasses and fall into one's plate if it is to stand. Decide all these little points in the light of "What is the thing used for? Where is it to be used? By whom is it to be used? What is the most suitable, practical, simple, orderly, and historical method of producing it?"

7

LAYOUT

The layout in its many forms can be an idea, a map, or a finished drawing of the page to be printed. It must do much more than simply show all the elements of the page in position. The layout process finalizes an accurate visual statement of every typographic and design choice that has been made to establish the voice and mood of the page. Typefaces, measures, linespaces, design elements, and type sizes should be immediately discernible to the client, typesetter, mechanical artist, and, if necessary, camera person, stripper, and pressman.

Symmetric versus Asymmetric Typography

Before creating the layout, the typographer must choose a particular method. *Modern layout,* or asymmetric typography, is much different from classical layout techniques. The dominant force in today's typography, asymmetric typographic principles were employed by the Bauhaus and were later taken up by New Wave and post-modernist typographers.

Symmetric typography is based upon the principle of centering. Before 1920, virtually all typeset lines were centered on the page. Critics like Jan Tschichold argued that symmetry did not allow sufficient room for typographic invention. The result? Typographers, Tschichold claims, use decorative typefaces and ornamention to permit stylistic distinction.

The asymmetric typographers of the Bauhaus declared their intention to free typography from decoration. By stressing the functional aspect of type, they placed a new importance on the type itself. The basic idea is that a choice must be made. Our pages can be either symmetrical and decorated or asymmetrical and simple. The theory of asymmetric typography argues that type can stand on its own if it is not hindered by the demand for centering (figs. 7-1 and 7-2).

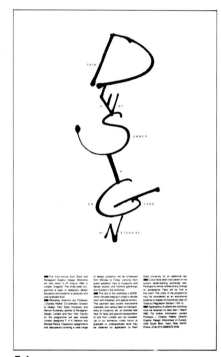

7-1.

Asymmetric typography by Pentagram Design Group.

7-2.

Asymmetric typography of the Bauhaus.

Many typographers, then, do not center all typography on the page, although this is certainly still an option, especially in book typography. Modern layout permits movement while retaining legibility. Rather than automatically place headlines in the optical center, the designer may specify that type be set on a diagonal, in a corner, or in a very large size. In defense of symmetric typography, however, classic patterns were created specifically with legibility and attractiveness in mind. Today's typographers often switch allegiances between the modern and classic, realizing that competing theories may coexist.

The multiplicity of possible approaches is the reason typography and graphic design are creative professions. We do not have to work within static guidelines. However, it is often easier if we do. Typography does not have to be novel to be excellent, and design does not have to be idiosyncratic to be modern. There are existing patterns within which many typographic designers choose to fit their work. The beginning typographer should master the principles that have formed those patterns. Of course, the first step after learning the patterns may well be to break new ground.

ELEMENTS OF CLASSIC SYMMETRY

In classic symmetric typography, four basic elements contribute to the effective coexistence of illustrative and textual elements: harmony of shape, harmony of tone, contrast, and balance.

Harmony of shape is determined by a shared geometry of the page and text (fig. 7-3). For example, the golden section discussed in chapter 5

7-3.
Symmetric typography.

7-4.
Symmetry, Turgeon Wine & Food Society.

7-5.

Centering.

harmonizes the shape of the text with the shape of the page. This principle applies to typefaces as well. Condensed type works best in a narrow column; expanded faces should be set in wide measures.

Harmony of tone is closely related. The tone of body type is gray. Unless emphasis is required, the other elements on the page should have a similar tone. Emphasized type or logos may be laid out in full blacks or bolds to provide the page with an element of *contrast* to the page (fig. 7-4). Indeed, the larger, bolder letterforms of display type are purposely selected to be set apart from the gray body. Minor decorative elements, on the other hand, should not call attention to themselves by being a jarring black.

Balance is another consideration. The page should be optically rather than mechanically balanced. In order to understand balance, one must understand the concept of the *optical center,* or the first point on the page where the eye will focus. The eye tends to move naturally in a downward direction and toward the right—away from the center unless directed back by an advertisement or some other aspect of the layout that has been placed, for instance, in the lower lefthand corner of the page. The pointing index finger was one of the first devices to direct eye movement. Today, more subtle approaches produce the same effect. For example, a photograph or illustration of a person should be laid out with the subject's eyes facing toward the page rather than away from it.

The optical balance of the page may be achieved formally, through the simple symmetry of centering (fig. 7-5), or informally, through boldface type or decorative elements (fig. 7-6). Boldface letters set only at the top of an advertisement will present a visual imbalance that must be counterpoised by an illustration or logo at the bottom.

7-6.

Balance.

7-7.

Four-point layout.

ELEMENTS OF MODERN ASYMMETRY

Asymmetric layout creates a typographic *shape*. The vertical rectangle is exchanged for a newer, more interesting form. Perhaps the most popular technique used to create modern typographic patterns is the *four-point* system, which calls for each of the four points of the page, top, bottom, left, and right, to be approached by design elements only once (fig. 7-7). Four-point is especially notable in advertising typography.

Tilt is a second principle. Modern typography permits baselines and illustrations to be tilted onto a diagonal (figs. 7-8 and 7-9). Because the slant requires the viewer's attention to be taken to the extreme, tilt is obviously related to *eye movement*. The asymmetric devices most often used to foster eye movement are the horizontal and vertical rule (figs. 7-10 and 7-11). Since it is difficult for the eye to avoid moving down the path of a straight line, the rule should be used by the typographer to direct attention appropriately.

Decorative devices, supposedly rejected by the asymmetric typographers, definitely survive in a simple restrained fashion.. Geometric shapes, tints, drop shadows, and bands of rules are the most popular (figs. 7-12 and 7-13). The triangles and squares dropped about the pages shown here are not intended to increase legibility. They are blatant attempts to attract

7-8.

Tilt.

7-9.

Tilt.

C O V E R

Six flat match colors, two screens, double bump
flat match blue background and overall gloss varnish.
Ghost relief bars used to offset blue build-up
around illustration. Graphic based on early Kellar
promotional poster shown performing his
famous levitation illusion. One that always got a rise
out of his audiences. And his assistants.

S E V E N

Conventional 150 line screen black on black
duotones dry trapped over solid metallic gold and image
gloss varnished. Original archive prints were
photographed to create duplicate prints. Duplicates
then retouched to increase contrast and sharpness before
separations were begun.

T H R E E

Three-color process screen combinations, black
line, flat match orange, match purple mezzotint and black
halftone combination and image gloss varnish.
Adapted from antique PR photo of Houdini rarely seen in
magic publications. Originally photographed on
textured background, figure was masked with vignette
knock-out at separation stage. All combined, the
image is startling. As if Houdini is disappearing before
your very eyes.

C E N T E R

Eight flat match colors, two screens and metallic silver
foil hot stamp. Opaque white added to ink formulations
and colors run dense for smoother solids on
uncoated side of sheet. Fit on lady's hair and other areas
is deliberate to create highlights and to duplicate the
characteristic color register of woodcut illustration style.

F I V E

Scanned 175 line screen four-color process,
color register emboss and image gloss varnish. Cyan and
magenta negatives combined for brass die
detail on shells embossing. An effect certain to create
an outstanding impression on your customers.

T E N

Scanned 175 line screen four-color process and
image gloss varnish. Reproduced from 35 mm chrome
of rare Thurston promotional poster. Various
imperfections were corrected and color was enhanced
at separation stage. The devils, now redder than
ever, were a trademark of Thurston's promotional graphics.
They symbolized a certain supernatural quality his
shows mysteriously possessed.

7-10.

Horizontal rule.

7-11.

Vertical rule.

industries, approximately 50% in
molten form. Molten aluminum
reduces the customers' melting requirements, thereby saving energy
and production costs. Wabash pioneered the delivery of aluminum in
molten form in 1964 and has since
delivered over one billion pounds of
molten aluminum.

The recycling of aluminum requires
only about one-twentieth of the
energy needed to produce primary
aluminum. Industry use of the
100,000 tons recycled by Wabash
in 1981 saved 85,000 barrels of oil.

Despite the relatively low rate of
automobile production in 1981,
Wabash's results showed improvement over 1980, due to development of new markets and increased
penetration of existing markets.
The company expects to achieve
comparable results in 1982.

Mayville Metal Products Co., with
manufacturing plants in Mayville,
Wisconsin, Lomira, Wisconsin, and
Casa Grande, Arizona, fabricates
custom metal components for the
business machine, data processing,
electronics, office equipment, communications, and medical equipment industries.

Mayville's Casa Grande facility,
serving the expanding southwest
and west coast markets, was placed
into service during 1981. This new
facility, housed in a 127,000-square-
foot building on a 20-acre site, is
capable of all operations performed
at the company's Mayville plant.

Mayville's Casa Grande plant is now
fully operational and is expected to
show a positive contribution to the
company's results in 1982.

Ortner Freight Car Co., of Cincin-
nati, Ohio, with plants in Mt. Orab,
Ohio, and Covington, Kentucky, engineers and builds various types of

A t Mayville
Metal Prod-
ucts' new
facility in
Casa Grande,
Arizona, an
employee performs
a grinding operation
on a computer periph-
eral frame. Mayville's
127,000-square-foot
Casa Grande facility is
convenient to the grow-
ing markets in Arizona,
Colorado, and Califor-
nia. The Casa Grande
plant made its first
shipment in June, 1981,
as Mayville Metal Prod-
ucts evolves from a
primarily regional to a
national manufacturer.

20

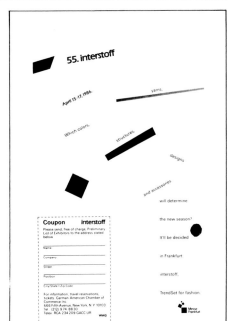

7-12.

Geometric shapes.

7-13.

Drop shadows.

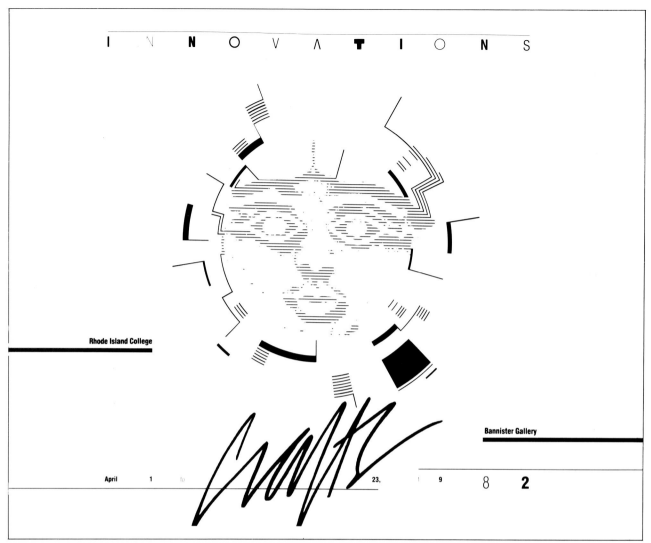

7-14.

Bleed.

7-15.

Kerning.

the reader away from the words and toward the design. The typography, and not the typesetting, is the message.

Bleeds, the fourth layout element, are textual and illustrative elements that fall off the edge of the page. Once again exaggerated by the practitioners of the postmodern and New Wave styles, the bleed's popularity is relatively new. Classic symmetry shunned diagonal rules, letterforms, or photographs that moved off the page into a hidden end. Contemporary typographers have explored new ways to use the bleed for maximum effectiveness (fig. 7-14).

What remains? In classic typography, letterspacing and wordspacing values were simplistic, with clearly defined values that all typesetters knew, understood, and used. The letterspacing of asymmetric typography, however, is wildly subjective: typographers choose from the severest of kerning to the wide open spaces of recent typography (figs. 7-15 and 7-16). Type patterns have also changed: type may be repeated to create a design, or flush left/ragged right typography may be specified.

The typographic designer has matured with asymmetric typography. Before the Bauhaus and asymmetry, the master typographer merely used the golden section for layout and had the relatively simple task of selecting a typeface, type size, and linespace. The front and back matter of a book had to be designed, but even that typography usually followed classic patterns.

Today, after the typeface, type size, linespace, and measure have been selected, the job has just begun. Decisions must be made concerning the letterspacing and wordspacing values, whether to use justified or ragged type patterns, whether to design symmetrically or asymmetrically, and on and on. As new typographic theories have been created, the duties of the typographer have grown. Increased attention to layout is among the most important of these new, and now more complicated, responsibilities.

7-16.
Letterspacing of the New Wave.

The Layout Process

After discussing the job with the client and determining the kind of layout to be created, the typographer will usually follow a three-step design process: the thumbnail layout, the rough layout, and the finished comprehensive. These steps may not all be completed by the typographer. In a large advertising agency or design firm, the art director will do thumbnails. Roughs and comprehensives will be executed by layout artists.

THUMBNAILS

Rapidly sketched on a layout pad, the back of an envelope, or any other space available, thumbnails contain only the most basic elements of the page (fig. 7-17). Although technical skill will be important later, when the design is executed, this is the point when the designer's creative ability is more important than his or her technical mastery.

In advertising typography, a hundred or more thumbnails may be drawn for a single project. Usually about 2 inches square, the thumbnail should be *quickly* drawn in pencil. A wide range of design strategies and placements should be tried. An atrociously designed thumbnail may lead to more positive results, as the ideation process leads from concept to concept. Little time should be spent on neatness or skilled drawing (many typographic designers, in fact, are poor renderers). The idea, and not the execution, is the essence of the thumbnail. Beginning typographers often spend too much effort nicely finishing off the details of these sketches, but technique is meaningless here. The goal is to find the creative flash, the insight, the novel approach.

7-17.

Thumbnails, Valerie Ferenti. Project: Famous Designer's Series, SUNY College at Fredonia, 1986.

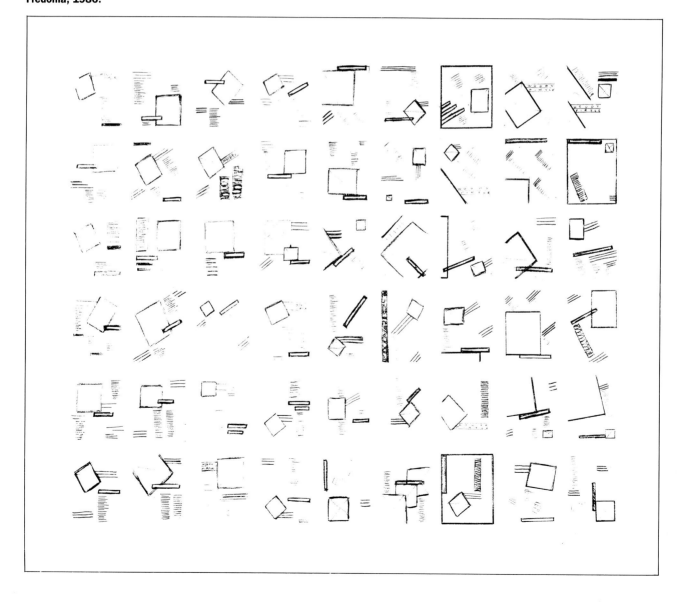

ROUGH LAYOUTS

After the thumbnails have been created, the typographer or art director selects the most effective sketches and develops them into rough layouts. Roughs follow the patterns created by the thumbnail but are rendered much more carefully (fig. 7-18). Because the rough may be the first layout actually shown to and approved by the client, the typographic elements of the page are presented in their proposed sizes and positions: display and body type are shown as they are intended to be set. Letterspacing and wordspacing values are carefully illustrated, as are the position and cropping of photographs.

Advertising agencies and design firms may actually set display type in-house and incorporate it into the roughs. A more common approach is the penciled rough, where display type is painstakingly traced or copied from the specimen pages of typebooks. The latter method requires the typographer to ensure that serif shapes are clearly defined, ovals are obvious, and letters are sharply focused. Special attention must also be paid to spacing variables.

7-18.

Roughs, Valerie Ferenti.

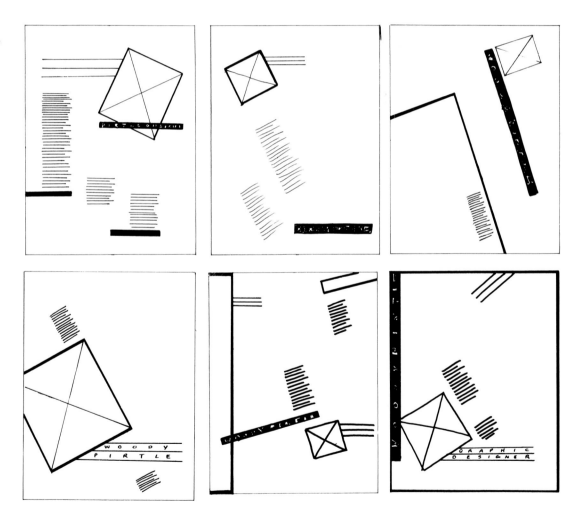

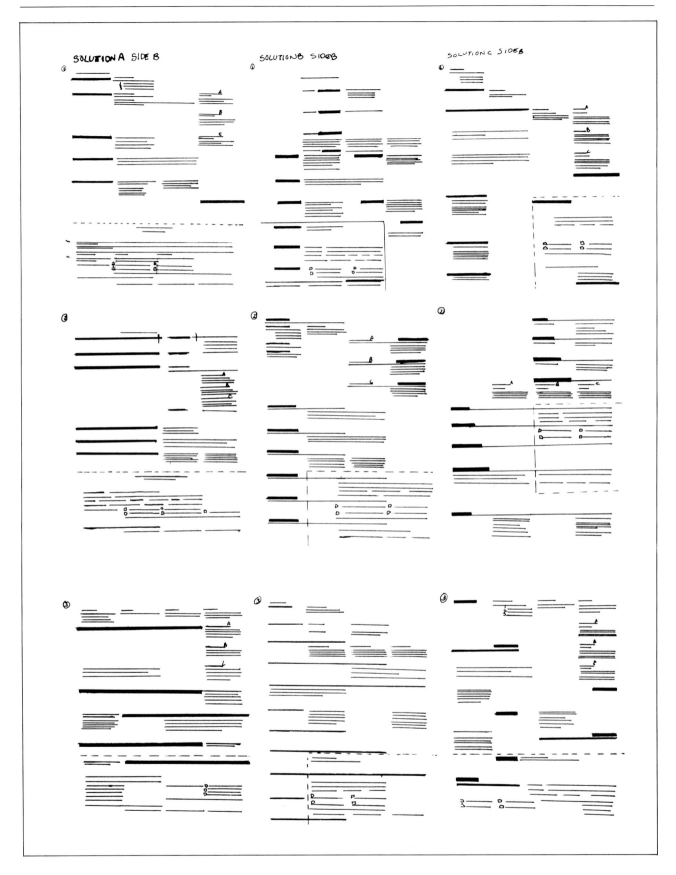

7-19.
Comping body type.

Many typographers use a 2B or HB pencil for tracing display lettering. Letters may then be inked or painted over with a brush or technical pen. The precision of line and oval, however, are more important than simple density.

Several methods may be used to show the position of body type. The easiest is simply to draw a single line representing each baseline. This style, however, does little to illustrate the density of the typeface chosen. Other methods require two lines or a single broad line showing the x-height (fig. 7-19). The x-height is a better indicator of apparent size than are type size and linespace. Elegant roughs, such as those often required in advertising, demand a strict indication of the x-height to demonstrate the apparent size of type most effectively. For jobwork or book typography, the quicker single-line method may be used.

The rough layout will follow the job through the typesetting and printing processes, serving as a guide in actual production.

COMPREHENSIVE LAYOUTS

After the client selects the rough layout, the designer will create a *comprehensive,* or *comp.* The finished comp is intended to resemble as closely as possible the actual printed page. Several different artistic processes may be used to produce comps (figs. 7-20 through 7-22). *Pantone sheets* are sheets of adhesive-backed acetate available in dozens of colors. The layout artist applies the sheets to the board to create a facsimile of the intended design. Display type is comped either by inking or by using transfer lettering. Body type may be transferred from *greeking sheets,* lettering sheets that are printed with body type in different sizes and weights.

Color key and *chromalin* (chromes) are proofing methods that are often used to produce four-color comps. If the illustration for an ad is a color photograph, a chrome produces a high-quality visual very similar to a printed piece.

Marker comps are drawn with art markers. Usually produced when

7-20.

**Pencil comp,
Valerie Ferenti.**

7-21.

**Finished comp
rendered through
the greeking method.**

7-22.

**Finished comp
showing type in
position.**

an illustration is required, they are rendered by a professional illustrator or designer. Type is carefully positioned and drawn to match the typographer's rough layout.

In book typography and publication design, the typographer often creates comps by using photocopies of galley type. The photocopies are pasted into position with rubber cement. Photostats or photocopies of the illustrations are mounted into position to complete the design.

After the comps have been completed, the client must once again approve the art. If the client does not approve it, additional comps must be made. For the safety of both the typographer and the client, it is essential that several stages of approval (and communication) take place. If the client does not like the printed piece after approving a finished comp, the blame lies with the client and not the typographer.

THE DUMMY

In bookwork, publication design, and some types of jobwork, the typographer will often create a *dummy,* or a collection of layouts, in correct imposition, of an entire book, periodical, or brochure. The completeness of the dummy will depend on the project. For a novel, the typographer should create layouts of the jacket, cover, front and back matter, and first few pages of text. It makes little sense to spend hours dummying up page after similar page. For a history of art with hundreds of illustrations, however, an accurate layout of each text page will be required.

The purpose of the dummy is somewhat different from that of the layout. The layout is prepared, in part, to receive the approval of the client. The dummy is a comprehensive guide used in the preparation of mechanicals, the final camera copy. How are four illustrations on one page to be arranged? What are the relationships between chapter opening pages and illustrations? Must the chapter openings begin on the recto? These are the kinds of questions the dummy answers for the typographer and mechanical artist. The dummy need not be as technically precise as the finished comprehensive. The mechanical artist and others who work with the dummy in the printing process are using it for placement purposes only. The dummy should be accurate, clean, and complete.

A dummy should be prepared whenever a job requires a fold, even if only one fold is necessary. Dummies of brochures, folders, greeting cards, flyers, and newsletters reduce the possibility of printing the job in incorrect page order. This is especially important when folios are not used (as in several of the examples just listed).

Even if the typographer is planning to prepare the mechanicals for a job, he or she should still make a dummy. Without one, the typographer, no matter how experienced, can face pages in the wrong mechanical order. Mechanicals will also be executed more quickly because the dummy ensures that design decisions are properly made.

8

SPECIFYING TYPE

One of the most basic typographic skills is the accurate specification of typesetting parameters. If type is not specified correctly, the result is often surprising and almost always unsatisfactory. Poor typography is caused far more often by a lack of communication than by the shoddy work of a type house. Of course, in order to communicate effectively, one must establish a common semantic ground. For typography, this semantic ground is called *typographic notation,* a system that communicates the essential information that determines what your job will look like.

The typographer or designer must supply specifications for six essential parameters: typeface, type size, linespace, measure, letterspacing, and wordspacing. These notations are usually written directly on the manuscript in a process called the *markup* (fig. 8-1). The markup serves as the typographic map for the typesetter. The original instructions for, as well as any changes in, typeface, size, and leading must be clearly indicated, so that as the job is keyboarded, the typesetter will recognize and incorporate the information.

Typographic notation should be easily distinguishable from other notations on the manuscript. Many designers and typographers use a pencil color different from that used by the editor when marking up copy. Pencil is best to allow for erasures and corrections.

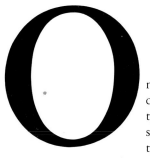

ACM stands for area composing machine. This is a very versatile unit because it can be used as a direct entry unit, it can accept paper tape and it will accept a mini-disk. There are two film strips on the machine at all times which is a total of eight fonts of type. Sizes range from six to 72 point or 12 standard sizes. It is very essential that the copy be marked-up for typesetting before sitting down at this keyboard. The machine requires information such as point size, font #, line space and line length before actual typesetting begins. In the manual mode the operator must make all end-of-line decisions, such as justified, quad left, quad right, or quad center. After selecting one of the above, the operator then hits the return key. The paper on which the type is set is call Ektamatic. It is eight inches wide and must be taken out of the machine for processing.

MDT (Mini Disk Terminal) Keyboard

This unit is used to set type on a mini-disk. It is a video display terminal with a small screen similar to a TV. 14 lines of type can be seen when the screen area is full. About 85,000 characters can be stored on the disk. It is very easy to add or delete information and several jobs are usually on file. This unit represents our newest method of typesetting and the system is very popular in the graphic arts industry.

8-1.
Markup.

Most notations should be placed neatly in the left margin, as close as possible to the applicable copy. Assume you are typesetting a manuscript with body copy specified to set in Times Roman and subheads in Times Bold Italic. That information should be written next to the actual copy. Whenever notations are made, the specification will remain in effect until changed. If the body copy is not respecified as Times Roman, in this example, the typesetter may continue to set the body copy in Times Bold Italic after the first subhead. Although the careful typesetter will probably understand the intention of the notation and revert to Times Roman, the notation should be correctly specified to avoid possible confusion.

In bookwork, typographic notation of heads and subheads is often given by keying a specific pattern of parameters with a letter or number. In the example just cited, for instance, the subhead might be labeled *A* and the body *B.* If there are several levels of heads and subheads (as in this book), each is assigned a different letter. Keying the copy saves hours of markup time. As the book is set, the operator will simply follow the key and change parameters accordingly.

The designer specifies typefaces by writing out the names. Shorthand is acceptable, as in "Helv" or "Times B.I.," but care should be taken to ensure that the name is both legible and unmistakable.

Typeface

ITALICS AND PSEUDO-ITALICS

Watch these fingers dance
Watch these fingers dance

8-2.

Italics versus pseudo-italics.

When specifying italic typefaces, the designer must be certain that true italics are received. One result of the manipulations available via digital typesetting is the *pseudo-italic* (fig. 8-2), which is merely a slanted version of a roman typeface.

Pseudo-italics may be slanted at various degrees of bias. A 15-degree slant is visibly different from a 20-degree slant. If an italic is specified, a true italic (and not a pseudo-italic) should be set. If a pseudo-italic is specified, the degree of slant must be included in the specification. The typesetter must be certain that the desired degree of slant is supplied.

More problematical, pseudo-italics do not look like true italics. In serif typefaces especially, italic letters such as *a, t, f,* and *v* possess very different letterforms from their roman counterparts. Specialized italic letterforms are easier to identify and more attractive than pseudo-italics.

Pseudo-italics are not acceptable for serif typefaces. When sans serif typefaces are used, pseudo-italics may or may not be satisfactory, depending on the typeface chosen. The designer should carefully examine specimens before accepting the pseudo-italic as a substitute.

CONDENSED AND EXPANDED TYPEFACES

Digital technology is capable not only of slanting but of condensing and expanding versions of typefaces automatically. As with italics, these manipulations are not identical to a true condensed or expanded typeface created by a typeface designer who has painstakingly reworked each letterform.

The degree to which typefaces may be condensed or expanded is variable and usually expressed as a percentage of the original design. For example, condensed versions are from 50 to 99 percent as wide as the original; expanded variations may be ordered from 101 to 150 percent wider than the parent design. Because of the many variables, the typesetter must supply the face as specified. Although digitally condensed or expanded typefaces may produce excellent typography, the designer must consult a specimen sheet before ordering them.

THE TYPEBOOK

The single most important tool of anyone specifying type is the *typebook,* a set of specimen pages of various typefaces set in different sizes (figs. 8-3 through 8-6).

A typebook must be functional—a display of what the type house has to offer to the customer. To that end it must also be attractive; indeed, many such books are typographic masterpieces.

Some type houses simply purchase specimen pages from the typesetting equipment manufacturers, like Mergenthaler or Compugraphic, or from third-party suppliers. Other companies design and produce their own specimen pages. Whichever method is chosen, the type specifier depends on the typebook for accurate, precise information. Many designers use the books as tools in comping type (a process discussed in chapter 7). The constant attention given to the specimens usually leads to sales for the type house, so the typebook should be created with the designer in mind:

- The type house may not be able to include every typeface in its large type library, but a reasonable collection should include a complete family of the historical classics, such as Baskerville, Times, and Helvetica. Contemporary faces should also be included, although many designers concentrate on using a relatively small number of faces.

8-3.

Typebook.

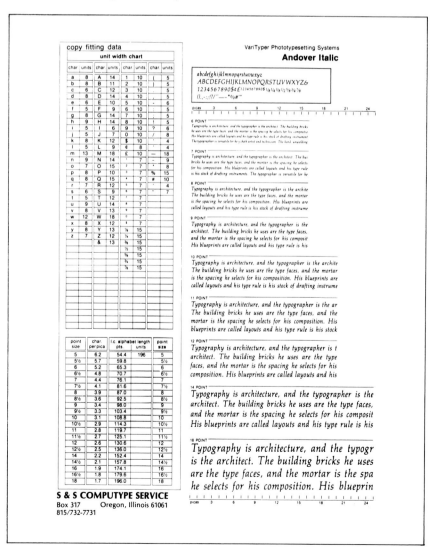

- The typebook should also include a complete alphabet of every display type available from the type house. Display type need not (indeed, cannot) be shown in every size, given the multitude of sizes available in digital typesetting. A single size is adequate, and should be shown in a squarish block so that the designer can enlarge or reduce the type on an art viewer.
- Body copy should be shown in only three or four sizes. Many typebooks include 6-point type, despite the fact that 6-point is rarely specified. A specimen showing 8-, 10-, 12-, and 14-point is far more valuable. The typebook should include examples of body type set both with one and two points of lead, the most common choices.
- Finally, the typebook should be packaged in a three-ring binder that allows pages to be removed for updating, for comping, or for use in an art viewer.

The student typographer should ask area type houses for a copy of a typebook. In addition to specimen pages, the typebook may also include other useful proofreader's marks, interfacing information, notes on typeface classifications, a quick primer on typographic basics, and other useful information.

Type Size and Linespace

Typographers always specify typesize and linespace together using one of several designations. No matter which method is chosen, the type size is *always* given first, followed by the linespace.

Assume, for example, you wish to have 12-point type set with a 14-point linespace. To specify this type, you can write *12 on 14, 12/14,* or *12-14.* Alternatively, some designers use the phrase *12 with 2 points of lead; 12/2* and *12-2* are other possibilities. Of these notations, *12/14* is the most popular, but all are acceptable. The designer and typesetter should be certain that a common understanding has been reached. Confusion is possible, especially when one sets display with large amounts of linespace: *36/36* may mean 36-point set solid or 36 on 72-point, depending on whether the second number is the linespace or the lead.

The technology also creates difficulties in specifying linespace correctly. Many of the newly digitized typefaces are created with a "built-in" half point of linespacing. Thus, if 12 on 14 type is specified, the type will actually be set 12 on 14.5; the difference in visual spacing is noticeable. More important, if you want to have type set solid, you may have to specify negative linespacing, such as *12 on 11.5.*

Finally, additional linespace is routinely required between textual items. Examples include spacing between body copy and a subhead, between a chapter title and body copy, and between body copy and a footnote. Where such spacing is warranted, the type specifier should write the number of points of space required along with the symbol for space (#), and circle the notation (fig. 8-7).

8-4.

Typebook, Graphics of Utica.

8-5.

Typebook showing various x-heights.

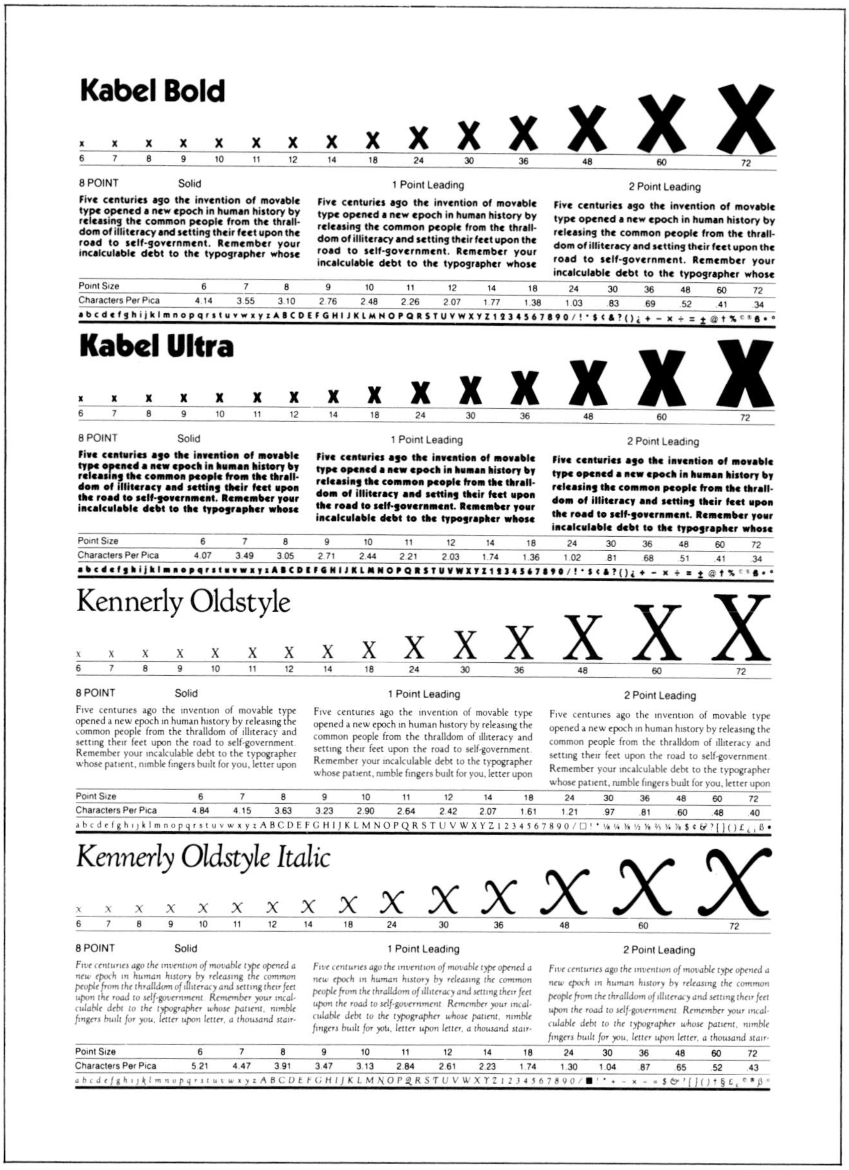

Kabel Bold

x	x	x	x	x	x	X	X	X	X	X	X	X	X	X
6	7	8	9	10	11	12	14	18	24	30	36	48	60	72

8 POINT · Solid · 1 Point Leading · 2 Point Leading

Five centuries ago the invention of movable type opened a new epoch in human history by releasing the common people from the thralldom of illiteracy and setting their feet upon the road to self-government. Remember your incalculable debt to the typographer whose

Five centuries ago the invention of movable type opened a new epoch in human history by releasing the common people from the thralldom of illiteracy and setting their feet upon the road to self-government. Remember your incalculable debt to the typographer whose

Five centuries ago the invention of movable type opened a new epoch in human history by releasing the common people from the thralldom of illiteracy and setting their feet upon the road to self-government. Remember your incalculable debt to the typographer whose

Point Size	6	7	8	9	10	11	12	14	18	24	30	36	48	60	72
Characters Per Pica	4.14	3.55	3.10	2.76	2.48	2.26	2.07	1.77	1.38	1.03	.83	.69	.52	.41	.34

abcdefghijklmnopqrstuvwxyzABCDEFGHIJKLMNOPQRSTUVWXYZ1234567890/!`$¢&?()¿+—×÷±@†%°¢§•*

Kabel Ultra

x	x	x	x	x	x	X	X	X	X	X	X	X	X	X
6	7	8	9	10	11	12	14	18	24	30	36	48	60	72

8 POINT · Solid · 1 Point Leading · 2 Point Leading

Five centuries ago the invention of movable type opened a new epoch in human history by releasing the common people from the thralldom of illiteracy and setting their feet upon the road to self-government. Remember your incalculable debt to the typographer whose

Five centuries ago the invention of movable type opened a new epoch in human history by releasing the common people from the thralldom of illiteracy and setting their feet upon the road to self-government. Remember your incalculable debt to the typographer whose

Five centuries ago the invention of movable type opened a new epoch in human history by releasing the common people from the thralldom of illiteracy and setting their feet upon the road to self-government. Remember your incalculable debt to the typographer whose

Point Size	6	7	8	9	10	11	12	14	18	24	30	36	48	60	72
Characters Per Pica	4.07	3.49	3.05	2.71	2.44	2.21	2.03	1.74	1.36	1.02	.81	.68	.51	.41	.34

abcdefghijklmnopqrstuvwxyzABCDEFGHIJKLMNOPQRSTUVWXYZ1234567890/!`$¢&?()¿+—×÷±@†%°¢§•*

Kennerly Oldstyle

x	x	x	x	x	x	X	X	X	X	X	X	X	X
6	7	8	9	10	11	12	14	18	24	30	36	48	60	72

8 POINT · Solid · 1 Point Leading · 2 Point Leading

Five centuries ago the invention of movable type opened a new epoch in human history by releasing the common people from the thralldom of illiteracy and setting their feet upon the road to self-government. Remember your incalculable debt to the typographer whose patient, nimble fingers built for you, letter upon

Five centuries ago the invention of movable type opened a new epoch in human history by releasing the common people from the thralldom of illiteracy and setting their feet upon the road to self-government. Remember your incalculable debt to the typographer whose patient, nimble fingers built for you, letter upon

Five centuries ago the invention of movable type opened a new epoch in human history by releasing the common people from the thralldom of illiteracy and setting their feet upon the road to self-government. Remember your incalculable debt to the typographer whose patient, nimble fingers built for you, letter upon

Point Size	6	7	8	9	10	11	12	14	18	24	30	36	48	60	72
Characters Per Pica	4.84	4.15	3.63	3.23	2.90	2.64	2.42	2.07	1.61	1.21	.97	.81	.60	.48	.40

abcdefghijklmnopqrstuvwxyzABCDEFGHIJKLMNOPQRSTUVWXYZ1234567890/□!`¼½¾⅛⅜⅝⅞$¢&?()£¿•*

Kennerly Oldstyle Italic

x	x	x	x	x	x	X	X	X	X	X	X	X	X
6	7	8	9	10	11	12	14	18	24	30	36	48	60	72

8 POINT · Solid · 1 Point Leading · 2 Point Leading

Five centuries ago the invention of movable type opened a new epoch in human history by releasing the common people from the thralldom of illiteracy and setting their feet upon the road to self-government. Remember your incalculable debt to the typographer whose patient, nimble fingers built for you, letter upon letter, a thousand stair-

Five centuries ago the invention of movable type opened a new epoch in human history by releasing the common people from the thralldom of illiteracy and setting their feet upon the road to self-government. Remember your incalculable debt to the typographer whose patient, nimble fingers built for you, letter upon letter, a thousand stair-

Five centuries ago the invention of movable type opened a new epoch in human history by releasing the common people from the thralldom of illiteracy and setting their feet upon the road to self-government. Remember your incalculable debt to the typographer whose patient, nimble fingers built for you, letter upon letter, a thousand stair-

Point Size	6	7	8	9	10	11	12	14	18	24	30	36	48	60	72
Characters Per Pica	5.21	4.47	3.91	3.47	3.13	2.84	2.61	2.23	1.74	1.30	1.04	.87	.65	.52	.43

abcdefghijklmnopqrstuvwxyzABCDEFGHIJKLMNOPQRSTUVWXYZ1234567890/■!`•—×−÷$&?()†§¿°•*

8-6.

Specimen page uniformly set solid.

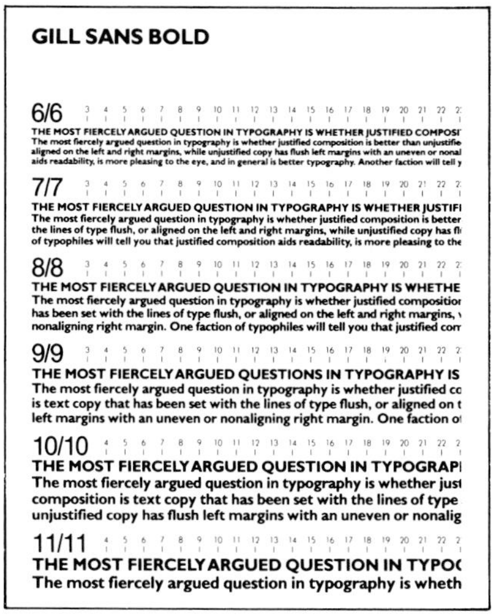

GILL SANS BOLD

6/6 3 4 5 6 7 8 9 10 11 12 13 14 15 16 17 18 19 20 21 22 2
THE MOST FIERCELY ARGUED QUESTION IN TYPOGRAPHY IS WHETHER JUSTIFIED COMPOSI
The most fiercely argued question in typography is whether justified composition is better than unjustifie
aligned on the left and right margins, while unjustified copy has flush left margins with an uneven or nonal
aids readability, is more pleasing to the eye, and in general is better typography. Another faction will tell y

7/7 3 4 5 6 7 8 9 10 11 12 13 14 15 16 17 18 19 20 21 22 2
THE MOST FIERCELY ARGUED QUESTION IN TYPOGRAPHY IS WHETHER JUSTIFI
The most fiercely argued question in typography is whether justified compositi
the lines of type flush, or aligned on the left and right margins, while unjustified copy has fl
of typophiles will tell you that justified composition aids readability, is more pleasing to the

8/8 3 4 5 6 7 8 9 10 11 12 13 14 15 16 17 18 19 20 21 22 2
THE MOST FIERCELY ARGUED QUESTION IN TYPOGRAPHY IS WHETHE
The most fiercely argued question in typography is whether justified composition
has been set with the lines of type flush, or aligned on the left and right margins, v
nonaligning right margin. One faction of typophiles will tell you that justified com

9/9 4 5 6 7 8 9 10 11 12 13 14 15 16 17 18 19 20 21 22 2
THE MOST FIERCELY ARGUED QUESTIONS IN TYPOGRAPHY IS
The most fiercely argued question in typography is whether justified co
is text copy that has been set with the lines of type flush, or aligned on t
left margins with an uneven or nonaligning right margin. One faction o

10/10 4 5 6 7 8 9 10 11 12 13 14 15 16 17 18 19 20 21 22 2
THE MOST FIERCELY ARGUED QUESTION IN TYPOGRAPH
The most fiercely argued question in typography is whether just
composition is text copy that has been set with the lines of type
unjustified copy has flush left margins with an uneven or nonalig

11/11 4 5 6 7 8 9 10 11 12 13 14 15 16 17 18 19 20 21 22 2
THE MOST FIERCELY ARGUED QUESTION IN TYPOG
The most fiercely argued question in typography is wheth

8-7.

Typographic notation of linespace.

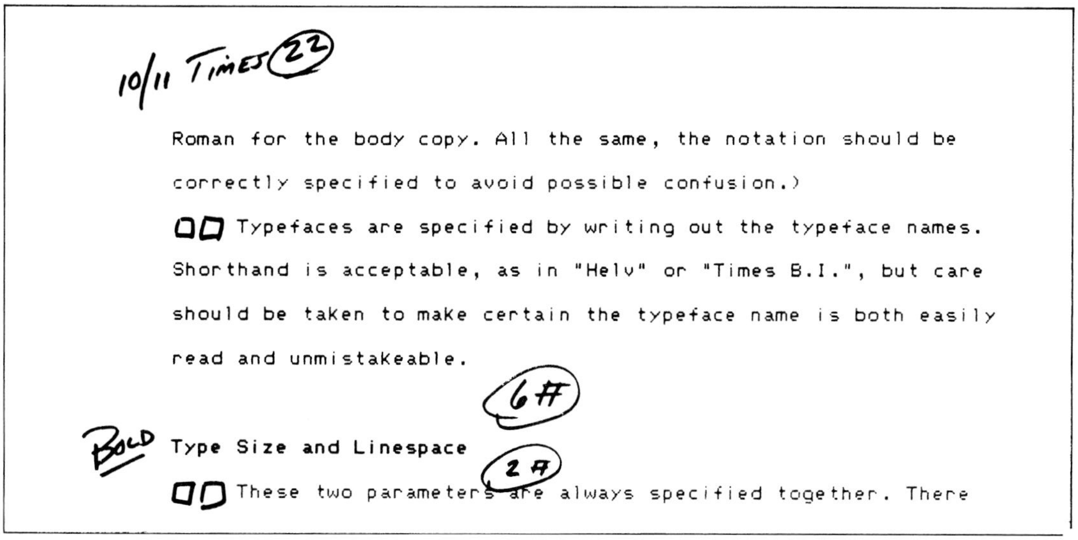

10/11 Times ②②

Roman for the body copy. All the same, the notation should be correctly specified to avoid possible confusion.)

□□ Typefaces are specified by writing out the typeface names. Shorthand is acceptable, as in "Helv" or "Times B.I.", but care should be taken to make certain the typeface name is both easily read and unmistakeable.

⑥#

BOLD Type Size and Linespace ②#

□□ These two parameters are always specified together. There

Measure

As with type size and linespace, measure may be specified in a variety of ways. For example, 12 on 14 type set on a 26-pica measure could be written as any of the following:

12/14/26   12-14 x 26   12/14 x 26

Other methods include circling the measure or adding a small triangle after the number of picas. Again, whenever changes in the measure are necessary, be certain to revert to the standard measure after noting the deviation. Heads and subheads are an exception to this rule—the typesetter will follow the typographer's initial instructions regarding how wide these are to be set.

Letterspacing and Wordspacing

Although the typesetter specifies minimum and maximum letterspacing and wordspacing values in terms of units (fig. 8-8), the designer usually uses more imprecise terms: very tight, tight or normal, loose, and very loose (fig. 8-9). Loose letterspacing and wordspacing are usually unsightly in text type.

"Tight" letterspacing can mean different things to the designer, the typographer, and the typesetter. Worse, its definition may also vary from one type house to another. The best way to communicate letterspacing and wordspacing values is to specify from samples contained on specimen sheets.

Proof Marks

Proofreaders' marks are used both in specifying type and in reading typeset galleys. The copy editor, who is responsible for reviewing the manuscript before it is sent to the type house, uses proofreader's marks to indicate additions, deletions, and corrections in the material. Figure 8-10 shows a complete set of proof marks. These are the most commonly used:

Carat. The carat is a small arrow (/\) that alerts the typesetter to the placement of inserted material. It is written along the baseline, and the text to be added is penciled above the x-height or in the margin..

Insert space and close up space. Space to be added between words or characters is designated by a crosshatch (#). Conversely, if space is to be closed up, a turned set of parentheses is used (⌒).

Stet. When stet, meaning *let it stand,* is written in the margin of a manuscript, the typesetter has been instructed to disregard changes made in a particular part of the text (distinguished by a series of penciled dots at the baseline) and to set the material as originally typed.

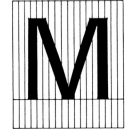

8-8.

The 18- and 36-unit systems.

Instruction	Notation in margin	Notation in type	Corrected type
Delete		the ~~type~~ font	the font
Insert	type	the font	the type font
Let it stand	stet	the type font	the type font
Reset in capitals	cap	the type font	THE TYPE FONT
Reset in lowercase	lc	the type font	the type font
Reset in italics	ital	the type font	the *type* font
Reset in small capitals	sc	See type font	See TYPE FONT
Reset in roman	rom	the type font	the type font
Reset in boldface	bf	the type font	**the type font**
Reset in lightface	lf	the type font	the type font
Transpose	tr	the font type	the type font
Close up space		the ty pe	the type
Delete and close space		the type fo nt	the type font
Move left		the type font	the type font
Move right		the type font	the type font
Run in	run in	The type font is Univers. It is not Garamond.	The type font is Univers. It is not Garamond.
Align		the type font the type font the type font	the type font the type font the type font
Spell out	sp	3 type fonts	Three type fonts
Insert space	#	the type font	the type font
Insert period		The type font	The type font.
Insert comma		One two, three	One, two, three
Insert hyphen		Ten point type	Ten-point type
Insert colon		Old Style types	Old Style types:
Insert semicolon		Select the font spec the type	Select the font; spec the type.
Insert apostrophe		Baskervilles type	Baskerville's type
Insert quotation marks		the word type	the word "type"
Insert parenthesis		The word type is in parenthesis.	The word (type) is in parenthesis.
Insert en dash		Flush left	Flush–left
Insert em dash		Garamond an Old Style face is used today.	Garamond — an Old Style face — is used today.
Start paragraph		The type font is Univers 55.	The type font is Univers 55.

Typography

Typography

Typography

Typography

Typography

8-9.

Various letterspacing values: touching, very tight, tight, normal, and loose.

8-10.

Proofreaders' marks.

Delete copy. The mark used to delete copy is a short irregular stroke
(✐). If words or sentences are to be removed, the copy editor will first
place a line through the offending word or sentence, and then finish the
line with the deletion stroke.

U&lc. The typesetter will assume that text is to be set with uppercase and lowercase characters unless he or she is otherwise instructed. However, when type set in all uppercase or all lowercase is specified for certain
elements of the text, *U&lc* must be written in the margin to indicate a
reversion to the standard style. When letters are typed in a manuscript in
uppercase and are to be set lowercase, the letter is slashed (as in A̸).

Indents. The typographer should show em indents by placing a sequence of squares at the beginning of the paragraph. One box (□) means
one em; two boxes (□ □) mean two ems; and so on.

Transposing copy. When copy is to be transposed, the proofreader
must use two marks. The transposition symbol, a stroke that encompasses
the textual elements to be reversed, is placed directly on the copy ("Four-
score and seven ago years"). To make the intention completely clear, *tr* is
written and circled in the margin.

Circled copy. Circling words means two different things. If copy is
circled in the text, the typesetter should spell out the words, as in *Mister*
instead of *Mr.,* or *President* instead of *Pres.*

However, if the editor or proofreader wishes to make a specification clear or raise a question, care must be taken not to confuse copy that is
to be set with a query. The comment is penciled in the margin and circled.
The typesetter will recognize the circle as a flag indicating that either a
question is being raised or a specification is being changed.

Underlining copy. There are five different proofreaders' marks that
are placed directly below the copy. The dotted line already discussed means
stet. A single solid line means *change to italic,* a double solid line means *set
copy in small capitals,* and a triple solid line means *set copy in all caps.* A
single wavy line means *change to boldface.* If the single wavy line is used, the
copy editor should also write the letters *bf* in the margin.

Indicating the end of copy. The author or editor should signify that a
manuscript is complete by writing *-30-,* three crosshatches (###), or simply *The End.* The *-30-* symbol is often used in newspaper work.

The typesetter will learn most of the many proof marks through
practice. A good set of proof marks, included in many dictionaries, should
be within easy reach of every typesetting device.

9

COPYFITTING

Copyfitting determines how much space body type will consume after it is typeset. This information is absolutely necessary when the typographer works with large amounts of type because the typeface, type size, linespace, and line length selections have a significant impact upon the ultimate length of the printed work.

The decisions of the typographer are most often based on two considerations: space and cost. In the first case, especially important in advertising typography, copyfitting will determine what parameters may be specified to fit a given number of characters successfully in a given space. In the second case, any manuscript set in 8-point type will obviously take up less space than the same pages set in 12-point. The selection of typographic parameters will be significantly influenced by the publisher's decision as to how many pages should be printed. Copyfitting is the only way in which the typographer can be certain the chosen book length will be realized.

Every typographer must know how to copyfit, though many prefer to avoid the simple mathematics required. Designers and art directors often write the notation *set to fit,* meaning that the typesetter should fit the copy into the block that has been created.

Many devices, including slide rules, copyfitting wheels, and even handheld calculators, are sold to make copyfitting easier. However, such devices only complicate a simple procedure. Instead of equipment, the typographer merely needs a method that is easy to learn and use.

Typebooks include information about the amount of space a particular typeface, set in a particular size, takes up on the page. The space consumed varies according to the width of the letters, which, as noted, may have very little to do with type size (fig. 9-1). Thus, 20 letters set in 12-point may take up as much as 20 picas or as little as 12 picas of horizontal space.

First examine how typebooks present copyfitting information to the typographer (fig. 9-2). The number of characters per unit of space is called the *character count.* There are several possible formats: characters per pica, per 10 picas, or per a given line length are the most popular. This discussion will be based on the per-pica method. The other methods are easily adaptable to the copyfitting steps that follow.

9-1.

Various widths of a 60-point *m*.

The Copy

Before you determine how much space your typesetting will require, you must assess how long the typewritten manuscript is. To do this, you must count the characters, but, frequently, you will not have to count *every* character in the manuscript. Usually the copy has been typed consistently in one of two standard typewriter styles: pica and elite. Pica type invariably has ten characters to the inch. If you measure an inch of copy with a ruler and find it has ten characters, *every* horizontal inch of that copy will have ten characters. *Elite* typewriting is slightly smaller—there are twelve characters to the inch—but the same principle applies. If you count twelve characters in one inch of copy, every inch of that copy will have twelve characters.

    Proportionally spacing typewriters complicate matters because they produce copy that looks like typesetting. An *m* is wider than an *l;* a *k* is wider than an *i* (fig. 9-3). Where these machines are used, every character in a line must be counted to ensure accurate copyfitting. In the rare cases when a typographer works from a handwritten manuscript, the same principle will apply: each character in the line must be counted individually.

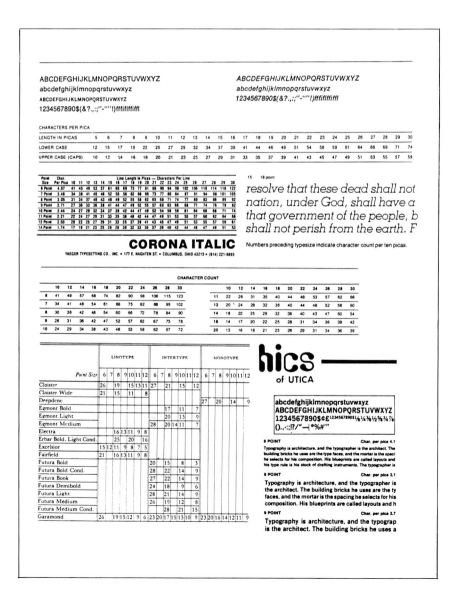

9-2.

Copyfitting charts.

Step One: Counting One Line

The first step in copyfitting is to count the number of characters in a *single line*. You can do this either by counting the number of characters in one inch and multiplying that figure by the number of inches in the line, or simply by counting each character.

Using figure 9-4 as your copy, pick a line of average length. The character count you will be computing is an average. A very short or very long line will skew the average either high or low. *Remember* also that when counting characters for copyfitting, you must count letters, figures, punctuation marks, *and* spaces between words. When you have finished the character count for one line, write down the number.

9-3.

(from top) Pica, elite, and proportionally spaced typewriting.

123456789**1**123456789**2**123456789**3**123456789**4**12345
123456789**1** 123456789**2** 123456789**3** 123456789**4** 12345678**95**1234
123456789**1**123456789**2**123456789**3**123456789**4**123456789**4**123456789**5**12345678

A dominant recent theme in art, the relationship of one shape to another, has moved into typography and type design increasingly since World War II. In a paradoxical way, it reverses prior emphases on the shape of a letter's lines. Now, with quite subtle and sophisticated changes of the letter forms, emphasis is on the white space, to make it more powerful to the eye than the lines themselves, creating an excitement while it achieves the harmony and unity a typeface needs. The simple lines allow great opportunity for opening up the counters and the space around the letters. One general effect has been the widening, even squaring, of letters. These sans use Roman proportions and rounds, and are now considered standard display faces. They reflect the times, and fit well with modern architecture and abstract art.

But the supporters of the sans insisted on its use as a body type as well, and this is where a controversy occurred. Opponents insisted it was not readable in large bodies of text, because the serif serves three functions: to cut down the reflection of light from around the letter into the reader's eye (halation), to link the letters in a word, and to help distinguish one letter from another. In this connection is not the problem with reading a word such as Illinois without serifs! Nor, said the opponents, is readability the only consideration. Except for a few faces only technically sans serifs, such as Optima (Oracle), the sans serifs are monotonous and nonhuman. Sans serif used exclusively gives the cold feel of an automated factory, they said.

10|13
Optima
23

Set flush right

on Trendsetter

+ 4 pts.

9-4.

Copy.

Step Two: The Page Count

After you have counted the number of characters in one line, it is easy to compute the number of characters on one page. Count the number of *lines* on the page, ignoring very short lines. Multiply that number by the character count determined in step one. This is the *page character count*.

If your manuscript has more than a single page, the page character count is first computed as outlined above. But you must then determine the number of *full* pages of manuscript. Pages with one or two lines may be ignored; if two chapters each end with a half page, the two half pages are counted as a single page. After you have determined the number of full pages, multiply the page character count by the number of full pages to obtain the *manuscript character count*, the number of characters in the complete manuscript.

Examine figure 9-5 to see how a copyfitter has computed the values for figure 9-4 and compare them with your character count. Remember that this is an average: if your computations are within 30 characters of the count already determined, they are accurate.

Step Three: Copyfitting Charts

Before you can go further in your copyfitting, the typesetting specifications must be established. Assume, for example, that the type is to be set in 10-point Helvetica with an 11-point linespace on a 20-pica measure. The information for 10-point Helvetica is given in the copyfitting chart shown in figure 9-6. Notice that the *character-per-pica* value for 10-point type is 2.68. Write this down.

If the measure is 20 picas, how many typeset characters will be in one line of type? You know two things: there are 2.68 characters in every pica and there are 20 picas. Multiply the *character-per-pica* value by the *measure*. The result will be the number of characters that will appear in each line of typesetting.

Step Four: Number of Typeset Lines

You now know the number of characters in the job as well as the number of characters in one line of typesetting. With these two values, you can determine the *number of typeset lines*, the information you will need to make certain that the type will fit the layout. Each typeset line is represented by a line drawn as body copy on the layout.

To determine the number of lines, divide the number of typeset characters in one line *into* the total page (or manuscript) character count. Remember that you are now dealing with typeset, and not typewritten, characters. Use the value you determined in step three using the copyfitting chart. As a simple example, if a document has 100 characters and there are 20 typeset characters in each line, the typeset job will have five lines. Try this with the example given in figure 9-4, and check your calculations against the copyfitting results in figure 9-5.

Step Five: Vertical Depth

After you have determined the number of typeset lines, the copyfitting exercise is basically completed. The layout artist, in principle, could now draw the number of computed typeset lines. But there are two more steps to round out the job.

9-5.
Copyfitted text.

[Handwritten annotations:] 10/13 Optima · ㉓ · Set flush right on Trendsetter · ✓ 62 Char · ① 62 × 26 lines / 372 / 124 / 1612 Total Char · ② 2.68 CPP × 23 P / 804 / 534 / 61.44 char PER LINE · ③ 61)1612 26.4 ... = 27 lines · ④ 27 × 13 linespace / 81 / 27 / 351 pts · ⑤ 12)351 29 picas / 24 / 111 · 29 picas total depth · +4 pts.

A dominant recent theme in art, the relationship of one shape to another, has moved into typography and type design increasingly since World War II. In a paradoxical way, it reverses prior emphases on the shape of a letter's lines. Now, with quite subtle and sophisticated changes of the letter forms, emphasis is on the white space, to make it more powerful to the eye than the lines themselves, creating an excitement while it achieves the harmony and unity a typeface needs. The simple lines allow great opportunity for opening up the counters and the space around the letters. One general effect has been the widening, even squaring, of letters. These sans use Roman proportions and rounds, and are now considered standard display faces. They reflect the times, and fit well with modern architecture and abstract art.

But the supporters of the sans insisted on its use as a body type as well, and this is where a controversy occurred. Opponents insisted it was not readable in large bodies of text, because the serif serves three functions: to cut down the reflection of light from around the letter into the reader's eye (halation), to link the letters in a word, and to help distinguish one letter from another. In this connection is not the problem with reading a word such as Illinois without serifs! Nor, said the opponents, is readability the only consideration. Except for a few faces only technically sans serifs, such as Optima (Oracle), the sans serifs are monotonous and nonhuman. Sans serif used exclusively gives the cold feel of an automated factory, they said.

9-6.
Copyfitting chart for Helvetica.

CHARACTERS PER PICA BY POINT SIZE

Helvetica
ABCDEFGHIJKLMNOPQRSTUVWXYZ
abcdefghijklmnopqrstuvwxyz
$1234567890

	6	7	8	9	10	11	12	14	16	18	20	24	30	36
ABC	3.12	2.67	2.34	2.08	1.87	1.70	1.56	1.33	1.17	1.04	.93	.78	.62	.52
abc	4.48	3.83	3.36	2.98	2.68	2.44	2.24	1.91	1.67	1.49	1.34	1.12	.89	.74

Helvetica Italic
ABCDEFGHIJKLMNOPQRSTUVWXYZ
abcdefghijklmnopqrstuvwxyz
$1234567890

	6	7	8	9	10	11	12	14	16	18	20	24	30	36
ABC	3.16	2.71	2.37	2.10	1.89	1.72	1.58	1.35	1.18	1.05	.94	.79	.63	.52
abc	4.34	3.72	3.26	2.89	2.60	2.37	2.17	1.86	1.62	1.44	1.30	1.08	.87	.72

Helvetica Bold
ABCDEFGHIJKLMNOPQRSTUVWXYZ
abcdefghijklmnopqrstuvwxyz
$1234567890

	6	7	8	9	10	11	12	14	16	18	20	24	30	36
ABC	3.07	2.63	2.30	2.04	1.84	1.67	1.53	1.31	1.15	1.02	.92	.76	.61	.51
abc	4.07	3.48	3.05	2.71	2.44	2.22	2.03	1.74	1.52	1.35	1.22	1.01	.81	.67

First, remember that the linespace has been specified as 11 points. To make certain that the type will fit your layout, you must compute the total depth of the typesetting. If one line takes up 11 points, multiply the number of typeset lines determined in step four to compute the *total depth in points*.

Total depth expressed in points, however, is not particularly useful. It is difficult to visualize what a depth of 351 points, for example, means (it is as if a person were to refer to his or her height as 70 inches, rather than 5 feet 10 inches). For better comprehension, the copyfitter should convert depth in points into *depth in picas*. Since there are 12 points in a pica, the conversion is quite simple: divide the depth in points by 12. If you wish to go one step farther, you may also determine *depth in inches* by dividing the depth in picas by 6.

Book typographers should compute the number of pages in the typeset book. The publisher may then decide to make the book larger or smaller by adjusting specifications. To compute the number of typeset pages, determine how many lines of typesetting will be on each page (by counting the number of lines on your layout) and multiply the number of characters in one typeset line (the result of step three) by the number of lines. This is the number of characters on each typeset page. Divide by the total manuscript character count and you will have determined a reliable estimate of the number of pages consumed by text. To ensure an accurate page count, remember to add necessary pages for art, front matter, and back matter.

Now you can verify whether the type fits the space allotted for it in the layout. If the type fits the space, simply specify the typesetting parameters you have selected. If not, adjust your specifications. When making changes, keep in mind that there is no difference in the depth consumed by justified and ragged right composition.

Copyfitting prevents the page from designing itself. The type should not simply consume whatever space it happens to require. The typographer must *control* the page.

A Recap

Here is a roundup of the copyfitting steps:

1. Count the number of characters in an average line of typewriting.
2. Count the number of lines in the manuscript.
3. Multiply the number of characters in one line by the number of lines. This is the total number of typewritten characters.
4. After specifying your type, consult a copyfitting chart. Find the per-pica value for typeface and type size chosen.
5. Multiply the character-per-pica value by the measure you have specified. This is the number of characters in one typeset line.
6. Divide the number of characters in one typeset line by the total number of typewritten characters in the manuscript. This is the number of typeset lines.
7. Multiply the number of typeset lines by the linespace. This is the total depth in points.
8. Convert depth in points into depth in picas by dividing by 12. If you wish, convert depth in picas into depth in inches by dividing by 6.

10

TYPESETTING OVER THE GENERATIONS

The Linotype, although a major improvement in technology, was not a revolution in typesetting methodology. A new tool had been invented but only well-trained, highly specialized craftsmen could use it.

In the 1950s, the early phototypesetters were just as difficult to use and required as much training as the Linotype. By 1970, however, the computer joined forces with phototypesetting technology, and a real revolution in typesetting occurred. The computer made phototypesetting machines *easy* to use. The industry quickly discovered that simplicity offered both advantages and disadvantages.

Computerization has created a confusion of roles. Typesetters no longer need to study the art of typography to make equipment work. Indeed, in many shops, the "typesetter" is nothing more than a typist, producing keystrokes as rapidly as possible while a computer program hyphenates, justifies, changes measure, and adjusts linespacing automatically.

The job description of the "typographer," however, has not changed. No matter how advanced the technology is, typography is still only as good as the person producing it. Though an artform, typography is nevertheless affected by advances in technology. The expert typographer must be aware of those changes, taking advantage of the ones that result in better work and avoiding the ones that create aesthetic problems.

Technological Advantages

The advances in typesetting of the last 25 years can be divided into five basic categories: sharper image, reduced expense, better working environment, greater variety of fonts, and more efficient production.

Sharper Image. Letterpress printing ink tends to spread, obscuring the printed image (fig. 10-1). Moreover, the individual metal letters and

10-1.

(from left) **Results of relief, gravure, and offset lithography.**

slugs wear out as the repeated pressure of letterpress printing destroys fine strokes and serifs. Phototypeset letters, on the other hand, are always newly set. Film strips and digital patterns do not wear out. Every letter is perfectly formed. Offset printing reproduces those letters crisply and exactly as the type designer intended them.

Expense. The initial investment required for phototypesetting, since 1970, has completely altered the industry. Technology has made equipment increasingly affordable, creating a new world of typesetting: in-house shops, one-person type shops, and quick printers are all new members of the industry. Today many more typesetters are working within in-house shops than are working for type houses.

Environment. Three major changes have occurred in the typesetting work environment. First, there is much less noise. With a dozen machines run by levers, pulleys, rods and cams, all with metal striking metal, linotype shops could be literally deafening. Phototypesetting is a much quieter process; digital typesetting is completely silent.

Second, the fumes and heat produced by molten lead have been eliminated. Comparatively safe photochemicals have replaced the hazards of hot metal. More than one linecasting typesetter suffered severe burns when handling newly cast lines of type.

Third, many more women are now typesetting than ever before. Thousands of secretaries and word processors learned to operate typesetting equipment in the 1970s. There were very few women linecasters, whereas, today, typesetting is becoming a profession populated primarily by women.

Fonts. Many more type fonts and typefaces are available now than ever before. A digital typesetter is capable of producing type in every size from 5- to 72-point, typically in tenth of a point increments. Thus, whereas hot-metal typesetting was limited to 16 or fewer type sizes, digital typesetting offers 670. The "family" has been remarkably widened: a complete collection of Helvetica's 36 variations in 670 sizes is more than 24,000 fonts.

Because film strips are conveniently stored (and are less expensive than hot-metal fonts), type houses are able to offer selective typographers hundreds more choices than in the past.

Finally, phototypesetting and digital fonts do not have to be cast from expensive matrices. Today's original letter is photographed. Type design is therefore simpler, resulting in the creation of original typeface designs at an unprecedented rate.

Production. Perhaps the most obvious production advantage is speed. The fastest digital typesetter produces type at the rate of 6,000 lines per minute. Current typesetting systems also afford greater control than had been formerly available. Letterspacing, linespacing, and measure can be adjusted in increments of a tenth of a point. In addition, kerning pairs (fig. 10-2) are automatically kerned when the two letters are typed together.

AC AL AN AO AT AV AW AY
Av Aw ac af ao at au av
aw ax ay
CA CO CT CY Co Ce
DY du
ew ex ey
FA FG FO F, F. Fa Fe Fo Fu
GY
KE KO ke ko ku
LA LI LL LO LS LT LV LW LY
Ma mu
NT nu
OA OT OV OW OY
PA PE PO PR P, P. Pa Pe Po Pr
Qu
RA RO RV RY ra rc re ro
SA ST SY sys st
TA TC TE TO TS TW TY T, T.
Ta Te To Tr Tu Tw Ty
VA VO VY V, V. Va Ve Vo
WA WO WV WY W, W. Wa We
Wh Wi Wo Wr wa we w, w.
YA YO YS Y, Y. Ya Ye Yo
ya ye yo ys y, y.
ZA

10-2.

Kerning pairs.

Phototypesetting and Offset Lithography

Technology, then, has provided advantages so desirable that the typesetting industry has been forced to retool itself. Although some type houses and newspapers did move from the Linotype to the laser literally overnight, the general transition to current technology was more gradual.

The possibility of setting type photographically was discussed as early as 1887. The first attempts to actually implement the idea did not take place, however, until 1920. The 1921 edition of *The Penrose Annual*, a technological review serving the printing industry, featured a description by Arthur Dutton of the *Photoline*, a primitive phototypesetter adapted by Dutton from a linecasting machine. Photocomposition was still in its infancy, but William Gamble, the review's editor, continued to document developments. The 1926 volume reported that the August-Hunter Photocomposing Machine might revolutionize methods in several industries. Those revolutionary features included a metal master *film font* (30 feet long) and electronic, rather than manual, typewriter keys.

The same issue of the *Penrose Annual* advertised another phototypesetter, the Typary. Throughout the 1930s, the Monotype and Linotype companies, both manufacturers of hot-metal typesetters, experimented with photographic composition. In 1937, the Orotype became the first phototypesetter to be placed on the market, but it was not until after World War II that Intertype produced the Fotosetter, the earliest commercially successful phototypesetting machine (see fig. 1-8). First demonstrated at the U.S. Government Printing Office in 1947, the Fotosetter was sold by the hundreds in the early 1950s. Technologically, it did not move far beyond the hot-metal linecaster, for it merely replaced hot-metal matrices with individual photographic negatives. Since the 1950s, however, typesetting technology has radically changed in each decade.

The changes in typesetting technology have helped to foster a change in printing technology as well. There are three basic printing methods: raised (or relief) printing; recessed (or intaglio) printing; and flat (or planographic) printing. The most important raised printing method is letterpress. The most significant planographic technique is offset lithography.

In the last 40 years, the relative popularity of letterpress and offset lithography has reversed. Government studies point out that over 60 percent of commercial printing is now offset whereas only 25 percent is achieved through letterpress. Why has printing changed so dramatically?

For five hundred years, from the time of Gutenberg until the 1950s, typesetting had produced a raised surface (metal letters) that was printed by a raised printing method (letterpress). Phototypesetting is planographic (it produces type as a flat surface), but it did not doom relief printing (fig. 10-3). In the 1950s, several methods were developed that combined flat phototype and raised printing. For a time, it made sense for major newspapers and printers to use these methods—retooling huge letterpresses to offset lithography was very expensive. As letterpresses wore out, however, they were replaced by offset lithography presses (fig. 10-4).

Certainly, phototype and offset lithography are obvious partners: they are both planographic. Moreover, as phototypesetting technology was perfected, printers no longer needed to invest large sums in linecasters (which cost tens of thousands of dollars in the mid-1950s), handsetting equipment, or retrofitted letterpresses. By the 1960s, offset lithography had begun its slow ascendency. Economics and the comparative ease of the offset litho process created a printing boom throughout the past three decades. Total printing sales grew from less than $2 billion in 1947 to more than $10 billion in 1970. The 1984 *U.S. Industrial Outlook* projected an annual total of over $80 billion in the 1980s.

Although all printing historians refer to the development of typesetting technology in terms of generations, there is no real consensus as to how many generations have evolved—any number from four to dozens has been suggested. For the purposes of this book, generations will be divided by decades: the first generation emerged in the 1950s; the second generation in the 1960s; the third generation in the 1970s; and the fourth generation in the 1980s.

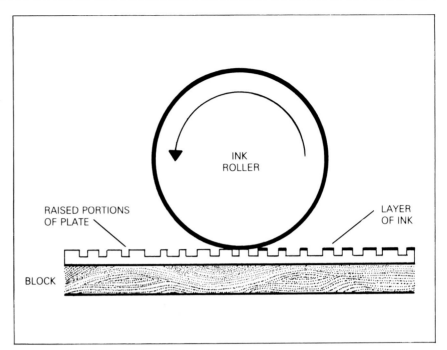

10-3.

Schematic of the relief printing process.

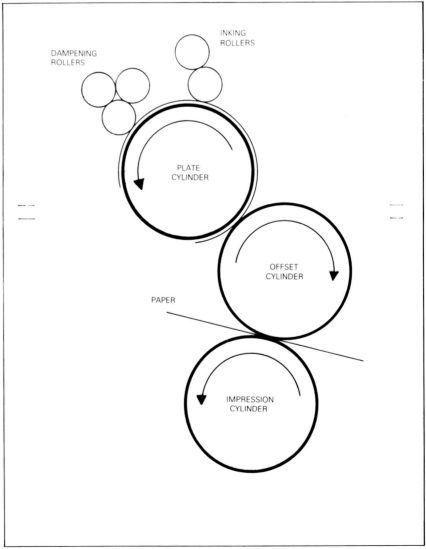

10-4.

Schematic of the offset litho printing process.

10-5.

First-generation phototypesetter.

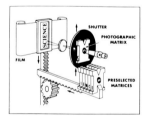

10-6.

Phototypesetting matrix.

THE FIRST GENERATION

The phototypesetters of the first generation operated entirely on mechanical principles. Like the Linotype and the Monotype, upon which they were based, these machines depended upon levers, pulleys, and gears that had been perfected earlier. As noted, the Fotosetter and the Monophoto, the first machines of this generation, were both produced by the companies that pioneered the first linecasting machines (fig. 10-5). The Fotomat photographic matrix works in exactly the same way as a Linotype matrix (fig. 10-6). A keyboard similar to a typewriter is operated by a compositor. As the operator manipulates keys, the Fotomat matrices are released from the magazine and drop onto an assembly elevator. As with the Linotype, when the matrices have filled out a line, the operator pushes a lever, mechanically moving the Fotomats into the photo unit for setting the line.

Unlike the Linotype, which uses hot metal to create lines, the photo unit of the Fotosetter exposes one letter at a time by raising the Fotomats into position before a light source. The light travels through a lens and then exposes photographic paper, which receives the image.

After photographing the negative matrices, the rack holding the complete line of mats is lifted to a distributor bar. The Fotomats make their way to the top of the machine, falling back into the channels from which they began. The serrated teeth of the Fotomats, like those of the hot-metal matrices, each find their own groove. They then recirculate to form additional lines of type.

The system of levers and bars that moves matrices about the machine means that first-generation phototypesetting is comparatively slow. The best operators, waiting for the Fotomats to be lifted out of position or the distributor bar to be moved, set type at the rate of about four lines per minute. The primary asset of the machine was planographic typesetting that complemented offset lithography.

Today, some printers continue to work with hot-metal type, but anyone using phototype has graduated to more efficient and economical methods. Nonetheless, the earliest phototypesetters contained the basic parts of later, more sophisticated, systems: a master negative font, a light source, and a lens.

Toward the end of the 1950s, first-generation typesetting was revolutionized by the earliest use of memory. Documents were stored on *paper tape* (fig. 10-7). Before this innovation, precision on the part of the compositor was essential. If errors were made, the only way to correct the line was to reset it. After the development of memory, however, compositors could manipulate the keyboard with less worry about mistakes, which could be easily corrected later on. The process was nevertheless limited by the slowness with which the machine itself operated, regardless of the compositor's speed.

THE SECOND GENERATION

The second generation of phototypesetters is characterized by the use of electronics to enhance what had formerly been a process of complicated moving parts. Although most type houses and printers did not incorporate this technology until the 1960s (some waited until the 1970s), the first second-generation machine, the Photon, was developed as early as 1954. Today, the second generation represents the lowest level of technology in use. Nonetheless, second-generation machines are responsible for much, if not most, of the phototypeset material created. Because of their ubiquity, a full discussion of these phototypesetters is in order.

The Second-Generation Phototypesetting System

All second-generation phototypesetters are composed of three parts: the keyboard, the computer unit, and the photo unit.

10-7.

Paper tape on which first-generation memory is stored.

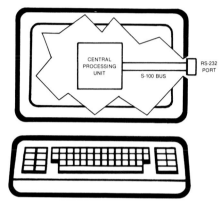

10-8.

Keyboard and video display terminal.

Keyboard

When an operator uses the keyboard of a phototypesetter, he or she supplies information to the machine. The data can be typeset immediately or stored in memory for later use. This information consists of the actual words to be set, along with typographic information, such as line length, linespace, typeface selection, and point size. The second-generation keyboard is often connected to a *cathode-ray tube* (CRT) for visual display of the text. The combination of CRT and keyboard is known as a *video display terminal* (fig. 10-8).

A *direct-entry* machine, such as the Compugraphic Execuwriter, does not use memory. As each line is keyed, the lines of type are set immediately after the operator signals the computer unit with a return. Because the operator is typesetting line by line, display of the full page on a video screen is unnecessary. Typical direct-entry phototypesetters feature a display of no more than 40 characters (fig. 10-9).

A formidable drawback of direct-entry typesetting is that it does not permit on-the-spot editing. If a mistake is made, the line must be retyped. Even so, some shops continue to use this outdated technology.

Today's far more popular method is *off-line* typesetting. Several typists produce input on different machines that are not directly connected to a central output unit (fig. 10-10). The information is stored, and when output is required, the memory system—either paper tape or *magnetic media*—is carried by the operator to a tape or diskette drive in the output photo unit. The drive reads the memory, and type is produced.

10-9.

Character display is a feature of the Compugraphic CompuWriter IV. Photo courtesy Compugraphic Corporation

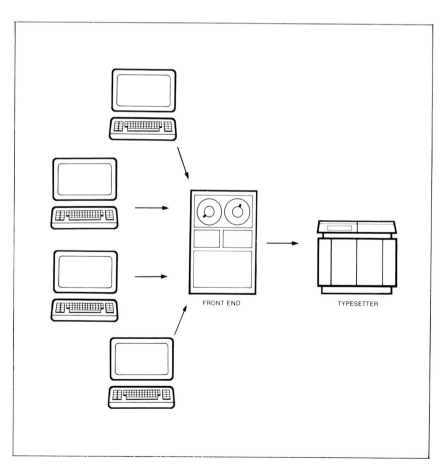

10-10.

Off-line typesetting.

Direct-entry and off-line typesetting have created two kinds of keyboards: counting and noncounting. The *counting keyboard* assesses the space taken up by each letter in a line and signals the operator when a designated limit is about to be reached. The operator must then decide precisely where that line will end. That decision is indicated by depressing a "return" or similar key. In direct-entry typesetting, the line is set immediately. In off-line keyboarding, a *justified tape* or magnetic media is produced that can be taken to the photo unit for output.

Noncounting, or "idiot" keyboards, by contrast, do not require the operator to pause with every line. After the entire job has been typed on the keyboard, the system's computer makes end-of-line decisions as the job is being set. Obviously, this innovation permits much faster input and more efficient off-line typesetting. Once the faster second-generation systems replaced operator decisions with computerized ones, typesetting output increased from a maximum of four to more than two hundred fifty lines per minute. Type houses and larger printers interested in speed moved to noncounting keyboards in the 1960s.

Computer Unit

As the description of noncounting keyboards suggests, the computer unit is the brains of the typesetting system (fig. 10-11). Apart from end-of-line decisions, it performs two decisive functions: hyphenation and justification (h&j).

The *hyphenation logic* is a set of rules programmed into the computer unit that determines where a hyphen should be placed in a word that is broken at the end of a line. For example, two of the most common instructions in the program are to hyphenate before the syllables *-ing* or *-tion* to produce such word divisions as *row-ing* and *automa-tion.* Ironically, the very efficiency of the system results in errors, for no program can instruct the computer to follow every nuance of word division. Even monosyllabic words, such as *swing* and *thing,* will be hyphenated as *sw-ing* and *th-ing.* Such errors may be corrected by the *exception dictionary,* a list of correctly hyphenated words. When the hyphenation logic program is about to make a hyphenation decision, the exception dictionary (a second program) is crossed-referenced to make sure the word being hyphenated is *not* included. Often, the exception dictionary can be expanded as hyphenation problems are discovered. If the operator is diligent in adding mistakes to the dictionary, the number of errors can be greatly reduced over time. Some errors are inevitable when a computer makes hyphenation decisions. Nevertheless, the time saved by increasing the operator's input speed exceeds that lost by making corrections after the type has been set.

Hyphenation is required to allow for proper *justification.* If lines are to be set evenly on the right margin, words must often be broken at the ends of lines. Otherwise, the lines can be justified only by adjusting spaces between words and letters, which often results in a poorly composed page (fig. 10-12).

For justification and end-of-line decisions, the typesetting operator advises the computer unit, either directly or through memory, of the line length designated for a particular job. The computer unit then counts character widths in each line of type. It automatically makes the end-of-line decision when no further words or syllables can be included in the line. The copy is justified by distributing the amount of remaining space evenly between words and letters, according to maximum and minimum specifications determined by the typographer. Thus, the computer unit decides how many words will fit into the line and how much space to insert between words.

10-11.

The Alphatype CRS 9900. Photo courtesy Alphatype Corporation

It seems   probable that   the Chinese have long been in possession of the art of printing, though from whence derived it cannot now be ascertained. Possibly   it may have been from the practices   adopted by the   Ninevites and Babylonians. The art never advanced beyond the style of the   block books of England

10-12.

Poor wordspacing in justified copy.

10-13.

Photo unit: the Berthold tpu 3608. Photo courtesy Berthold Group

Photo Unit

Phototypesetting output is produced in the photo unit (fig. 10-13). There are several types of photo units, but all employ the same basic technique: a high-intensity light beam is flashed through a master film negative containing all the characters of the selected typeface. The beam exposes a light-sensitive medium on which the images of the characters are produced.

Depending on the system, the master negative (known as the *film font*) may take the shape of a disc, grid, or strip (fig. 10-14). The film font either revolves on a drum-shaped *image carrier* within the machine or the light source moves from letter to letter while the font remains stationary. In either case, the individual letters are correctly positioned with respect to the light source (fig. 10-15). In most machines, the movement of the font drum or light source is controlled by an electronic sensor, which determines that the correct letter is in position before a signal is sent to the photo unit to expose the character. Naturally, the more automated the system, the greater the speed with which type can be set.

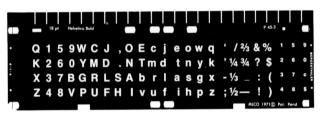

10-14.

Font strip.

10-15.

Action of font strip in second-generation phototypesetting.

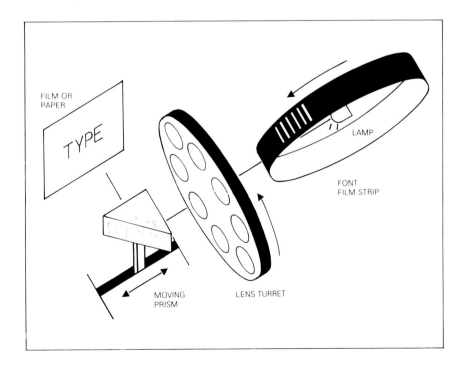

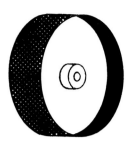

10-16.
Font drum.

Because of the variety of competitive second-generation systems available, several different combinations of film fonts and accompanying image carriers have been created. Perhaps the most popular is the one alluded to above—a plastic *film strip* attached to a *font drum.* The drum rotates at great speed within the light-tight photo unit, bringing the strip into the appropriate position for setting each letter (fig. 10-16). In an alternative system, disk segments or complete disks are connected to the drum (fig. 10-17). Many font drums hold more than one (and as many as 16) different type styles, thus saving the time of stopping the machine and changing the film fonts whenever a different type style is required. One common strategy is to engineer the film font so that it contains more than one complete typeface. The number of type styles that can be held on the font drum at one time is known as the number of fonts *on-line.*

Several Mergenthaler machines use a grid system (fig. 10-18). Letters and other characters are imprinted in various locations on the grid. When typesetting occurs, the entire grid is illuminated. If, for example, the letter *A* is to be typeset, the other characters on the grid are masked off and only the *A* is exposed. The grid system is slower than systems employing a rotating font drum with an attached film font.

Once a beam of light has passed through the film font, it does not immediately strike the photographic paper, but passes through a lens and a series of mirrors. The system's optics allow different sizes and even variations of type to be set (see fig. 10-15). When different sizes of type are used in the same job, the photo unit signals the lens to move nearer to or farther from the light source, as required, to produce the correct type size. Instead of a single moving lens, some machines employ several lenses: one for 8-point type, another for 10-point, another for 12-point, and so on. This second strategy tends to produce slightly sharper type, but the number of available type sizes is limited by the number of lenses. Optical systems perform a second function as well. In some systems, moving mirrors ensure that lines of type are set from left to right. The lens and font strip do not move laterally; only the mirror moves, thus preventing individual letters from being superimposed on one another.

The optical systems of the second-generation machines are in large part controlled by electronics. Computerization of the photo unit produced absolutely straight baselines and perfect justification by the 1960s. Com-

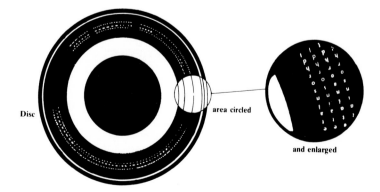

10-17.
Disk font and disk segment.

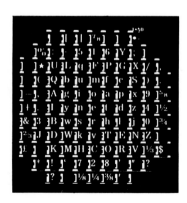

10-18.
Phototypesetting grid.

10-19.

Magnetic cartridges. Photo courtesy 3M Corporation

bined with the perfected mechanics of a rotating font drum, electronics allowed for unmatched typesetting speeds. A human being, however, could not possibly keyboard 150 lines per minute to match the average rate at which the machines set type. Only the final element of second-generation typesetting, memory, would allow printers to exploit the improvements in their systems.

Second-Generation Memory Systems

Two major kinds of memory are available in second-generation phototypesetters: paper tape and magnetic media.

Similar to the Braille system employed by the blind, paper tape stores information by a series of coded holes. Each letter is represented by a unique pattern of perforations (see fig. 10-7). Paper tape was first used by newspapers in the 1940s. The Teletypesetter, a machine that received newswire reports, automatically coded the information on tape, which was then inserted into a specially adapted Linotype for decoding and output. Only the last of the first-generation typesetters, such as the Intertype Foto-matic, introduced paper tape to commercial typesetting.

A major advantage of any form of memory is versatility. If an error is discovered, one ought to be able to change memory without retyping a line, a paragraph, or worst of all, a whole job. Yet the holes punched into paper tape cannot be changed: if corrections are needed, a new tape must be created. Tapes are fragile; they can be damaged as they are being fed through a paper tape reader and must be safely stored when not in use. Finally, it is sometimes difficult to determine whether a tape represents an original or corrected version of a job. Typesetters resorted to using different colored tapes for different proofing stages.

By the 1960s, a better method of storing information had been developed: *magnetic media*. The range of materials includes magnetic tape, floppy disks, diskettes, cards, cartridges, and cassettes (figs. 10-19 and 10-20). Magnetic (or mag) tape and floppy disks are by far the most popular storage media used in typesetting today.

All magnetic media are constructed from plastic that has been coated with iron oxide. Each is inserted into a *drive unit* (different kinds are manufactured for the different media) containing a *read/write head* (fig.10-21).

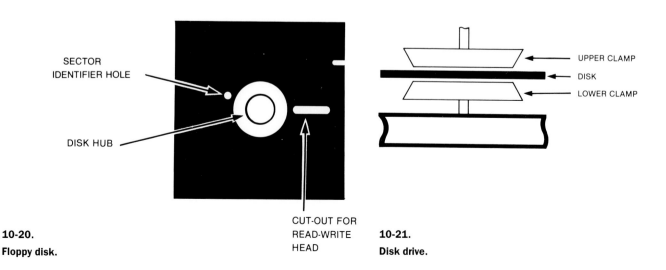

SECTOR IDENTIFIER HOLE

DISK HUB

CUT-OUT FOR READ-WRITE HEAD

UPPER CLAMP

DISK

LOWER CLAMP

10-20.

Floppy disk.

10-21.

Disk drive.

Impulses, produced through the magnetization of the iron oxide, form invisible patterns comparable to the perforations in paper tape. The read/write head not only imposes the patterns onto the medium, but is capable of decoding them and retrieving data that had been previously created. When the input is edited, the new magnetic patterns of the edited copy are written over the previous copy.

Mag tape is stored on reels that are usually 9 inches in diameter and capable of holding hundreds of thousands of words. As with paper tape, jobs are stored in the order in which they are created. Thus, an operator who wishes to edit a particular document usually must look through a sequence of other jobs before he or she finds the one needing corrections. Floppy disks store information using a *random access memory*. This means that a specific job can be accessed, or retrieved, immediately.

Disks, like tapes, hold vast amounts of data. The capabilities of different magnetic media vary, but one 8-inch floppy disk can usually retain as much as 500 pages of information. Diskettes, which look a lot like 45 RPM records, are, along with disks, the most popular storage media for phototypesetting. Diskettes, as their name implies, are basically smaller (5¼-inch square) versions of disks. Priced at under five dollars, disks and diskettes store information much more cheaply—and much more efficiently—than paper tape. They are also reusable; when a job has been completed, it can be erased from the disk and new information can be stored. Editing is much simpler, and duplicate back-up copies can be made quickly and inexpensively. For the 1980s and 1990s, disks and diskettes are the preeminent media.

THE THIRD GENERATION

Typesetting engineers did not stop at 150 lines per minute. As part of the information explosion of the 1960s and 1970s, typesetting technology moved farther and faster. Indeed, the experimental third generation of the 1960s was really just a precursor of the fourth- and fifth-generation machines, which can set type at the rate of 6,000 lines per minute.

The third generation still uses photo optics, but the role of the film font has changed. In 1967, Mergenthaler Linotype, in cooperation with CBS Laboratories, announced the Linotron 1010 and CRT scanning, an ingenious substitute for second-generation technology.

As noted, a CRT is a cathode-ray tube, similar in appearance to the picture tube of a television set. A typical television screen image is composed of lines called *rasters* or dots called *digits* (fig. 10-22). In America, television images are made up of 525 horizontal lines per inch. CRT typography creates letters in the same way, but in much greater detail, using as many as 2,600 lines per inch. Typesetting that creates letters from individual dots is called *digital* or *digitized* typesetting (fig. 10-23).

Letters are transformed into digital images through a process called *scanning*. The first step is to project a letter on the surface of the CRT via a photographic negative . Then the scanner "reads" the pattern of the letter and converts it into digits or rasters. Finally, the lens receives the image from the CRT screen and projects that image, in one photographic exposure, on phototypesetting paper (fig. 10-24). The digits of the typeset image are not visible . Nonetheless, at very high typesetting speeds, the quality of the image can suffer. Speeds of 3,000 lines per minute and more are often used only to produce quick proofs; slower speeds are used for reproduction-quality type.

10-22.

Low, medium, and high resolution.

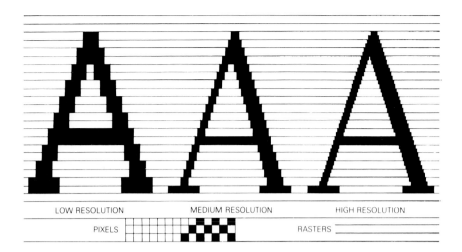

LOW RESOLUTION   MEDIUM RESOLUTION   HIGH RESOLUTION

PIXELS   RASTERS

10-23.

Digital composition creates letters by combinations of dots.

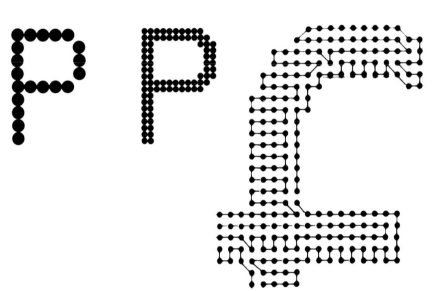

10-24.

Third-generation system: Alphatype Mini Multiset. Photo courtesy Alphatype Corporation

CRT typesetters constitute the third and fourth generations of typesetting machines. This more sophisticated technology has not yet *superseded* the technology of the second generation, however, primarily because of the cost of the newer machines. Since speed is the greatest advantage of the equipment, only the busiest type houses and printers have enough work to justify the expense. Yet cost considerations aside, the CRT is desirable for several other reasons:

- Moving parts are virtually eliminated; fewer moving parts means a concomitant decrease in needed repairs.
- Type can be immediately extended, expanded, or slanted without the use of special film fonts.
- Special logos and ideographs can be stored and reproduced as necessary.
- Because photographs are normally reproduced through halftone dots, digital halftones can be incorporated directly into the typeset image.

By the 1970s, many companies were producing CRT typesetters. Mergenthaler is still a leader in the field, but Monotype, Intertype, Compugraphic, and Berthold are other major manufacturers (fig. 10-25). In the 1980s, prices for digital typesetting have steadily decreased. Compugraphic, AM, and several other manufacturers now sell third- and fourth-generation units for less than $30,000.

10-25.

Mergenthaler Linotron 1010. Photo courtesy Allied Linotype

THE FOURTH GENERATION

Because the fourth generation comprises a second group of typesetters based upon the CRT, some historians consider this generation to be a subgroup of the third. But an important change characterizes fourth-generation technology: the photographic film font has been completely scrapped. Instead, the images created on the CRT are transmitted as video signals directly from the *VDT*.

When the CRT typesetter was "trained" to paint rasters or digits on the CRT screen, the last moving part—the photographic master—could be discarded. The photographic negative was thus eliminated, but photography was not—digital images were still exposed onto photosensitive paper. The important innovation of this generation is that the "master" is a digital pattern stored in the computer unit of the typesetting system (fig. 10-26). An image sent by the operator to the photo unit is translated into video signals. The CRT then deciphers those signals to recreate the page. The scanned image is immediately projected onto photographic paper or film.

If you do not require third- or fourth-generation speed, the less expensive second-generation machines are still available. The marketplace is fractured because the technology has, to a very great degree, outrun the needs of many potential buyers. In the 1980s and 1990s, the third- and fourth-generation machines will take over because their costs are consistently declining—to the extent that they are now competitive with the second generation.

The earliest fourth-generation machines made their way onto the market in the late 1970s. Compugraphic's MCS 8000, Itek's Mark 8, Mergenthaler's Linotron 202, and Autologic's APS series are among the competitors (fig. 10-27).

10-26.

The digital scanning of fourth-generation typesetting.

10-27.

The MCS 8000. Photo courtesy Compugraphic Corporation

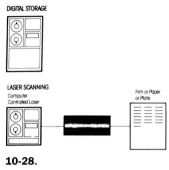

10-28.

Fifth-generation typesetting.

10-29.

The Lasercomp. Photo courtesy Monotype International

THE FIFTH GENERATION

Typesetting technology has followed a logical course. Photographic negatives were eliminated in the third generation; photo optics was discarded in the fourth; and all photographic techniques were completely abandoned in the fifth, although the term *phototypesetting* is still often used. Fifth-generation machines continue to use light to set type. The difference, however, is that the light is produced by lasers and the type is physically scorched onto the paper.

The laser image is created by direct impulses from the computer unit. When signaled by memory, the computer retrieves a digitally stored pattern and communicates it to the laser unit, which immediately reproduces the pattern in horizontal rasters at speeds that usually range from 500 to 1,500 lines per minute (3,000 lines per minute is the maximum) (fig. 10-28). Because laser scanning patterns are directly output onto paper, there is no need for traditional photoprocessing techniques.

Laser typesetting quality is expressed in terms of dpi, or dots per inch. The quality produced by laser output units varies tremendously, from less than 100 to over 2,000 dpi. Professional-quality laser typesetting has been defined by the Typographers International Association as a minimum of 1,000 dots per inch.

Laser typesetting's greatest advantage is that many different kinds of images can be digitally created. Photographs, logotypes, and all other artwork need not be added at later stages in the production process, but can be simultaneously incorporated with the text. Complete pages may be created more quickly than in other composition methods. The specially treated paper used in laser typesetting is not as expensive as photographic paper. Depending on the nature of the laser typesetting equipment, savings in paper costs may justify the costs of the machines. There is a broad diversity of capabilities among laser typesetters. *Desktop publishing* output units are available for under $5,000. Professional type houses spend hundreds of thousands of dollars for more sophisticated equipment.

Fifth-generation typesetters were first made available for commercial use in the early 1980s. Two of the earliest examples are the Monotype Lasercomp and the Mergenthaler Omnitech/2000 (fig. 10-29). Type sizes vary from 5- to 256-point. Because no film font is used, the complete complement of available type sizes and typefaces is on-line at all times.

NEW GENERATIONS

One can safely predict several new technological routes for the next 15 to 20 years. Two of these developments will be expensive alternatives limited to heavy-volume typesetters, at least in the near future. Two others have already changed input methods.

First, today's automated page layout systems are now producing complete pages intact (fig. 10-30). These machines will be further developed into perfected *direct-to-plate* typesetting systems, which will complete the erosion process of traditional typesetting technology, resulting in the elimination of the typesetter altogether. With a direct-to-plate system, input produced on a standard video display terminal will be photographed directly on plates. All of our current production steps will be eliminated. In fact, this technology has already been established. The *Observer-Dispatch* of Utica, New York, has successfully used the first direct-to-plate system in the world.

A second, and more remote, innovation is *voice-activated typesetting*. During the early 1980s, several typewriter manufacturers consistently promised, but never produced, a typewriter that would accept voice input. Computers that can "understand" several words do exist, but the problems of context, dialect voices, and similar-sounding words are enormous. How is the machine to know whether one is saying *two, too,* or *to?* These and other problems have relegated voice input to the status of an interesting possibility, not expected technology. However, if solutions are found, the look of typesetting rooms will be changed radically.

Third, and most important for the 1980s, is the development not of new technological hardware but of new applications. As discussed, technology has developed to the point that the latest machines can actually do

10-30.

Automatic page layout system.

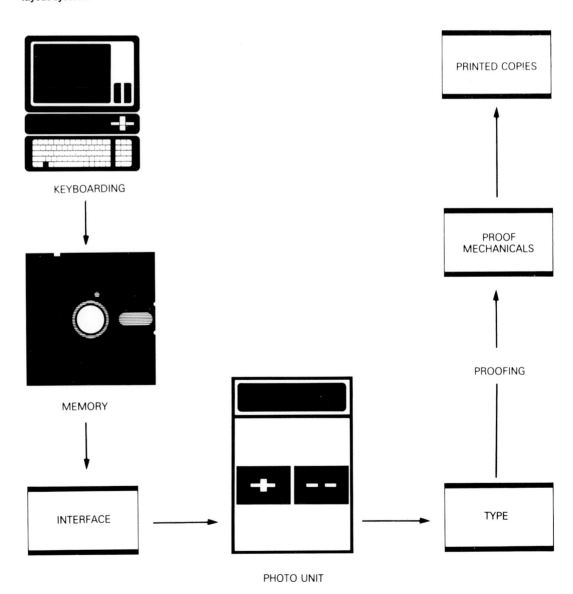

KEYBOARDING

MEMORY

INTERFACE

PHOTO UNIT

TYPE

PROOFING

PROOF MECHANICALS

PRINTED COPIES

more than is required of them. Over the next decades, we will explore the ways to use existing technology rather than create new machines.

Among the most important of those applications is *interfacing*, the transmission of data from one computer to another. Today, most typeset documents are keyboarded on word processors or personal computers. Stored in computer memory, these documents can be sent to the typesetter electronically, via telephone calls or magnetic media, instead of as paper copies. (See chapter 13 for a full discussion of interfacing methods and possibilities.)

In the mid-1980s, hundreds of type houses and thousands of type users established interfaces: up to a 50 percent savings in type costs has been predicted by the National Composition Association. If recent trends continue, interfacing will become increasingly popular. In 1973, only 1 percent of all typeset documents did not require retyping. By 1983, over 30 percent of all jobs were interfaced and industry experts expect that figure to jump to as high as 80 percent by 1993.

Desktop publishing is the second innovation which has already had great effects. Introduced in 1985 by Apple Computers, it has been very popular among type houses as a proofing method and among in-house production facilities as an inexpensive technology. Priced at under $10,000, desktop publishing units generate output at 300 dots per inch. The quality is not high enough for professional typesetting but it is acceptable for many in-house applications.

Display Typesetting

One area that the new technology will not drastically affect is the typesetting of photodisplay letters. Machines designed specifically for setting headline type have undergone few significant changes in the past twenty years.

Display type can be set in three ways: with a text phototypesetter that simply enlarges the size of body type; with a display phototypesetter that uses automatic letterspacing; and with a display typesetter that uses manual, or *visual*, letterspacing. Of these options, the first is the least desirable; although most machines that set 8-, 10-, and 12-point body type can also set display, they do not adjust readily for kerning, or spacing between characters. Thus, when certain letters, such as *T* and *y*, are juxtaposed, they appear too far from one another (fig. 10-31). A text typesetter is capable of varying letterspace, but perfect results require superior ability on the part of the operator and, even then, several proofs are needed. Kerned pairs that are set on a display machine that allows for visual space adjustments look much better. And, although this slower process may seem to be a costly alternative, in actual practice setting display lettering on a machine specifically developed for that purpose is cost-effective as well as aesthetically advantageous.

Most photodisplay machines set type on 2-inch-wide strips of photographic paper (figs. 10-32 and 10-33). Available type sizes vary, but 18- to 144-point is a common range. The operator adjusts type size by turning a dial on the machine that moves a lens into the appropriate position. The type font is either a strip or disk. Individual letters are exposed through one of two processes: *contact-printing*, in which the font comes into direct contact with the paper; or *projection-printing*, in which light is projected through the negative letter. In the former process, only one type size is available per type font, whereas in the latter, the machine can adjust for many different sizes. After exposure, the photo paper is developed either directly in the machine or in an independent processor.

Type
Type

10-31.

Display versus text type.

10-32.

AM Varityper Headliner disk.

AUTOMATIC LETTERSPACING DEVICES

Automatic letterspacing machines can be operated in normal light (rather than darkroom) conditions. They enable the operator to predetermine the spacing values that will appear between all letters and words in a job. The machine itself has the task of imposing those values in a consistent fashion —as each letter or word is selected and set, the spacing values are automatic. Indeed, they cannot be altered easily. Two of the most popular automatic letterspacing display devices are the Varityper Headliner and the Compugraphic 7200 (fig. 10-34).

The Headliner can produce type sizes ranging from 6 to 84 points. The operator sets letters manually by moving the font wheel, approximately the size of an LP record, to the appropriate position, and then pressing an exposure switch. Each wheel contains one film font capable of producing only one type size. Because the Headliner uses contact printing,

10-33.

Phototypositor typesetting strip.

10-34.

AM Varityper Headliner photodisplay device. Photo courtesy AM Varityper

letterspacing, wordspacing, and film processing are automatic. The operator has initial control over letterspacing values but does not control spacing between individual letters. This feature allows typesetting display to be produced quite simply, but the type quality is usually inferior to that produced by machines using *visual letterspacing,* the process by which the operator, rather than the machine, makes spacing decisions. When the desired display line is completed, a lever is lifted to cut the type and begin automatic processing. The Headliner is thus a self-contained unit. No further equipment is needed to produce type.

The CG 7200 is similar to the Headliner in that letterspacing and wordspacing values are initially programmed by the operator. The major difference between the two devices is that the 7200 is keyboard controlled; instead of pushing a switch to set each letter individually, the CG 7200 operator types lines on a keyboard, which are then composed by projection through film strips. Thus, many sizes are available in each typeface. When the setting of display is completed, photographic paper is automatically moved into a light-tight cassette, which eliminates the need for darkroom processing. The paper must be developed in a photostabilization processor available from Compugraphic and other manufacturers.

Although the Compugraphic 7200 seems more versatile than the Headliner, the Headliner has been very popular: the machine and the font wheels are relatively inexpensive, and the automatic processing capability makes display typesetting easier.

VISUAL LETTERSPACING DEVICES

Machines that allow visual letterspacing are preferable to automatic letterspacing devices if quality, rather than speed, is most important to the buyer. Popular visual letterspacing machines include the Phototypositor (fig. 10-35) and the StripPrinter (fig. 10-36).

The Phototypositor is manufactured by Visual Graphics Corporation. It is similar to the Headliner in that many models are available and type is automatically processed within the machine. Projection exposures are used to create type from 2-inch-wide film strips. The operator inserts a strip into the machine and moves the appropriate letter into position. Each letter is exposed with a flip switch, after which the operator uses levers to carefully move the photo paper the precise amount of letterspace desired. With some practice, it is possible to produce perfectly spaced type. Typographers are able to choose any amount of word- and letterspacing (fig. 10-37). Many typefaces are available in sizes ranging from 18 to 144 points. Condensed, expanded, slanted, and curved type is possible with special distortion lenses. Because the position of the typesetting paper can be adjusted, one can also produce type set on curved, staggered, and angled baselines. Finally, type can be double-exposed to produce shadowed or background effects.

The StripPrinter also uses a film strip. Type sizes typically vary from 6 to 96 points, but a special model, the StripPrinter 90, sets type as large as 180-point. This machine differs from the Phototypositor in that the type is contact-printed, so each font strip is capable of producing only one type size. The operator preselects a letterspacing value as a guide to accurate spacing between all letters. Guidelines on the film strips can be used to advance each character. Those guides, however, can be "violated" whenever kerning is required. After exposure, development and fixing of the paper is completed with a photostabilization process.

Many other photodisplay units are available. Visual letterspacing devices include the Filmotype, the Staromat, the Morisawa, the Typro, the

10-35.

The Phototypositor. Photo courtesy Visual Graphics Corporation

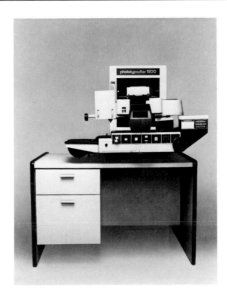

A B C D E F G H I J K L M N O P Q

10-36.
StripPrinter font.

Typography
Typography
Typography
Typography
Typography

10-37.
Letterspacing values in display type.

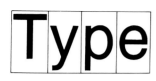

10-38.

Visual versus automatic letterspacing.

Protype, and the Visutek. Although several of these machines are no longer manufactured, they continue to be used by many type houses and printers.

Automatic letterspacing display units tend to be less popular among type houses because the same quality can be produced more quickly with text typesetting systems. Differences in quality between visual and automatic letterspacing are not difficult to discern (fig. 10-38). Although many advertising agencies and book typographers will accept nothing less than the high quality achieved by visual letterspacing, newspapers and the producers of newsletters and catalogs often use the less-expensive automatic letterspacing devices.

Disadvantages: Typesetting with Care

Any new technology can be misused, and certainly typesetting equipment is no exception. Both in the mid-1970s and mid-1980s, the typesetting industry suffered through eras of some alarmingly poor work. As untrained operators learned how to use increasingly sophisticated equipment, the simplification of typesetting technology created a class of operators who were able to use the machines, but could not use them well.

Many of the errors made by new operators are simple mistakes of ignorance. But there are several new pitfalls created by the technology: fake faces, blurring, and typeface distortion.

Fake Faces. Some typefaces available from equipment manufacturers are only vaguely similar to original versions. Fake faces (fig. 10-39) come in two varieties: poor reproductions of classic typefaces like Caslon, Bodoni, and Baskerville, and "clones" of contemporary faces that have been created to avoid payment of a royalty to the original type designer. Both the novice and experienced typographer must be careful when ordering type, especially since clones are sometimes advertised as the original faces.

Blurring. Phototypesetting output may create slight variances in typeface designs due to several causes. A face may be distorted if, for instance, a film font is improperly loaded on the font drum. In addition, overexposure, underexposure, and imperfect alignment of mirrors or prisms will cause blurring of the typeset image. Finally, changes in humidity, extreme temperatures, potent chemicals, and old phototypesetting paper all may contribute to blurring.

Typeface Distortion. The typesetter must be specifically instructed to set type without variation. Some type houses routinely condense or expand certain typefaces.

10-39.

Pseudo-Helvetica.

ABCDEFGHIJKLMNOPQRSTUVWXYZ
abcdefghijklmnopqrstuvwxyz   0123456789
ABCDEFGHIJKLMNOPQRSTUVWXYZ
abcdefghijklmnopqrstuvwxyz   0123456789

TYPESETTING INPUT AND OUTPUT

In a phototypesetting system, input requires two different talents of the operator. Copy must first be introduced into the system, either by keyboarding or, recently, by one of several data transmission methods. The operator, however, must also properly encode the document to meet the typographer's specifications. The often complex typographic coding required is the basic difference between keyboarding and typesetting. Those who typeset documents understand typography and typographic requirements and are able to convert those demands systematically into phototypesetting commands.

Output choices are less complex. If input is still a process of constant human decision on a day-to-day basis, output is a computerized matter. After a button or two is pushed, output units are self-regulating producers of type that seldom fail to function. The only significant skill involved is selecting machines with the features and capabilities required.

Using a Typesetting Keyboard

Understanding technical terminology is the first step toward becoming a skillful typesetter. It is not possible to present a complete course in typesetting in one volume. Each manufacturer supplies manuals and technical data sheets, which are the best sources of information about specific systems. It is possible, however, to present a list of commands that any computerized phototypesetting system is programmed to understand.

A *keystroke* is the result of the physical act of hitting a key on the terminal to create a letter, give a command, or elicit a response. The keyboard can be divided into seven categories: alphanumeric keys, spacing keys, pi font keys, typographic command keys, editing keypad, user-defined keys, and file management keypad. *Keypads* are specific, segregated portions of the keyboard that perform a single function (for example, file management).

11-1.

Typesetting alphanumerics.

ALPHANUMERICS

Alphanumeric keys correspond to all characters, including the 26 letters of the alphabet, the numbers 0 to 9, and punctuation marks (fig. 11-1). Although the alphanumeric keypad usually contains several extra punctuation marks, and fractions other than the standard ¼ and ½, it is otherwise very similar to the typewriting keyboard and completely different from the Linotype keyboard (fig. 11-2).

The current "qwerty" key pattern is sensible because many of today's typesetters have begun their careers as typists or word processors. This pattern was not always the standard, however. As the linecasting machines were replaced by phototypesetters, the "etaoin shrdlu" keyboards featured on the Linotypes and Intertypes were changed as well. The entire

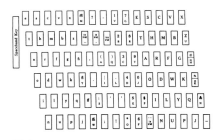

11-2.

Linotype keyboard.

typesetting industry retrained as it retooled in the 1950s and 1960s.

Ergonomics is the science of industrial design devoted to creating machines and tools that humans can use simply and efficiently for maximum benefit. The qwerty keyboard was *not* ergonomically designed. In fact, it was designed in the nineteenth century with the express purpose of slowing down typists who jammed their machines because they typed too quickly. In the advent of phototypesetting, the qwerty choice was made because it was the standard typewriting keyboard design. There is little doubt that other systems would allow for faster input, but retraining the entire industry to use a new keyboard design will not happen again soon. The qwerty keyboard is with us and will most likely remain the standard.

The alphanumeric keypad is itself divisible into several sections. The alphabet, numbers, and common punctuation marks, such as the comma and period, are all in precisely the same places as in the qwerty keyboard. The dollar sign, plus sign, and other symbols that are used less often are scattered throughout. Keyboarders quickly develop a feel for the particular keypad being used.

SPACING KEYS

Every typesetting keyboard has a minimum of four spacing keys: the spaceband, the em space, the en space, and the thin space.

Usually located at the bottom of the alphanumeric keypad, the spaceband is used for wordspacing, *never* for indentation. Word processors and typists often indent five spaces for paragraphs, but this is absolutely forbidden to typesetters. Also, whereas word processors and typists insert two spaces after periods, typesetters must not follow this practice.

Spacebands are used to justify type. When a computer unit is making end-of-line and hyphenation and justification decisions, it counts the number of spacebands (or, in ordinary terms, the number of spaces between words). The width of each spaceband is determined by dividing the amount of available space by the total number of spacebands in a particular line. The amount of actual space taken up by a spaceband will therefore vary from line to line, depending on how much space the computer unit must fill out to justify each line. Thus, if five spacebands are regularly used for a paragraph indent, the indent will vary from paragraph to paragraph because the spacebands will be larger in some lines, smaller in others (fig. 11-3). Similarly, if two spaces are consistently typed after a period, when the computer unit substitutes its return codes for the last spaceband in each line (known as *stripping out* the spacebands), one space will remain and the line will not be justified (fig. 11-4).

The *em space, en space,* and *thin space,* known together as the *fixed spaces,* are used to avoid difficulties caused by the variable spacing of the spaceband. The typographer, who usually specifies the paragraph indent to be used, typically calls for two ems (the em is sometimes called the *Mutt* or *Mary*). This means that the typesetter presses the em space key twice before beginning to type the first word of each paragraph. Because the em is a fixed space, the double em will take up precisely the same amount of space each time it is used and every paragraph will be evenly indented.

Occasionally a typographer may wish to have paragraph indents with slightly less space (especially when a short line length is being used, as in newspaper columns). In those cases, a combination of ems and ens may be used. The en (known as the *nut* or *Nancy*), is half the width of the em. It is useful in situations where a unit of smaller space must be consistently imposed. For example, figure 11-5 shows a table in which quantities

11-3.

**Fixed versus
variable spacing as
paragraph indents.**

Since his street photographs became widely known in the mid-1970s, Joel Meyerowitz has rightly been recognized as a master of color photography.

At a time when ''art'' photographers were just beginning to work with color, Meyerowitz's brilliant color of the medium set a standard of excellence. A standard that has rarely been surpassed.

The artist's work has changed since those early days of color, when the hustle of New York street life were his themes. For a number of years he has been operating in a mellower mode, and examining the Cape Cod landscape.

Since his street photographs became widely known in the mid-1970s, Joel Meyerowitz has rightly been recognized as a master of color photography.

At a time when ''art'' photographers were just beginning to work with color, Meyerowitz's brilliant color of the medium set a standard of excellence. A standard that has rarely been surpassed.

The artist's work has changed since those early days of color, when the hustle of New York street life were his themes. For a number of years he has been operating in a mellower mode, and examining the Cape Cod landscape.

11-4.

**Justification
problems caused by
double-spacing
after periods.**

As in many of his earlier works, the French composer seems to equate religious ecstasy with fortissimos, especially percussive fortissimos. That predilection lends a certain sameness to his "St. Francis" music—at least so far as could be heard on this occasion. Always a more interesting composer and a less ideologically rigid one than some of his followers, such as Pierre Boulez, Mr. Messiaen does know how to make a joyous racket unto the Lord. That cannot be denied him.

11-5.

**Alignment of
figures with fixed
spacing.**

Five years ended the last day of February In millions of average fiscal year 1982 dollars, except per share data	1982	1981*	1980
Revenue and other income			
as reported	$ 769.3	$ 653.5	$ 556.3
in constant dollars	769.3	718.0	691.2
Net income			
as reported	12.4	7.7	
in constant dollars	5.3	.4	
at current cost	7.2	.7	
Net income per share of common stock			
as reported	2.04	1.23	
in constant dollars	.77	(.05)	
at current cost	1.10	(.02)	
Net assets (shareholders' equity) at year end			
as reported	80.7	71.6	
in constant dollars	111.0	107.0	
at current cost	114.6	112.1	

There was a letter from a banker in Denver:

Although I have made many presentations in my life. I cannot imagine doing anything as terrifying as being a sports commentator, and I really admire you for being a contestant.

Mr. Talerico, you were quoted as saying you had never done anything constructive in your life. [But] you had a very constructive effect on me and have made me reevaluate my current situation. You exhibited persistence and stamina by studying so hard and traveling so far for the audition, grace under pressure by performing so well during the audition, and good sportsmanship by congratulating the winner. I wish that more of the people I worked with exhibited these qualities, and I wish that I exhibited them more often myself.

And then there was the letter from Olympic champion gymnast Bart Conner:

It seems every so often, perhaps not often enough, we are reminded of how fortunate we really are. Today I read [the column] about Greg Talerico's dream to be a TV color commentator. Thanks for helping me to remember that I am a very lucky man.

I happened to win a couple of gold medals in the Los Angeles Olympics. Because of that success plenty of opportunities have come my way—one of them being a spot as a CBS-TV commentator. And yet I only won the gold by .025 in parallel bars—it was very close! Just because I won by .025 points does it mean that my opinions carry any more weight than Greg Talerico's?

Life is strange and very unfair. The tears that welled in my eyes for Greg Talerico reminded me that I'm a very lucky man.

ESQUIRE/AUGUST 1986

11-6.

Alignment of text with fixed spacing.

ABCDEFGHIJKLMNOPQRSTUVWXYZ
1234567890 1 ´ ` ˆ ˜ ¨   ˊ ˇ ˘ ˙ ˚ , . : SC 1234567890
Ææ Œœ ßℝ©%‰$✂☎✿ fififfififlfif
◄ ► ▲ △ ♦ ◊ ● ○ ● ● ● ← ↓ ↑ → ¡¿ – — —— /&‖ _ ● × □

11-7.

Pi font.

that are expressed in four or fewer digits are aligned in vertical columns. In order to maintain a consistent width, the typesetter had to add space to quantities with fewer than four digits, compensating for the absence of numerals. Each space added is thus a unit of fixed space equal to the widths of the digits themselves and much smaller than a typical em space—the width of this dash. That unit is the en space. Indeed, numerals are almost invariably designed to be the width of an en to make alignment easier.

Often equal in width to the comma and period, the thin space traditionally has been half the width of an en. Many contemporary phototype systems, however, use a thin space that is slightly larger, one-third (rather than one-quarter) the width of the em. Like the en, the thin space is used for numerical alignment; for example, the quantities in figure 11-5 that have decimal points occupy a width equivalent to four ens and a thin space.

The en space and thin space are also used for indentations in an outline format. If a variable space is inserted after the outline number or letter, the outline body copy will not align (fig. 11-6). At times, the typesetter will use a thin space after periods to provide perfectly symmetrical spacing (sometimes known as French spacing). Some typesetting systems allow the operator one "fixed space" key, which can be defined according to individual need. One-and-one-half and two ems are frequently used.

The most common error of typists and word processors who keyboard for typesetting is excessive use of the spaceband. A general rule to keep in mind is that whenever you type two successive spacebands, you are making an error.

PI FONT KEYS

Pi (π) is a Greek letter used in the formula for the radius of a circle. Since this and many other characters are often used in technical typesetting, the term *pi character* has grown to include any mathematical and scientific symbol, punctuation mark, foreign language character, and diacritical mark that is not necessary in ordinary typing. (Such characters are called "sorts" by some typesetters because handsetting required that they be sorted out of a common area of the job case.) A complete collection of pi characters is called the *pi font* (fig. 11-7).

Typesetting manufacturers have created several ways to access pi characters. If a complete collection is needed, as in scientific typesetting, the best method is simply to purchase a ready-made font that contains the set. In second-generation typesetting, font strips are manufactured with four tracks, each consisting of a different typeface or variation. For scientific typesetting, the first two tracks will often be the roman and italic versions of a face—Baskerville, for instance. The third track will be devoted to a display sans, such as Helvetica. The fourth and last track will be filled with pi characters: a mathematical symbol will be substituted for the *A*, a diacritical mark will take the place of a 7, and so on. In later typesetting generations, a digitally stored font of pi characters is purchased and loaded on-line along with several other fonts.

Type houses specializing in technical typesetting may also order fonts constructed to meet their specific needs. Such fonts may include original art, trademarks, and customer logotypes. However, custom-made pi fonts can easily cost more than $1,000, as opposed to $100 to $400 for ready-made fonts.

A second, less expensive alternative is to use special keystrokes to access pi characters. The typical track of a font may have as many as 120 spaces for characters. After devoting 52 to the alphabet (uppercase and lowercase), 10 to numbers, and perhaps another 28 to punctuation marks, one can fill the remaining 30 or so spaces with pi characters. A digital typesetter allows as many as 256 spaces and thus offers greater accessibility to special characters.

If a special pi font is not used, depressing the *a* or *b* key will not suffice to access the pi characters (you will simply access the *a* or *b*). Instead, special keystroke combinations must be used, which have various names, depending on the manufacturer: *precedence keys* (Compugraphic) and *supershift* (AM Varityper) are two of the most common. The precedence key works in the same way as the shift key. If you wish to type the capital *A*, you depress the shift key, hold it down, and type the *a* key. Likewise, when you wish to access a supershift or precedence character, you type the supershift or precedence key followed by the character identified on a chart supplied by the manufacturer (fig. 11-8). *Precedence A* may be a dagger, a Greek letter alpha, or a mathematical symbol, depending on the individual chart, which of course must correspond to the geography of the actual font.

If few pi characters are necessary, standard manufacturers' charts and fonts can be purchased. If a customized pi font is required, the type house must construct its own chart.

The names and functions of many pi characters may be unfamiliar (fig. 11-9). A large solid dot, often used to separate the items in a list, is called a *bullet*. The open square that serves the same purpose is called a *ballot box. Ampersands, daggers,* and *double daggers* may be more recognizable. The ampersand (&) is a favorite among type designers. Dozens of different styles exist, and some typographers even "collect" them. Any complete font will have a *registration mark* and a *copyright symbol.* Brackets, braces, and other typographic ornaments are less popular now than in the nineteenth century. The ornaments shown in figure 11-10 are called *dingbats.*

There are also special typographic constructs that are not pi characters. The *ellipsis* is a row of three dots signifying a pause (as in . . .). Lines set below words for emphasis are *underscores.* A straight line set for ornament or to separate text on a page is a *rule* (fig. 11-11). A row of dots used to draw the reader's eye from one item of information to another across the page is called a *leader.*

11-8.
Pi chart.

11-9.
Pi characters.

11-10.
Dingbats.

11-11.
Rules.

TYPOGRAPHIC COMMAND KEYS

The simplest typographic commands are those that determine the typesetting parameters of the copy being set. Line length, linespace, typeface, and type size must be keyed into the electronic memory for output on the photo unit. To this end, two methods are popular: specific keys and alphanumeric mnemonics (figs. 11-12 and 11-13).

There are dozens of specific keys for typographic commands, each of which is dedicated to a major function. In many systems, linespace is controlled by the *linespace* key, type size by the *size* key, and typeface selection by the *font* key.

Some less-imposing keyboards are not so specific. Instead, they feature one key, perhaps a supershift, to allow access to many typesetting codes. If the operator wishes to establish a type size, he or she may issue a command sequence such as *supershift, T,* and *S,* followed by a number and ending with a closing *supershift.* This strategy, called *mnemonics,* does not require dozens of specific keys. A chart featuring the different codes is supplied by the manufacturer. Codes that are commonly used are quickly memorized.

One advantage of specific keys is that they are actually easier to use. Once the operator has undergone an initial training session to become acquainted with the function of each key, he or she simply types the appropriate command rather than consult a chart to figure out a complicated mnemonic sequence. Also, a single specific key command is quicker than a mnemonic sequence of several keystrokes.

Specifying Typographic Patterns

Although many typographic command keys (or mnemonic sequences) exist, the most important control typographic patterns on the page, spacing, tabular composition, and special characters.

There are four basic typographic patterns: justified, flush left/ragged right, flush right/ragged left, and centered (fig. 11-14). The specific key that controls flush left/ragged right composition (typesetting that is unjustified on the right and justified on the left) may be labelled *FL* (flush left), *left, QL* (quad left), or may simply be an arrow pointing to the left. If mnemonics are employed, similar letter combinations are required. A very different strategy is used by systems that have an *insert space* key. If a line is to be set ragged left/flush right, the insert space key is typed at the beginning of each line. Instead of justifying the line by counting the spacebands and distributing the space equally, the computer unit will distribute *all* available space in the line wherever the insert space character appears (in this case, at the extreme left). In ragged left/flush right composition, the result is a series of lines that are even on the right and uneven on the left. For centering, two insert space keys are used, one at each margin. The computer unit of the typesetter automatically divides the available space in the line equally, distributing half to the right and half to the left.

Every typesetting keyboard provides a flush left key, often located just to the right of the return key (fig. 11-15). In most typesetting systems, all lines of type will be set justified on the given line length unless the operator specifies otherwise. A common error of apprentice typesetters is neglecting to set the last line of each paragraph flush left, with poor wordspacing as the invariable result (fig. 11-16). The proper sequence at the end of paragraphs is the final period, a flush left code, and a return code. Unless the operator is making end-of-line decisions, the return code is used *only* at the ends of paragraphs or individual lines (and not lines of a

11-12.

Phototypesetting keyboard with command keys.

11-13.

Simplified phototypesetting keyboard.

Phototypesetting

Prior to World War II, several typesetting machines were constructed employing photographic principles, but the first successful machine of its kind was the Fotosetter, introduced to the printing trade in 1950 by the Intertype Company after three years of successful field testing.

Phototypesetting

There had always been a possibility of combining photography and typesetting even before the days of Mergenthaler. Luther Ringwalt's *Encyclopedia of Printing*, published in 1871, included an account of a process called "phototypography."

Phototypesetting History

After the successful introduction of the Intertype Fotosetter, competing firms also developed photographic machines. The English Monotype Company marketed the Monophoto. Like the Fotosetter, it was a variation of the original hot-metal machine.

Phototypesetting

The ultimate use was rapidly changing from the age-old procedure of relief printing to photomechanical printing in which a plate is substituted for metal printing type. Photography was introduced.

11-15.

Flush left and return keys.

With a great many health plans, many of the complications arise after surgery.

Before they've taken any of the dressings off, you find yourself up to your neck in red tape: endless forms to fill out, deductibles, co-insurance. You're hardly finished with the doctors and it seems like now you need a lawyer or an accountant.

But US Healthcare performs a minor miracle when it comes to major medical problems.

11-16.

The last line of each paragraph must be flush left.

11-14.

Typographic patterns: *(from top)* flush right/ragged left, flush left/ragged right; centered, and justified.

Dropping out of a photo school that "restricted his personal creativity," New York fashion photographer Ian Miles learned the craft by reading the entire Time-Life series. Seven years later, as he was flipping through a photo magazine, he spotted an ad for the new edition of the encyclopedia.

11-17.
End-of-line decisions are best made by the end-of-line logic of the computer unit.

paragraph). Otherwise, copy is automatically "wrapped around" from line to line until the end of the paragraph is indicated by the sequence just described. Those who attempt to make end-of-line decisions using non-counting keyboards are often confronted with terrible results (fig. 11-17). If flush left/ragged right copy is specified, a special code is typed at the beginning of the job to override the justification mode until the job is completed.

Hyphenation and Dashes

Four keys perform hyphenation and dash functions: the hyphen, the dash, the discretionary hyphen, and the em baseline underscore.

The hyphen should be used between words, such as *on-line,* that appear in the middle of a line. It should never be used to end lines. The hyphenation logic and exception dictionary of the computer unit will make hyphenation decisions as necessary. If the hyphenation logic makes an incorrect choice, the error will be noticed. For example, the computer's logic may hyphenate the word *swinger* incorrectly as *sw-inger,* so the *sw-* appears at the end of a line. This error, referred to as a *bad break,* must be corrected by placing a *discretionary hyphen* between the syllables of a word that ought to be hyphenated, overriding the hyphenation logic. Careful typesetting operators will often anticipate possible errors and place discretionary hyphens in words to avoid bad breaks before they are made. In this case, if the word does not appear at the end of a line, the discretionary hyphen is not needed and the computer logic ignores the code. In certain words, such as *swing,* a discretionary hyphen may be placed at the beginning of the word to signal the computer logic that that word should not be hyphenated.

In addition to hyphenation codes, the keyboard will have two keystrokes that are one em in width but have different functions. The *em dash* key allows for a dash between words at approximately the top of the x-height (fig. 11-18). The *baseline em underscore* key, used to create rules and underscores, is accessed by pressing the shift key and 6 key at the same time.

Tab Keys

Typesetting in columns, known as tabular composition, is among the most difficult to perform. Of the several keys that are dedicated to easy tabbing, the most important is the tab key itself, which moves the position of the cursor from column to column. The cursor is a blinking box or underscore that provides a visual display of the typing position on the CRT screen. Other tabular keys that may appear on the keyboard include the *tab return,* which provides space between lines but allows the operator to remain in the tab field being used; the *call tab* key, which permits the operator to move directly to a specific table; the *carriage return* key, which moves the cursor to the left margin, outside the tabs, as in typewriting; the *set tab* key, which allows the operator to create tab fields of given lengths and patterns; and the *clear tab* key, which eliminates all previous tabs, cleaning the slate for more composition.

Spacing Keys

Apart from the keys for linespace and the special em, en, thin, and fixed spaces, many systems provide keys that further control letterspacing and

Now is the time—

Now is the time‗‗‗‗‗

Now is the time

11-18.
(from top) Em dash, rule, and underscore.

wordspacing by setting minimum and maximum values. For instance, if slightly extra (or slighly less) space is needed between lines of type, *plus point* or *minus point* keys are useful. Some systems feature *plus linespace* and *minus linespace* keys as well. Several AM Varityper products have a *secondary linespace* key, which allows the operator to set two different linespaces in the same job; primary linespace might be 12 points in 10-point body type, while a secondary linespace of 18 points might be indicated for the space between display type and body.

The *no flash* or *space only* keys tell the photo unit to move over the width of the character but *not* to photograph it. In figure 11-19, the *space only* command has been issued twice (notice the commands *SO,* or space only, and *SX,* or space only off). The first word actually to be set is *Massachusetts;* the *no flash* command was used to move over the width of the 36-point *MIT* before setting *Massachusetts* in 8-point. That command sequence was repeated in the second line, which contains the word *Institute.* Finally, the last line to be set was a flashed 36-point bold *MIT* followed by the 8-point roman of *Technology.* In most systems, the *no flash* command stays in effect until it is removed by a special command, such as *space only off* in the example shown. *No flash* is sometimes referred to as *no escapement,* because escapement is the mechanism used to move the photographic lens and mirror of the photo unit.

The *no space* key performs the opposite function. It is an instruction to the photo unit to set the character following the command but *not* to move over after flashing. The result is that the next character is set over the one just exposed—the desired consequence when building a fraction such as $\frac{27}{64}$ or placing a foreign language accent above a letter (fig. 11-20).

11-19.

No space.

KEYBOARDING INSTRUCTIONS		TYPESET COPY
₅P36 SL080 F4 SM1800₅ ↵		
₅SO₅ MIT ₅SX P08 F1₅ □ Massachusetts QL ↵		**MIT** Massachusetts Institute of Technology
₅P36 F4 SO₅ MIT ₅SX P08 F1₅ □ Institute QL ↵		
₅P36 F4₅ MIT ₅P08 F1₅ □ of Technology QL ↵		

11-20.

A *no space* command is issued to set the umlaut over the capital O.

11-21.
Editing keypad.

EDITING KEYS

To edit copy, the operator must be able to move it about the screen. Four essential keys devoted to screen movement are usually labeled as arrows that point left, right, up, and down. These keys automatically move the cursor in the direction indicated. The *home* key moves the cursor directly to the top left corner of the screen being displayed. Some systems provide for scrolling, meaning that the cursor will automatically move beyond the current screen to the beginning or end of the document (fig. 11-21).

Several keys allow the operator to actually make corrections. The *backspace* key is used while copy is being input to erase the keystroke displayed just before the cursor. *Delete character, delete line,* and *delete paragraph* keys enable the typesetter to correct errors detected in the first proof. An *insert* key permits words or phrases to be added to existing copy. When the insert key is struck, the insert mode is immediately invoked, and any copy that is typed will be added at the location of the cursor. After the insert is completed, the typesetting terminal may be returned to the replace mode, which means that any new copy typed over existing characters will replace those characters rather than be inserted between them.

USER-DEFINED KEYS

Many typesetting terminals allow the operator to program several keys to serve as a form of shorthand for inputting information. The two most important applications of these user-defined keys (UDKs) are initial formatting and the quick repetition of words or phrases.

Programming of a UDK is quite simple. The operator strikes the *format* command key, one of the user-defined keys, and the desired sequence of characters to be stored. Thereafter, each time the UDK is struck, the sequence will be repeated. For instance, a pattern consisting of a 30-pica line length, 10-point type size, and 12-point linespace, set flush left, may be programmed as one UDK. A second UDK containing different parameters may be programmed for the same job. Especially in jobs where two distinct type patterns are repeatedly used, the work saved in not having to type out each change in typeface, line length, and linespace can be tremendous.

The UDK is also used for storing repetitive phrases. If *Mohawk Valley Community College* will be used seven times in an article to be set for a local newspaper, a shorthand UDK will permit one keystroke to be defined as the four-word string. Thirty-one keystrokes are converted into the one keystroke of a UDK, obviously increasing the operator's typing speed.

FILE MANAGEMENT KEYPAD

In computerized typesetting, a document or typesetting job is called a *file.* The operator is able to command the terminal to manipulate files through the file management keypad (fig. 11-22). Although some systems are engineered with other file management functions, at least six keys are essential to all.

Enter File

The terminal screen uses a memory independent of the permanent magnetic memory system being used. This screen memory is volatile, meaning that if the terminal is turned off, the memory will be lost. Some method is required to move documents from the volatile screen memory to the perma-

11-22.
File management keypad.

nent magnetic memory. After a document is keyboarded on screen, the operator strikes the *enter file* key, types in a file name, and presses a *command* or *execute* key. The last signals the terminal to perform the function at hand, whether storing, deleting, or setting. In this case, the file will be entered in permanent memory. Novice typesetters often make the frustrating error of neglecting to include a file name in the sequence. Some "user-friendly" systems alert the typesetter to the error; many do not. If the error is made on the latter machines, the entire document is lost and must be rekeyboarded.

Call File

After a job is typed and stored in memory, a proof is made and corrections are indicated by a proofreader or editor. The operator's next function is to edit the job to correct these errors. To do so, he or she must call the document to the screen memory by striking the *call file* key. A typical pattern is to strike the call file key, type the file name, and strike the execute key. Corrections can then be made with the editing keypad.

Replace File

Corrections that are made when one edits a file on screen are not automatically incorporated into the computer's permanent memory. In fact, a common error for beginning typesetters is to correct a file but neglect to replace the incorrect version with the correct version on screen. The appropriate process, common to virtually all systems, requires the operator to make all corrections, move to the end of the screen file, strike the *replace file* key, and then strike the execute key. Some typesetting terminals require that the cursor be placed at the end of the file because these systems will truncate the file *wherever* the cursor appears. "User-friendly" systems do not require any particular placement of the cursor.

Delete File

At some time after the last proof has been corrected and the final galley typeset, the document will be deleted from memory. Erasures should be performed only when it is absolutely certain that no further setting will be necessary (it is best to wait until the job has actually been printed and approved by the customer). Insuring against overzealous deletions is not expensive: diskettes that hold hundreds of pages of memory cost less than five dollars. A representative keystroke sequence for the deletion of a file is to strike the *delete file* key, type the file name, and press the execute key. In many cases, files are never deleted from memory. Annual directories, college catalogs, revised editions, and price lists are often permanently stored so that, when minor changes are required, only editing, and not complete keyboarding, is necessary.

Call Index

The list of files that are stored in memory is known as the *index*. If several disks are used at the same time, they must be differentiated. When a file is to be edited or set, the correct disk will then be immediately handy. Numbering, alphabetizing, or simply writing file names on the disk itself are all useful methods. If the operator is uncertain as to whether a particular file is on a disk, the *call index* key will bring a complete list of all files on the disk to the screen.

11-23.

The typesetting system. Photo courtesy AM Varityper

Mark File

The *mark file* key distinguishes for the computer unit the particular file that must be set. In systems like Compugraphic's MDT (fig. 11-23), a visible x appears next to the appropriate marked file. The disk is then removed from the MDT and inserted into an independent computer unit, which reads the magnetized mark on the disk and orders the photo unit to set the designated job. If several files are to be set, a *queue* is automatically created by the computer unit. Each file waits its turn according to its position in the file index.

If a *standalone* unit like the Mergenthaler CRTronic or AM 510-II is being used (fig. 11-24), files can be moved directly from the screen to the photo unit. After the *typeset file* key is struck and the appropriate file name or number is typed, that file is immediately moved to the typesetting queue. If no other files are in queue, typesetting of the file begins instantly. A critical consideration when purchasing standalone units is the manner in which jobs are queued. Some systems allow the operator to continue keyboarding new files as edited ones are being typeset. Other, less economic, systems tie up the screen memory during typesetting, needlessly consuming many hours of valuable keyboarding time. This thwarts—and bores—operators who are interested in retaining a smooth job flow.

11-24.

The standalone. Photo courtesy AM Varityper

Proofing Input

After a job is keyboarded and typeset, the typesetting operator makes, or *pulls,* a series of proofs. A *proof* is a copy of the typeset image that is checked for errors before moving through the succeeding steps in the production process. The phrase *pulling proof* is a reminder of hot-metal typesetting, when a single sheet of proof paper was physically pulled through a special press.

The first proofing stage, called *galley proofs,* are photocopies of typesetting output. The customer receives the galley proof along with the original copy for the job, compares the two, and makes corrections or additions on the galley proofs, using the standard proofreader's marks discussed in chapter 8. Proofreading is a skill demanded of editors both in book and magazine publishing. Some companies also employ specialist proofreaders who are particularly competent in discovering errors and marking proofs.

A second galley proof may or may not be required, depending on the number of errors and changes in the first proof. After all galley proofs have been corrected, the job will be reset. Mechanicals are then created by graphic artists who use wax or rubber cement to affix the parts of the page onto heavy boards. *Page proofs,* photocopies of the mechanicals, allow the customer to perform two tasks. The proofs are checked to ensure that all specified corrections have been made. In addition, the customer will see type in page position for the first time. The page proof is the last relatively inexpensive place to make changes. The cost of corrections increases geometrically with each successive stage: galley proofs are very cheaply repaired; page proofs are more expensive; and later proofs are prohibitively costly to correct.

Changes in page proofs usually do not require new galleys. Corrected lines are individually reset and fixed into position over errors. Professional type houses often supply two sets of corrections because a single line of type may be damaged or lost by the mechanical artist. If several corrections are necessary in a paragraph, it is often simpler to reset the entire paragraph. Even when only one correction is required, the operator must be certain that the addition of words in a line does not affect the number of lines in the paragraph. If a correction takes up two lines where the original galley proof contained one, the correction will obviously not fit. The entire paragraph—and perhaps a page—will have to be reformed.

After the page proofs are checked, negatives, from which printing plates are eventually made, are shot from the mechanicals. The third proofing stage, *blueprints* or *blues,* are photographic contact prints of the negatives. Any correction made at this point is very expensive: new type, new mechanicals, new negatives, and new blues will all be required. Because any changes other than corrections of the typesetter's errors are charged to the customer, those who demand extensive revisions at the blues stage are charged rightfully high prices.

For some jobs, the customer may also require a *press proof,* the last possible proofing stage. In the offset lithography process, the press proof is the first impression of the actual printing press run. The proof is therefore available only from the printer. Designers or editors ordering the proof are usually interested primarily in approving color reproduction quality.

Correcting Input

Professional typesetters produce galleys that are often remarkably free of errors. Although speed is important, many type houses and printers recognize that corrections are often more time-consuming than the original keyboarding. Keyboarding for typesetting, then, should be as accurate as possible. A quick check for errors before outputting is cost-effective in the long run, and fewer mistakes in the galley proofs inspire greater confidence in the customer.

A common misconception about typesetting, however, is that it *primarily* involves keyboarding. Efficient use of the keyboard's command keys, an understanding of proof marks, and the talent to edit galleys quickly are each at least as important as raw typing speed. Of course, the fewer errors one initially makes, the quicker one edits. You should always keyboard within your own typing speed; slower typists can be superior typesetters by using the full capabilities of their system. Perhaps the most useful editing function keys are those that permit *search and replace* (fig. 11-25).

SEARCH AND REPLACE

As errors are detected, they are marked in proof. When the typesetting operator calls a file to the screen and begins to make corrections, one strategy is to use the directional keys to move the cursor through the document so that changes are made as they are located. However, if there are only a few errors (as there should be), a far quicker way to edit is to use a search function, which finds all instances of a programmed series of letters. The operator types the *search* key followed by the word or phrase that must be corrected (some systems limit the number of characters in a search to eight). The *central processing unit* (CPU) of the terminal immediately institutes a search for the given set of characters. When each instance of the character is found, the cursor stops, enabling the operator to make the correction.

11-25.

Search and replace keys.

Perhaps editors have decided the word *glamour* should be spelled *glamor*. A difficult name or foreign word may have been frequently misspelled in manuscript. The solution is to use *global search and replace,* an even faster function than a simple search. The operator first types the command or key for global search and replace, and then types the offending string of characters. The memory of the file is scanned and each error is corrected as it is found until all such errors have been eliminated. The obvious advantage is that if an error is made consistently, a global search saves time. The typesetting operator makes the correction once and the power of the computer takes over. Some systems even permit the global search and replace to correct errors throughout an entire disk. This is a useful feature if the document being set requires more than one file (such as a book or a long magazine article).

The global search can also facilitate the initial inputting of a document. Suppose the job is a brochure that is being produced for a pharmaceutical firm, and a quick glance at the manuscript reveals that the phrase *deoxyribonucleic acids* appears in the six pages of manuscript a minimum of eight times on each page. Complicated chemical and technical terms are difficult to type; even the fastest typists slow down considerably when keyboarding unfamiliar words. The experienced typesetting operator realizes this and may well decide to type *dx,* or some other abbreviation, every time the troublesome *deoxyribonucleic acids* is used.

If that decision is made, a global search and replace can be performed to substitute the appropriate string of characters for every instance of *dx*. By exploiting the technological capability of the machine, the operator can increase his or her productivity, saving 20 keystrokes each time *dx* is used, for a minimum total of 960 difficult keystrokes in one job.

One must be cautious, however, when creating patterns of characters that will be globally replaced. If you are typesetting an article about the history of typography, the letters *cm* could be used to mean *Caroline Minuscule*. But remember that *every* instance of *cm* will be replaced by the global search and replace function. Thus, the sentence, *This face is the acme of medieval calligraphy* will become, *This face is the aCaroline Minusculee of medieval calligraphy*. It is best to use combinations of consonants that never appear together.

Not all typesetting systems allow for global search and replace. Some permit a search with no replacement, whereas others perform the function only once, forcing the operator to retype the search and replace sequence for repeated errors. Although the function is not indispensable, it is a valuable feature of better typesetting systems.

FILE SIZE

A computer stores information in the form of *bytes*, each of which is made up of eight *bits*. In general, one byte of computer storage is required for each character typed on the screen. Memory capacity is usually expressed in K, or thousands of bytes. As a rule of thumb, each K of memory is equivalent to about one-half of a typewritten, doubled-spaced 8½- by 11-inch page. A system that allows for a 10K file size will therefore permit files that are a maximum of five pages long.

Those who use typewriters, naturally type to the bottom of the first page and then begin another. But novice typesetters who follow the same pattern create editing problems. If the entire character space of a file is consumed, there is no room for a sentence, or even a word, of copy that the customer may wish to add. One can, of course, divide the file into two files and add the copy. But file names may then become confused.

The better practice is to always leave a buffer of memory when typing files. The terminal display line keeps a running count of the number of characters remaining in the file (fig. 11-26). Most systems will signal the typesetting operator when that number has dwindled below several hundred characters. When the signal (usually an audible tone) is given, the operator should stop input at the end of the nearest paragraph, store the file, and begin a new one. The files will thus be conveniently numbered and allowance will be made for future additions. Files should be stored in complete paragraphs, because the operator has no idea where ends of lines

11-26.

Third- and fourth-generation devices provide a running character count to the typesetting operator.

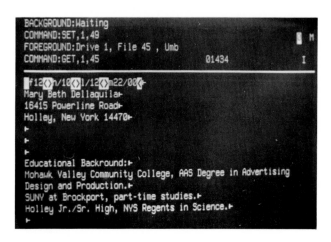

will occur within the body of a paragraph. Again, the only time returns should be used when setting body copy are at the ends of paragraphs.

File sizes can range from 10K to the entire disk storage space, which may be as much as 800K. If the latter option is available, the operator should again be prudent. When files are constructed of 125 pages, it may take several minutes to scroll through several dozen pages before reaching a particular one where a correction should be made. File lengths of less than 20 pages are more handy.

REVISIONS

A revision involves more than a few corrections or additions to a manuscript. In fact, one must decide early on in the revision process whether it is less time-consuming simply to retype an entire job.

Customers are usually unaware of the intricacies of file editing and may believe a revision will save money. However, because type houses bill at an hourly rate, customers must take special care to estimate the total amount of time needed to revise existing memory. They must also keep in mind that handwritten revisions, no matter how neat, take longer to keyboard than typed manuscript.

The yes-or-no revision debate is usually decided by two considerations. First, and most obvious, how much of the material needs to be revised? If more than 50 percent of the matter to be set is new copy, editing stored memory will probably cost the customer more than retyping will. Not only is it more difficult (and therefore slower) to keyboard handwritten revisions, but more time must be devoted to proofreading and editing the job. If less than 25 percent of the copy consists of new material, however, the process may be cost-effective.

A second consideration regards the kind of material that is being revised. There are three types of composition. *Straight matter* is simple body copy, for example, the paragraphs that appear in a newspaper, magazine, or novel (fig. 11-27). *Tabular composition* consists of tables, charts, and graphs (fig. 11-28). The most difficult of all is *technical type,* which includes mathematical, scientific, and financial typesetting (fig. 11-29). As figure 11-30 shows, technical type is not as easy to produce as it may appear on the printed page. The typesetting operator must make literally hundreds of coding decisions to set one complicated equation.

Straight matter by far involves the simplest choice: editing is relatively easy, and if the amount of revised copy is reasonable, the revision process will be less expensive than retyping. Tabular composition and technical type, on the other hand, are both more difficult to revise. Moreover, that difficulty is compounded if the person doing the revisions did not originally set the type. Like other craftspersons, typesetters incorporate a personal style into the creation of technical matter: one typesetter's obvious pattern might appear to be jibberish to another. Since technical type rates can range from $30 to as much as $85 per page, anything other than straight matter should be rekeyboarded unless the revisions are minor. If, for instance, the structure of a complicated multilevel fraction is changed, it should not be revised. Whichever the decision, formulas, technical language, tables, graphs, and fractions are never inexpensive to produce.

11-27.

Straight matter.

While foundry types and those produced on Monotype equipment differ physically, there remains some confusion of terms, as well.

Type metal consists of varying amounts of lead, tin, and antimony. Foundry type also contains a minute amount of copper, and more tin and antimony than types cast in Monotype machines. However, several firms that cast types from Monotype matrices to sell to printers at rates below those of regular typefounders, also rightfully call themselves founders.

In the United States such types are not generally considered "foundry" types even though they may contain a greater amount of tin and antimony (for durability) than the standard Monotype faces. The only traditional typefounder currently producing types in this country is the American Type Founders Company. This in no way denigrates production techniques of such firms as MacKenzie & Harris, Baltimore Type, and Los Angeles Type Founders, which fulfill a most necessary function.

The basic physical differences between foundry type and standard Monotype is the latter's lack of the groove. An exception is the type of the Thompson Typecaster, a machine manufactured by the Monotype Company until 1967. Thompson-cast type retains the groove at the bottom but at the back of the letter rather than in the center, as in the standard foundry type.

Numerous European typefounders still operate as noted on the list on page 120. Most of these firms sell type for the American market through agents in the United States. Some European type sold here is cast upon the Didot body, and although originally of a different

11-28.

Tabular composition.

STATISTICAL PROCEDURES

FIGURE 4.1
T-TEST — MALE AND FEMALE APTITUDE TEST SCORES

Male (X_{i1})	$(X_{i1} - \overline{X}^2)$	Female (X_{i2})	$(X_{i2} - \overline{X}_2)^2$
80	$(80 - 82.857)^2 =$ 8.16	90	$(90 - 80)^2 =$ 100
95	$(95 - 82.857)^2 =$ 147.45	75	$(75 - 80)^2 =$ 25
85	$(85 - 82.857)^2 =$ 4.59	90	$(90 - 80)^2 =$ 100
80	$(80 - 82.857)^2 =$ 4.59	65	$(65 - 80)^2 =$ 225
80	$(80 - 82.257)^2 =$ 8.16	80	$(80 - 80)^2 =$ 0
80	$(80 - 82.257)^2 =$ 8.16		
75	$(75 - 82.857)^2 =$ 61.73		
$\Sigma X_{i1} = 580$	$\Sigma (X_{i1} - \overline{X}_1)^2 = 242.84$	$\Sigma X_{i2} = 400$	$\Sigma(X_{i2} - \overline{X}_2)^2 = 450$

11-29.

Technical type.

$$\dot{M}_f = \frac{\dot{Q}_c + \dot{Q}_g - \dot{Q}_b + \Sigma \dot{Q}_1}{H_f + (M_a/M_f)(\overline{C}_p)_a(T_a - T_r) - (M_e/M_f)(\overline{C}_p)_e}$$

where:

$\dot{M}_f$ = fuel flow rate, kg/h (lbm/h)

$\dot{Q}_c$ = net glass-chemical reaction energy J/h (Btu/h)

$\dot{Q}_g$ = throat glass energy flow, J/h (Btu/h)

$\dot{Q}_b$ = batch energy flow, J/h (Btu/h)

$\Sigma \dot{Q}_1$ = summation of energy-loss flows, J

H_f = fuel net heating value, J/kg (Btu/

(M_a/M_f) = air-to-fuel mass ratio

$(\overline{C}_p)_a$ = mean specific heat of air, J/kg·°C

T_a = incoming air temperature, °C (°F)

T_r = reference temperature, °C (°F)

(M_e/M_f) = exhaust-to-fuel mass ratio

$(\overline{C}_p)_e$ = mean specific heat of exhaust, J/k (Btu/lbm·°F)

T_e = exhaust temperature, °C (°F)

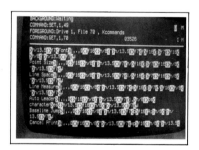

11-30.

Technical type on screen.

Output: Papers and Film

Output options are not limited to the hardware discussed in chapter 14 on typesetting equipment. After the equipment decision is made, a typesetting manager must choose, from among several possibilities, the actual medium on which output will be produced.

Decisions about output material depend in part upon the typesetting system selected. Some systems permit output on conventional papers, photographic papers, and lithographic film. Others limit the typesetting manager to one or two materials.

PHOTOGRAPHIC PAPERS

It is possible to use conventional high-contrast photographic paper in devices that produce display lettering. The paper, however, is not light-sensitive enough to be used in text typesetters (which depend on far faster exposure times). The long developing, fixing, and drying times necessarily rule out hand processing. On the other hand, automatic processors cost a great deal of money, offsetting any economic benefits one might obtain from using this less costly material. Thus, whether processed manually or automatically, conventional photographic paper is false economy.

A better choice is RC (in this case, resin-coated, not rapid contrast) paper. Slightly more expensive than commercial, high-contrast paper, it is also more durable. The resin coating resists processing stains. Moreover, images produced on RC paper last indefinitely, whereas output on other paper fades or becomes discolored within two to three months. If, as often happens, the gap between typesetting and other phases of the production process is extended, the permanent RC output eliminates the need for a time-consuming and expensive resetting of the type. Finally, RC paper dries more quickly than other papers, an advantage important to advertising typographers and in-house production facilities interested in a quick turnaround.

The major disadvantage of RC paper is that it requires an automatic processor costing from $3,000 to $5,000 (fig. 11-31). The paper is developed, stopped, fixed, and washed in the processor's four baths.

S-grade (stabilization) paper costs about the same as RC paper, but the processor is less expensive—about $750 (fig. 11-32). Developing agents are embedded in the paper's photographic emulsion. Upon processing, an activating agent produces an image, and development stops after the paper is immersed in a second bath, the stabilizing agent. Yet, in spite of its name, stabilization paper is not stable very long. Images fade quickly (usually within three months) because the paper is not fixed to remove all chemicals. The typeset image will last longer if care is taken not to expose the processed paper to normal light.

Newspapers are an ideal candidate for S-processing: mechanicals are used only once and then discarded because news obviously must be recomposed each day. Documents that may be revised, on the other hand, or advertisements that will be run repeatedly over the course of months or years, should be set on RC paper. The majority of the industry is moving either to RC or various hybrid papers that have greater permanence than stabilization papers but can be processed in the inexpensive S-processor. Otherwise, RC papers are not compatible with S-processors.

Produced in 150-foot rolls, typesetting paper is manufactured in 2-inch, 4-inch, 6-inch, 8-inch, and 12-inch widths. Many machines cannot hold paper that is wider than 8 inches. However, newspapers with short column lengths use the 2- and 4-inch widths. For a long time, Kodak was

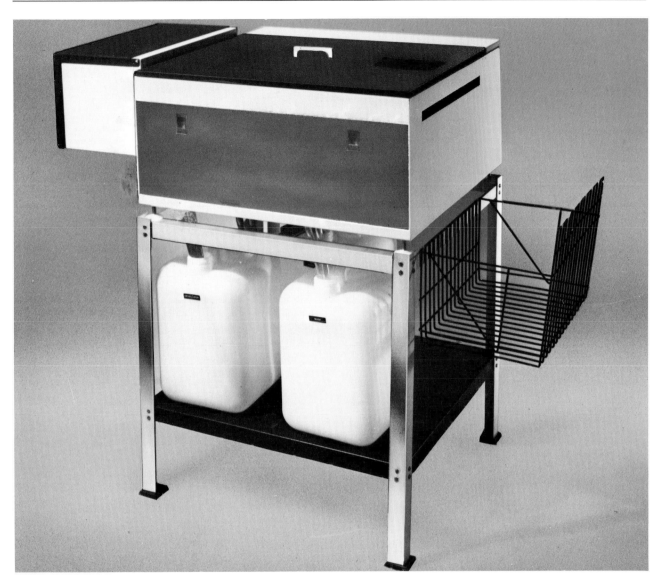

11-31.

ML-314 RC processor. Photo courtesy Allied Linotype

11-32.

Kodak Ektamatic processor. Photo courtesy Thomas Maneen

virtually the sole manufacturer of phototypesetting paper, but, in the last five years, many companies have begun to sell competing products.

RC- and S-grade papers both sell for about $45 per 150-foot, 8-inch-wide roll, or about 30 cents per foot. A book typographer will use dozens of rolls per month. Because of the various proofing steps involved, the type house, on average, will output every job at least twice—meaning that a single 300-page book will require about 4 rolls of typesetting paper. Because of the expense, type houses and other heavy-volume users are constantly looking for ways to cut paper consumption.

LITHOGRAPHIC FILM

Lithographic film is the final photographic product that can be used in typesetting systems. In the 1960s, film was a popular material because of the higher-quality image it produced. That advantage has waned, however, with advances in paper products. Furthermore, film costs nearly twice as much as paper and must be developed in an expensive automatic processor. When lithographic film is used, the output is a negative version of that produced on photographic paper. Photocopying as a method of making proofs is therefore impossible because the result would be an illegible negative. *Diazo proofs,* made by contact printing litho film onto specially treated paper, are more time-consuming and expensive than photocopies.

NONPHOTOGRAPHIC MATERIALS

A very popular recent method to cut costs involves the use of computer printers. Documents are sent to the printers via electronic cable. After the electronic interface is completed, cheap printouts serve as initial proofs (fig. 11-33). This method enables the typesetter to correct obvious typographic errors and omissions before typesetting with the more expensive photographic paper. The quality produced by computer printers is not nearly good enough for reproduction.

As discussed, digital laser phototypesetters require a special non-

11-33.

The Digitek 3000 with laser printer for first proofs. Photo courtesy Itek Composition Systems

photographic paper. This paper is less expensive than any other output material. The savings, however, could not begin to justify the cost of a sophisticated laser typesetting system—until 1985, when desktop publishing offered a new nonphotographic alternative. *Laserwriting,* though not phototypesetting, produces near "typesetting-quality" output on ordinary paper. More than 15,000 desktop units were sold in the first six months after they were introduced. Most were purchased by type houses and printers who discovered an ideal, cheap proofing system.

Processing Photo Papers

The first step in processing typesetting is to remove the paper from the photo unit. With the exception of those photodisplay machines that automatically process type, all typesetters store exposed photographic paper or film in a similar device: the light-tight cassette (fig. 11-34).

There are many varieties of cassettes, but they all work on the same principle. As type is produced, the photo unit automatically feeds paper into the cassette (fig. 11-35). After typesetting is completed, the paper is cut, and the cassette is lifted from the photo unit and carried to the processor. Because several inches of paper must be manually pushed toward the rollers before the rollers begin to pull the paper into the processor automatically, the operator *must* feed extra paper into the cassette. Otherwise several inches of imprinted rather than blank paper will turn completely black when developed (fig. 11-36). Also, the cover of the typesetter should be left open to ensure that the cassette is in place before the next galleys are set. If not, the paper will be exposed when the cover is opened.

After feeding paper into the processor, the operator must close the processor cover quickly to expose as little paper as possible. S-processors are invariably tabletop models. The automatic RC-processors can be divided into two categories: those that use straight-through processing and those that do not. Straight-through processors are engineered in such a way that the paper is processed in a straight line, moving horizontally through the rollers with no vertical movement. Alternatively, some processors are more complicated arrangements of top and bottom roller systems; paper is more likely to jam as it is moved up and down through the many roller stations. All S-processors move paper using a straight-through pattern.

Both kinds of processors can be equipped with drying units. If a drying unit is not used, galleys are clipped or pinned to a line for air drying. RC paper dries slightly faster than S-grade papers.

Whether RC- or S-grade processors are used, the equipment must be frequently cleaned and the chemicals changed periodically. When one is setting corrections to be stripped over mechanicals, it is especially important to control development. Exposure is rigidly controlled by the photo unit (although the light source in the photo unit can change exposure values over a long period of time). If the chemicals are not changed often enough, alterations in type weight are likely, and the corrections will be lighter or darker than the original typesetting. To avoid this problem, processor manufacturers recommend frequent checks of development power. Some processors automatically replenish each chemical after a given period of time; others recirculate chemicals continuously.

Apart from exposure and development, other factors may affect type quality. Humidity and temperature should be controlled within the parameters specified by the manufacturer of the photo unit. Air conditioning may be required. Ventilation is always necessary to avoid any concentration of vapors from the photochemistry.

11-34.
Phototypesetting cassette.

11-35.
Cassette in photo unit.

11-36.
Phototypesetting paper is fed into processor.

Maintaining Equipment

The processor itself is primarily a series of rollers that should be cleaned at least weekly. Many type houses, however, change chemicals and clean the processor daily. An accumulation of chemical sludge on the rollers causes streaking, poor density, and inadequately stabilized (or fixed) galleys. Manufacturers provide troubleshooting charts and guides if these or other problems occur.

The photo unit must be maintained as well. Dust and dirt particles that collect on film fonts may obscure the photographed image and should be wiped with a chamois and a special film cleaner (fig. 11-37). The photo unit itself must be cleaned and serviced only by trained technical personnel. The most important element the type house or printer can provide is as dust-free an environment as is feasible.

A dedicated electrical line is necessary to minimize surges in electrical power that will cause problems for the keyboards and the photo unit. Static electricity can be troublesome and may be reduced with sprays, if the photo unit is located in a carpeted room. However, the most suitable place for the unit is a ventilated room with tiled floors. The unit should not be placed near a window through which direct sunlight may cause stray exposure of the photographic paper.

Finally, proper care should be taken in disposing of photo chemicals and the potent solutions used in cleaning the processor. Toxic chemicals should not be carelessly poured down a drain. If typesetting personnel are uncertain about the proper procedure for disposal, local printing plants or professional associations will supply information. In some places, local ordinances *require* special disposal methods.

11-37.

Cleaning the font strip.

THE PROFESSIONAL ROLE OF THE TYPE HOUSE

The relationship between the type house and the customer is based upon two factors: product and price. The product, obviously, is type. The type house (or, in the case of in-house typesetting, the graphics shop) must provide quality output irrespective of the acumen of the customer. Indeed, many customers know little or nothing about design or typography; they simply ask the type house to "make it look good." It is the professional responsibility of both type house and typographer to make certain that all type meets internal quality standards. As Goudy might have put it, the typographer is the guardian of type—caring about (and furnishing) quality whether or not the customer knows and demands it.

Type professionals are aware of both the aesthetic and psychological advantages of type. Many reject, for instance, today's laser printers capable of "near-typesetting quality." But the professional has a responsibility to educate the user—to inform him or her about how well a job is being done.

That care and education, of course, has a price: the difference between professional type house rates and discount typesetting. Different type houses use varying methods to compute prices. All professionals, however, must make basic decisions as to how much the customer should—and will—be told about the business of type.

New Technical Capabilities

Many experienced typographers believe that the new capabilities offered by technology are unnecessary. Questions are raised as to whether 24,000 fonts, or 61.7-point Helvetica, are ever really advantageous.

There may indeed be occasions for 61.7-point Helvetica. In advertising typography, for instance, the designer may require type to be set exactly 36 picas wide; the use of 61.7-point type may be perfect for this application.

But other, more important, questions remain. An experienced typographer has been trained to combine type sizes, typefaces, spacing, and other elements to produce a suitably designed page. The typesetting customer, however, is usually not aware of the new-found capabilities.

Typographers must decide how much customers should know about the possibilities of that technology, and will often use several capabilities the customer may not have requested. Many graphic designers use terminology such as *set to fit* when specifying body type. The basic responsibility of the typographer is to provide excellence. The "hidden" arsenal of that expertise includes a knowledge of the following design elements.

KERNING AND LETTERSPACING

Unless otherwise specified, good typography dictates that type be set according to general principles of kerning pairs and minimum letterspacing. Some typefaces must be kerned more than others (fig. 12-1). Photographic typesetting allows better control by making kerning simpler: letters are simply photographed closer to one another.

The most important kerning pairs are shown in figure 10-2, but there are hundreds of others. A basic rule to remember is that the letters, *Y, W, T, P, y,* and *w* are involved in most kerning pairs.

VISUAL LINESPACING

Recall that linespacing is measured in points from the baseline of one line of type to the baseline of the next. In body copy, linespacing rarely needs adjustment. Visual linespacing, however, is mandatory for the setting of display type. Each display line will have a different number of ascenders and descenders, which will affect the apparent distance of the line from those above and below. Whether or not it is requested by the customer, spacing must be adjusted so that all lines *appear* to be the same distance from one another (fig. 12-2). The minute adjustments permissible by phototypesetting systems allow the experienced typesetter simple and effective visual linespacing.

a

COMPETITIVE CAMERA CORP.
b

12-1.

**Kerning in *a.*
handsetting and *b.*
photocomposition.**

VERTICAL
ALIGNMENT
OF LINES
SHOULD BE
OPTICAL.
BUT
THIS IS

NOT A
PROBLEM WHEN
LETTERS
HAVE STRAIGHT
FEATURES
LIKE B, D,
E, F, ETC.

12-2.

**Visual linespacing
in display.**

WORDSPACING

A minimum and maximum wordspace value should be specified. Nearly every typesetting system will "default" to some standard value if the typesetter does not take control of wordspace values. The default value may or may not be appropriate.

The perfect word space for any type size is the width of the lower-case letter *i*. Minimum and maximum word space values should be specified to ensure the frequent occurrence of that word space.

INDENTS

Paragraph indents should always be fixed combinations of em spaces, en spaces, or thin spaces. If a manuscript is received that does not specify indents, the indent should be proportional to the measure. For instance, a 20-pica line measure should be indented at least one em.

OPTICAL ALIGNMENT

Characters must be set to align in three different cases. First, when you set display type flush left, the letters on the far left must align optically, not mechanically. Certain letters, such as *A, J, O, T, V,* and *Y,* present special problems (fig. 12-3). Unless adjusted, they will not appear to be aligned. Second, if you are setting a series of single display characters directly above one another, the letters must always be set centered rather than flush left. Third, certain punctuation marks (such as hyphens, parentheses, and quotation marks) should be set outside the paragraph body. Sometimes called hanging punctuation, this practice contributes to the appearance of perfect justification. In all three cases, phototypesetting, because it permits greater control of spacing than does handsetting, allows for better results if used properly.

12-3.

**Optical alignment
in display.**

Lines of type which have many ascenders and descenders will appear to be closer together than lines having very few such letterforms.

There are some lines, in some cases in the same paragraph, where spacing will seem uneven even if space between lines is consistent.

ORPHANS AND WIDOWS

Perhaps the simplest rule of typography to remember is never to permit a line of less than two or three words to end a paragraph. These short lines, called orphans, are unsightly. It is the typesetter's responsibility to "repair the damage" whether or not the correction is demanded by the customer. When a digital typesetter or phototypesetter is being used, the orphan can often be avoided altogether by adjusting letterspace and wordspace. If this is impossible, the orphan should be hidden toward the middle of a page. In bookwork, another solution is to set several facing pages one line short or one line long, thus eliminating an orphan at the bottom of the page. *Never* allow an orphan to appear at the top of a page. This is properly called a widow, and typographers consider it one of the cardinal sins of the craft.

PUNCTUATION

A number of typographic rules govern the setting of punctuation and mathematical symbols. Many are descended from handsetting and linecasting, but several have evolved with the new technology.

Dashes. There are three distinct types of punctuation that appear to be similar: the hyphen, the en dash, and the em dash. The hyphen is the shortest and should be used only within or between words, as in *in-house* and *time-consuming.* En dashes are the width of an en and one-half the width of an em dash. They should be used between numbers, as in 1987–88. They are also specified by those who prefer shorter dashes in body copy. En and em dashes are sometimes called short and long dashes. Their specific uses are typographic fine points that are too often neglected. Each should be used correctly by the typesetter whether specified or not.

Figures. There are two types of figures: old style and modern, or lining (fig. 12-4). Modern figures are the size of uppercase letters; old style figures have ascenders and descenders. Figures should be set as specified. Because of the larger number of characters in the phototypesetting font, both styles are usually available.

Underscores and rules. These are among the most difficult pi characters to specify because there is no standard by which customers can order the rule width they require. The best solution is to refer to a set of standard rule widths, which should be made available in the type house's typebook. If the customer does not order a specific width, a hairline or one-point rule

1 2 3 4 5 6 7 8 9 0

1 2 3 4 5 6 7 8 9 0

12-4.
Old style (top)
and modern lining
figures.

is often used. If an underscore is specified, care should be taken to avoid running the line through descending letterforms. There are two possible solutions: breaking the underscore before the descender and then resuming it afterward, or setting the underscore one or two points below the bottom of the descending letterform. The latter strategy tends to work well only in display typography.

Superiors and inferiors. Floating above the x-height or slightly below the baseline, superiors and inferiors are a little smaller than the *x*. They are often used in mathematical and scientific typesetting, but, beyond those technical applications, the most common use is as building blocks of fractions. Fractions should not be set with a slash (as in 1/2). Rather, a true fraction should be created with an en dash, a superior, and an inferior (as in $\frac{1}{2}$). Building fractions is a daunting task for handsetters; it is not particularly difficult for phototypesetters.

Ellipses. An ellipsis is three periods (. . .) used as a pause in a sentence. The ellipsis must be created by typing a period, a thin space, a period, a thin space, and then a third period. Operators should never set an ellipsis with more than three dots.

Ligatures. Ligatures are two or more letters set as one character, including *ff, fi, fl, ffi,* and *ffl* (there are, in addition, several foreign language ligatures called diphthongs, for example, *ae* and *oe*). Traditionally used to avoid unsightly spacing between letters, ligatures are still respected as an elegant touch in fine typography. They should not be set in advertising typography unless specifically requested. However, they should always be used in bookwork whenever a serif typeface is specified.

Bullets and ballot boxes. Bullets are solid dots often used to signify items in a list. They are available to the phototypesetting operator in two sizes, the en and em of each type size. Ballot boxes are closed boxes that are usually a square of the type size. Because phototypesetting offers such a wide variety of type sizes, bullets and boxes may be set in many more sizes than were previously available. Care should be taken that the characters are the correct size. For example, 10- or 12-point body type may require boxes that are set in 18- or 24-point type. The bullet, on the other hand, is usually set in the same size as the body copy.

Estimating Type

Estimating is the process of developing a logical and fair pricing structure. The written estimate is a legal document binding the relationship between the typesetting supplier and buyer.

Many methods of calculating prices exist in industry, and it is unlikely that one particular strategy is used by a majority of type houses. At some type houses, in fact, estimating is predominantly guesswork based upon experience. Such estimates can be problematic, however, because only with a reliable system can the type house avoid jobs that actually lose money. Estimating standards enable a business to concentrate sales on those jobs that are most profitable.

In spite of the complexities involved in establishing a workable procedure, typographic estimating is relatively simple compared with estimates made in other areas of the printing industry. There are few variables and many fixed costs. The estimating procedures discussed below are used by many type houses in the industry, and the beginning typographer should be aware of them. Knowledge of cost breakdowns and pricing structures may save the client an unnecessarily high typesetting bill.

KEYSTROKES PER HOUR

Most type houses bill their services by the hour; the basic unit of work in the typesetting industry is the keystroke. A rational pricing structure can be based upon the amount of work the typesetting operator can produce in an hour.

The estimator must determine the operator's average keyboard speed. Assume, for example, that an operator's speed is 20 words per minute (typesetting operators keyboard more slowly than typists because they must continually make typographic decisions). That speed must be converted into keystrokes per hour in order to be useful to the estimator. To begin the conversion, multiply the operator's keyboard speed by six (because five letters and one spaceband are required for the average word). The product, 120, is the operator's speed expressed in keystrokes per minute.

Continuing the conversion, multiply the keystrokes per minute times 60 to determine the keystrokes per hour; in this example, 7,200 is the total.

COST PER UNIT

All estimates require a cost per unit, or the price of one unit of work. As noted, for typesetters that unit is the keystroke.

The management will necessarily have to make a decision at this point. The estimator must discover what dollar figure is necessary to pay for equipment leases (or amortization), employee wages and benefits, taxes, supplies, rent, and utilities, to make a reasonable profit. The average type house charges $50 per hour.

To develop the cost per unit, divide the keystrokes per hour (the type house's unit) into $50. In this example, the cost per unit will be $.007, or seven-tenths of a cent per keystroke. This information can be used to develop consistent prices.

PRICING

It is now very simple to quote prices. After a job is copyfit, the estimator multiplies the number of keystrokes required to typeset the job by the cost per unit. The result is the estimated price for the job.

As an example, assume that a manuscript of 1½ pages has 370 words, or about 2,200 keystrokes. The price would be 2,200 times $.007, or $15.40—which happens to be a fair market price for a job of this length.

It must be remembered that the developed pricing structure will be applicable only to straight matter, not technical type or tabular material. Furthermore, the example of $50 per hour is hypothetical; actual costs may be higher or lower, depending upon the cost per unit and the charge per hour.

QUOTES

The per-keystroke method is only one of several ways that a job can be quoted. Whatever method is chosen, the cost per unit must still be developed and integrated into the quote to ensure fair pricing.

Hourly Rates. Many type houses use hourly rates internally. An experienced estimator will quickly be able to approximate the time needed to typeset a job and convert that time into a quote based, for instance, on a $50-per-hour rate. Quoting from this rate is one of the poorest of methods, because the customer may be distressed by what appears to be a high hourly rate—$50 per hour seems a higher price than $15.40 for a job.

Keystroke Rates. Although the cost per unit must be developed, the keystroke rate is usually not recommended for jobwork typography because it is too open-ended. If a customer is quoted a rate of $.007 per keystroke for one job, he or she may assume that this is the rate for every job when, in fact, it may be appropriate only for straight matter.

Per-Line Rate. If the customer is quoted a per-line rate, the type house again must be careful to make certain the customer understands that this applies only to straight matter. The type house develops the per-line rate by multiplying the cost per unit times the number of units (keystrokes) in an average line. This method affords several advantages: it is easy to understand; it does not sound expensive to the customer (35 cents per line, for instance, is a typical rate); and it makes for easy calculations.

Per-Page Rate. Book typographers must often quote on a per-page basis, assuming that the page is legible, uncomplicated straight matter. The average cost per page is from $10 to $15, although some type houses charge much less. The per-page rate is often mandated when bids are required by book publishers in search of a type house.

Per-Job Rate. The per-job rate is the most problematic for the type house. It is, however, the most helpful to the customer and continues to be the method most often used.

However a price is quoted, type houses always offer their customers quantity discounts. Regular customers, or those who supply an extraordinarily large job, will receive, as a rule, a lower per-unit rate.

THE DIFFICULTY FACTOR

Some manuscripts need very few font changes, others require some tabular work, and still others contain several complicated equations. The estimator accounts for variations in complexity by calculating a difficulty factor into the costs of setting any material that is not pure straight matter. For example, if the material is fairly straight, the job may be assigned a difficulty factor of 1.3. After a price is computed on a per-keystroke, per-line, or per-page basis, the result is multiplied by 1.3 to produce a fair price.

Technical type and tabular copy, which are the hardest materials to set, may require a difficulty factor of 3.0 or 4.0. The estimator must, of course, create a range of factors, each corresponding to a different kind of manuscript. Some research may be required to determine the sorts of jobs that require the most keyboarding and typesetting time.

DISPLAY TYPE

Machines specifically manufactured to produce quality display type must be operated slowly by highly trained personnel, which means that display rates are much higher than text or even technical rates.

The type house specializing in advertising typography may charge a dollar or more per letter for a high-quality product with optical letterspacing set exactly as specified.

MINIMUM CHARGES

The typesetting customer must assume that all type houses will charge a minimum rate for every job. For instance, if a type house were to set the type for a single business card at a per-keystroke rate of $.007, the bill would be under a dollar, which is far less than the costs consumed by any job, no matter how small.

The minimum charge is usually from five to ten dollars. The designer in need of a small amount of type should add several often needed names, addresses, telephone numbers, and so on to a job for later use. Also, if two sets of galleys are routinely requested for every job, a helpful library of type will be developed for use in emergencies.

ALTERATIONS

Once the type house has provided the customer with galley proofs, any further changes from the original manuscript are *author's alterations,* or *AAs*. The AA is chargeable to the customer at a fixed rate determined by the type house. Rates vary from fifty cents to two dollars per line.

A second kind of correction is the *printer's error,* or *PE,* which is a mistake made by the type house. Examples include misspelled words, type set out of font, and errors in technical typesetting. The customer is not charged for the correction of printer's errors.

13

COMPUTERS AND COMMUNICATIONS

Although new technological capabilities have affected the design of our pages, the equipment and practice of typesetting is now entirely based upon the computer. Because of the extent of that dependence, the typographer and, especially, the type house manager must have a basic understanding of what the computer is, how it works, and how it affects design.

Digital Computers

Computers work on principles of applied electronics that have not radically changed since 1946, when ENIAC, the first computer that could be programmed (instructed to do various tasks), was invented. Despite its 18,000 vacuum tubes and unwieldy size, ENIAC was based on the same technological theory that applies to the newest IBM PC or Apple Macintosh.

Digital computers use sets of numbers to represent words, keystroke commands, and whatever else is contained in a document. The basic idea is that computers understand *only* two digits, 0 and 1, and thus may be compared with a huge bank of light switches that are either switched on (1) or off (0). The light switches are an especially good analogy because, in fact, the computer understands 0 as a voltage level of zero volts and 1 as a voltage level of five volts. The most complicated coding is simply a combination of on and off switches producing the appropriate voltage series.

In 1946, when ENIAC was built, the vacuum tube was the fastest possible switch. By the early 1950s, the transistor had been invented and soon replaced the vacuum tube in the aerospace and broadcasting industries, as well as in computer technology. Unlike a light bulb or vacuum tube, transistors require no heating element and work with less voltage. Consequently, they are smaller, cheaper, and more dependable.

Technology continued to develop throughout the 1960s, when *semiconductors* were the major innovation. An electrical conductor is a substance through which charged atomic particles flow readily in any direction. Semiconductors are similar to conductors in this regard, but with one peculiarity: a strong flow is permitted in one direction yet inhibited in the other (as though in that reverse direction, the material were an insulator and not a conductor).

The most common semiconductor is silicon, a plentiful element developed by technologists of the 1960s as a raw material in electronic components. *Integrated circuits* (ICs) were the next development: two or more transistors were combined, or integrated, on the same silicon semiconductor. As tinier and tinier transistors were produced, it seemed logical to make even this Lilliputian world more productive. ICs, or *chips,* are now the predominant circuit in all electronics (fig. 13-1).

Since the 1960s, chips have progressively grown in power and complexity but not in size. A single chip is capable of holding thousands of transistors, each of which is photoetched onto the silicon substrate.

Around 1970, engineers produced chips capable of much more than simply turning dishwashers on and off. Called *microprocessors,* chips were developed that could actually read information and make "decisions" (fig. 13-2). With this innovation, the computer as we use it today became possible. Every computerized device used in word processing and typesetting is based upon the microprocessor.

CENTRAL PROCESSING UNIT

The two parts that form the essence of a computer are the central processing unit (CPU) and the *main memory.* The CPU is one or several chips, no larger than the eraser on the end of a pencil, which do the computer's real work (fig. 13-3). Often referred to as the "brains" of the computer, the CPU processes commands and moves information by way of voltage switches in strings of 0s and 1s. Common microprocessors are the Intel 8080 and 8088, the Motorola 8080 and 68000, the Zilog Z80, and the MOS Tech 6502.

Microcomputers, personal computers, minicomputers, and even the largest mainframes all use microprocessor chips. In the larger minis and mainframes, the CPU is constructed of several chips mounted on a single unit known as a board.

How important was the chip to the computer revolution of the 1970s? In 1950, $2.61 was the average cost of storing one character in a computer, in part because of the expense of the central processing unit. In the 1980s, the cost has dropped to less than one-tenth of a cent per character, while capacity has mushroomed. The 1950s computer had a CPU capable of holding 20,000 characters at one time. Today's CPU holds millions.

MAIN MEMORY

Internal memory is stored on chips within the computer, whereas external memory is stored on tape, diskettes, and other magnetic media. Main memory, the programs and information necessary during a particular computing session, is stored in internal memory in two different ways: *RAM* (random-access memory) and *ROM* (read-only memory).

A computer either can read from its memory to perform a particular function or store memory for later use. These functions differentiate RAM from ROM, which, for explanatory purposes, are often compared to a

13-1.

Template used to produce microchip. Photo courtesy Motorola

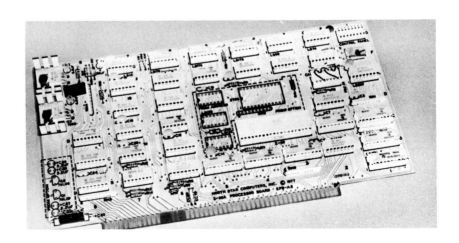

13-2.

Microprocessor. Photo courtesy Motorola

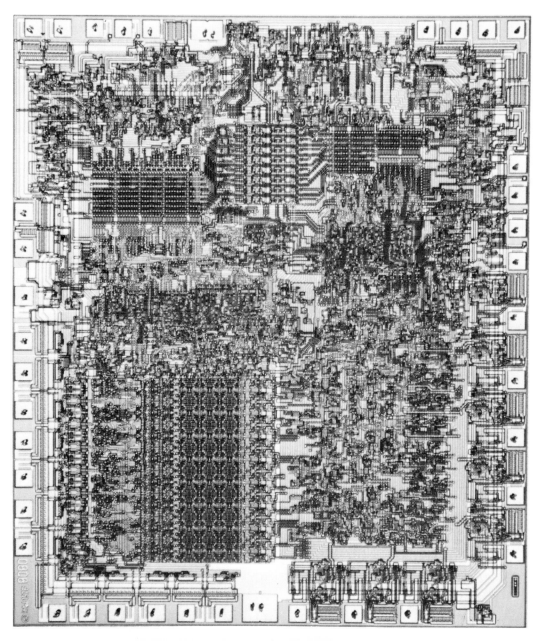

13-3.

Microprocessor size. Photo courtesy Motorola

phonograph record and a cassette tape respectively. A phonograph record has a "memory" that cannot be changed by the user: a Pavarotti aria cannot be erased to become a Bob Dylan song. That is the way ROM works. The memory is programmed as a permanent part of the computer's internal memory and cannot be edited.

RAM is like an audio cassette. Any tape can be erased and another recording dubbed in its place. Similarly, with RAM, new instructions or documents can be written over previous information. RAM is used to store operating programs for the specific jobs one is doing at any particular time, to store data before moving it to external memory, or to store user-developed programs.

I/O: The Display

The CPU and memory are the essential components of a computer. However, in order to construct a computer system that will be useful, you will require more hardware. The computer itself does not include devices for creating, storing, or moving information. Among the most important peripherals are the I/O devices—input and output equipment.

Input devices include calculator keyboards and window-display systems; terminals (fig. 13-4); and such devices as paper tape readers that move information from external memory into internal memory. There are, of course, many types of storage. The basic decision is between paper and magnetic media.

13-4.
Video display terminal. Photo courtesy ITT

PAPER MEDIA

In the 1970s, the *Hollerith card* (fig. 13-5) was the paper media most familiar to the general public. Also known as the IBM or punch card, Hollerith cards are rarely used today except for some data processing tasks.

   Paper tape was more often seen in typesetting rooms of the 1960s and 1970s than in computer centers. As noted in chapter 10, it was the first popular way to store information for computerized typesetting (see fig. 10-7). The tape memory is read by a tape reader as a particular sequence of six vertical holes. The letter *A,* for instance, is two holes at the top, three positions unpunched, and then one hole at the sixth and final position.

MAGNETIC MEDIA

After paper tape, the next revolution in memory was magnetic media. Packaged in several ways, these media are all understood by the CPU in the same way: recorded impulses are deciphered to create output. An *A,* for instance, is represented by the sequence impulse, impulse, no impulse, no impulse, no impulse, impulse. Put into computer vernacular, the sequence is understood as 110001 (the 1, again, being the "on" switch position, and the 0 being "off").

   There are many different magnetic media. The least powerful are *magnetic cassettes and cartridges* (fig. 13-6), rarely used by sophisticated typesetters. *Magnetic cards,* on the other hand, are still employed in the various

13-5.
Hollerith card.

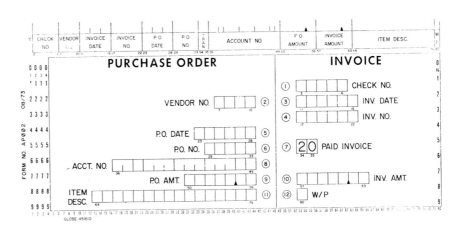

13-6.

Magnetic cassette.
Photo courtesy 3M

13-7.
The MT/ST direct-impression typesetting system. Photo courtesy IBM

13-8.

Magnetic tapes and reels. Photo courtesy 3M

direct-impression devices manufactured by IBM (fig. 13-7). In fact, *only* typesetters with IBM equipment use these thin, unprotected mag cards.

The largest computers and typesetters use *magnetic tape* as a storage medium (fig. 13-8). The major advantage of magnetic tape for the typesetter is its capacity to store a large amount of information handily: 2 million punch cards would be required to hold the memory retained on one tape.

Rigid disks are similar to magnetic tape reels in their large storage capacity. The most powerful hold up to 90 megabytes of information, or roughly 45,000 pages of typewritten manuscript. Also known as platters, hard disks, and Winchester systems, rigid disks are used throughout the typesetting industry in *front-end systems,* in *standalones,* and even in *desktop publishing* units (fig. 13-9).

The most popular magnetic medium, however, is the *floppy disk* or diskette (fig. 13-10). Generally 3½ inches, 5¼ inches, or 8 inches in diameter, disks and diskettes are read after they are inserted into a *disk drive* of the appropriate width (fig. 13-11). Unfortunately for typesetters who wish to move information from one computer to another, there is no generic floppy disk. They are system-dependent, lacking "coherence," or the ability to be formatted by one computer and read by another.

Floppies are system-dependent because of variations in their sizes and structures. A diskette always looks like a 45 RPM record, but it may be single-sided or double-sided, meaning that either or both sides may be magnetized. Diskettes are also available in single density, double density, and quad density. *Density* refers to the amount of data that can be stored on one side of a diskette. Single-density disks tend to be more reliable, but hold half as much information as double-density. Dual-density diskettes can function either as single- or double-density. Quad-density disks are those that are double-density *and* double-sided.

Diskettes are also either *hard-sectored* or *soft-sectored.* Every disk or diskette has a large hole in its middle called the disk hub. When inserted into the disk drive, the disk is rotated on its hub, allowing the read/write head of the drive to access different stored documents (see fig. 13-10). Soft-sectored disks are divided by electromagnetic sector marks that appear when the disk is first formatted by a computer. Hard-sectored disks are punched with a series of small holes that mark the beginnings of new sectors. Hard-sectored disks do not work in soft-sector drives, and vice versa.

CARE AND STORAGE

All magnetic media are vulnerable. Disks, cartridges, and tapes must be kept away from sources of electromagnetism—meaning a wide variety of appliances, such as televisions, fans, telephones, typewriters, loudspeakers, and air conditioners—or memory may be scrambled. Care must also be taken to avoid touching the iron oxide coating of disks and tapes. Finally, temperature extremes can erase memory.

All documents that are stored should be copied at least every day. Called the *back-up,* the second copy insures the user against potentially disastrous losses of memory.

Output: Printers

After a job is typed, the document is stored. In order to produce paper copies, an output device is necessary. Although the distinction is blurred by desktop publishing, there are three kinds of output device used by typesetters: letter-quality printers, dot matrix printers, and, of course, typesetting machines.

13-9.
Rigid disk.

13-10.
Floppy disk
schematic.

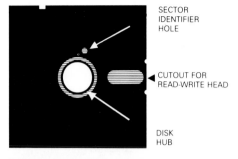

SECTOR
IDENTIFIER
HOLE

CUTOUT FOR
READ-WRITE HEAD

DISK
HUB

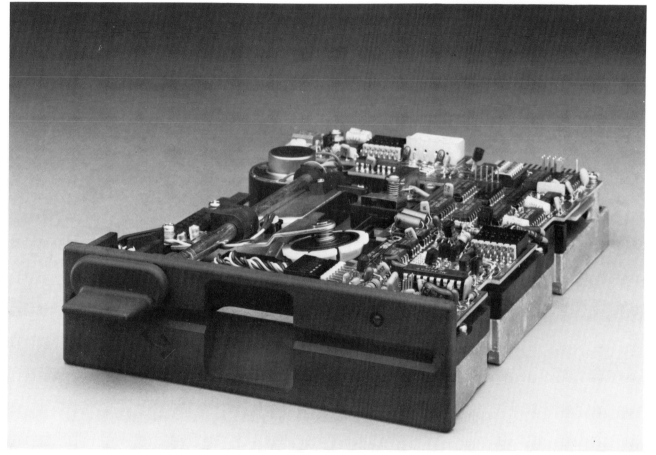

a

13-11.
a. **Floppy disk drive.**
Photo courtesy ITT
b. **Schematic with**
diskette.

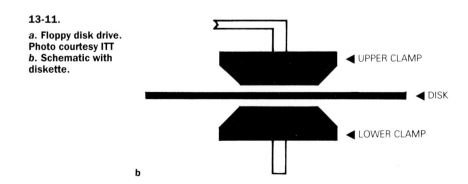

UPPER CLAMP

DISK

LOWER CLAMP

b

LETTER-QUALITY PRINTERS

Letter-quality printers are often called *impact printers* because, as in typewriting, they create an image by the direct impression (or impact) of ink on paper. Indeed, the first letter-quality printers were IBM Selectric typewriters converted to serve as printer/terminals. By using the Selectric connected to an IBM, one could communicate directly with the computer while producing "hard" (paper) copy. Today, many electronic typewriters double as computer printers.

Typewriters, however, are not suited to the needs of typesetters who use printers to output first proof. First, they are very slow: IBM Selectrics print at the rate of 15 characters per second, which seems fast when compared with a typist's speed, but actually means that it takes about three minutes to print a standard 8½- by 11-inch manuscript page. A document that is 50 pages long would thus require more than two hours to be transformed into hard copy. Second, typewriters cannot be run hour after hour, day after day, without needing frequent repairs.

The only letter-quality option occasionally used by type houses is the *daisy-wheel printer*. Composed of several dozen spokes, or petals, converging in a central hub, daisy-wheel fonts are interchangeable (fig. 13-12). The wheel rotates and individual petals strike ink onto paper. Though faster than typewriters, daisy-wheel printers still depend on moving parts and are thus comparatively slow.

DOT MATRIX PRINTERS

Faster, more economical, and quieter than daisy wheels, dot matrix printers are manufactered in two varieties: impact and nonimpact.

Dot matrix impact printing involves an inked ribbon that is struck by a bank of small hammers to create letters, which are "stored" electronically in the printer's computer chips. For example, when the letter *q* is required, the printer recalls the pattern (matrix) of small dots that will produce a *q*, and then orders the hammers to strike that pattern (fig. 13-13). The quality of this connect-the-dots technology is based upon the number of hammers used. A standard matrix is 7 by 9 dots per letter. If the density of dots is increased, each individual dot becomes less visible. This question of resolution is one of the basic differences between dot matrix printing and digital typesetting.

Impact printers obviously use mechanics, striking ink onto paper with moving parts. The newest generation of printing devices, the nonimpact printers, are much faster because of their reliance upon electronics. There are three types of nonimpact printers: heat-sensitive, ink-jet, and electrostatic. Heat-sensitive papers are treated with special chemicals before printing. Output is achieved by scorching the paper in dot matrix patterns. In ink-jet printing, tiny droplets of ink are sprayed in dot matrix patterns to produce letters. Both of these methods, however, are less popular than the third option. "Intelligent copiers," the fastest of the nonimpact electrostatic printers, produce copy at the rate of 20,000 lines per minute by combining electronic images with laser printing (fig. 13-14). A document is sent through an *interface* to the CPU of the copier, which converts the electronic manuscript into dot matrix patterns. Although the price tag was originally out of the range of most printing companies and type houses, this technology is now the basis of laserwriting, a cornerstone of desktop publishing. A scaled-down version of electrostatic printing is thus the single most popular proofing method in the typesetting industry today.

13-12.
Daisy-wheel elements.

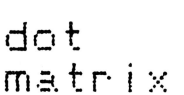

13-13.
Construction of letters through a dot matrix.

13-14.

Xerox intelligent copier. Photo courtesy Xerox Corporation

Optional Hardware

The basic computer hardware is the keyboard, video monitor, printer, and CPU. Beyond the basics, however, several peripheral devices are often necessary.

A *line-voltage regulator* is an inexpensive device that controls electronic glitches, the surges of power that disrupt the electromagnetic impulses on your media and scramble memory. By controlling brown-outs and voltage surges, the regulators eliminate electrical noise—the static you hear on your AM radio.

If communications are to be established, interfacing hardware—cables, phone equipment, and connecting devices—may be necessary. There are cartridges, trays, and binders designed to hold diskettes and other media. Special floor mats are available that prevent static electricity from being conducted into the CPU. Extra daisy wheels, printer paper, color graphics monitors, light pens, and voice and speech synthesizers (the first allows you to speak to your computer, and the second lets it talk back) can be purchased.

But what can the type house now do with a computer? Hardware alone is useless without the human element of the computer system. The computer cannot act without the directions, or *programs, called *software.*

Software

The first rule regulating the purchase and use of computers in the 1980s is that software development is not a mechanical science; it is a creative expression. Software quality ultimately depends on the skill of the programmer. A program can be easy to understand and use, or klutzy (as the programmer calls it, a "kluge").

What do programs actually do? The answer to that question depends upon the type of software that has been purchased. The first, and most essential, is the program that makes hardware intelligent: the *operating system* (OS). Sometimes called the *firmware,* because it is a permanent fixture of the computer, the OS is the organized collection of directions that tell the computer how to process jobs, understand the various keystrokes, and communicate with peripherals, such as keyboards, printers, and the like. If you had to tell the CPU how to work every time you turned the computer on, you would not only become very frustrated, but would waste a great deal of time. In the early days of mainframe computers, operators had to load CPU instructions *every* time a new job was begun and clear the CPU of any data after it was finished. With OS programming, the computer has a permanent system: the OS manages the computer's time and processing schedule so that more than one job can be run simultaneously. These master control programs are the roads that all other programs follow.

There are two types of operating systems: those contained on disks (the DOS, or disk operating systems) and those loaded on the CPU by other means. Because of the blind devotion of the operating system, the particular one your computer uses might seem unimportant. But the choice of an operating system has substantial consequences: programs that perform such functions as word processing and data processing are often written to be used on a specific operating system.

Among the several very popular operating systems, the best known for use with the widely adopted 8080 chip is Digital Research's CP/M. Its popularity is based in part on history: CP/M was the first and only OS in the mid-1970s, when microcomputers were first developed. Moreover,

CP/M supports many popular *computer languages,* including Basic, Fortran, Pascal, APL, Cobol, and C.

The most important competitors on the microcomputer market are MS-DOS, used in the IBM Personal Computer and in all of the many PC clones, and AppleDOS, used in the Apple II series of Macintosh computers. Dozens of *proprietary operating systems,* like Radio Shack's TRSDOS, have been manufactured to accompany a particular computer.

In the world of the larger minicomputers, the operating systems include UNIX, which was developed by Bell Labs in the late 1960s and then sold by AT&T to the general public because of its power and easy interactivity. UNIX was first designed for use with Digital Equipment Corporation (DEC) computers. The PDP series, the first minicomputers, has since been replaced by the very popular VAX line of computers, but UNIX continues as a successful operating system (both in the universe of minicomputers and, more recently, in microcomputers as well). Digital itself produces its own operating system for the VAX computers, VMS. At Data General, the Nova microcomputers are run with MP/OS, upgradable to Eclipse, the operating system which runs the machine described in Tracy Kidder's best-selling book, *The Soul of a New Machine (1981).* IBM, of course, produces its own operating systems for use with its computers, as does every other computer manufacturer.

The Binary System

As you type a program or use a word processing software package to create manuscripts, the characters entered on the keyboard immediately appear on-screen. But the computer understands letters only in a coded language called *binary,* a language that has only two "words," 0 and 1. As discussed earlier in this chapter, these binary digits are interpreted by the computer, not as numbers, but as the state of an electronic impulse: on or off.

The binary code is used to express letters, numbers, and, eventually, complicated concepts to the computer (fig. 13-15). Numbers are expressed in powers of 2, just as numbers in the decimal system are expressed in powers of 10. Thus, the number 10 in binary means (reading from right to left) zero plus two to the first power, or zero plus two, or, expressed in the decimal system, 2. Because we are not familiar with binary, examples seem to be complicated at first, but the system is really just another way of expressing numeric values.

For example, how is a decimal number like 70 converted to binary? Begin with the largest power of 2 that is less than 70. Sixty-four is two to the sixth power ($2 \times 2 \times 2 \times 2 \times 2 \times 2$). But you must still account for the remainder of six after you have subtracted 64 from 70. Six,

13-15.

How binary code works.

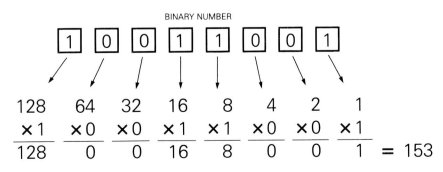

of course, is two to the second power (2 x 2, or 4) plus two to the first power (2). So, to express the decimal number 70 in binary, you will have to include in a series of zeros and ones the codes for two to the sixth, second, and first powers.

> Your value for two to the zero power: 0
> Your value for two to the first power: 1
> Your value for two to the second power: 1
> Your value for two to the third power: 0
> Your value for two to the fourth power: 0
> Your value for two to the fifth power: 0
> Your value for two to the sixth power: 1

Starting from the bottom of your list of zeros and ones, and remembering to read from left to right, with the leftmost number being two to the sixth power, you will note that the binary number for decimal 70 is 1000110.

Unfortunately, one computer's binary system is not necessarily the same as another's. Binary is not, strictly speaking, the translation of a computer language, but the dictionary. Each computer manufacturer creates different *code sets*, so binary patterns mean different things in different manufacturers' "languages." As a result, one machine using one code set cannot "talk" to another using a second set. Interfacing, discussed later in this chapter, bridges the language gap between different machines.

User Programs

When the CPU is loaded with an operating system, it is then ready to process information. But information processing requires a user program, which can be written either by you or by software manufacturers. Examples of user programs include WordStar (a word processing package), Lotus 1-2-3 (a data-base management system), and TypeLink (a telecommunications utility).

Computer Languages

User programs are written in computer languages, the most popular being those that are the simplest to learn and use. BASIC is a standard among what are called the high-level programming languages—easy-to-use languages that are based on English. Other popular high-level languages include Fortran, C, Cobol, Forth, and Pascal.

Today, only programmers must master computer languages. They are not necessary for those who want to be able to "turn a key" and have the computer work for them. There are literally thousands of software options on the market. Most type houses and printers prefer to buy one of these "canned" programs to save time and development costs. Canned software can be purchased in source code (English), which can be edited by the user, or in machine code (binary), which cannot be edited easily, but is used in less-expensive programs.

Processing Information

Once hardware and software have been purchased and the operating system is loaded you are ready to type on a terminal. Assume you have typed the X key. The result, of course, is that the letter X appears on the terminal screen. But what did the computer actually do?

First, the pressure you created by striking the keystroke *X* was a switch that sent an electronic signal to the CPU. The *X* has been understood by the computer as a series of binary digits, in this case, 10001000. After the CPU correctly interprets that sequence, it sends a signal to the monitor, and the screen glows, creating a dot matrix pattern that makes up the letter.

But where did 10001000 come from? The code is a peculiar form of binary called a *binary coded decimal,* or BCD for short. This BCD is a binary interpretation of the decimal number 88, whose digits have each been converted to their binary equivalent. A decimal 8 is equivalent to a binary 1000, so 88 has in this case been translated as 1000 1000. This discovery, of course, begs the question: knowing that 10001000 means 88 gets us no closer toward solving the riddle of its origin. The answer is based in the different code sets being used by computers to interpret binary digits.

ASCII AND EBCDIC

Although programs can be written in English, the computer can read them only in binary. Translations from English to binary are therefore necessary, but it is very difficult for programmers to write in binary code—each letter requires eight binary digits, so a six-letter word must be expressed in a string of 48 zeros and ones. These long rows of numbers are difficult for programmers to write and read correctly, and many mistakes are made. An intermediate code between binary and English is needed, a code that can be easily understood both by people and computers.

The perfect answer would be a single, universally accepted numeric code as a go-between for binary and English. And it could well be ASCII (pronounced "as-key"), the American Standard Code for Information Interchange (fig. 13-16). Known internationally as CCITT Alphabet Number 5, this 8-bit code was originally developed for telegraphs and teletype machines. In the 1950s, teletypes were used as terminals for computers, so ASCII was a logical choice for a translating code set.

Several other codes have represented characters in data transmission. Morse code and Baudot, employed in American networks serving the deaf, are too clumsy to be used for word processing or typesetting. But a relatively new code named EBCDIC (Extended Binary Coded Decimal Interchange Code, pronounced "eb-see-dick") directly competes with ASCII: some computers use one code, some the other, but no computer can use or understand both. Many computer professionals believe that the creation of a competitive code set was an action by major computer manufacturers to write the rules of the game. Whatever the intention, the result is that we have two major codes.

If there were only two codes, interfacing between EBCDIC-based equipment and ASCII-based equipment would be simply a matter of one translation. Even the New International ASCII of 1978, which further confuses the situation, is not an overwhelming obstacle. The major communications barrier rests with our keyboards.

Take a look at any typesetting keyboard. You will find an em space, a linespace key, perhaps a precedence uppercase and lowercase key, an insert space, and, of course, a quad left key that automatically pushes words to the left margin. Most typesetting keyboards share those specific, or similar, keystrokes. Now, look at a word processing keyboard. No quad left keys here, but there is a control, a line feed, a backslash, and perhaps an escape key, none of which appears on the typesetting keyboard.

Binary	Decimal	Octal	Hexadecimal	ASCII	EBCDIC	TTS
00110110	054	066	36	6	UC	Shift
00110111	055	067	37	7	EOT	Lower Rail
00111000	056	070	38	8		M
00111001	057	071	39	9		
00111010	058	072	3A	:		X
00111011	059	073	3B	;		1
00111100	060	074	3C	<	DC4	V
00111101	061	075	3D	=	NAK	Quad Center
00111110	062	076	3E	>		Unshift
00111111	063	077	3F	?	SUB	Delete
01000000	064	100	40	@	SP	
01000001	065	101	41	A		
01000010	066	102	42	B		
01000011	067	103	43	C		
01000100	068	104	44	D		
01000101	069	105	45	E		
01000110	070	106	46	F		
01000111	071	107	47	G		
01001000	072	110	48	H		
01001001	073	111	49	I		
01001010	074	112	4A	J	¢	
01001011	075	113	4B	K	.	
01001100	076	114	4C	L	×	
01001101	077	115	4D	M	(	
01001110	078	116	4E	N	+	
01001111	079	117	4F	O			
01010000	080	120	50	P	&	
01010001	081	121	51	Q		
01010010	082	122	52	R		
01010011	083	123	53	S		
01010100	084	124	54	T		
01010101	085	125	55	U		
01010110	086	126	56	V		
01010111	087	127	57	W		
01011000	088	130	58	X		
01011001	089	131	59	Y		
01011010	090	132	5A	Z	!	
01011011	091	133	5B	[	$	
01011100	092	134	5C	\	*	
01011101	093	135	5D	]	)	
01011110	094	136	5E	^	;	
01011111	095	137	5F	_	¬	
01100000	096	140	60	`		
01100001	097	141	61	a	/	
01100010	098	142	62	b		
01100011	099	143	63	c		
01100100	100	144	64	d		
01101001	101	145	65	e		
01100110	102	146	66	f		
01101011	103	147	67	g		
01101100	104	150	68	h		
01101101	105	151	69	i		
01101110	106	152	6A	j		

13-16
Conversion chart for several computer codes.

Constructing translations of keys that do not exist on typesetting keyboards (and vice versa) is difficult enough, but there is a second stumbling block: even if ASCII or EBCDIC is used, manufacturers need not strictly adhere to the industry standard for either code. Indeed, because each keyboard is different, the ASCII "standard" is something of a fiction. Virtually every hardware manufacturer deviates (sometimes slightly, sometimes dramatically) from the ASCII norm. So, even if the typesetter and the word processor are both using ASCII, one will not necessarily be understood by the other.

STANDARD PRACTICE

The manufacturer of the word processing or typesetting hardware determines what code will be used with the equipment. Whichever version is selected, all operations at the level of binary and machine code are relatively similar. Assume, for example, that you have typed the word *ABOUT*. By looking at the ASCII chart (see fig. 13-16), you can determine the BCD (binary coded decimal) for the first letter, *A*. To do that, you will have to convert *A* into the decimal figure given to it on the ASCII chart. That number is 65.

But if you look more closely at the chart, you will see that other numbers are available: 41 and 101. In this case, 41 is the *hex code* number for *A*. Hex is short for *hexadecimal*. Like binary and decimal, hex is simply another way of expressing a quantity, in this case, by powers of sixteen rather than two or ten. The number 101 is an *octal* code—yet another counting system, which expresses numbers in powers of eight.

The hex code is used for most interfacing applications, primarily because it can express up to 256 characters using no more than two digits or a digit and a letter. Decimal, on the other hand, can express only 100 characters: from 00 to 99. The 16 characters used in expressing hex codes are 0, 1, 2, 3, 4, 5, 6, 7, 8, 9, A, B, C, D, E, and F. When all of the 256 possible permutations of those characters are constructed (for example, 1A, 2B, 3F), you have more than enough to give every character on any keyboard its own two-character hex code—which is essential to avoid confusion in translation. Decimal and octal simply do not have enough characters to do the job.

Yet another type of notation, *binary coded hexadecimals*, can be used by interfacers. Similar to BCDs, binary coded hexadecimals are assigned codes. The letter *A*, in this case, has been assigned the hex code 41, which is translated in exactly the same way as the BCD 0100 (meaning 4) and 0001 (meaning 1). Put the two codes together, and you have the standard ASCII binary code for *A:* 01000001.

The binary code also can be converted into and from decimal code. Compute the value of 01000001 in decimal codes, recalling that this apparently obtuse string of zeros and ones is actually a binary number equal to two to the zero power plus two to the seventh power, which is 1 plus 64, or 65. Check the letter *A* in figure 13-16 and you will see the decimal value 65. What that means is that you can think of ASCII binary codes either in straight decimal equivalents *or,* if you prefer, in terms of binary coded hexadecimals. It does not matter, because 01000001 will mean *A* both in hex (as 41) and in decimal (as 65). You can use either system.

Continuing our example of *ABOUT,* we must translate the second letter, *B*. Hex code for *B* is 42, which converts into binary 0100 (4) and binary 0010 (2), or 01000010. The next letter *O*, however, is slightly different: its hex code is 4F. Because *F* is part of the hex code, we cannot treat it as a binary coded hexadecimal and translate it as two sets of four binary digits (F is not a binary digit and thus cannot be immediately translated). This is where the table of equivalents comes in handy, because the solution is to revert to decimal coding. The decimal code for *O* is 79. So, rather than convert 4F (a hex) into binary, just convert 79 (a decimal) directly: 79 is 64 + 8 + 4 + 2 + 1, so our binary code for *O* becomes 01001111. Since we know by our earlier example that decimal 79 is indeed equivalent to hex 4F, we can be sure that we have arrived at the right binary sequence.

To complete the example, the hex code for *U* is 55, or binary 0101 0101, and the hex code for *T* is 54, or binary 01010100. The entire word, in ASCII, thus looks like this:

A	B	O	U	T
01000001	01000010	01001111	01010101	01010100

Putting this string together, *ABOUT* is 0100000101000010010011110101010101010100, a complicated sequence that makes it simple to understand why an intermediary code is needed between binary and English. In hex, *ABOUT* translates as 41424F5554, a string that is not immediately understandable but is at least decipherable.

Given the number of keyboards currently in use, the number of different manufacturers of computer systems, and even the existence of totally new keyboard layouts, the standardization of ASCII or any other code set seems impossible. Therefore, we must learn to use hex so we can translate the various versions of ASCII and EBCDIC that have been created.

If the process seems confusing, remember that most of the time, the computer is doing these translations for you. However, there will be occasions during interfacing when translations will have to be made in hex.

Interfacing Networks

Type houses interested in creating communications between computers must establish a *network,* a collection of electronic devices linked together and capable of communicating with one another (fig. 13-17). Common examples are networks used for airline reservations and, of course, for long-distance telephoning. There are basically two types of networks: *point-to-point* and *multiplexer* (figs. 13-18 and 13-19). The *front-end* system in a type house is a point-to-point network, connecting terminals directly with the CPU via *ports* located at the back of the computer. Multiplexing networks are larger and more powerful. They first connect terminals to intermediaries, known as multiplexers, which are in turn connected to the host computer.

Any network is dependent upon a successful *interface,* the direct transfer of information from one computer to another without retyping. Simple interfaces occur between computer terminals and printers. More complicated communications, such as between a word processor and a typesetting machine, continue to transform the industry . As mentioned, by 1992, 80% of all typesetting will be interfaced from a word processor or PC.

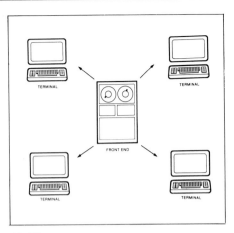

13-17.

Satellite networking.

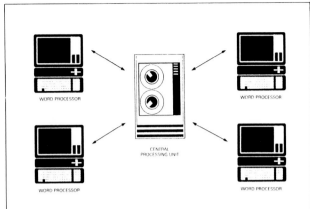

13-18.

Point-to-point networking.

13-19.

Multiplexer networking.

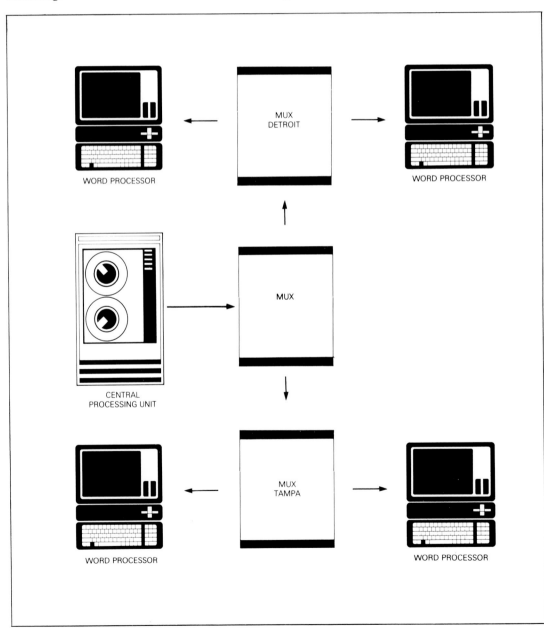

Advantages of Interfacing

SAVINGS IN PRODUCTION

Interfacing is most often incorporated into the traditional work flow as a cost-saving measure. Because keystrokes are captured and communicated, documents need not be retyped by the typesetter. Moreover, the keystrokes that are captured can be cheaper: rather than pay type house rates of $50 and more per hour for the relatively easy job of keyboarding, word processing personnel can do the same work for six or seven dollars per hour. Type houses are then paid only to ensure that the typeset pages are correctly positioned, spaced, and designed.

Depending on whether the customer encodes documents with typographic parameters or simply communicates raw words, interfacing can substantially reduce customer costs. A National Composition Association (NCA) report broke down the typesetting job into six areas (fig. 13-20). Interfacing enables the customers to cut costs in all areas except makeup (the mechanical). Keyboarding, the most expensive aspect of a job, is subject to the greatest savings. The costs of proofreading and correcting are likewise minimized, and money is saved in typesetting and materials through the elimination of second and third proofs. Although the NCA estimates that it is possible to save 50 percent or more through interfacing, and some customers report savings in excess of 70 percent, 20 to 30 percent is a more realistic estimate.

CHEAPER HARDWARE

Beyond savings in the overall typesetting budget, interfacing can reduce expenditures on equipment. Terminals dedicated to typesetting systems often cost $5,000. An industrywide solution to this expense is PC-based composition, an interface to cheaper, quite serviceable keyboards manufactured as personal computers.

TYPE QUALITY

Because interfacing has made professional typographic quality less expensive, many organizations are typesetting documents that were formerly typewritten. Beyond pure economics, there are aesthetic advantages: typesetting is often more legible and always makes a better, more professional, impression than typewriting.

COMPACTION

On average, 40 percent less paper is used with typesetting than with typewriting. Interfacing long technical reports or technical manuals may be justified on the basis of reduced costs of paper alone.

SPEED

When deadlines are an issue, jobs that are already typewritten on a word processor need not be retyped. The savings in time provides clear advantages to advertising agencies, daily newspapers, and other organizations facing frequent deadlines.

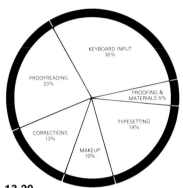

**13-20.
Interfacing cuts costs in several areas of the typesetting process.**

Four Ways To Interface

Of the four possible methods of interfacing, the options are quite clear: two methods are *indirect*—meaning that computers do not communicate directly with one another—and two are *direct*—involving unmediated lines of communication. Indirect routes have been available longer and are less complicated for the consumer but they are also less cost-effective. Direct interfacing offers the only access to the maximum possible savings.

OCR: THE FIRST INDIRECT ROUTE

Optical character readers (OCRs) convert typewritten copy into digital codes, which are then sent directly to the typesetting machine by means of a cable (fig. 13-21). Once the manuscript has been keyboarded on a typewriter or word processor, it need not be retyped. The OCR scans the page and transfers what it has "read" to the photo unit for hard copy.

    Optical scanning is a valuable technique only if manuscript preparation is rigidly controlled. But there are disadvantages. First, some OCRs successfully scan only specially designed type styles, called OCR-readable faces. In addition, documents must be formatted correctly: no mix of single- and double-spacing is permissible, and there can be no underlining and certainly no smudged characters. If corrections are required, full pages must be retyped. Penciled additions are not possible. Worst of all, optical character readers are the most expensive of the interfacing options. Prices start at over $25,000 and easily extend to as much as $100,000.

    Several scanners, notably the Kurzweil, are able to read any typeface (fig. 13-22). Although this new generation of "intelligent" OCRs is still more expensive than other interfacing hardware, many type houses are willing to invest in the ultimately rewarding equipment. Customers are able to purchase OCR services from one of the many typesetting companies that feature them. In general, optical scanning is primarily for the high-volume type buyer producing straight matter (simple text). Complicated technical material filled with equations and tables is much more difficult to scan than simple paragraphs.

MEDIA CONVERSION: THE SECOND INDIRECT ROUTE

Media converters solve the problem of media inscrutability by translating digitally stored memory from one format to another (figs. 13-23 and 13-24). Theoretically, these machines are able to read the magnetic media used by *any* computer. After the magnetic disk or tape is read, information is converted into a format understandable by a typesetting machine. In most cases, the media converter is wired to a front-end system and transmits word processing documents via telecommunications cable.

    Unfortunately, although diskettes can be formatted only in a limited number of ways, the many manufacturers of typesetters and word processors each format differently, so that number is still substantial. The media converter must be programmed (in other words, software must be written) to permit each connection to work. For instance, in order to interface with a Mergenthaler typesetter in a large metropolitan area, a typesetting company with a media converter must have a program to interface Apple with Mergenthaler, another to interface KayPro with Mergenthaler, yet others to interface IBM, Altos, Radio Shack, and Digital with Mergenthaler, and on and on.

    When a typesetting company wants to interface with all possible customers, it is faced with a tremendous capital outlay. The most popular

13-21.
The Scanner 2000,
an OCR device.
Photo courtesy
Compugraphic
Corporation

13-22.

Kurzweil optical
character reader.
Photo courtesy
Kurzweil

13-23.

Applications of
OCR and media
conversion.

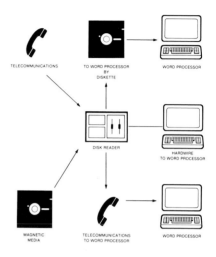

13-24.

Shaftstall 5000
media converter.
Photo courtesy
Shaftstall

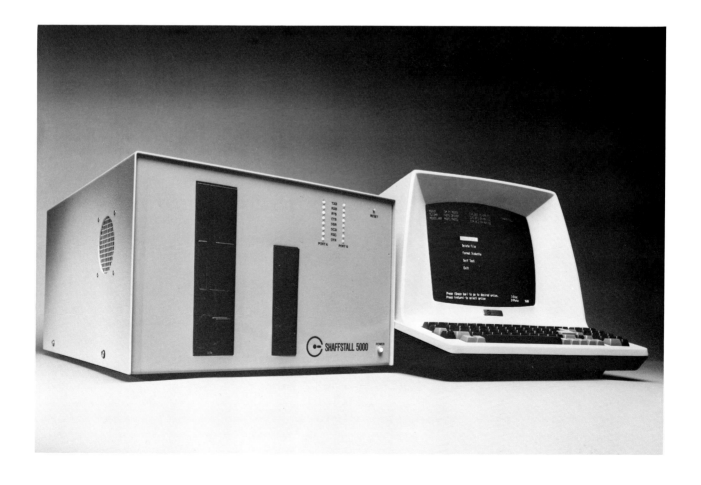

media converter in the 1980s, the Shaftstall, requires a $1,200 surcharge for each program application. Indeed, the software costs for a well-equipped media converter can exceed $40,000, while the machines themselves cost from $6,000 up to $25,000.

For the customer, the advantage of media conversion is that there is no out-of-pocket cost. The type house pays for the converter, and customers pay for conversion services. However, for the typesetter interested in establishing interfacing, the cost of purchasing a well-equipped media converter will become increasingly expensive as more and more companies enter the microcomputer and word processing equipment markets. AT&T and Sperry joined the fray as late as 1984, adding another two obligatory conversion packages at $1,200 each.

The question for typesetters is whether to participate in a universal interface and keep all of their marketing options open, or to focus on a limited group of companies using one machine, the equipment-specific interface. Media conversion is an excellent option for typesetters who are certain of never interfacing with a large and varied universe of computer users. If, for instance, one's seven largest type customers all use Apples, media conversion is an excellent choice.

HARDWIRING: THE FIRST DIRECT ROUTE

Hardwiring is simply using communications cable to connect two computerized devices so that information is sent directly from one machine to the other. The most common application for typesetting is the front-end system, in which many terminals are wired to a single photo unit.

The method may seem easy and obvious, but it does have limits. Some manufacturers specify that cabling cannot exceed 25 feet (others say 125 or even 150 feet). Boosters may have to be bought to amplify electrical signals and increase the distance between machines. Finally, cabling requires the purchase of special hardware and software (fig. 13-25).

The necessary hardware is a *null modem,* which is a cable that basically emulates *telecommunications* (fig. 13-26). The word processor and typesetter react as though telecommunicating, but the process is simplified because one organization controls the entire interface.

Hardwiring is the system of choice for any company that sets its own type in an in-house graphics shop. For commercial typesetting shops, the only meaningful hardwiring application is in wiring input stations to the existing typesetter. It is simply impossible to hardwire with customers.

TELECOMMUNICATIONS: THE SECOND DIRECT ROUTE

Typesetting through telecommunications is an interface dependent on either common telephone or satellite communications. Special equipment is necessary, but, when compared with potential savings, the equipment cost is a minor concern. *Acoustic couplers* and *modems* (an acronym for modulator/demodulator) are telephone devices that convert electronic signals generated by the computer into tones similar to those we use in speaking over the telephone (figs. 13-27 and 13-28). The signals are sent over telephone lines (or via telecommunications satellites) to a second modem or acoustic coupler, which then converts the tones it "hears" back into the electronic signals understandable by the second computer (fig. 13-29). Acoustic couplers differ from modems in that they require a handset from a standard telephone to be fit into the coupler created for that purpose. Modems simply connect to a port at the back of the computer and require no telephone.

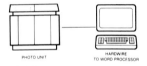

**13-25.
Hardwiring.**

**13-26.
Null modem. Photo
courtesy Thomas
Maneen**

13-27.

Telecommunications.

13-28.

a. **CAT acoustic coupler. Photo courtesy Novation** *b.* **Acoustic coupler schematic.**

13-29.

Hayes SmartModem. Photo courtesy Hayes

With modems, a word processor sends documents directly to a communicating phototypesetter through the RS-232 connector, one of the few widely accepted standards of the typesetting industry. Other standard "plugs" are the IEEE Standard and GPIB Standard. All work similarly to create a *serial interface* (see next section). If a document is prepared well, personnel at the type house may send the job immediately to be typeset without further keyboarding. Proofs are often sent to the customer the same day that the job is received.

Serial and Parallel Transmission

There are two types of computerized transmission: serial and parallel. In order to understand these methods, imagine a busy railroad yard. There are eight tracks; each is continually occupied. But this is a strange railroad: the eight tracks coming into the station converge into a single track going away from the station. Furthermore, as the station manager switches the trains onto the one available track, he does so at precise intervals. The space between trains is rigidly controlled.

Coming toward the station, the trains are taking the parallel route; several trains (or bits of information) move at the same time on different tracks. Going away from the station, the trains (bits) are carried serially, all on the same track at specific time intervals. If it were possible, eight tracks would be built to carry the trains out of the station as well as in, but that is out of the question because of the expense involved.

Hardwire interfaces are typically serial. One-way printer cables are usually parallel. Because a sixteen-track (eight tracks in each direction) parallel communication channel is very expensive, telecommunications is serial. But the CPU of a word processor sends and understands signals on parallel tracks.

The RS-232 is the switching device that moves eight tracks of information into one channel. If both the word processor and the typesetting equipment have RS-232 ports, as is usually the case, communication is possible.

Translation Tables

Serial communications works most of the time, but, if one interfaces between two different keyboards that understand a specific key in two different ways, the method will not be adequate. Instead, translations must be designed to accommodate unusual characters, such as em spaces and quad left keys. This is not to say that simple serial transmission is utterly unfeasible, but serial will not enable the word processor to encode typesetting information into the word processing document. The word processor will be able to send only letters and numbers and, as any typesetter will tell you, those characters are by far the simplest part of the typesetting process. A maximum of 10 percent of the expense is saved by telecommunicating characters alone and thereby delegating the most challenging input decisions to the typesetter.

Fortunately, manufacturers supply sample translation tables. Many type houses have refined those tables to establish easy-to-use guidelines. There are several ways in which word processing customers can encode typographic information in their documents. Perhaps the simplest is the mnemonic substitution of existing keystrokes for necessary typesetting commands. For example, $LL22 might be used to signify a line length of 22 picas.

Electronic versus Paper Manuscripts

The most important advantage that telecommunications offers is the universality of its communications capability. Telecommunications, unlike media conversion, OCR, and hardwiring, does not limit the type house to a particular stable of customers.

Many type houses, however, choose both direct and indirect methods of interfacing. Because it is a direct method, telecommunications cannot be controlled as easily as media conversion or OCR—a customer who telephones and wants to interface immediately unilaterally restructures the type house's work flow.

Paper copy is giving way to electronic manuscripts. In publishing, many authors have already converted, delivering a manuscript not as 500 pages of paper but as a couple of diskettes. By 1993, 80 percent of all typeset jobs will be interfaced.

The Computer and the Typesetting Industry

Technology has changed the business of typesetting as well as the craft. There are more members of the industry setting more type in more ways.

TYPE HOUSES

The major type house has become a service bureau providing a variety of software functions. From interfacing, telecommunications, and data-base typesetting to electronic printing and publishing, the type house is no longer a manufacturing facility. Technology has created a new set of demands that center upon software manipulation rather than keystroking.

In attempts to solidify marketing positions, many more type houses have begun to specialize in such areas as advertising, bookwork, and technical type. Type houses have also branched into camera work, color separations, and other production processes formerly reserved to the printer.

COMMERCIAL PRINTERS

The availability of inexpensive technology has created new profit centers for commercial printers. Twenty-five years ago, printers worked from slugs if the printing method was letterpress, or repro proofs if the printing method was offset lithography. Most commercial printers themselves offer typesetting to their customers, not as a source of profit but as a means to attract clients for long-term gains.

JOB SHOPS AND QUICK PRINTERS

With desktop publishing, even the smallest quick printer can now afford the price of typesetting technology. These shops concentrate on jobwork: brochures, newsletters, business cards, letterheads, and posters.

IN-HOUSE SHOPS

The most dramatic new development, however, has been the growth of the in-house shop. Large corporations, government agencies, nonprofit institutions, and national associations are all establishing these facilities for four basic reasons.

Lower Production Costs. As general typesetting and production costs rise, type houses must pass on costs to their customers, and do-it-yourself options become more and more attractive. Indeed, an organization that spends $100,000 a year on typesetting can save at least $25,000 the first year, *after* paying installation costs and salaries.

Profit from Sales. Another way to combat high prices is for the in-house agency to sell type to its own customers. Many shops contract work from other agencies and set type for their own customers during lull periods.

Control. Many organizations that are concerned with controlling the quality of the work they produce have joined the independent typesetting movement. Type house type may not be good enough—or it may be too good. There is little sense in paying type house prices for work that any competent in-house shop could do.

Turnaround. For many companies, a quick turnaround is crucial. When an in-house shop is created, an organization can rush important jobs through the shop in an emergency and avoid paying the high rates many type houses charge for producing work on short notice.

Purchasing Equipment

Typographers must often become resident experts in typesetting technology. As such, one of the talents required of many supervisory typographers is the ability to purchase appropriate equipment. Buying technological solutions means new decision making. The type supervisor using hot-metal had no such difficulties: there were only two suppliers of a linecaster, and they both supplied the same machine.

The following steps will supply the typographer with sufficient information to make an intelligent decision.

1. Consider the equipment recommended to meet specifications, including the FOB (freight on board) location, terms, and conditions. Quote any available options.
2. Find out the approximate delivery date of all equipment after you receive a binding order.
3. Examine all lease and/or rental arrangements available from the equipment manufacturer.
4. Examine a copy of a service maintenance agreement, including the cost on the recommended equipment.
5. Make a list of the people within a 100-mile radius who are trained to repair the recommended equipment.
6. Find out the number of similar systems installed within a 100-mile radius.
7. Make a list of locations from which parts must be drawn to repair the equipment.
8. Find out how many backup systems are available within a 100-mile radius.
9. Find out the approximate time necessary to draw parts from the repair location.
10. Consider the procedures covered under the preventive maintenance visits. How frequent are such visits?
11. Find out the average response time to a service repair call. List the hours during which service is available.
12. Consider any additional items that may be required in order to make the system operational.
13. Find out what kind of training will be provided to your personnel,

including the length of initial training and the comprehensiveness of all instructional manuals. Note any "hot-line" training advice that may be available.

14. Find out whether any additional support is available.

15. List the names, addresses, and telephone numbers of at least three customers within a 100-mile radius. Include a contact at these firms.

16. Determine specifications (by piece of equipment), including the dimensions, weights, electrical requirements, BTU output, static sensitivity, and specialized plugs required. Find out whether equipment requires a dedicated electrical line.

17. Check a sample of output.

18. Consider the point sizes available on the output unit, including the method of achieving those sizes.

19. Find out the number of faces on-line.

20. Find out whether any reprogramming or mechanical operations will be required for font changes.

21. Investigate the hyphenation and justification logic used by the recommended equipment.

22. Find out the rated speed of the output unit.

23. Find out the method of mixing sizes and styles of type, both inter- and intraline.

24. Find out the range of linespacing available, including the incremental values.

25. Find out whether there are reverse leading features.

26. Find out how many lines of type will be visible on the screen at one time.

27. Investigate the editing procedure.

28. Find out the coding structures for specialized functions, including point size, linespace, and line length.

29. Determine the maximum number of input stations that can be attached to the system.

30. Determine the maximum number of output stations that can be attached to the system. Determine all current output units capable of being attached.

31. Find out the minimum and maximum distances permissible between the input units and output units.

32. Consider any restrictions to cabling in plans for installing the equipment (for example, cable must always be available to service personnel; it cannot be buried in the wall or ceiling; and it cannot be near electrical or telephone wires).

33. Find out what kinds of material will be available as output.

34. Find out whether output requires special processing and consider what additional equipment may be necessary.

35. If a processor is to be purchased, find out whether it will require plumbing. Find out whether a temperature mixing valve and filtering system will be necessary.

36. Consider the prices of all supplies that would be required for the operation of the recommended system.

After the research is done, an intelligent purchase can be made. When doing that research, a comprehensive look at the typesetting industry will be necessary. The basic technology of typesetting is shared—the products offered by two different companies are often similar. Yet careful examination of the industry is necessary to make the best choice. Certainly, in the equipment market of the 1980s, there are dozens of possibilities from which to choose.

14-1.

**AM Comp/Set
standalone. Photo
courtesy AM
Varityper**

14

TYPESETTING EQUIPMENT: AN OVERVIEW

From the 1960s through the 1980s, type rooms have radically changed every few years. In the 1960s, the greatest of changes, from hot-metal machines to cold type, had begun. In the 1970s, early phototypesetting technology was beginning to be replaced by computerization. By the late 1970s, phototypesetting networks that are directed by intelligent front ends had been introduced.

The improvements of the 1970s and 1980s have been of degree rather than kind. The machines of the 1970s, the standalone phototypesetting unit and the mini-network, are not technologically obsolete. Rather, large-volume typesetting users have found newer technology that better suits their needs, while smaller-volume users continue to employ the less expensive, but suitable, technology of earlier decades. In practice, this means that typographers can choose from among standalones, direct-entry devices, intelligent terminals, slaves, personal computers as input, auto-pagination, and phototypesetting systems. In addition, several major companies manufacture competing products in each category. An in-depth look at what is available—and what is no longer manufactured but still being used—will be a survey of today's type rooms.

The basic choice is simple. There are smart machines (those that make end-of-line, hyphenation, and justification decisions) and there are dumb machines (those that do not). The latter will be discussed first.

Direct Entry and Slaves

Phototypesetters are categorized according to performance and price. The least-expensive machines are the descendants of the first phototypesetters of the 1950s and 1960s. Direct-entry typesetters, such as the Compugraphic Execuwriter and the AM Comp/Set 3510, lack memory capacity (fig. 14-1). As the operator enters lines on the machine's keyboard, they are immediately typeset.

For production typesetting some form of memory is necessary, but direct-entry devices have not yet outlived their usefulness. Many companies purchase these relatively inexpensive machines for their own typesetting work. The price tag, $10,000 and less, is well suited to the budgets of smaller printers who typeset business cards, letterheads, flyers, and short brochures as a service to their customers. More technologically up-to-date graphics firms use direct-entry devices as slave printers, sending data to the typesetter through an interface. The only limitation is the amount of photo paper that can be moved into the light-tight paper cassette during one interface session. A major advantage to direct-entry interfacing is that personnel need not supervise the process. Some companies send information to these devices after normal working hours, and the typesetting operator simply processes the exposed phototypesetting paper in the morning.

The main drawback is the lack of memory (some of the machines can be updated with memory, but they then are no longer direct-entry devices). Equipment is slow, comparatively unreliable, and irritating. Because it is also inexpensive, it will continue to be used. There are better and faster ways to typeset, but few cost so little.

Direct Entry II

By the 1970s, a new set of direct-entry typesetters created startling changes in the industry. Sharp cuts in prices, versatility, and ease of operation were the principal reasons for the explosion of in-house graphics shops in the 1970s and 1980s. In the 1950s and 1960s, a nonprofit organization or small industrial manufacturer could not participate in what was essentially a closed craft. Typesetting required long years of training in the handling of foundry type, the use of a linecasting machine, and the correct way to lock up pages. In addition, the initial investment was prohibitive: a single linecasting machine cost $20,000 or more in the 1960s, and anyone who established a type shop also had to purchase lead, type fonts, type cases, a proof press, and a variety of other equipment and supplies.

14-2.
The EPICS composition system. Photo courtesy AM Varityper

The machines of the 1970s, with easy-to-use technology, changed typesetting forever. The industry grew from a relatively small group of typesetting companies to a huge number of type houses, commercial printers, duplicating services, in-house shops, and quick printers setting type. The major advances that fueled the change were the standard typewriter keyboard, the VDT, and the reduced cost of equipment. Priced at under $15,000, typesetting technology became affordable to many companies formerly unwilling to make an investment.

These machines connected input and output in one device. When memory was added in the form of a diskette to the machines of the 1980s, input was separated from output and the phenomenon of typesetting networks was created (fig. 14-2). Intelligence and adaptability have made the basic standalone the best-selling phototypesetter in history. Priced between $10,000 and $30,000, thousands of these machines are still in use.

Indirect-Entry Systems

Basically there are two types of indirect-entry "systems." The lower-priced versions are standalones that have been upgraded to create multi-user networks. These low-cost systems allow an organization the advantage of an extra two or three input stations. Terminals are purchased for about $5,000 and networked to the existing photo unit (fig. 14-3). By retrofitting a standalone photo unit, an organization needing four input stations may purchase four terminals (at $5,000 each) instead of four standalone typesetters (at $20,000 each). The system makes obvious economic sense (fig. 14-4).

The second type of indirect system is the super network, often simply called the *phototypesetting system*. Usually priced at over $100,000, this equipment is affordable only for type houses and major type users such as newspapers. Bedford, Penta, Autologic, and CCI are some of the manufacturers who specialize in supplying hardware to newspaper and magazine publishers (fig. 14-5).

The manufacturers of these machines developed *autopagination* technology, meaning that pages are set—and can be viewed on screen—exactly as they will appear in printed form (fig. 14-6). Phototypesetting systems

14-3.

Typesetting network costs.

Typesetting Network Costs

Example: a five workstation network, using third-generation typesetting technology and microcomputers for input.

Front End

Photo unit	$25,000
Software	8,000

Input

5 Microcomputers, $2500 each	$12,500

Output

Processor	$4,000

Total	**$49,500**

Note: Total does not include costs of phototypesetting chemistry, diskettes, and other miscellaneous supplies. This is a start-up cost.

Standalone Typesetting Costs

Example: five third-generation standalone units.

Standalones

5 typesetting machines, at $20,000 each	$100,000
Software	2,500

Output

Processor	$4,000

Total	**$106,500**

Note: Total does not include costs of phototypesetting chemistry, diskettes, and other miscellaneous supplies. This is a start-up cost. Also note that such a system of five standalones does not support interactive communications without extra cost.

14-4.

Standalone typesetting costs.

14-5.

The Penta integrated publishing environment.

14-6.

Atex software allows for pagination using microcomputers. Photo courtesy Atex

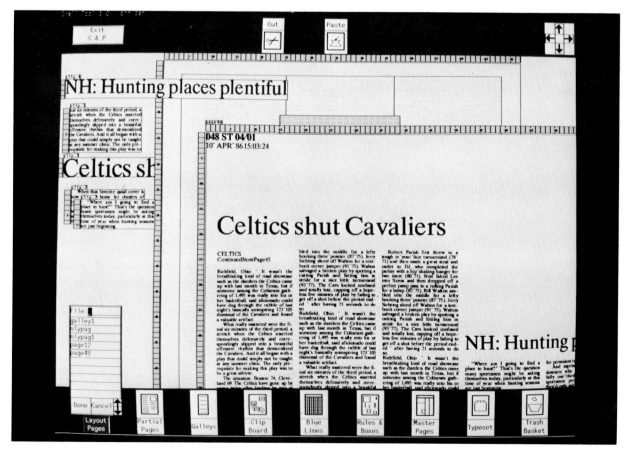

have two components: the *front end,* or information processor, and the *back end,* or photo unit. The front-end system is run by a powerful minicomputer, such as a Digital VAX or Data General. Autopagination decisions are made for copy received from perhaps dozens of input terminals, known as slaves because they make no decisions of their own (fig. 6-8). From 1982 through 1986, sales of the autopaginating front ends exceeded $1.1 billion on the U.S. market alone. Because it is built around an expensive minicomputer, a typical front-end system costs hundreds of thousands of dollars.

Information is moved from the back end to the front end via electronic cables or by inserting memory disks into a back-end disk drive. Since networks of a dozen or more terminals are not unusual, the back ends set the work of many keyboarders, and the output speed must be fast enough to service that workload. The fastest machines are able to produce type at rates of 6,000 lines per minute.

Because the technology of the front and back ends is so very different, manufacturers of front ends, such as Bedford and Penta, usually do not manufacture back-end output devices. The reverse is also true. A typical type house, then, will have a Penta or CCI front end "driving" a Mergenthaler Linoterm or Itek photo unit.

In the 1980s, front ends contributed to the revival of an employment practice that was especially popular in the last century: the cottage industry. Formerly, textile and other industry workers performed their jobs at home (in the cottage), for which they were paid piecework wages rather than salaries. Today, many type houses supply terminals to employees who wish to keyboard at home according to their own schedules. Periodically, the employee delivers the keyboarded memory (via diskette) to the type house and picks up new material. The advantage for the employee, of course, is that scheduling is self-directed. Within the guidelines constructed by the employer, the employee can work many more hours one day and fewer the next. The keyboarder can also generate extra income, depending on the number of hours he or she wishes to work. Meanwhile, the employer eliminates the need to house a staff in a large physical plant that must be air conditioned in the summer and heated in the winter. More important, because of the flexibility allowed in maintaining a work schedule, it is not as difficult to retain excellent employees. Finally, because work is usually keyboarded on a piece rate (per page or per line), costs are easily calculable. Typesetting prices can therefore be estimated more efficiently.

Equipment Manufacturers and Products

The most popular standalones are manufactured by AM, Compugraphic, Mergenthaler, and Itek. The more expensive multi-user systems offered by Alphatype, Berthold, and CCI represent one terminus of a spectrum occupied at the other end by the *very* costly Bedford and Penta front-end systems. Mergenthaler is the leading manufacturer of the back-end photo units. In addition, the newspaper and publishing composition market is a huge independent enterprise. Itek, EIT, Newspaper Electronics, and Harris are among the companies that offer publishing systems. An overview of the various competing hardware options is a synopsis of today's output possibilities.

14-7.

The VIP 7245 photo unit. Photo courtesy Allied Linotype

MERGENTHALER

After Gutenberg, Mergenthaler is the oldest name in typesetting. Founded nearly a hundred years ago to market the linecaster invented by Ottmar Mergenthaler, the Mergenthaler company is well known for the excellent typography produced by its machines. Printers and typesetters favor Mergenthaler equipment for its dependability, quality, and precision engineering. In the past, Mergenthaler typesetters have been comparatively expensive. Today, however, several of the company's newer products are both cost-competitive and technologically up-to-date.

For years, the VIP was the standard throughout the industry (fig. 14-7). Yet, recently, several new members of the Mergenthaler family have superseded it in popularity.

CRTronic

A first for Mergenthaler, the CRTronic is a standalone unit that can also serve as the output hub of a minisystem (fig. 14-8). The least expensive version of this series is the CRTronic 100, which, priced at $20,000 (with a Linotype Communications Interface [LCI] adding another $4,000), is aimed at the small printer, quick print shop, in-house graphics facility, and educational market.

One of the new generation of inexpensive digital typesetters, the CRTronic may proliferate in the 1980s. Digital scanning priced at $20,000 was a dream in 1982. By the end of the decade, prices may come down even farther. The CRTronic is equipped with a dual computer: one unit operates the front end of the standalone, the second conducts back-end operations. The 200 model operates at three typesetting speeds, with the fastest speeds usually used for proofs and the slower speeds for quality

14-8.

CRTronic 150. Photo courtesy Allied Linotype

typesetting. Many of the features of the very expensive front-end systems—including user programming, autopaginated typesetting, and a dedicated back end—are available in the CRTronic.

The CRTronic is typical of the current standalones in that it is well equipped to communicate with other computerized equipment. The machine can either display documents on screen or store memory directly on a disk for typesetting later. Though typical, the CRTronic will not be found at many major type houses. For $24,000, it is impossible to buy a machine with the terrific speed required by professional typographers.

Linotron and Linoterm

14-9.

Linotron 606. Photo courtesy Allied Linotype

The Linotron and Linoterm are dedicated purely to output. Typesetters with heavy type demands may purchase several units like the CRTronic. But those systems do not have a shared logic or shared memory. The preferred strategy is to interface several typesetting terminals with a sophisticated photo unit.

Combined with MVP/2 terminals supplied by Mergenthaler or with third-party terminals manufactured by other suppliers, Mergenthaler photo units offer a variety of options. The Linotron 101, for instance, is capable of speeds ranging from 30 to 125 lines per minute, depending upon the quality of type that is desired. The Linotron 606, on the other hand, sets up to 3,000 newspaper lines per minute (fig. 14-9). The newest output units, the Linotronics, were introduced in 1984.

Because type is not photographed through negatives, these machines (and most of their competitors) are capable of setting a wide variety of type sizes. The Linotron 101 sets type from 4½ to 127 points in one-half-point increments. The CRTronic sets in increments of a tenth of a point. Beginning typographers should be wary of misusing this type size capability. The sixteen standard type sizes have for centuries been capable of filling the needs of virtually any job. For the most part, the standard sizes should be used even when hardware allows deviations from the norm.

Omnitech 2000

14-10.

Omnitech 2000. Photo courtesy Allied Linotype

When the Omnitech appeared in 1981, it was among the first typesetters equipped to communicate with other computers. The WPI, a word processing interface, was developed by George Smith of G. O. Graphics, a hardware/software supplier, which, in the early 1980s, created telecommunications devices for Mergenthaler, Compugraphic, *and* AM. Starting in 1984, the devices were sold directly by G. O. Graphics. All work according to similar technological principles.

The Omnitech, like other competitive photo units, is capable of outputting to photo paper, dry-processed paper, film, or even paper printing plates. It costs about $30,000. Billed as the first fifth-generation typesetter, Omnitechs are not found in many in-house shops because of their relatively high price. Organizations with a workload requiring several input terminals are most interested in these faster machines (fig. 14-10).

The Omnitech is a glimpse at what the most sophisticated machines may be like throughout the 1980s: digital typesetting, inexpensive paper output, a wide variety of type sizes, vertical and horizontal ruling, slanted type versions, autopagination, expanded and condensed variations, reverse video (setting white type on a black background), and interfacing capability.

COMPUGRAPHIC

Compugraphic does not have as long a history in typesetting hardware as Mergenthaler. Established in the 1960s, the company has developed a reputation as a supplier of the workingman's typesetter. Less expensive than Mergenthaler products, Compugraphic equipment populates the service type shops at small to medium-sized printers, advertising agencies, and in-house graphics shops. In schools that have typesetting labs and tight budgets, Compugraphic machines are by far the most common hardware.

The reason for Compugraphic's success is a combination of quality and competitive prices. One of the infamous ways that the company managed to keep prices down was by deciding early on to create its own versions of popular typefaces. By designing Helios as a substitute for Helvetica, Oracle as a substitute for Optima, and English Times as a substitute for Times Roman, CG saved the customer the expense of paying royalties to the type designer. But the company also earned the enmity of many designers and typographers who bemoaned the butchering of their beautiful faces. Lately, Compugraphic has mended its ways and offers the classic letterforms in their original stylizations. Many typographers nevertheless view the damage as irreparable.

As the following discussion of individual machines demonstrates, Compugraphic revolutionized the industry by creating in large part the impetus toward both in-house typesetting and interfacing.

EditWriter 7500

In the 1970s, the EditWriter 7500 took the typesetting world by storm. It was a standalone typesetter that had a standard keyboard, worked under normal light conditions, and could be operated without a 500-page instruction manual. Companies that formerly paid for type bought typesetting machines by the thousands. New positions in typesetting were created (and the demand for typesetting operators continues to rise). Compugraphic had helped to expand the narrow, specialized base of the typesetting industry by reducing investment costs and simplifying equipment.

Then, two months into the 1980s, Compugraphic engineered another coup. A computer board, the Intelligent Communications Interface, was introduced for the EditWriters. Less than a year after the ICI made its debut, over 700 were sold, a remarkable figure given that less than 150 interfacing devices had been sold by Compugraphic in the previous five years.

Within a year, interfaces had been established between the EditWriter and nearly 150 different word processors and computers. In 1981, 73 percent of the interfaces were with minicomputers, 18 percent were with mainframes, and only 9 percent were with micros. By the mid-1980s, during the personal computer revolution, those figures would reverse in favor of the microcomputer. Figure 14-11 lists the most popular microcomputers in the United States.

14-11.

Most popular PCs in the United States, 1984.

MCS

EditWriters can support systems populated by 1750 and 2750 terminals, but they were originally designed as standalones with independent terminals, and they continue to work best in that configuration. Recognizing that the EditWriter could not reach the output speeds necessary to support three or four terminals, Compugraphic has produced several photo unit/terminal combinations. From the ACM 9000 through the Trendsetter and

Unisetter, CG has moved from a direct-entry device capable of reading paper tape and diskette memory to a second-generation typesetter. The ACM 9000, one of the most versatile photo units, can be operated as a direct entry-device, receive data through paper tape, or generate type from diskette memory (fig. 14-12). Indeed, its versatility is one reason the ACM, though somewhat slow and difficult to service, continues to survive in some shops. Printers who continue to use paper tape do so because large jobs, such as annual catalogs, have been stored on that media for years. Since it can be expensive to convert paper tape to diskette memory, terminals such as the AM Varityper AKI, which are capable of editing paper tape memory, are still sometimes used (fig. 14-13).

The MDT, or minidisk terminal, is a simple multiterminal system. Operators keyboard documents onto diskette memory at one of several input stations. After the job is typed, the disk is inserted into a detached photo unit and the type is set. The simplicity and expandability of such systems have made them very popular both in education and industry (fig. 14-14). Compugraphic no longer manufactures the ACM or the MDT 350. Instead, the company has moved to a newer network, replacing the MDT/Trendsetter photo unit concept with the more sophisticated MCS, or modular composition system. MCS is centered around a series of digital photo units priced from under $25,000.

Flexibility is the key to these systems. The MCS's options include a computer printer for cheap proofs, a preview screen that allows entire pages to be viewed and edited on screen, a 5-megabyte rigid disk drive, and an interfacing device. Pushing the modular concept to its current technological limit, Compugraphic has created a system that is priced as low as $25,000 (although with options, the cost of equipment can far exceed that figure) (fig. 14-15). The advantage of modularity, of course, is that each customer is able to buy precisely what is required.

MCS offers the Advanced Communications Interface (ACI) for those interested in links between computerized data bases. Taking a cue from the AM interface, the ACI allows information to be transmitted from sender to receiver and back again. Priced at less than $5,000, the ACI is included in more than 40 percent of all MCS systems currently sold. Those sales figures mean that type houses will be full of ACI devices. Expandability is the key selling point that attracts typesetting managers to the MCS. Because of the many options in photo units, and the ability to purchase additional keyboards and disk drives, a company can easily enhance its equipment whenever necessary. But the initial investment can be less than $30,000.

14-12.

The ACM 9000 keyboard photo unit. Photo courtesy John Devecis

14-13.

The AM Electroset paper tape terminal. Photo courtesy John Devecis

14-14.

The Trendsetter photo unit. Photo courtesy John Devecis

14-15.

MCS composition system. Photo courtesy Compugraphic Corporation

14-16.

**PCS. Photo
courtesy
Compugraphic
Corporation**

14-17.

**Quadritek 2500
phototypesetting
system. Photo
courtesy Itek
Composition
Systems**

PCS

A more recent Compugraphic device is the Personal Composition System, a combination of an Apple Lisa computer and an MCS photo unit. Introduced in 1984 and taken off the market by 1986, the PCS was a business failure. But the technology gave a glimpse of the future.

The PCS is an interface (fig. 14-16). A "mouse" (hand-held controlling device) is touched to a tablet to move text, edit, and file documents. As in the desktop publishing that followed it (and, indeed, desktop may have been one of the reasons for its decline), PCS uses a microcomputer for input, a digital output unit, and new, easier ways to operate both machines.

ITEK

Returning to interfacing's distant past, in 1977, Itek made news that received the attention of very few. It introduced the DCI, or Data Communications Interface, which was a true pioneer, one of the first commercial interfaces available for *any* typesetter.

In the late 1970s and early 1980s, many typesetting companies that wanted to develop communications packages as a marketing tool simply went ahead and made their own. Several media converters and OCR devices began as successful in-house experiments.

If you had a Quadritek typesetter manufactured by Itek, you were fortunate (fig. 14-17). The DCI was available and it addressed a communi-

cations need that was not filled by other equipment manufacturers. For 1977, the telecommunications capability of the DCI was revolutionary.

Since 1977, microcomputers and telecommunications technology have evolved concomitantly with interfacing devices. The DCI, for instance, communicated alphanumerics effectively, but was limited to a maximum of 30 translations of technical type sequences and typographic commands. DCI interfacing worked, but certainly not as well as the interfaces to come later.

The DCI succeeded because of the Quadritek market. At a maximum speed of 50 lines per minute, the 1200, 1400, and 1600 series were not fast enough to be used by professional type houses or even by most newspapers. The Quadritek's marketing position was exactly correct for the DCI; the buyers of this equipment did not require as sophisticated an interface as did type houses and major printers.

Mark IX

With a maximum speed of 600 lines per minute, the Mark IX photo unit is the heart of several systems specifically designed for newspaper production. Communication links between remote news bureaus and a central office are bidirectional, sending and receiving information either way. The Mark IX is very competitive in an especially high-tech market that has developed many of the innovations type houses and in-house shops benefitted from years later.

AM VARITYPER

AM's equipment has long been known as an economical option. A Comp/Set 510-II, a basic beginner's machine with memory but no frills, sells for less than $15,000. AM produces more direct-entry options than any other manufacturer. Do you need terminals? Choose from the 4800, the 5404, the 5414, the 5618 (with or without the Image Previewer). Are standalone phototypesetters what you want? AM offers the 500, the 510, the 510-II, the 3510, the 4510, the 5310, the 5410, the 5810, the 5900, the 6300, and the 6400. Moreover, most of the standalones can be used with several terminals to create systems. If they do not fill your needs, AM's newest offering, the EPICS multiterminal system, is another option.

For the most part, AM machines vary essentially in their options. One can select digital output units, photographic photo units, slower or faster speeds, or more or fewer lines per screen on the video display terminals. But all AM machines interface.

The AM version of the G. O. Graphics telecommunications board is called the TeleCom. There are actually two different devices, one designed for the Comp/Edit series and a second for the Comp/Sets. Compared with their higher-priced cousins, the Comp/Sets are slower yet more popular machines (figs. 14-18 and 14-19). Price is AM's most important selling point.

By 1981, AM had developed bilateral communications. If a typesetter received copy that later required editing, changes could be made at the typesetting end on the VDT. Copy was then telecommunicated back to the customer for on-screen proofing. By 1984, the AM advantage had been lost. Every major typesetting terminal could be equipped with one or more of the popular microcomputer operating systems. As a result, typesetting terminals were no longer dumb, dedicated slaves. With appropriate software, they could be used for business applications, word processing, and many other purposes.

14-18.
AM Varityper 6850.
Photo courtesy AM Varityper

14-19.
The Comp/Edit 6400 CRT typesetter. Photo courtesy AM Varityper

14-20.

AM Graphics Text Organizer. Photo courtesy AM Varityper

14-21.

NewsPro. Photo courtesy Crosfield Hastech

14-22.

Camex Breeze terminal. Photo courtesy Camex

Autopagination Systems

Dozens of excellent typesetting packages are available. Any front-end manufacturer will offer computer interfacing opening up a line of communication between the front end and the terminals of the back end. This equipment is directed to two general markets: newspaper and publishing composition and commercial typesetting. Newspapers and magazines, which must adhere to strict deadlines, are interested in raw speeds. Expensive autopagination systems are well worth the price if a 4,000-line-per-minute overdrive is required. Of course, dependability and service are also important considerations. A fast typesetter that cannot be serviced is of no use to a newspaper editor striving to make a daily deadline.

Type houses, on the other hand, are more concerned with type quality and ease of operation. Whereas newspapers rarely feature graphs or tables and almost never print equations, a type house sets technical type every day. Its manager, more than the newspaper production manager, is interested in a machine that makes difficult copy easier to input. However, because newspaper publishers and typesetters alike deal with hundreds of pages of copy every day, each requires the speed of the autopagination system.

THE NEWSPAPER MARKET

There are actually several newspaper markets. Weeklies and small daily newspapers do not require the speedy machines used by a large metropolitan newspaper with a daily circulation in the hundreds of thousands. They use second- or third-generation equipment to typeset the relatively few pages that make up each issue. As a result, many of these papers do commercial typesetting as a sideline.

On slightly larger papers, with circulations in the tens of thousands, time becomes an important consideration. Daily newspapers have punishing schedules; every minute saved in the setting of type can be applied to the collection and dissemination of news. The quickest way to create pages is to set them automatically. Pasteup is a timely process that many newspapers simply cannot afford.

Most medium-sized papers invest in equipment such as the AM Graphics Text Organizer, the Harris 2220 Video Layout System, the Crosfield Hastech NewsPro, the Minitek manufactured by Itek, the Camex Breeze terminal and 3100 BitCaster, and the Micronews produced by Newspaper Electronics Corporation (NEC) (figs. 14-20 through 14-23). All of these products are scaled-down versions of large systems and all sell in the $20,000 to $30,000 range. The price makes the systems affordable within the budgets of smaller papers, yet, like their larger cousins, they can produce pages of type automatically.

Large papers, which can afford to be more selective, may choose from a wider range of autopagination systems specially designed for newspapers. All allow typesetting operators to keyboard on screen interactively, meaning that as type is set or ads are created, the operator sees the type on screen just as it will appear in proof. If corrections are needed, the operator edits the copy and the correction immediately appears on screen. The technological advantage of interactivity is that operators see the results of typographic changes as they are making them. Preview screens, on the other hand, involve sending the job to the screen, noting changes that must be made, doing the required corrections on a terminal, and then previewing the job a second time. Whether or not the system is interactive, headlines, columns of type, photographs, and ads are all shown in position.

14-23.

Camex 3100 BitCaster. Photo courtesy Camex

14-24.

AdPro. Photo courtesy Crosfield Hastech

14-25.

Pagination system. Photo courtesy Interleaf

14-26.

The 4500 Ad Makeup station. Photo courtesy Information International

14-27.

The COMp 808/3 Universal Pagesetter. Photo courtesy Information International

14-28.

Front-end typesetting system. Photo courtesy Compugraphic Corporation

The options in this market include the Mergenthaler System MVP, 5/10, 5/30, and 5500 newspaper typesetting/publishing systems; the Information International 4500 Ad Makeup station and COMp 808/3 Universal Pagesetter; the Itek Mark IX phototypesetter, Pagitek and CPS 1000 series copy processing systems; the Harris 2200 and 3300; the Logicon TPS 6000 text processing system; the Mycro-Tek Mycro-Comp 1000 front end; the Raytheon Graphic Systems Raycomp 100 System with AdSet, the RayPubs text processing system and RayComp II; the ONE System's bcw System, Power Editor terminal, and One/Series; the High Technology Solutions FastWord, FastPage, and MPS1000; the DECset Integrated Publishing System and CMS-11 Classified Management System offered by Digital Equipment Corporation; the Hastech AdPro and PagePro layout systems; the Newspaper Electronic Corporation News III and Amicus systems; and the Xyvision—among many others (figs. 14-24 through 14-27). In a recent issue of *TypeWorld,* a periodical devoted to high-technology hardware for typesetters, seven new autopagination systems and terminals were discussed. *TypeWorld* is published every three weeks and new options are announced in every issue. By the 1990s, autopagination and area composition will probably become standard practice in the typesetting industry, just as they are in the newspaper industry of the 1980s.

Area composition systems for newspapers vary in price from $20,000 for a single terminal to hundreds of thousands of dollars for a multiterminal system with on-line output (which means that after a job has been typed and approved, it can be immediately typeset without the intervention of a typesetting operator). Large newspapers have networks of hundreds of terminals all in communication with a front-end computer, which sends data to a slave phototypesetting unit (figs. 14-28 and 14-29).

THE TYPESETTING MARKET

Like *direct entry,* the meaning of the term *area composition* has changed in the last twenty years. In the 1960s, area composition meant that the operator was able to control typesetting. Compugraphic's ACM 9000 was a departure from the idiot keyboards then prevalent because it enabled the operator to set type justified or unjustified, as the parameters demanded. In the 1980s, area composition means the ability to keyboard type in the same size, style, and position in which it will eventually be set.

Typesetters and commercial printers interested in the speed and accuracy of autopagination have three options: area composition terminals, preview screens, and the more expensive front-end systems. A front-end system can cost more than a quarter million dollars; the first two options are less than $20,000.

Area composition terminals and preview screens perform similar functions. Both allow the operator to see a "soft copy" version of a galley before it is typeset onto paper, or "hard copy." Soft copy enables the operator to correct any errors *before* the job is actually set. However, area composition terminals are interactive; preview screens are not. In addition, area composition terminals are input devices. Operators are able to strike a key and record characters in memory. The preview screen, however, has no accompanying keyboard. Instead, it is attached to the terminal via electronic cable. When the operator wishes to preview a job, the data on the terminal screen is sent to the preview screen with a keystroke command. The preview screen displays the type as it will be set, but no editing can occur. On the whole, preview screens are more clumsy but less expensive than area composition terminals.

Standalone typesetters, such as Mergenthaler's CRTronic, allow for

14-29.

Newspaper typesetting system.

14-30.

CRTronic screen structure. Photo courtesy Allied Linotype

14-31.

Preview screen. Photo courtesy Compugraphic Corporation

14-32.

The Alphatype Action Composition System, an interactive system. Photo courtesy Alphatype Corporation

14-33.

Digitek Preview terminal. Photo courtesy Itek Composition Systems

autopagination but are not area composition terminals. Type appears on screen in a complicated format that is common to most typesetting terminals (fig. 14-30).

The true area composition device allows for autopagination in photosetting *and* soft-copy pagination on screen. There are many terminals from which to choose. Those produced by typesetting systems manufacturers are usable only by purchasers of that company's equipment. Several generic area composition terminals that are manufactured by third-party companies can be used in conjunction with a variety of different systems.

Compugraphic has at least five different products: the AdVantage, the EditWriter PreView, the Quadex PreView terminal, the MCS Power-View 10, and the PCS. The EditWriter PreView screen was made available in the early 1980s as part of Compugraphic's Display Composition System (DCS). Like the Quadex Preview, it is not interactive and does not allow for operator input. The AdVantage, PowerView, and PCS all permit interactivity (figs. 14-31 and 14-32). The AdVantage was one of the first typesetting machines specifically engineered to be run without complicated typesetting coding. Ad layout artists working with a light pen simply touched the screen display of ordinary English commands such as *Start Job* and *Write for Typesetting*.

The EditWriter Preview screen image resembled most early products that offered soft copy. The words and phrases on screen are certainly discernible, but serifs are blurred, type styles are limited, and many pi characters are obscured. Later machines, especially the front-end systems, perfected the screen image.

The Itek Preview terminal was manufactured to be used in conjunction with Itek's Quadritek phototypesetting systems (fig. 14-33). One thousand characters per second are moved from the typesetting screen to the preview terminal, so that the entire screen is displayed in about 15 seconds. Like the Compugraphic Preview, the Itek Preview displays only

14-34.

**Linotype TypeView
300 soft copy
display monitor**

two generic type styles, a serif and a sans. But, also like the Compu-graphic, the Itek price makes previewing affordable for advertising agencies that use the terminal as a layout tool or for typesetters interested in saving the costs of wasted photographic paper and manual paste-up.

Many other preview screens are available. Mergenthaler offers a preview screen option that works in conjunction with the CRTronic series (fig. 14-34). Preview screens are generally used in standalone configurations. Because a standalone is a complete unit with a built-in terminal, interactive graphics can be updated only with a second screen.

However, a more powerful multiterminal system ideally includes terminals that have graphics capabilities—the interactive area composition terminals. Input terminals manufactured by third-party companies include High Technology Solutions' MPS terminal, Xenotron Corporation's AVC-2, the Texet Document Machine, and AKI's Optimix. These machines can be used in any typesetting system, but every major typesetting photo unit manufacturer also offers its own area composition products. Berthold, for instance, produces the ADS-3000 input station, an interactive terminal that can be used with a variety of Berthold photo units (fig. 14-35).

The Digiskop is an area composition terminal engineered to drive Digiset typesetting units. Digiset typesetters are manufactured in Germany and distributed in North America by HCM Graphic Systems. The Lino-screen Composer is used with many Mergenthaler photo units. The Comp/Set 4800 is similar in that it is engineered to be used with any of AM's Comp/Set or Comp/Edit typesetting systems. The 2020 Page Layout Station is an integral part of the VideoComp 570, a typesetting system manu-factured by Information International. All of these terminals share interactivity and automatic pagination. Again, in the 1990s, interactive screen displays with easy correcting features will be common equipment throughout the industry.

14-35.

**Berthold apu 6016.
Photo courtesy
Berthold Group**

14-36.

Multiset III Minicomputer System. Photo courtesy Alphatype Corporation

Front-End Systems

The most expensive typesetting option is the front-end system, produced specifically with typesetters and publishing companies in mind. The major competitors in this market include Bedford, Penta, CCI, Alphatype, Electronic Information Technology, Itek, and AKI. (A complete list is not possible because new manufacturers and new products are introduced every month.)

The AKI UltraType 4000 system is typical of the genre in that it is based on a powerful Digital Equipment Corporation minicomputer, programmed with kerning, hyphenation, justification, and pagination software, which drives a photo unit and dozens of input terminals. Typographic excellence is thus determined by initial programming instead of line-by-line decision making. As a fail-safe, the terminal screens are interactive; if a program does make an error, the operator can detect the problem and manually correct it.

Alphatype's Multiset III is a relatively inexpensive mini-front-end system with two terminals, which can be expanded to include others (fig. 14-36). Although this machine is not as powerful as other front ends, it does make many features available to those who do not need (and cannot afford) the power necessary to drive dozens of input terminals. Even less expensive is the Alphatype Mini Multiset, a system that can be used with one terminal. In both systems, the Alphatype SoftVu preview screen is available as an option.

Several other companies offer front-end systems designed, like Alphatype's, for the relatively low-volume typesetter. Itek's Pagitek and Minitek, and the TS-1 by Electronic Information International, are systems that are less expensive and less expandable than the larger front ends, and are thus appropriate for smaller type houses and publishing companies. The Alphatype system is expandable to ten terminals, the Minitek to eight, and the TS-11 to six.

The CCI system manufactured by Computer Composition International is more powerful: a network of as many as 28 terminals and eight different photo units can be built around a single front end. For major type houses, that power and easy expandability justify the larger purchase price (fig. 14-37).

Several dozen input and output options are available, including the ActiView soft copy area composition terminal, a line printer for inexpensive computer printout proofs, color printers, word processors, and the PageView preview screen. Software options include TypeLink, a program that permits interfacing with customers' word processors, PageBuilder, which automatically paginates copy, and TechPage for pagination of technical typesetting. For those who cannot afford the CCI 400, the CX 1000 is a smaller, less expensive version of the standard front end.

Autologic produces several different front-end systems in its popular APS series. Because all are expensive, they are marketed only to type houses, publishers, and large commercial printers.

PentaVision is the interactive system manufactured for the Penta front end (fig. 14-38). Like the APS, CCI, and Bedford, the Penta page displayed on screen closely approximates the final typesetting output. Run on a Data General Nova or Eclipse minicomputer, software includes PentaPage, an automatic pagination program; PentaQuick, which allows Penta front ends to process text at speeds of up to 1,000 characters per second; and VeriQuick, which verifes corrections after proofreading. Available hardware includes line printers, interfacing devices, interactive terminals, and the PentaComm bidirectional editing terminal (fig. 14-39).

14-37.

CCI 400 system. Photo courtesy Computer Composition International

14-38.

Penta pagination and editorial system based on 32-bit microcomputers. Photo courtesy Penta

14-39.

Penta System's Composition team. The PentaSaturn IV intelligent composition terminal and the PentaVision make-up terminal. Photo courtesy Penta

Bedford Computer Corporation is a major competitor in the large front-end market. Its Vision Network System combines IBM personal computers for input, Bedford Meteor/Star and Meteor pagination and area composition terminals, and a Bedford digital typesetter for output. The Bedford system offers extremely good interactive graphics and amazing expandability. A network can be configured with an incredible 254 input and output stations, a very long way from the standalone typesetters of the 1970s.

Finally, some front ends are manufactured for specialized typesetting tasks. Most type houses with the Bedford, Penta, APS, or CCI front-end systems produce technical type or huge amounts of text. Their investment in the equipment, amounting to hundreds of thousands of dollars, must be recouped by producing either expensive jobs or tremendous volume. The last front end to be discussed, the Purup PE 4000, is among the most expensive. The system features an interactive front end that required six years of research for the full development of a solution to one specific problem: forms. The composition of business forms is a growing typesetting subindustry, just as the printing of forms is an important specialization within the printing industry as a whole.

A Danish company that has just recently moved into the American market, Purups Electronics is little noticed in most of the typesetting industry because of this market niche. Purup typesetters are digital laser units that are among the fastest available output devices today.

The Software Option

There is one more way to establish an interactive relationship between the typesetting operator and the computer terminal. Rather than creating specific hardware to accomplish the task, a growing number of companies are producing software that allows existing terminals to be updated with interactivity and autopagination features.

The CS V software produced by Informatics General Corporation is specifically designed for in-house publishing. Created to be used with the most popular mini-based word processing systems, the Wang VS, CS V allows Wang users to move from word processing to page processing. Its features include automatic justification and hyphenation, indexing, footnotes, and heads. After the material is produced with the CS V programs, output is possible on AM, Autologic, VideoComp, Compugraphic, Mergenthaler, and other typesetters. Camera-ready pages can also be produced with the Xerox 8700 and 9700 digital printing systems.

It is not necessary to own an expensive minicomputer to produce autopaginated type with a word processor. By the middle of the 1980s, dozens of programs allowed the owners of IBM, Apple, Radio Shack, and other personal computers to justify, hyphenate, and paginate copy automatically (see fig. 14-6). A representative member of this group, Westminster Software's PagePlanner, is engineered for IBM and IBM-compatible computers (including the Compaq, Televideo, Columbia, Hewlett-Packard, Eagle, and Sperry) using the MS-DOS operating system. PagePlanner pages were first output to Mergenthaler equipment, but typesetting by AM, Compugraphic, Itek, and Autologic photo units is also possible.

A quick printer or small type house interested in inexpensive autopagination simply purchases the PagePlanner software and, rather than using a typesetting terminal for input, keyboards on an IBM or IBM-compatible personal computer. After keyboarding, the job is interfaced from the personal computer to a phototypesetter, a technique that is now called *PC-based composition*. Typesetting with personal computers—either by PC-based composition or by desktop publishing—will be the most important technological trend to affect typography in the late 1980s and 1990s.

As with hardware, several software programs are manufactured for specific applications. Docuflex, created by Image Sciences, is analogous to the hardware used in the composition of business forms. A major difference, however, is that Docuflex is based upon a new industry, *electronic printing and publishing.* This involves creating documents on personal computers and printing them on demand with digital copiers (see fig. 13-15). The "intelligent copiers" receive data through telecommunications and produce as many copies as needed.

Docuflex software creates a form or a document on an interactive terminal, stores it in a permanent memory, and accesses copies through communications with the intelligent copiers. Multiple copies of documents that emulate typesetting are produced without a typesetter *and* without a printing press. Docuflex and similar programs are especially useful for companies that produce technical documents. Only one copy of a technical report or insurance rider needs to be generated, and no warehouse storage or delivery is necessary. Perhaps more important, if a form or document must be updated, the job can be edited on screen and restored to memory. Any new copies will be edited copies. New galleys, new proofs, new mechanicals, and new prepress operations are never necessary. Electronic printing will be an important option in the 1990s, especially for short-run documents printed in press runs of 500 copies or fewer.

Desktop Publishing

The newest technology is a combination of electronic publishing and interfacing. Created by Apple Computer, desktop publishing originally consisted of an Apple Macintosh microcomputer attached to a digital laser printer. This hybrid advancement combines three technologies: character generation with a microcomputer, digital output onto paper, and WYSIWYG (what you see is what you get) technology. The revolutionary aspect of desktop publishing is the price: less than $10,000 for equipment and software that would have cost $250,000 in 1984.

Introduced in 1985, the LaserWriter is revolutionary because of a page description language called PostScript. Manufactured by Adobe Systems, PostScript allows the operator to create intact pages, thus eliminating the paste-up stage. More important, however, is the method used to generate fonts: PostScript stores one matrix (or bit map) for each typeface and then magnifies the matrix as required to produce different type sizes, in an imitation of digital typesetters.

This means that the Apple LaserWriter can produce output from a variety of digital devices. For proofs, customers can use their own LaserWriter printer based on the Canon LBP-CX. For commercial-quality typesetting, customers are able to interface autopaginated input with a variety of different typesetting machines, including the Linotype L100.

In a very short time, desktop publishing has become a tremendous success. Indeed, there are now several different levels of this new technology. *Personal desktop publishing* uses a microcomputer to produce pages and simple illustrations. MacDraw and MacPaint software, for instance, allow the production of charts, graphics, and forms. Computerized clip art is also available. PageMaker, MacPublisher, and other pagination programs are priced at less than $500. *Professional desktop publishing* fills the design and editing system needs of more sophisticated users. Software options from such companies as Bestinfo, Interleaf, Studio Software, and Magna Computer Systems accommodate a variety of page styles and provide such typographic niceties as linespacing control, multiple tabs, and hyphenation dictionaries. Software costs range from $2,500 to $10,000. *Multiuser desktop publishing* has proven popular with magazines and newspapers. Several personal computers are networked together to form a desktop system based upon professional desktop software and telecommunications. The price is between $25,000 and $50,000, depending upon the photo unit. Basic autopagination, editing, and text and graphics integration costs about $25,000.

Currently, about 80 percent of all graphics is processed traditionally: paste-up is still a manual process. By 1992, that percentage will be reversed. Desktop publishing is one of the reasons. The customer will create pages and the type house will be a service bureau, setting galleys as required. For those occasions where quality typesetting is not required, the customer can also use the output produced by the LaserWriter as camera-ready copy. Though not as good as professional typesetting, the output is certainly good enough for newletters, internal reports, and price lists. Desktop output will take the place of typewriting.

The type house of the 1990s will undergo radical changes. The typesetter will become a programmer instead of a keyboarder. The type house manager will become systems- and software-oriented. Customer service will become far more important than keyboard speed. But then, as now, there will always be a demand for the *knowledge* necessary to produce quality typesetting.

GLOSSARY

AA. *See* Author's alteration.

Acoustic coupler. A device used in telecommunications to transmit data through standard telephone analog signals.

Agate. A unit equal to $\frac{1}{14}$ of an inch, used in measuring newspaper advertisement space.

Alphanumerics. Alphabetic or numerical characters, often used to facilitate input.

Arabic numerals. The ten digits 0 through 9.

Ascenders. The parts of letters that rise above the x-height.

ASCII. American Standard Code for Information Interchange. The standard code set, established by the American National Standards Institute, for transmission of telecommunicated data.

Asymmetric typography. A theory espoused by Jan Tschichold and other members of the Bauhaus that attacked the classic typographic style of centering all copy on the page. Also called modern typography.

Asynchronous transmission. Data transmission that is not regulated by a timing source. The beginnings and ends of blocks of data are signalled by start and stop bits.

Author's alteration. In proofing, a change made by the customer in typeset copy, the cost of which is borne by the customer.

Autopagination. The ability of software to access pages set intact from the photo unit of the typesetter.

Back end. That part of a typesetting system dedicated to the input of characters into memory.

Back matter. The parts of a book that appear after the body. Includes the appendix, glossary, bibliography, index, and colophon.

Backup. Copies of programs or data safely stored in the event that originals are mistakenly destroyed.

Ballot box. A typeset character that is an open square.

Banner. The name of a publication as it is displayed on the cover.

Baseline. The imaginary line that all letters rest upon.

Baseline em underscore. The typesetting key that accesses a line that is even with the baseline and one em in length.

Basis size. The standard size at which paper is manufactured.

Bastard title. *See* Half title.

Bauhaus. An artistic movement, founded by Walter Gropius shortly after World War I, that stressed function and the elimination of decoration.

Binary. A number system with a base of two. Binary uses only the digits 0 and 1.

Bit. Abbreviation for binary digit, either 0 or 1. A unit of computer memory storage.

Black letter. The gothic type style popular in Germany in the fifteenth century.

Bleed. Type or art that extends to the edge of the printed page.

Blueprints. Photographic proofs received by the customer after page negatives are assembled.

Body type. Type that measures from 6 to 14 points. Also known as text type.

Bold. A heavy version of a regular typeface.

Boustrophedonic. The ancient Greek method of writing in alternating directions, from left to right and then from right to left.

Bowl. The curved stroke that creates a counter in such letters as *a, b, c, d, n,* and *o.*

Broadside. A large printed sheet, folded.

Bullet. A large solid dot, usually either one em or one en in diameter, often used to demarcate items in a list.

Byte. A group of bits (usually eight) representing a character.

California job case. Used in handsetting, a type case with a specific compartment for each letter.

Calligraphy. Elegant handwriting of various styles, many based on classic examples from the fourteenth through eighteenth centuries.

Cancellescara. The Renaissance chancery script upon which Griffo based the Aldine italic.

Canned software. Ready-to-use computer programs.

Captions. Short descriptions, often with citations, accompanying an illustration.

Caroline minuscule. The first set of letters designed with lowercase instead of all caps. Created by Alcuin of York for Charlemagne, who had decreed the development of a standard writing style.

Case. (1) In handsetting, a wooden or metal tray which is used to store letters. (2) Hardcover binding. The pages of the book are sewn together, glued into the "case," and secured by the end papers.

Casting. A method of producing hot-metal type. Molten metal is forced into molds called matrices (mats). The resulting lines of type are called slugs.

Cathode-ray tube. A vacuum tube that displays information on a computer screen.

Central processing unit (CPU). The part of the computer responsible for the interpretation and execution of instructions. *See also* Computer unit.

Chapter heading. The title and number of a chapter, located on the chapter opening page.

Chapter opening page. The first page of a book chapter.

Character. A letter, figure, punctuation mark, accent mark, or any other member of a font.

Character count. An estimate of the number of letters, figures, punctuation marks, and spacebands in a given space.

Chase. The metal frame into which foundry or linecast type is placed after handsetting.

Chip. A silicon wafer on which integrated circuits are etched. In a microcomputer or dumb terminal, a complete central processing unit may be stored on a single chip.

Chromalin. A proofing method used to produce four-color comps.

Cicero. The basis of a system of measurement used by some European typographers. There are 13 points in one cicero; six ciceros to the inch.

Circulating matrix. The essential principle of the successful linecasting system. Matrices are returned to the magazine after the line is cast.

Code sets. Systems used to interpret binary codes when translations are necessary to allow communications. ASCII and EBCDIC are two major examples.

Cold type. Type that is not set via molten metal: photocomposition and typewriter composition are two examples. *See* Hot type.

Colophon. Brief information, usually located as back matter, pertaining to the typography and production of a book.

Color key. A method of proofing pages intended to be produced by the four-color printing process.

Column inch. An area one column wide and one inch deep, often used in selling publications ad space.

Comp. *See* Comprehensive.

Composing stick. In handsetting, a small, hand-held tray into which letters are placed after their selection from the case.

Composition. Synonym for typesetting.

Comprehensive. A layout, complete with accurately sized type and art, that clearly shows the typographer's intentions.

Computer language. A system of commands understandable by the CPU, including binary and machine code.

Computer unit. The central processing unit of a computerized typesetting machine. Controls end-of-line and hyphenation and justification decisions.

Condensed variations. A narrow version of a typeface.

Contact printing. Photography in which the negative is placed atop the material being exposed.

Continuous transmission. Transmission of data that is not paced by time or on/off codes, but continues until all data are sent.

Control codes. A keyboard character or sequence of characters that initiates, stops, or modifies a particular function.

Conversion service. A company that converts information stored on a computer from one medium to another; for instance, from magnetic cartridges to magnetic disks.

Copyfitting. A method used to determine the amount of space that will be required for a specific quantity of typeset copy in a given typeface and size.

Cost per unit. In estimating for typesetting, the cost for one keystroke.

Counters. The hollow parts of such rounded letters as the *a, e, o,* and *p.*

Counting keyboard. A keyboard that adds up the space remaining on a line as each character is typed, enabling the operator to make end-of-line decisions based on this information.

Cursive. A typeface designed to resemble handwriting in which the letters do not touch when typeset. *See* Script.

Daisy-wheel printer. A printer with fonts consisting of single-character spokes radiating from a central hub.

Debug. To eliminate errors either from a program or from a communications routine.

Dedicated. Referring to a word processor, typesetting keyboard, or other device permanently assigned, either by software or by the user, to one task.

Delimiter. A code marking the beginning or end of a message.

Descenders. Parts of letters that extend below the baseline. Type size is measured from the top of an ascender to the bottom of a descender.

Desktop publishing. A system composed of a microcomputer and a laser digital printer that produces autopaginated output on plain paper.

Digital. Information that is coded in binary numerics.

Digital typesetting. Third-generation typesetting characterized by the elimination of film fonts, the storage of digital codes by the computer unit, and the production of characters in the form of microscopic dots or lines.

Digitized typesetting. *See* Digital typesetting.

Dingbat. A specialized character, such as a star or pointed finger, which is not usually part of a standard font.

Direct-entry typesetting. Characterizing first-generation typesetters, which set a letter immediately after a key is struck, and more sophisticated machines that store jobs in memory for later typesetting by the photo unit.

Direct impression typesetting. Typesetting by the physical impact of ink on paper. Also known as typewriter composition and strike-on typesetting.

Direct interfacing. Interfacing methods involving a direct electrical connection, for example, hardwiring and telecommunications.

Direct-to-plate typesetting. Typesetting by exposure of a printing plate, which eliminates several steps in the production process.

Discretionary hyphen (D/H). A hyphen placed by the typesetting operator in a word. Directs the hyphenation logic to hyphenate, if necessary, only where the key has been placed.

Disk. A flat, circular magnetic storage medium that is rotated, like a phonograph record, in a disk drive. Disks are either rigid or floppy.

Disk capacity. The amount of information that may be stored on a magnetic disk at one time.

Disk drive. A device equipped with a read/write head that allows information to be stored on or read from a disk.

Diskette. A cheap storage medium, usually either 8-inches or 5 1/4-inches square, used in many typesetters and microcomputers. Also called a floppy disk.

Display type. Type that is larger than 14-point.

Dot leader. A row of dots used to join two bodies of copy on a page.

Dot matrix printer. A nonimpact printer that produces characters by using a matrix of small dots. The quality is poorer than that produced by daisy-wheel printers.

Downtime. The amount of time a computer is inoperative because of failure. Usually expressed as a percentage of the total time the computer is used.

Dumb terminal. *See* Slave keyboards.

Dummy. A layout produced to show the imposition and design of a book, publication, or brochure.

EBCDIC. Extended Binary Coded Decimal Interchange Code. The code set used by IBM to represent data.

Electronic manuscript. A document sent to a typesetter or type house in electronic, rather than paper, format.

Electronic printing and publishing. A comprehensive term used to describe those devices which output type or art without an original paper manuscript. Pages are delivered to output devices through electronic, rather than paper, manuscripts.

Electrostatic printers. Copiers that convert telecommunicated data into dot matrix patterns.

Elite typewriter. A typewriter that produces 12 characters to the inch.

Ellipsis. Three dots signifying a pause or an omission.

Em dash. A horizontal printed line the length of an em.

Em indent. An indent the width of an em. *See* Em space.

Em space. A fixed space equal to the width of an *m* in the type size being used.

En indent. An indent the width of an en. *See* En space.

En space. One-half the width of an em space.

End-of-line decisions. Decisions made by a typesetting machine to end justified lines.

End papers. Folded sheets pasted between the boards and first signature of a book, securing the book within the covers.

Estimating. In printing and typesetting, the process of developing a price for a job.

Evocative printing. The typographic theory of William Morris, which asserts that type should create a suitable mood for the fullest partaking of a message.

Exception dictionary. Software that contains a list of words that should not be hyphenated.

Expanded variations. A widened version of a regular typeface.

Face. A typeface.

Family. All available typefaces and type sizes based on a single design.

Figures. Numbers. *See* Lining figures and Old style figures.

File. A collection of data treated as a unit.

File size. The amount of information, usually expressed in kilobytes, that can be placed in a file.

Filmstrip. A plastic strip containing negatives of each character in a typeface.

Firmware. Programs that cannot be edited by the user.

Fixed space. A space, such as the em or en, of fixed width, the value of which is determined by the typesetting operator.

Flaring. A letterform that is thinner at the middle than at the top or bottom.

Floppy disk. *See* Diskette.

Flush left. A type pattern in which material is aligned with the left margin but ragged on the right. The opposite of flush right. *See* Justified margins.

Folio. (1) The page number of a book. (2) A single sheet folded once to create two leaves and four pages. (3) A large book.

Font. A complete set of all characters in one typeface in one size. Includes letters, figures, symbols, and punctuation marks.

Font drum. In photo units, the round cylinder that revolves, bringing the appropriate letters of an attached font strip before a flashing light source, which makes the exposure.

Font strip. A plastic strip containing a complete negative collection of all characters in a typeface's font.

Foot. The bottom of a book page.

Formatting. In telecommunications, a coding system that requires the customer to insert format codes, such as F1, to mean a combination of previously determined typesetting parameters.

Foundry type. Individual pieces of metal type used for handsetting.

Front end. In phototypesetting, that part of a system which makes pagination, end-of-line, hyphenation, and justification decisions.

Front-end system. The combination of typesetting terminals and output units controlled by a front end.

Front matter. The parts of a book that appear before the body, including the half-title page, title page, copyright page, preface, foreword, table of contents, list of illustrations, and dedication.

Frontispiece. In a book, an illustration facing the title page.

Galley. (1) Raw output of a phototypesetting device, usually in the form of single columns on long sheets. (2) A long, shallow metal tray used to store and proof handset type.

Galley proof. The first appearance of typeset copy, photocopies of the galleys.

Generations. A series of technological breakthroughs defining the evolution of phototypesetting devices.

Golden section. A typographic theory used by medieval scribes and redis-
covered in this century by Jan Tschichold. The theory dictates that margins of the page be laid out in a 2:3:4:6 ratio.

Gravure. The most important commercial application of intaglio, or recessed, printing. The plates are copper cylinders in which tiny wells
forming the pattern of the image are etched. After the copper cylinder is
inked, paper is pressed onto the cylinder and an impression results. Because the copper cylinders are expensive, gravure printing is limited to
relatively large press runs (usually over 100,000).

Greeking sheet. A transfer lettering sheet used to create a facsimile of
body copy in layouts.

Grid theory. A layout system that requires the typographer to create a
uniform grid into which all design elements are placed.

H&J. *See* Hyphenation and justification.

Hairline. A fine-lined rule.

Half title. The first printed page in a book, containing only a shortened
version of the book title. Also called the bastard title.

Handsetting. The first typesetting method. Letters are individually selected from cases and placed into composing sticks.

Hard disk. A magnetic disk permanently encased in a cylinder, useful
because of the large storage capacity provided. Also known as a rigid
disk.

Hard returns. Return codes that are mandatory, such as at the ends of
paragraphs. *Compare* Soft returns.

Hardware. Mechanical, electronic, and magnetic components of any computer system.

Hardwiring. Connecting two computers with communications cable and
sending information through the cable.

Head. (1) The top of a book page. (2) Abbreviation of heading.

Heading. Display type appearing at the beginning of a chapter, preface, or
other section of a book.

Headline. Headings in periodical publications.

Headline schedule. In newspaper typography, a list of headline weights
that enables editors to assign headline type sizes and variations according
to the relative importance of the stories.

Hexadecimal codes. Usually abbreviated as *hex,* a numerical system based
on 16 digits. Useful in telecommunications as an intermediary code between machine code and human languages.

Hieroglyphics. A system of writing, used in ancient Egypt, which incorporated pictographs, ideographs, and phonograms into an alphabet.

Hollerith cards. Paper storage medium. Cards are perforated with coded
patterns that are interpreted by paper punch readers.

Horizontal flow. The capability of a typeface to carry the eye from the left
to the right, allowing for greater legibility.

Hot type. Type produced from molten metal.

Hung initial. An indented first letter of a chapter that drops down
through an indent of several vertical lines.

Hyphenation and justification. Two decisions, made by the front end of
a phototypesetting device or by the typesetting operator, which determine the width of letterspacing and wordspacing.

Hyphenation logic. The program used by the computer unit of a typesetting device that determines if and how a word will be hyphenated.

Ideograph. A picture or symbol that represents an idea.

Image carrier. Any surface, such as an offset lithography printing plate or
gravure copper cylinder, which serves as the original from which impres-

sions are made.

Impact printer. Any printer that produces characters by striking individually inked letters onto paper.

Imposition. The pattern in which pages will be properly sequenced when printed, folded, and trimmed.

Incunabula. Books printed before 1500.

Indirect interfacing. Interfacing methods that do not involve a direct connection between communicating machines.

In-house shop. A department in a corporation, institution, or governmental agency devoted to the production of graphics for the parent organization.

Initial. A specially set letter starting a body of copy.

Input device. Any device capable of moving data into a computer. Input devices include terminals and key punch machines.

Integrated circuit. A silicon circuit containing thousands of transistors on a single wafer. Synonym for chip.

Interface. Any hardware, software, or system that allows information to be shared between two computerized devices. Indirect interfacing methods (involving intermediate translating devices) include optical character recognition and media conversion; direct interfacing methods include hardwiring and telecommunications.

Italic. A typeface variation created by Aldus Manutius in which the type slants to the right.

ITC. International Typeface Corporation.

Jacket. The removable outer cover of a casebound book.

Jobwork. Design and printing of a variety of commercial items.

Justified margins. Vertically aligned margins on both sides of a typeset column.

Justified tape. In typesetting, a paper tape that contains letter- and word-spacing to justify each line.

K. *See* Kilobyte.

Kerning. Adjusting letterspace between specific characters known as kerning pairs.

Kerning pairs. Two letters which, when juxtaposed in copy, should always be set close together. Examples include *Ve* and *To*.

Keyboard. That part of the terminal where characters are typed to create a document. Similar in appearance to the typewriter.

Keyboarding. Typing on a keyboard.

Keystroke. One character typed on a keyboard.

Kill. To erase memory or destroy copy that is no longer needed by the type house or client.

Kilobyte. Two to the tenth power, or 1,024, bytes.

Laser typesetting. A nonphotographic typesetting technique in which images are imprinted directly onto paper by a light source.

Layout. (1) The typographer's plan for a page existing in several stages, including thumbnails, roughs, and comprehensives. (2) The process of creating such plans.

Lead. The difference between the type size and the linespace. In common notation, 10/12 means a type size of 10 points and a linespace of 12 points, or 2 points of lead.

Leader. *See* Dot leader.

Leading. *See* Linespace.

Leaf. A single sheet of paper in a book. Contains two pages (front and back).

Legibility. The capacity of a well-set letter, line, or page to be easily read.

Letterspace. Space between typeset letters.

Ligatures. Two characters set as one unit.

Lightface. A lighter version of a regular typeface.

Linecasting. A hot-metal typesetting method. *See* Casting.

Line length. *See* Measure.

Linespace. Measured in points, the distance from one baseline to the next.

Lines per minute. A speed rating given to all typesetters. Expressed in terms of the number of lines set in 8-point type, 11-picas wide, in one minute.

Line-voltage regulator. A device that controls surges of power disruptive to computer memory.

Lining figures. Sets of numerals that are all of equal height.

Linotype. The first successful linecasting machine.

Lowercase. Small letters, also called minuscules.

Magazine. In linecasting, the part of the linecaster that stores the matrices.

Magnetic media. Any form of computer storage that has a magnetic surface to retain data, including cartridges, cassettes, disks, and tapes.

Magnetized (map) cards. Computer storage system often used in electronic typing systems.

Mainframe. Powerful computers that are usually dedicated to data processing or networking.

Major strokes. The heavier, more pronounced strokes of a letter. Also called thicks. *See* Minor stroke.

Majuscules. *See* Uppercase letters.

Marker comp. A comprehensive layout prepared with an art marker.

Markup. Procedure for noting the typographic specifications for a job directly on the manuscript as a guide to the typesetter.

Massaging. Adding keystrokes to, editing, or repairing errors in an interfaced file.

Matrix (mat). In hot-metal typesetting, the mold from which a line or character is cast.

Measure. The length of a typeset line, expressed in picas.

Mechanicals. Boards containing the elements of the page prepared for reproduction. In offset lithography, often called pasteup.

Media. The various ways in which computer memory is permanently stored, including paper tape, Hollerith cards, and all forms of magnetic media.

Media conversion. An indirect interface in which media are converted from an unintelligible to intelligible format by an intermediate device. *See* Media converter.

Media converter. A device that converts unintelligible magnetic media into usable information. Programmable converters allow the purchaser to program the device to access information from many different computers.

Megabyte. Two to the eleventh power, or 1,048,576, bytes.

Memory. The capacity of a computer to store binary coded information.

Menu. A list of commands displayed on screen.

Microchip. *See* Integrated circuit.

Microcomputer. A computer, selling for under $30,000, based upon a single microprocessor.

Microprocessor. One of several different computer chips (for example, the Z80) that support a particular operating system.

Minicomputer. Intermediate priced (and powered) computers that cost between $30,000 and $300,000.

Minor strokes. The less pronounced strokes of a letter. Also called thins. *See* Major strokes.

Minuscules. Lowercase letters.

Mnemonics. Symbolic names for instructions, commands, or phrases, used to encode various kinds of information.

Modem. Acronym for modulator/demodulator. A device that converts and interprets audio and electromagnetic signals. In interfacing, most often used in converting and translating telephone communications.

Modern layout. *See* Asymmetric typography.

Modern romans. Roman typefaces designed after 1750 that are characterized by great contrast between major and minor strokes. Bodoni and Didot are examples.

Modern typography. *See* Asymmetric typography.

Mouse. A handheld device that controls a menu on screen.

Movable type. Individual letters used in handsetting that can be positioned and repositioned.

National hands. Styles of handwriting that were used in various parts of Europe in the Middle Ages. The three that most influenced the later history of typography were the Celtic (from Ireland), the Gothic (from Germany), and the Roman (from Italy).

Networks. Computer systems that allow several terminals to exchange data through the sharing of a common CPU. There are two kinds: point-to-point and multiplexer.

New Style. A typographic movement begun in the 1920s that stressed legibility and timelessness. Important advocates included Eric Gill, Stanley Morison, and Beatrice Warde.

New Wave. A typographic style of the late 1970s and early 1980s that stresses the visual, rather than the verbal, message.

Noncounting keyboard. Keyboards that do not count the spacing consumed from line to line and therefore do not require the operator to make end-of-line decisions.

Nonimpact printer. A printing device that creates letters or images without striking paper. The dot matrix and ink-jet printers are examples.

Null modem. The communication cable used in hardwiring.

OCR. Optical character recognition.

Octavo. (1) A sheet folded three times, producing 16 pages. (2) In the United States, a book measuring six by nine inches.

Off-line. The state of an independent device capable of operating without direct communication with a more powerful computer.

Offset lithography. The most popular printing method in the United States today. The offset principle involves transferring the inked image from an intermediate cylinder before impressing it onto paper. The ink moves from plate to offset cylinder (called the *blanket*) to the paper. The lithographic principle, perfected for printing by Alois Senefelder in 1796, is that grease and water do not mix. In lithography, an oil-based ink is used to ink a greased image area (the nonimage area is kept wet with water). Offset lithography is the combination of both principles.

Old Style. The first of the roman typeface classifications. Letters have rounded stress and little contrast between major and minor strokes.

On-line. (1) The number of fonts that can be accessed from the photo unit at one time. (2) Terminal or other device that is in direct communication with the CPU.

Operating system. An organization of software that controls the overall logic and operation of the computer.

Optical alignment. In display type, the setting of letters so that the eye perceives them to be aligned, although they may not be aligned geometrically.

Optical center. A position on the page slightly above the physical center, perceived as the center of the page.

Optical character recognition. A technology that enables computerized devices to read typed characters and convert them into magnetic data.

Optical scanning. The method used in OCR to "read" characters. Pages are scanned for specific programmed patterns, which, when identified, are stored in memory.

Orphan. A single word or short line that ends a paragraph. *See* Widow.

OS. *See* Operating system.

Output device. Any device that is capable of converting memory into printed or displayed form.

Page. A single side of a sheet of paper.

Pantone sheets. Colored adhesive-backed sheets used to produce one form of comprehensive layout.

Paper tape. The earliest form of typesetting memory. Information is coded via patterns of perforations.

Pasteups. *See* Mechanicals.

PC-based composition. Typesetting using a personal computer as an input device.

PE. *See* Printer's error.

Perfect binding. A method of binding, often used in paperback books, that employs glue.

Peripherals. The various input and output devices, storage units, and other hardware forming a computerized system.

Personal style. A typographic movement begun in the 1920s that held that typography should reflect the time in which it was created.

Photodisplay unit. A phototypesetting machine that produces optically spaced display lettering.

Phototypesetting system. A network of devices dedicated to the input and output of phototype.

Pica. A unit of measurement. There are 12 points in one pica and approximately six picas in one inch.

Pica typewriters. Typewriters that produce 12 characters to the inch.

Pictographs. Symbols that represent objects.

Pi font. A collection of pi characters—mathematical symbols, accent marks, and technical symbols that are not part of the normal type font.

Point. A unit of measurement. There are 12 points in one pica. One point is approximately $1/72$ of an inch high.

Press proof. In the offset lithography process, one of the first actual printed copies of the press run.

Preview screen. A video display terminal that allows the operator to examine type in position and correct size before it is set.

Printer's error. Mistake made by the typesetter for which the customer is not charged.

Private Press Movement. A typographic movement, founded by William Morris with his Kelmscott Press of the 1890s, that stressed a return to the methods and paradigms of traditional printing.

Programs. Software. Instructions that tell the CPU to perform a specific task.

Progressive margins. A layout theory stating that the sizes of margins on a page should increase progressively, beginning with the inner margin, and moving in order to the top, outer margin, and bottom of the page.

Proofreaders' marks. A group of symbols used to mark errors and make changes in manuscript and composed copy.

Proofs. Photocopies of a work produced in various stages of the printing process (including galleys, mechanicals, negative assembly, and presswork) checked by the client or proofreader for errors.

Pseudo-italics. Slanted versions of regular typefaces formed by a digital typesetting command.

Publication design. The design of newspapers and magazines.

Punch cards. *See* Hollerith cards.

Quad. A piece of metal type used to fill out lines and spacing between words. The terminology has carried over to phototypesetting (thus the term "quad left" is sometimes used synonymously with "flush left").

Quarto. (1) A sheet folded twice, producing eight pages. (2) In the United States, a book 8½ by 11 inches in size.

Queue. In typesetting, a list of jobs that are held in memory for typesetting.

Ragged left. A pattern of lines that are ragged on the left and even on the right.

Ragged right. A pattern of lines that are ragged on the right and even on the left.

RAM. *See* Random access memory.

Random access memory. Memory that can be edited by the user.

Rasters. Microscopic lines that are combined by a printer to form a digitally produced image.

RC paper. Resin coated typesetting paper, which, unlike S paper, produces a permanent, nonfading image.

Read-only memory. Memory that can only be read, but not changed, by the user.

Read/write head. That part of the disk drive which rotates the magnetized surface of a disk either to read or write magnetic memory.

Recto. The right-hand, odd-numbered pages of a book.

Reverse type. Type set white on a black background.

Rigid disk. *See* Hard disk.

ROM. See Read-only memory.

Roman. (1) A serif typeface that evolved from the Roman national hand. (2) The vertical letterform, as opposed to the slanted italic.

Roman classifications. Three groups of serifs (the old style, transitional, and modern), which represent the evolutionary stages of that letterform from the sixteenth through eighteenth centuries.

Roughs. Full-sized pencil illustrations, the second stage in the layout process.

Rounded stress. The forming of a letter, such as the *o,* with curved, rather than vertical, counters. The stress closest to handwriting.

RS-232 port. A standard plug with 25 pins, used to connect computers and input/output devices.

Rule. A straight line typeset on the page. Rules are produced in various weights: hairline, half-point, 1-point, 2-point, and so on.

Running head. Information about a book, such as the title or chapter name, that appears at the top of each page.

S paper. Stabilization-grade phototypesetting paper.

Saccadic jumps. According to social science research, the method by which we perceive groups of words at one glance, moving on to the next group after the previous one is understood.

Sans serif. Typeface style without serifs.

Scribes. Medieval copyists who duplicated and illustrated books by hand.

Script. A typeface that looks like handwriting, characterized by letters that touch one another when typeset. *See* Cursive.

Serif. (1) Short cross strokes projecting from letters. (2) A typeface classification characterized by these strokes.

Set. (1) To produce type by hand, by casting, by photography, or by typing. (2) *See* Set width.

Set solid. Describing typesetting in which the type size and linespace are equal.

Set width. The width of the individual letters of a typeface design, programmed by software before computerized typesetting occurs.

Signature. (1) In book typography and publication design, a sheet of printed paper folded into a set of consecutive pages, usually 8, 16, 32, or 64. (2) The collection of such pages, folded, gathered together in correct order, and sewed or glued to form a book.

Slave keyboard. Keyboard having limited memory and processing power, dedicated solely to producing keystrokes to be manipulated by front ends. Also known as dumb terminals.

Slug. A line of type cast in a single piece.

Soft returns. Returns inserted by the software, such as those at the end of each line of text in a paragraph. *See* Hard returns.

Software. Programs, data, and routines for use in a digital computer, as opposed to physical components called hardware.

Spacebands. (1) In handsetting and linecasting, spaces between words. (2) In phototypesetting, the key, located at the bottom of the keyboard, that accesses wordspaces.

Specs. Shorthand for specifications. Typesetting parameters, including linespace, type size, measure, and typeface.

Square serifs. A typeface classification of the nineteenth century characterized by squared rather than barbed serifs.

Standalones. Computers or computerized devices that can operate without being connected to any other computer.

Stet. A direction by the proofreader to make no changes in the copy.

Stock. Printing paper.

Straight matter. Simple text that can be set with a minimum amount of special coding. *See also* Tabular matter; Technical type.

Strike-on typesetting. *See* Direct-impression typesetting.

Subiaco. The first roman typeface, developed by Sweynheim and Pannartz in 1465.

Subscripts. Small characters that are set below the baseline, often used in mathematical and scientific typesetting. *See* Superscripts.

Superscripts. Small characters that are set just above the x-height. *See* Subscripts.

Swash letters. Capital letters with long flourishes or tails.

Swiss Typography. A typographic theory of the 1950s and beyond that stressed clarity and clean lines. Closely related to the International Style.

Symmetric typography. The classic theory of layout in which all elements are centered below one another. *See* Asymmetric typography.

Tabloid. A newspaper size, usually about one-half the size of a broadsheet.

Tabular matter. Tables and charts to be typeset.

Tape drive. A mechanism capable of reading information from magnetic tapes and writing information onto them.

Technical type. Difficult typesetting consisting of, for example, multilevel equations, charts and graphs, superscripts and subscripts, pi characters. Typesetting composed of scientific or mathematical material.

Telecommunications. In typesetting, the transmission of information via telephones or satellite communications.

Terminal. A keyboard able to provide input to a computer.

Text type. *See* Body type.

Thin space. A fixed space less than the width of an en space.

Thumbnails. Small sketches that express only the idea for a page design.

Title page. In book typography, the page listing the title, the author's name, and the name of the publisher.

Transitional romans. The middle period (between the old style and the modern) in the evolution of the roman classifications, characterized by greater contrast between major and minor strokes.

Translation tables. Sets of equations that facilitate the interpretation of data sent from one computer to another.

Trim. To cut paper to a specific size.

Trim size. The final size of a printed piece.

Turnaround. The amount of time necessary, after the receipt of a manuscript, to complete and deliver the job.

Type. The proportionally spaced letters produced, in different typefaces and sizes, by composition methods and machines.

Typebook. A collection of type specimen pages showing all the faces available from a type house.

Typecasting. *See* Casting.

Type designer. Graphic designer who creates typefaces.

Typeface. A single style of type.

Type house. A company that specializes in typesetting.

Typesetter. (1) A person who sets type either by keyboarding or by hand. (2) Any machine used to set type.

Type size. The length from the top of an ascender to the bottom of a descender, measured in points.

Type style. *See* Typeface.

Typewriter composition. *See* Direct-impression typesetting.

Typo. *See* Typographic error.

Typographer. A designer whose medium is type.

Typographic error. An error made by the typesetter. Synonym for printer's error.

Typographic notation. Various systems used to express typographic specifications.

U&lc. (1) Type that is set with both uppercase and lowercase characters. (2) A specification indicating that copy should be set with upper- and lowercase letters.

UDKs. User-defined keys. *See* User programmable keys.

Uncial. A writing hand of the Middle Ages characterized by an elegant roundness.

Underscores. Rules set directly below typewritten or typeset characters. Often used for emphasis.

Unit system. A variable counting system used in phototypesetting to divide the em into a given number of portions. The 18-unit system is one of the most popular.

Uppercase. Capital letters.

User groups. Clubs and organizations devoted to a specific operating system, typesetting system, computer, or program.

User programmable keys. Keys on a terminal that may be programmed by the user to mean any string of characters (or program) desired. Also called UDKs.

Variations. Different weights and stresses of a regular typeface. Bold, italic, condensed, and expanded are examples.

VDT. *See* Video display terminal.

Venetian. Any roman typeface designed before 1500.

Verso. A left-hand, even-numbered, page of a book.

Vertical stress. A stress found in modern Romans (such as Bodoni) which, in letters such as *o* and *a,* is completely straight. *See* Rounded stress.

Victorians. Nineteenth-century typefaces noted for wildly floriated, flared, and novel letterforms.

Video display terminal. A connected CRT and terminal.

Visual linespacing. In display typography, typesetting with linespaces varied to achieve visual symmetry.

Voice-activated typesetting. A promised technology that would permit typesetters to input copy by speech.

Whitespace. The blank areas of a page. Along with type and art, the third element in any design.

Widow. A single word or less than a third of a line that appears at the top of a page. Typesetters will change wordspacing or letterspacing to avoid both widows and orphans. *See* Orphans.

Word processing. Using a computer to create, store, retrieve, and edit text.

Wordspace. In phototypesetting, the variable space between words used to justify type. The computer unit inserts more or less space between words, as necessasry, to bring each line to an even margin.

Word wrap. In word processing and phototypesetting, the ability of the computer to emulate a carriage return in typewriting: to end a line automatically (with a soft return) and then move the cursor immediately to the next line.

X-height. The height of the lowercase x.

BIBLIOGRAPHY

Chapter 1. Typography Today.

Carter, Rob; Day, Ben; and Meggs, Philip. *Typographic Design.* New York: Van Nostrand Reinhold, 1985.

Craig, James. *Designing with Type.* New York: Watson-Guptill, 1978.

Lewis, John. *Typography: Basic Principles.* London: Studio Books, 1966.

———. *Typography: Design and Practice.* London: Barrie and Jenkins, 1977.

McLean, Ruari. *Typography.* London: Thames & Hudson, 1980.

Printing Industry of America. *Graphic Arts Awards Annuals.* Washington: Printing Industry of America, 1985, 1986.

Roberts, Raymond. *Typographic Design.* London: Ernest Benn, 1966.

Ruder, Emil. *Typography:* New York: Hastings House, 1981.

Swann, Cal. *Techniques of Typography.* New York: Watson-Guptill, 1969.

Type Directors Club Staff. *Typography. The Annuals of the Type Directors Club.* New York: Watson-Guptill, 1980–1987.

Chapter 2. The Anatomy of Type.

Hewitt, Graily. *Lettering.* New York: Taplinger, 1981.

Kapr, Albert. *The Art of Lettering: The History, Anatomy, and Aesthetics of the Roman Letterforms.* Munich: K. G. Sauer, 1983.

Lawson, Alexander. *Printing Types: An Introduction.* Boston: Beacon, 1971.

Ogg, Oscar. *The Twenty-Six Letters.* 3d Rev. ed. New York: Thomas Y. Crowell, 1971.

Rosen, Ben. *Type & Typography.* Rev. ed. New York: Van Nostrand Reinhold, 1976.

Zapf, Hermann. *About Alphabets.* Cambridge: MIT Press, 1970.

Chapter 3. A Short History of Type.

Aldis, Harry. *The Printed Book.* Cambridge: Cambridge University Press, 1947.

Berry, W. Turner, and Poole, H. Edmund. *Annals of Printing: A Chronological Encyclopedia.* London: Blandford, 1966.

Blumenthal, Joseph. *Art of the Printed Book 1455–1955.* Boston: Godine, 1973.

———. *The Printed Book in America.* Boston: Godine, 1977.

Cave, Roderick. *The Private Press.* New York: Bowker, 1983.

Chappell, Warren. *A Short History of the Printed Word.* Rev. ed. New York: Arno, 1980.

Clair, Colin. *A Chronology of Printing.* London: Cassell, 1969.

Day, Kenneth. *Book Typography 1815–1965 in Europe and the United States.* Chicago: University of Chicago Press, 1966.

Denman, Frank. *The Shaping of Our Alphabet.* New York: Knopf, 1955.

DeVinne, Theodore. *The Practice of Typography.* New York: Century, 1907.

Diringer, David. *The Book Before Printing.* New York: Dover, 1982.

Dreyfus, John, et al. *William Morris and the Art of the Book.* New York:

Pierpont Morgan Library, 1976.

Eisenstein, Elizabeth. *The Printing Press as an Agent of Change*. 2 Vols. Cambridge: Cambridge University Press, 1979.

Febvre, Lucien, and Martin, Henri-Jean. *The Coming of the Book: The Impact of Printing 1450–1800*. London: Verso, 1984.

Goudy, Frederic. *The Alphabet and Elements of Lettering*. Rpt. ed. New York: Dover, 1963.

———. *Typologia*. Rpt. ed. Berkeley: University of California Press, 1977.

———. "William Morris: His Influence on American Printing." *Philobiblon* 7 (1934).

Grannis, Chandler, ed. *Heritage of the Graphic Arts*. New York: Bowker, 1972.

Johnson, A. F. *Type Designs*. London: Grafton, 1934.

Kelly, Rob Roy. *American Wood Type: 1828–1900*. New York: Da Capo, 1977.

Lehmann-Haupt, Hellmut. *One Hundred Books about Bookmaking*. New York: Columbia University Press, 1949.

———. *The Book in America*. New York: Bowker, 1952.

Levarie, Norma. *The Art and History of Books*. New York: James Heinemann, 1968.

Lewis, John. *The 20th Century Book*. New York: Van Nostrand Reinhold, 1984.

Lieberman, J. Ben. *Type and Typefaces*. 2d ed. New Rochelle: Myriade, 1978.

McMurtrie, Douglas. *The Golden Book*. Chicago: Pascal Covici, 1927.

———. *History of Printing in America*. New York: Bowker, 1936.

Meggs, Philip B. *A History of Graphic Design*. New York: Van Nostrand Reinhold, 1983.

Morison, Stanley. *The Art of the Printer*. New York: Simon and Schuster, 1925.

———. *The Typographic Arts*. Cambridge: Harvard University Press, 1950.

Morris, William. *The Ideal Book*. Berkeley: University of California Press, 1982.

Nesbitt, Alexander. *The History and Technique of Lettering*. New York: Dover, 1957.

Ogg, Oscar. *Three Classics of Italian Calligraphy*. New York: Dover, 1953.

Oswald, John Clyde. *Printing in the Americas*. New York: Gregg, 1937.

Printing and the Mind of Man. The Catalogue of the Exhibitions at the British Museum and at Earls Court, London, 16–27 July 1963. London: F. W. Bridges, 1963.

Provan, Archie, and Lawson, Alexander. *One Hundred Type Histories*. 2 vols. Arlington: National Composition Association, 1983.

Putnam, George Haven. *Books and Their Makers During the Middle Ages*. Rpt. ed. 2 vols. New York: Hillary House, 1962.

Rand, Paul. *A Designer's Art*. New Haven: Yale University Press, 1985.

Ransom, Will. *Private Presses and Their Books*. New York: Bowker, 1929.

Rogers, Bruce. *Paragraphs on Printing*. Rpt. ed. New York: Dover, 1979.

Snyder, Gertrude, and Peckolick, Allan. *Herb Lubalin: Art Director, Graphic Designer and Typographer*. New York: American Showcase, 1985.

Steinberg, S. H. *Five Hundred Years of Printing*. Rev. ed. London: Penguin, 1961.

Thomson, Susan Otis. *American Book Design and William Morris*. New York: Bowker, 1977.

Tschichold, Jan. *Treasury of Alphabets and Lettering.* Hertfordshire, England: Omega, 1985.

Updike, Daniel Berkeley. *Printing Types.* Rpt. ed. 2 vols. New York: Dover, 1980.

Wallis, L. W. *Type Design Developments 1970 to 1985.* Arlington: National Composition Association, 1985.

Warde, Beatrice. *The Crystal Goblet.* London: Sylvan, 1955.

Whitford, Frank. *Bauhaus.* New York: Thames & Hudson, 1984.

Wingler, Hans. *Bauhaus: Weimar, Dessau, Berlin, Chicago.* Cambridge: MIT Press, 1984.

Zapf, Hermann. *Ein Arbeitsbericht.* Darmstadt, FRG: Maximilian, 1985.

———. *Manuale Typographicum.* Boston: MIT Press, 1970.

———. *Typographic Variations.* New Rochelle, N.Y.: Myriade, 1977.

Chapter 4. The Art and Science of Legible Pages

Dowding, G. *Finer Points in the Spacing and Arrangement of Type.* London, 1966.

Hart, H. *Rules for Compositors.* London: Oxford University Press, 1978.

Rehe, Rolf. *Typography: How to Make It Most Legible.* Carmel, Calif.: Design Research International, 1974.

Ruzicka, Rudolph. *Studies in Type Design.* Hanover, N.H.: Dartmouth College Press, 1966.

Spencer, Herbert. *The Study of Legibility.* London: Royal College of Art, n.d.

———. *The Visible Word.* London: Lund Humphries, 1969.

Van Nostrand Reinhold Company, Inc. *The Type Specimen Book.* New York: Van Nostrand Reinhold, 1974.

Visible Language. Cleveland: The Cleveland Museum of Art, ongoing publication.

Zachrisson, Bror. *Studies in the Legibility of Printed Text.* Stockholm, 1965.

Chapter 5. Typographic Applications: Book Design

American Association of University Presses. *One Book Five Ways.* Los Altos, Calif.: William Kaufmann, 1978.

Hurlburt, Allen. *The Grid.* New York: Van Nostrand Reinhold, 1978.

Lee, Marshall. *Bookmaking.* New York: Bowker, 1979.

Rice, Stanley. *Book Design: Systematic Aspects.* New York: Bowker, 1978.

———. *Book Design: Text Formats.* New York: Bowker, 1978.

White, Jan. *Editing By Design.* 2d Ed. New York: Bowker, 1982.

Wilson, Adrian. *The Design of Books.* New York: Reinhold, 1967.

Chapter 6. Typographic Applications: From Newspapers to Jobwork

Arnold, Edmund. *Arnold's Ancient Axioms.* Chicago: Ragan, 1978.

———. *Designing the Total Newspaper.* New York: Harper & Row, 1981.

———. *Modern Newspaper Design.* New York: Harper & Row, 1969.

Bockus, H. William, Jr. *Advertising Graphics.* 4th Ed. New York: Macmillan, 1986.

Douglas, Torin. *The Complete Guide to Advertising.* London: QED, 1984.

Humbert, Claude. *Label Design.* Fribourg, Switzerland: Office du Livre, 1972.

Hurlburt, Allen. *Publication Design.* New York: Van Nostrand Reinhold, 1976.

Hutt, Allen. *The Changing Newspaper.* London: Gordon Fraser, 1973.

Kery, Patricia. *Great Magazine Covers of the World.* New York: Abbeville, 1984.

Nelson, Roy Paul. *The Design of Advertising.* 3d ed. Dubuque, Iowa: William C. Brown, 1978.

Updike, Daniel Berkeley. *In the Day's Work.* Cambridge, Mass.: Harvard University Press, 1924.

White, Jan. *Designing for Magazines.* New York: R. R. Bowker, 1982.

Chapter 7. Layout

Evans, Harold. *Newspaper Design: An Illustrated Guide to Layout.* New York: Holt, Rinehart and Winston, 1973.

Hurlburt, Allan. *The Design Concept.* New York: Watson-Guptill, 1981.

Koberg, Don, and Bagnall, Jim. *The All New Universal Traveller.* Los Altos, Calif.: William Kaufman, 1981.

McKim, Robert. *Thinking Visually.* Belmont, Calif.: Lifetime Learning, 1980.

Plumb, David. *Design and Print Production.* Middlesex, England: Workbook, 1978.

Silver, Gerald. *Graphic Layout and Design.* Albany, N.Y.: Delmar, 1981.

Spencer, Herbert. *Pioneers of Modern Typography.* Cambridge, Mass.: MIT Press, 1982.

Tschichold, Jan. *Asymmetric Typography.* New York: Reinhold, 1967.

Wills, F. H. *Fundamentals of Layout.* New York: Dover, 1978.

Wong, Wucius. *Principles of Two-Dimensional Design.* New York: Van Nostrand Reinhold, 1972.

Chapter 10. Typesetting over the Generations

Haley, Allan. *Phototypography.* New York: Scribner's, 1980.

McPherson, Michael. *Electronic Textsetting: The Impact of Revolutions in Composition on Typography and Type Design.* Unpublished thesis. Providence: Rhode Island School of Design, 1979.

Romano, Frank. *The Typencyclopedia.* New York: Bowker, 1984.

Seybold, Jonathan. *Fundamentals of Modern Photocomposition.* Malibu, Calif.: Seybold, 1978.

Chapter 11. Typesetting Input and Output

Craig, James. *Phototypesetting: A Design Manual.* New York: Watson-Guptill, 1978.

Heath, L. G., and Faux, Ian. *Introductory Phototypesetting.* Pittsburgh: Graphic Arts Technical Foundation, 1980.

Kleper, Michael. *Everything You Always Wanted to Know About In-Plant Typesetting.* Wilmington: Compugraphic Corporation, 1977.

Labuz, Ronald. *Typesetting Options: From Interface to In-House.* Washington, D.C.: Society for National Association Publications, 1984.

Lawson, Alexander. *Typography for Photocomposition.* Arlington, Va.: National Composition Association, 1976.

Printing Industry of America. *A Composition Manual.* Tools of Industry Series, Arlington, Va.: Printing Industry of America, 1953.

Rice, Stanley. *CRT Typesetting Handbook.* New York: Van Nostrand Reinhold, 1981.

Romano, Frank. *Automated Typesetting: The Basic Course.* Salem, N.H.: GAMA Communications, 1974.

Chapter 12. The Professional Role of the Type House

Buhl, Tom. *How to Start, Operate, and Enjoy a Successful Typesetting Business.* Santa Barbara, Calif.: Homefront Graphics, 1984.

Hoch, Fred. *Estimating Standards for Printers.* New York: Hoch Associates, 1952.

Post, Jack. *How to Earn, Control and Maintain Your Profits in Typesetting.* Salem, N.H.: GAMA Publications, 1983.

Ruggles, Philip Kent. *Printing Estimating.* Boston: Breton, 1979.

Chapter 13. Computers and Communications

Cook, William J. *The Joy of Computer Communications.* New York: Dell, 1984.

Labuz, Ronald. *Creating Translation Tables for Telecommunications.* Washington, D.C.: Typographers International Association, 1984.

———. *How to Typeset From a Word Processor: An Interfacing Guide.* New York: Bowker, 1984.

———. *The Interface Data Book for Word Processing/Typesetting.* New York: Bowker, 1984.

———. *Interfacing Basics.* Washington, D.C.: Typographers International Association, 1984.

Myers, Patti. *Telecommunications for Typesetting.* Arlington, Va.: National Composition Association, 1982.

Chapter 14. Typesetting Equipment: An Overview

Durbin Associates. *Interactive Layout System Comparison Charts.* Easton: Durbin Associates, 1986.

———. *Phototypesetter Comparison Charts.* Easton: Durbin Associates, 1986.

———. *Text Processing Computer System Comparison Charts.* Easton: Durbin Associates, 1986.

Gottschall, Edward. *Graphic Communication '80s.* New York: Prentice-Hall, 1981.

Powers, Jack. *1986 Composition Annual.* Arlington, Va.: National Composition Association, 1986.

The Seybold Report. Malibu: Seybold Publications, ongoing publication.

Periodicals

The following controlled-circulation periodicals are distributed free to all qualified subscribers (usually defined as subscribers with a bona fide interest in the subject).

American Printer. Maclean Hunter Publishing Corporation, 300 W. Adams Street, Chicago, Ill. 60606.

CG Magazine. Compugraphic Corporation, 200 Ballardvale Avenue, Wilmington, Mass. 01887.

Graphic Arts Product News. North American Publishing Company, 401 N. Broad Street, Philadelphia, Pa. 19108.

Graphic Arts Monthly. Technical Publishing, 875 Third Avenue, New York, N.Y. 10022.

In Plant Printer. P.O. Box 368, 425 Huehl Road, Building 11B, Northbrook, Ill. 60062.

In-Plant Reproductions. North American Publishing Company, 401 N. Broad Street, Philadelphia, Pa. 19108.

Ligature. The Typographic Communication Journal. World Typeface Center, 145 E. 32d Street, New York, N.Y. 10016.

Magazine Design and Production. Globecom Publishing Limited, 4551 W. 107th Street, Suite 343, Overland Park, Ks. 66207.

Newspaper Production. North American Publishing Company, 401 N. Broad Street, Philadelphia, Pa. 19108.

Plan and Print. The Magazine for Design and Reproduction Management. 9931 Franklin Avenue, Franklin Park, Ill. 60131.

Print and Graphics. 1200 29th Street, Washington, D.C. 20007.

Printing Impressions. North American Publishing Company, 401 N. Broad Street, Philadelphia, Pa. 19108.

TypeWorld: The Newspaper for Word Processing, Typesetting and Graphic Communications. 15 Oakridge Circle, Wilmington, Mass. 01887.

The Typographer. Typographers International Association, 2262 Hall Place, N.W., Washington, D.C. 20007.

U&lc. The International Journal of Typographics. International Typeface Corporation (ITC), 2 Dag Hammarskjold Plaza, New York, N.Y. 10017.

The following periodicals will also be of interest to typographers:

Communication Arts. 410 Sherman Avenue, Palo Alto, Calif.

Fine Print. The Review for the Arts of the Book. P.O. Box 3394, San Francisco, Calif. 94119. Cost: $48 per year.

Graphic Arts Abstracts. Graphic Arts Technical Foundation, 4615 Forbes Avenue, Pittsburgh, Pa. 15213. Cost: $40 per year.

Graphic Arts Literature Abstracts. Technical and Education Center of the Graphic Arts, Rochester Institute of Technology, One Lomb Memorial Drive, P.O. Box 9887, Rochester, N.Y. 14623. Cost: $60 per year.

Graphis. Graphis Press Corporation, 107 Dufourstrasse, CH-8008, Zurich, Switzerland. Cost: $59 per year.

HOW. Ideas and Techniques in Graphic Design. 355 Lexington Avenue, New York, N.Y. 10017. Cost: $21 per year.

Print. America's Graphic Design Magazine. 355 Lexington Avenue, New York, N.Y. 10017. Cost: $40 per year.

typographic i. Typographers International Association (TIA), 2262 Hall Place, N.W., Washington, D.C. 20007. Distributed to TIA members.

INDEX